T0299434

Images of the Multinational Firm

John Dunning (1927–2009)

It was with great sadness that we heard of the death of John Dunning while we were putting the finishing touches to this book. His contribution here, with Sarianna Lundan, is amongst the last in a long line of articles from a man who has been a leading light in the field of International Business. John successfully published, presented and taught for over 50 years. He was awarded numerous accolades from honorary degrees to lifetime achievement awards and most recently a well-deserved OBE. He was the very epitome of a successful scholar. But colleagues and friends are equally likely to remember him on a more personal level, as a gentleman.

Simon Collinson and Glenn Morgan

Images of the Multinational Firm

Edited by

Simon Collinson
Glenn Morgan

⊛**WILEY**

A John Wiley and Sons, Ltd., Publication

Other Wiley Editorial Offices

John Wiley & Sons Inc., 111 River Street, Hoboken, NJ 07030, USA

Jossey-Bass, 989 Market Street, San Francisco, CA 94103-1741, USA

Wiley-VCH Verlag GmbH, Boschstr. 12, D-69469 Weinheim, Germany

John Wiley & Sons Australia Ltd, 42 McDougall Street, Milton, Queensland 4064, Australia

John Wiley & Sons (Asia) Pte Ltd, 2 Clementi Loop #02-01, Jin Xing Distripark, Singapore 129809

John Wiley & Sons Canada Ltd, 6045 Freemont Blvd. Mississauga, Ontario, L5R 4J3 Canada

Library of Congress Cataloging in Publication Data
A catalogue record for this book is available from the Library of Congress

British Library Cataloguing in Publication Data
A catalogue record for this book is available from the British Library

ISBN   978-1405-14700-2 (P/B)

Typeset in 10.5/13pt Minion by Aptara Inc., New Delhi, India
Printed and bound in Great Britain by CPI Antony Rowe, Chippenham, Wiltshire

Contents

Notes on Contributors   vii

Preface   xi

1. Images of the Multinational Firm   1
   Simon Collinson and Glenn Morgan

2. The Regional Dimension of Multinationals and the End of 'Varieties
   of Capitalism'   23
   Alan Rugman and Alain Verbeke

3. The Innovative Multinational Firm: The Dispersion of Creativity,
   and its Implications for the Firm and for World Development   45
   John Cantwell and Yanli Zhang

4. The Multinational Firm as the Major Global Promoter of Economic
   Development   69
   Simon Collinson

5. The Multinational Firm as a Creator, Fashioner and Respondent to
   Institutional Change   93
   John H. Dunning and Sarianna M. Lundan

6. The Multinational Firm as an Evolutionary System   117
   D. Eleanor Westney

7. The Multinational Firm as a Distinct Organizational Form   145
   Richard Whitley

8. Multinational Firms as Societies   167
   Glenn Morgan and Peer Hull Kristensen

9. The Multinational Firm as a Contested Terrain   193
   Paul Edwards and Jacques Bélanger

10. The Multinational Firm as a Locus of Learning along Networks   217
     Ray Loveridge

11. The Multinational Firm as an Instrument of Exploitation
     and Domination   247
     Raza Mir and Diana Rosemary Sharpe

Index   267

Notes on Contributors

Jacques Bélanger is Professor in the Département des Relations Industrielles at Université Laval, in Quebec City. The results of field research he conducted on workplace relations, mostly within multinational firms, have appeared in various industrial relations and sociological journals. With colleagues, he recently undertook a large-scale survey of employment practices within MNCs in Canada. This ongoing work also opens up the opportunity to compare findings with parallel surveys conducted in several other countries. He is Co-Director of the Inter-University Research Centre on Globalization and Work (CRIMT).

John Cantwell is Professor of International Business at Rutgers University, Newark, NJ, USA. He was previously Professor of International Economics at the University of Reading, UK, and he has also been a Visiting Professor in Rome, Toulouse and Vienna. His research focuses on technological innovation and multinational corporations. He has been Program Chair of the Academy of International Business (AIB), President of the European International Business Academy (EIBA), and he is an elected AIB Fellow and EIBA Fellow. He has so far published 11 books, over 55 articles in refereed academic journals, and over 70 chapters in edited collections.

Simon Collinson is Professor of International Business and Innovation and Head of the Marketing and Strategic Management (MSM) Group at Warwick Business School (WBS), University of Warwick. He is also a member of the Board of Directors for the UK's Advanced Institute of Management (AIM). He has a DPhil from the Science Policy Research Unit (Sussex) and has been a visiting Professor at the Kelley School of Business (Indiana), AGSM (Sydney) and NISTEP (Tokyo). He has published widely, including articles in the *Journal of International Business Studies* and *Organization Studies*, and has received funding awards from the UK ESRC, DTI, Royal Society and CEC. With Alan Rugman he is also co-author of *International Business* (FT/Pearson, 2009, 5th edn).

John Dunning is Emeritus Professor of International Business at the University of Reading, UK and at Rutgers University, US. He is a British citizen. He earned his

PhD in Economics from the University of Southampton in 1957, and since then has received six honorary doctorates. He is an ex-President of both the Academy of International Business, and the International Trade and Finance Association. His research interests include the theory and international political economy of international business activity. He has written or edited 50 books and 250 articles in professional journals. He was appointed OBE in the Queen's Birthday Honours List in 2008.

Paul Edwards is Professor of Industrial Relations at Warwick Business School, University of Warwick. He is a member of a team that conducted the first representative survey of MNCs in the UK; this survey has been replicated in several other countries. His other research interests include employment relations in small firms. He is a Fellow of the British Academy and an Associate Editor of *Human Relations*. His most recent book (with Judy Wajcman) is *The Politics of Working Life* (Oxford University Press, 2005).

Peer Hull Kristensen is Professor of the Sociology of the Firm and Work Organization at the International Center for Business and Politics, Copenhagen Business School. His research interest is the comparative study of national business systems, labor markets, and the organization of multinational companies. His current focus is on how changing forms of work-organization enable new firm strategies globally, and how this again co-evolves with making novel use of institutions – in particular in the Nordic countries. He has published widely on these issues. His book with Jonathan Zeitlin, *Local Players in Global Games: The Strategic Constitution of a Multinational Corporation* (Oxford University Press, 2005), is seen as somewhat iconoclastic in international business studies.

Ray Loveridge is Research Fellow at Said Business School, Oxford University, Professor Emeritus, Aston University, and Visiting Professor at Doshisha University, Kyoto, Japan. He previously lectured at the London School of Economics, at London Business School and latterly was Head of Strategic Management and Technology Policy at Aston. Formerly on the Editorial Board of the *British Journal of Industrial Relations*, between 1989 and 2000 he was Chief Editor of *Human Relations* and, until recently, a trustee and council member of the Tavistock Institute. He is currently Editorial Advisor to *Asian Business & Management*. He has published widely on issues of industrial relations, work, technology, organizations and multinationals.

Sarianna Lundan is Associate Professor of International Business Strategy at the University of Maastricht in the Netherlands and Research Fellow at ETLA, the Research Institute of the Finnish Economy in Helsinki. She has published widely in journals and books, and is the co-author with John Dunning of the second edition of *Multinational Enterprises and the Global Economy*, a major reference work in the field of International Business. She has also contributed to several research projects funded by UNCTAD, UNU-MERIT and the Commonwealth Secretariat, including work on the environmental and social impact of multinational enterprises.

Raza Mir is Professor of Management at William Paterson University in New Jersey, USA. His research mainly concerns the transfer of knowledge across national boundaries in multinational corporations, and issues relating to power and resistance in organizations. He is an Associate Editor of the journal *Organization*, and the co-author of *Organizations, Markets and Imperial Formations: Toward an Anthropology of Globalization* (Edward Elgar Press, 2009).

Glenn Morgan is Professor of Organizational Behaviour at Warwick Business School, University of Warwick. He is one of the Editors-in-Chief of *Organization: the critical journal of organization, theory and society*. He is a visiting Professor at the International Center for Business and Politics at Copenhagen Business School. Recent book publications include the co-edited volumes *The Multinational Firm: organizing across institutional and national divides* (2001) and *Changing Capitalisms?* (2005) (both published by Oxford University Press). Journal publications have appeared in *Organization Studies, Human Relations, Journal of Management Studies, Socio-Economic Review, Scandinavian Journal of Management* and *Critical Perspectives on International Business.*

Alan Rugman is the L. Leslie Waters Chair of International Business at the Kelley School of Business, Indiana University. In Spring 2009 he will become Professor of International Business at the Henley Business School of the University of Reading. His research analyzes the strategies and performance of the world's largest multinational enterprises. His recent books include: *The Regional Multinationals* (Cambridge University Press, 2005); *Regional Aspects of Multinationality and Performance*, (ed.) (Elsevier, 2007); *Multinationals and Development* (Yale, 2008) and *Rugman Reviews International Business* (Palgrave Macmillan, 2009).

Diana Sharpe is MBA Programme Director at the Webster Graduate School, Regents College, London. Previously she has held positions at Monmouth University, USA, Warwick Business School, the University of Warwick and Birmingham Business School, the University of Birmingham. She received her PhD from Manchester Business School for a study of work relations inside the subsidiaries of Japanese multinationals in the UK and her research has been published in the Journal of International Management, Journal of Management Studies and the International Journal of Human Resource Management. She co-edited New Horizons in Asian Business and Management: Critical Perspectives and Emerging Issues (Palgrave Macmillan, 2007).

Alain Verbeke holds the McCaig Research Chair in Management at the Haskayne School of Business, University of Calgary. He has been a visiting professor at Dalhousie University, the University of Toronto and the Université Catholique de Louvain, as well as an Associate Fellow of Templeton College (University of Oxford). He is presently a Visiting Chair in Strategy and International Business at Rotterdam School of Management. Dr Verbeke is an elected Fellow of the Academy of International Business and has authored or edited 23 books and more than 160 refereed publications, including several articles in the *Strategic Management Journal* and the *Journal of International Business Studies*.

Eleanor Westney is Professor of Organizational Behaviour/Industrial Relations and holds the Scotiabank Professorship in International Business, Schulich School of Business, York University, Canada. She spent 25 years on the faculty of the MIT Sloan School of Management, where she held the Sloan Fellows Chair in the Strategy and International Management group. She received a PhD in Sociology in 1978 from Princeton University, and taught in the Department of Sociology at Yale University. She has published widely, including *Organization Theory and the Multinational Corporation* (Macmillan, 2005, 2nd edn), co-edited with Sumantra Ghoshal. She is a Fellow of the Academy of International Business and is currently the Dean of the AIB Fellows.

Richard Whitley is Professor of Organizational Sociology at Manchester Business School, the University of Manchester. He has recently held visiting positions at Erasmus University, Rotterdam and Hitotsubashi University, Tokyo. His most recent book is *Business Systems and Organizational Capabilities: the institutional structuring of competitive competences* (Oxford University Press, 2007). He has been Chair of the European Group on Organization Studies (EGOS) and President of the Society for the Advancement of Socio-Economics (SASE). His publications have appeared in many journals and edited collections. Until recently he was a Senior Editor for *Organization Studies*.

Yanli Zhang is Assistant Professor in the Management and Information Systems Department at Montclair State University. She graduated with a PhD in Management concentrating on strategy and international business from Rutgers University in May 2007. Her research interests are in technological innovation, networks and knowledge. Her paper *Inter-Firm Networks and Innovation* won the Doug Nigh award for the most innovative paper in the International Management Division at the Academy of Management 2007 annual conference. She obtained a BA in Economics from Beijing University, China; and has worked as an economic analyst in the Ministry of Foreign Affairs, China, and a management consultant in Accenture, Beijing office.

Preface

This book project has been some time in the making. We first discussed the idea with Rosemary Nixon when she was based at Blackwell Publishers and she has supported it from the beginning. The shift to John Wiley & Sons has worked smoothly for the book in the final stages of production.

The idea to draw contributors from a range of different disciplines was crucial to the purpose of the book. The editors come from different groups within the large and intellectually stimulating environment of Warwick Business School (Simon from Marketing and Strategic Management, Glenn from Industrial Relations and Organizational Behaviour). We are both engaged in a range of teaching at WBS across undergraduate, specialist masters and MBA degrees as well as supervising students and were therefore strongly conscious of the need to make the subject area and the book suitable for use by students. We had a personal as well as a professional interest in bringing together experienced scholars studying the same phenomenon in very different ways, to juxtapose their approaches, objectives and underlying assumptions. Being in different areas of the business school research community, we were able to draw on distinct but complementary networks of international scholars studying multinational firms. We thank our contributors very much for their willingness to participate in the project.

Rosemary Nixon facilitated a workshop in Warwick where most of the contributors presented early versions of their chapters and discussed the objectives of the book. The ESRC Centre for the Study of Globalization and Regionalization also provided support for the workshop. Simon was funded, for part of the project, by a Ghoshal Fellowship from the UK's Advanced Institute of Management (AIM). Secretarial and administrative assistance for the production of the manuscript was provided by Jo Sheehan from the Industrial Relations and Organizational Behaviour Group at Warwick Business School. We thank them all for their help.

Simon Collinson
Glenn Morgan
Warwick Business School
February 2009

Chapter 1 Images of the Multinational Firm

Simon Collinson and Glenn Morgan

Introduction

Multinational enterprises (MNEs) are everywhere, connecting people and places as product and service providers, employers, investors, brand promoters, lobbyists. The economic scope and geographic spread of MNEs is large and expanding. They are a central part of the process of globalization which has characterized social, economic and political development over the last 30 years. The rationale for their existence, their impact on societies and environments, their role in transferring technologies, people, skills and wealth across national boundaries, and their involvement in political debates places them in the centre of our experience of the modern world. For these reasons, discussions of multinationals appear in many academic disciplines and courses.

This creates a problem for students, teachers and the interested lay reader. How are they to get to grips with the range of different approaches to multinationals? If they approach the topic primarily from the perspective of economics, they will get one set of views of the MNE; if they examine the MNE from a sociological or political perspective, they will get another set of views. If they dig deeper they will often find that there are few linkages between the diverse literatures that examine MNEs. They tend to operate in particular enclaves (some larger and more populated than others) which are based on their own assumptions and express little interest in or knowledge of other traditions.

The main aim of this unique collection of articles is not to synthesize or summarize the multitude of case studies and data, methodologies, frameworks and theories that try to capture, characterize, explain or predict the MNE. Instead we have brought together some of the leading authors in the study of MNEs over the last few decades and asked them to encapsulate their view of how such organizations work. In this introduction, we discuss three aspects of this project. The first aspect concerns the

Images of the Multinational Firm   Edited by Simon Collinson and Glenn Morgan
© 2009 John Wiley & Sons, Ltd

value of bringing such diverse approaches together in this format. Here we explain our understanding of the value of analysing different 'images' of the MNE. The second aspect concerns why this approach is peculiarly useful to the study of MNEs. The third aspect describes how the various images relate together and how this book can be used.

Images: Why and What For?

An 'image' is a representation of a phenomenon. As with any representation, it offers us a particular view so that we can think of the phenomenon being represented in a new way. Images, of their nature, are not claims to transcendental 'truth'. We can think of multiple representations of the human body in art and sculpture. Some artistic representations may aim for 'realism' but they still remain the product of the artist and the artist's attempt at representation. Many other images of the body particularly in the modern era make no claim to realism and in fact explicitly reject its tenets. Thus images proliferate without any obvious constraints on them. What makes certain images powerful is less to do with their realism and more to do with how, in particular social and artistic contexts, these images provide a focus for diverse audiences to reflect upon the nature of aesthetics, the nature of the human and the nature of social order. Clearly one of the most important reflections that they force is into the nature of transcendental truth and its perceived enemy, 'relativism'. If all images are representations, where does truth lie? We are now used to this proliferation of images and reflections in many spheres of our lives and social theorists have broadly labelled this shift as a move towards 'postmodernism' (Lyotard, 1984) or in some authors 'high modernism' (Giddens, 1992) or 'hyper-reality' (Baudrillard in Poster, 2001). From this perspective, it is how images help us to think about ourselves that gives them power and relevance in particular contexts.

We remain less comfortable about the idea of images in the scientific arena, particularly in the social sciences where the inherent contestability of concepts makes diverse images endemic in many disciplines, thus undermining claims to scientific objectivity and in this way the legitimacy of access to large public research funds. Most social sciences disciplines therefore contain a substantial proportion of researchers committed to the search for truth and another group more likely to feel comfortable with the idea of alternative images or paradigms illuminating different aspects of social reality through the stimulation of reflection and debate. The balance between these two perspectives varies enormously. When Gareth Morgan first developed the use of the idea of images to study 'organizations', it was in a context where organization studies had been predominantly driven by claims to truth built on methodologies that reflected as far as they could more natural science approaches built in large numbers, and developing law-like generalizations (Morgan, 2006: originally published 1986). Morgan, building on his previous work with Burrell on 'sociological paradigms' (Burrell and Morgan, 1978), proclaimed the value of images of organizations as a means to reflect on and debate the nature of management, authority, control, values etc. Morgan found a receptive climate to his ideas as many others sought to broaden out the study of organizations to tackle new questions in new ways. The impact of postmodernist and poststructuralist philosophy within organization studies contributed further to this process.

For Morgan, the issue was what could be learned about organizations by developing particular images. How could particular images contribute to us understanding contemporary organizations and our role in them? Within this framework, it is possible to remain agnostic about the question of truth and relativism. The point of discussing organizations through the lens of 'images' is not to say an organization is 'a' or 'b' (and we can prove that according to scientific methodology); instead the question would be what if we think about an organization as *like* 'a' or 'b'? How does that resonate with our experience? How does it help us think about the organization? What questions does it open up that might be worth pursuing? How does it contribute to the debates which concern us about organizations – whether those are in terms of productivity or efficiency or more in terms of power and control? As Morgan states:

> 'a metaphor always produces one-sided kind of insight. In highlighting certain interpretations it tends to force others into a background role ... metaphor *always* creates distortions. We have to accept that any theory or perspective that we bring to the study of organization and management, while capable of creating valuable insights is also incomplete, biased and potentially misleading ... no single theory will ever give us a perfect or all-purpose point of view ... the challenge is to become skilled in the art of using metaphor: to find fresh ways of seeing, understanding and shaping the situations that we want to organize and manage'. (Morgan, 1997: 4)

It is in this spirit which we present this collection of essays. In effect, we put aside or bracket off questions about the nature of social reality (ontology) and acquiring knowledge of that reality (epistemology). It is not that we believe these to be minor issues or insignificant; on the contrary, as Burrell and Morgan (1978) demonstrated in their book, epistemological and ontological commitments in effect drive theorizing down certain channels and shape the sorts of concepts and methods which we use in our analysis. However, our purpose here is not to engage in a confrontation of different philosophical positions, useful and worthy as that might be. In some ways that might be a next step for anybody who really wants to understand what underpins the images which are discussed here. But for this project, our purpose is to present these images as clearly and carefully as we can. Each author or pair of authors makes their own case as to how the image which they present provides an insight into the multinational corporation. This in itself is sufficient for us in this project, not least because the diversity and breadth of authors who have contributed is unique as far as we are aware. There are no other collections of work on multinationals which place so many diverse perspectives side by side. So we have not sought to blur those distinctions or to create a different 'battleground of ideas' by simultaneously evoking the terrains of ontology and epistemology. The authors clearly take very different positions on these issues but as we have stated for the purposes of this project we have bracketed these questions off in order to concentrate on the images themselves. Anybody wishing for the 'truth' about multinationals will need to go elsewhere.

Finally, the need to reflect on the nature of images, or imagery, is heightened by their proliferation in the world around us. Particular implicit or explicit intentions, or agency, lie behind the presentation and dissemination of all kinds of images. The motivation underlying the portrayal of a specific image of an MNE may be political, social, economic or a combination of these. Whilst media, of whatever variety, has the primary function to attract attention, politicians, managers, trades unions and other interest groups have particular reasons for using media to portray certain images of MNEs. In the face of a real-world challenge to understand the nature, impact and future of MNEs some degree of reflection on the agency behind different images is necessary.

Images of Multinationals: Some Initial Considerations

According to UNCTAD's World Investment Report (UNCTAD, 2007) an estimated 37 000 MNEs, with 170 000 foreign affiliates, in the early 1990s, had grown to 77 000 parent companies with over 770 000 foreign affiliates by 2005. These affiliates employed about 62 million workers globally and generated about $4.5 trillion in value added. The amount of economic assets controlled through the activities of multinationals has often been compared to the GDP of countries. Anderson and Cavanagh (2000), for example, calculated that of the 100 largest economies in the world, 51 are multinational corporations and only 49 are countries.

Historically firms which could be described as multinational (in terms of having assets in different countries and trading across borders) have existed for centuries. Firstly they existed primarily as merchants or trading companies, e.g. the East India Company, the Hudson Bay Trading Company. In the nineteenth century, alongside the traders there emerged international companies seeking raw materials (such as oil, diamonds and gold, foodstuffs, minerals etc.) in different parts of the world. These activities were supported by a burgeoning network of international financiers and banks that facilitated the transfer of capital across national borders. In the late nineteenth century, the first manufacturing MNEs emerged, transferring technologies, capital and expertise across borders in order to access markets and reduce costs of production. Commentators such as Hirst and Thompson (1999) argue that the highly internationalized economy of the period up to 1914 under the hegemony of the British Empire and the pound sterling marked a high watermark of internationalization that, because of the catastrophes of World War One and the Depression of the 1930s, was not surpassed until the early 1990s.

Right from the start of these developments, commentators saw different consequences emerging from the expansion of FDI and multinationals. For many European imperialists of the nineteenth century, the 'white man's burden' considered in terms of bringing 'civilization' and 'Christianity' to the world more generally was accomplished by the extension of the principles of trade, manufacture and commerce to new areas. This was a vision of progress in which both sides were seen to benefit. The division of labour encouraged specialization; some countries specialized in raw material production; others in the production of manufactured goods. Trade between the two brought higher economic benefits to both. From this perspective, the internationalization of economic activity might generate certain problems of equilibrium but in the main this was the world of Adam Smith writ large – the invisible hand of the market working to the benefit of all concerned.

Others saw a very different picture. In his essay on Imperialism which was highly influential for over 50 years, Lenin saw the drive of companies to expand overseas as leading in a number of directions. The first was an effort to weaken the collective institutions of labour in the European heartland by increasing the 'reserve army of labour' available to capital in developing countries which lacked trade unions and had repressive labour regimes. The second was that these companies demanded that their home governments guarantee them access to the markets and resources of these new locations. Out of this grew the competition between European powers that was known as the 'scramble for Africa' and also saw the French and the British compete over lands in the Caribbean, China and India. This competitive struggle became more intense as Germany, Italy and Russia became unified states and the Ottoman Empire, that held most of South East Europe as well as the Levant, the Arab peninsular and Egypt, began to break apart. Lenin saw this as the roots of the First World War, a position shared by some liberal thinkers such as J. A. Hobson whose work on Liberal Imperialism inspired Lenin. Hobson was a liberal who believed that large conglomerates and their allies in government were pushing countries towards war. In his view, open competitive markets were a necessary antidote to imperialism. In later years, the *New York Times* journalist, Tom Friedman invented a new version of the Gladstonian liberal belief that free trade prevented war when he argued that no two countries that had McDonalds have ever fought a war with each other since both got McDonalds.

Right from the start, therefore, there existed these two distinct images about the nature of multinationals – one that they were broadly progressive in their economic impact, serving to distribute the gains of a global division of labour and bringing areas into the global economy in a way that would bring improvement to their populations. The other view was that MNEs were involved in maximizing the exploitation of the workforce wherever it was based and in order to achieve this they looked for governments that would protect and support them, thus fermenting international rivalries and the potential for war.

Across the sub-fields of management and business studies, including strategy, marketing, finance and accounting, human resource management and operations, two terminologies began to develop with accepted assumptions, an associated set of methodological approaches, and legitimized measures of empirical reality. These would characterize both academic studies of multinationals and the imagery employed by the media, the public and policymakers, for some time to come. One was around issues of performance, ownership, prices and costs, profit maximization, markets and hierarchies, internalization, rational agents and strategic intent; the other around issues of social relations, contexts, institutions, learning, interest groups, power, authority and exploitation.[1]

The economics discipline provided the concepts, theories and methods to anchor the approach taken by the first of these scholarly communities. It focused on issues of internal firm efficiency and organizational best practices, connected with a concern for optimizing external market positioning and relative competitive advantage in the context of firm internationalization. The latter group perceived multinational firms as organizational contexts for internal contests over goals, means and processes. A focus on conflicts between internal interest groups mirrored a concern over the contentious external political, economic and societal roles of multinational firms. Sociology and political science more loosely provided the theoretical foundations of this latter group, which has always been smaller and less coherent in its aims and approach than the former, more dominant paradigm. Although this portrayal suggests a clear-cut dichotomy, where there exists a continuum of perspectives and approaches to understanding the MNE, it is fair to say that studies have tended to cluster at the extremes of this range.

Theories of Multinationals: The Evolving Landscape

In the post-war period, these two views existed in different domains of academic study and policy discussion buttressed by distinctive methodological approaches. What is interesting, however, is how what for many years seemed to be an unbridgeable chasm has more recently become more like the development of a common ground of study even if there continues to exist a diversity of images. In some ways, the fact that this split became so deep is intriguing because in the 1960s and early 1970s two of the earliest significant influences on the debate on multinationals – Hymer and Vernon – sought to keep both sets of issues in view. Dunning (2001) in his survey of the key literature on IB activities describes how Hymer, as well as addressing the question of why firms should wish to control or coordinate activities across borders, also influenced Marxist scholars such as Baran (1966) and Radice (1975) as well as the dependency school of Andre Gunder Frank (1967) with his analysis of how the international firm was an exploiter and creator of monopolistic advantages. Similarly, Vernon, whose product life cycle theory explained how and why firms move across borders, produced a highly influential book entitled *Sovereignty at Bay* in which he tackled the question of the relationship between nation states and multinationals (Vernon, 1971). However, this sort of broad sweep approach to the study of multinationals began to be squeezed out as more specialist academic perspectives evolved.

For much of the period up to around 2000, it was the field of international business (derived initially from developments in economic analysis) which set the pace for understanding multinationals. Although studies of MNEs from more organizational or sociological perspectives did not die out completely, they were not very influential either in terms of the academic debate or policymaking. Instead the study of MNEs became increasingly oriented around two main themes. The first was around the economic factors influencing their growth and development – a theme which tended to dominate up to the early 1990s. The second was around issues of strategy and structure, a theme emerging more strongly in the 1990s. In the rest of this section we discuss these two developments and then explain the gradual tensions which emerged within the field as these approaches struggled to deal with the evolving landscape of globalization in the late 1990s. It was this tension that stimulated a reawakening of interest in a more sociological approach to MNEs which is discussed in the following section of this introduction.

Economic Theories of the MNE

The most significant of these in the 1970s was the establishment of the internalization paradigm building on the work of Coase and Williamson in transaction cost economics. Why was it that cross-national activities became coordinated through international firm structures rather than simply through markets? The internalization of transactions within firm hierarchies emerged as a rational economic response to the failure of other forms of organizing transactions over national borders. Dunning describes this as '*the* question of the day' in the 1970s. He states that 'for much of the last two decades ... the theory of internalization ... has been the dominant explanation for the existence and growth of the MNE. It has natural appeal to micro-economists, business historians and organizational theorists' (Dunning, 2001: 42). Buckley and Casson (1976) is often seen as the key milestone text linking the transaction cost approach and internalization theory to the study of international business. Hennart, another of the main authors in this approach, summarizes the argument as follows:

> 'An MNE will expand abroad when it can organize interdependencies between agents located in different countries more efficiently than markets. This implies that three conditions must be met: (1) interdependent agents must be located in different countries ... (2) the MNE must be the most efficient way to organize those interdependencies (otherwise we would have international market transactions) and (3) given condition (2) the costs incurred by MNEs to organize these interdependencies are lower than the benefits of doing so.'
> (Hennart, 2001: 132)

Hennart describes a number of phenomena that influence these decisions. In particular, he focuses on know-how. This has a broad meaning including knowledge per se and technology. Where know-how is to be transferred, only hierarchy (i.e. the creation of subsidiary relations) can ensure that it does not leak out to competitors (through opportunism or cheating), thus devaluing the proprietary knowledge of the firm. Similarly a firm's reputation can be devalued if it franchises its knowledge out overseas to others who do not have the same incentive to protect its reputation as the firm itself does, a problem also where marketing and distribution is not controlled inside the firm.

Internalization theory has been supplemented by a range of other approaches which have picked up in more detail the geographical and locational issues which arose out of this analysis. The most well-known attempt to expand this form of analysis, retaining the basic insights of internalization theory but locating it in a broader context, was Dunning's 'eclectic paradigm' of MNE activity. The 'eclectic theory' of multinational activity identifies three elements influencing the why and how of MNE development. The first element consists of the competitive advantages of existing MNEs; Dunning labels these as ownership (O) advantages. They reflect the capabilities developed by the MNE in its home base. Here, Dunning drew into the analysis the influential work of Penrose on why firms do what they do, which later became a component of the debate on the 'core competences' of the firm and the resource-based view of the firm. The second element consists of locational (L) advantages of particular countries in terms of access to skills, knowledge, markets, technologies, raw materials and other resources that the firm requires. The third element consists of internalization (I) advantages as discussed previously.

Dunning's OLI paradigm provides a broad framework for a number of other developments in theories of multinationals. One increasingly important set of concerns which emerged from this was the focus on locational advantages. In particular, questions about the development of new technologies, products and processes outside the home base became increasingly significant. A central part of locational attractiveness lies in the ability to access specialist knowledge and skills that have emerged in particular geographical contexts. Thus Dunning's ideas linked strongly to emerging discussion of industrial districts and clusters, suggesting that MNEs are keen to locate in such contexts in order to upgrade their own skills and knowledge. More recent work on these processes has revealed that there is quite a subtle form of learning and exchange which goes on in such contexts. In particular the MNE has to build social capital, trust and networks with local firms if it is to benefit from agglomeration effects. It also needs to develop its own absorptive capacity so that it can access the tacit knowledge which underpins specific forms of technology, skill and knowledge. This in turn raises questions that derive from the internalization approach concerning how networks are to be governed, how to build alliances and linkages as well as how to use the market to access these capabilities.

In his contribution to this book, Dunning and his co-author Lundan emphasize the significance of the widening geographic distribution of the sourcing and deployment of competitiveness enhancing assets for MNEs. Moreover, as these strategic assets have become more knowledge and information-intensive, there are important changes in the organizational demands on MNEs. Together these trends place institutions closer to centre stage in studies of MNES. The authors suggest that not only are national institutions now more important as an influence on behaviour of MNEs, but MNEs are exerting a greater influence on national level institutions, and thereby on the economic and social goals of countries. Dunning and Lundan present an image of the MNE as a 'creator, fashioner and respondent to institutional change'. Right from his earliest contributions, Dunning saw that the role of government was crucial in these processes. He was interested in how governments could shape a conducive environment for FDI and multinationals but also recognized that MNEs could affect the politics of the countries in which they were located. His arguments have been influential in policy circles such as UNCTAD and in more recent times he has explored issues of ethics (Dunning, 2005), a theme which he develops in his contribution to this book.

In his chapter, Cantwell, who has made a major contribution to understanding how technology and R&D interacts with the development of multinational corporations ('MNCs'), writing together with Yanli Zhang, considers the evolution of the 'innovative MNE'. The past 30 years have seen a structural and strategic shift from a situation where the main source of innovation and creativity in MNEs was at the centre, to one where innovation and competence creation is distributed across the MNE network. They examine the particular significance of this change for the role of MNEs in developing countries. The chapter re-evaluates Hymer's (1972) 'law of uneven development' which saw the dominant MNE role as reinforcing and perpetuating patterns of uneven development in the world. The interchange between MNEs and subsidiary locations, which have their own specific advantages, is more complex than Hymer proposed. Patterns of uneven development are therefore not as extreme or as self-perpetuating as Hymer suggested. Moreover, where it is linked to the activities of MNEs, uneven development does not result solely from centralized control in MNE headquarters. The fragmentation of production and modularization of technologies have created new opportunities for countries catching up technologically, and they have resulted in more complex 'bottom-up' links between 'centre and periphery' via the activities of MNEs.

In his contribution Collinson takes a similar topic, the role of MNEs in developing countries, and concludes that MNEs are major promoters of economic development. As noted by Dunning and Lundan, Collinson suggests that too little attention has been paid to the effects of MNEs on their host environments. He presents an image of the global firm as a key contributor to the innovative capabilities of host region firms in developing countries and therefore an important positive force for economic growth and social development in countries around the world. There is often a strong coincidence of interests between MNEs and host governments. However, he argues that MNEs usually perform this role unwittingly and often unwillingly.

Another significant figure in these developments has been Alan Rugman. Like Dunning, Rugman draws in an eclectic manner from different economic perspectives. In recent years, however, he has been particularly concerned to emphasize the regional nature of MNE activities. Developing his argument from a series of large scale databases which he has constructed, Rugman argues that the reality of MNEs is that most of their assets and markets are located within their home regions (defining these broadly as the Triad of the Americas, Asia and Europe; Collinson and Rugman (2008), Rugman (2005)). In his chapter in this book together with Verbeke, he develops this argument as a way to critique those authors who emphasize national varieties of capitalism. Rugman and Verbeke review empirical evidence on the world's largest 500 multinational enterprises and show a strong intra-regional pattern of sales and assets, rather than a global one. They present an image of the MNE as a regional organization that requires regional, not global strategies. Part of this image views home region governments focusing on policies of social, cultural, and political harmonization to develop internal markets, as in the EU, and working towards economic integration, as in NAFTA and Asia. At the same time inter-regional business is likely to be restricted by government-imposed barriers to entry. They use this empirical evidence to argue against the 'varieties of capitalism' approach to international political economy (IPE) most associated with Hall and Soskice (2001). Whilst it may be valid to differentiate country conditions, including institutions, culture and politics, the authors critique the highly stylized view of globalization put forward by varieties of capitalism approaches and the limited attention paid to the activities and effects of MNEs. The image they present is clear-cut in terms of which empirical dimensions best characterize the MNE as an organizational form. The distribution of assets and sales in their view captures much of what we need to know because it informs a long-running debate regarding the competitive advantages of MNEs, demonstrated by the limited geographical spread of what they own and what they can successfully sell in competition with local firms.

Multinational Strategy and Organization

Whilst there were clearly implications for the management of multinationals in the economic theories developed, these were not necessarily made explicit. By contrast, by the late 1980s, there was increasing interest in organizational and strategic questions concerning the development of MNEs. One of the most influential attempts to create an enduring framework for this type of analysis was Bartlett and Ghoshal's (1989) *Managing across Borders*.[2] Their framework built on the work of the economists but drew out the strategic and organizational implications for managers. However it also took two very significant steps beyond the economists, firstly by incorporating a much more dynamic sense of the globalization processes that were then emerging and secondly by appreciating early on the centrality of innovation, knowledge and learning to the development of the MNE.

In relation to their initial framework, this was a fairly standard contingency model. Using the economists' notions it began from the idea that certain sorts of markets 'fitted' particular sorts of internationalization strategy on the part of firms and this led to a particular organizational configuration. Where national markets were very distinctive from each other, it made sense to organize the firm in a decentralized way as a set of national units sensing and exploiting local opportunities. Somewhat confusingly they called this model a 'multinational' firm. Where national markets retained some elements of distinctiveness but there was also a commonality, then the firm was likely to be a combination of centralized and decentralized processes and functions, adapting and leveraging parent company competences as their key advantage. Thus knowledge developed at the centre would be transferred to overseas units. These firms they labeled as 'international'. Where markets were more or less standardized across countries, firms were likely to be highly centralized. Production was planned on a global basis to take advantage of economies of scale and then the outputs were delivered into national markets. These they labeled as 'global firms'.

Where they created new ground was with their fourth category – the 'transnational firm'. This firm sought to combine three advantages. It needed to be globally competitive so its production process had to achieve economies of scale, implying strong centralizing tendencies. However it also needed to be sensitive to local markets and responses to differences between contexts, implying elements of decentralization. Finally and most importantly, it had to leverage the knowledge and skills spread around its different parts in order to create learning and innovation. They therefore developed a vision of a firm which was global, dynamic, networked horizontally rather than just vertically and highly innovative (see also Nohria and Ghoshal, 1997).

The style of Bartlett and Ghoshal was to use simple case studies of companies in a rather unproblematic way (drawing evidence on the basis of unsystematic interviews and observations of senior managers). They could be justifiably criticized for what by most standards, even in the slippery world of business and management, could be described as 'methodological weaknesses'. However, in retrospect, it might be argued that they were producing their own 'images of multinationals'. They were not saying that all MNEs must be in one or the other category but rather that these types emphasize some interesting aspects of how MNEs are structured and are therefore good tools to use in looking in detail at any one particular case. Their concept of 'administrative heritage' emphasized that firms moved towards or away from these various models depending on their own history in terms of their founding contexts and the impact of early decisions on how to organize the firm. Their models are aids to thinking, not substitutes for it. In this respect they have been remarkably successful since their ideas continue to influence how MNEs are considered. What they did, however, was to identify the potential innovative capabilities of the MNE as lying in its very internal diversity. They recognized, that this potential was difficult to achieve and could result in a breakdown of the firm into competing units. So there had to be some delicate balancing between centralization and decentralization, between integration and responsiveness. Although organization structures played a part in this, they also emphasized the importance of creating a global management culture that kept the senior management of the transnational working together and coordinating the different parts of the firm. What was central here was their identification of the problem even if their solution did not go much beyond wishful thinking. Nevertheless the way in which they spelt out the problem has been fundamental to later developments.

Two strands emerged during the 1990s that developed these ideas. The first associated particularly with the work of Julian Birkinshaw concerned the relationship between subsidiaries and headquarters. The second was an attempt to bridge the gap between organization theory and the study of MNEs associated particularly with the work of Eleanor Westney but also developing further as the influence of neo-institutional theory became more profound in US business schools, e.g. through the work of Kostova and Guillen. Both of these developments could be said to start to reposition the study of MNEs in a space where it was open to wider influences than transaction costs economics or even Dunning's eclectic theory.

Birkinshaw's work evolved quite closely out of Bartlett and Ghoshal; later indeed he cooperated with them on a textbook on transnational management (Bartlett, Ghoshal and Birkinshaw, 2006). He was particularly interested in subsidiaries and the degree to which they were active in developing their own strategies. Previous work in this area had tended to emerge from slightly different concerns from those of Bartlett and Ghoshal. In particular the work of Taggart, Hood *et al.* in Scotland had been stimulated by debates on 'branch plant economies' (Birkinshaw and Hood, 1998). In a context where governments were increasingly active in seeking to per-suade multinationals to set up subsidiaries (by offering tax reliefs, cheap land and other forms of assistance), there was growing concern that MNEs were setting up subsidiaries for their own short-term advantage and that the MNEs were not gener-ating much in the way of positive effects for the locations in which the subsidiaries were established. It appeared in a number of cases that once the advantages were phased out (particularly those to do with tax breaks), MNEs were likely to look else-where and were willing to close down their subsidiary, particularly where labour laws (as in the UK by the late 1980s) made this a relatively easy and low cost option. What was it that made subsidiaries put down deeper roots, to stick in particular locations and generate longer term positive outcomes for localities? Clearly part of the answer already provided by Dunning and his colleagues was that the locality had to have assets worth staying for. However, another part of the answer lay in the strategies which were pursued by the local subsidiaries (Birkinshaw, 1997). Birkinshaw partic-ularly examined this point, labelling the process as 'entrepreneurship in the global firm', the title of his 2000 book. Birkinshaw's analysis was complex and consisted of trying to capture the dynamics of strategy formation in the headquarters, how this impacted on processes and structures inside the MNE and within this context how subsidiaries and their managers could strategize for advantage. Whereas in Bartlett and Ghoshal the internal environment of the MNE was diverse but essentially benign and cohesive, Birkinshaw produced a much more dynamic view of the internal struc-ture, one where 'gaming' was occurring as subsidiaries played against each other for resources held by the centre. In Birkinshaw, this was a positive process that could be likened to an internal market producing overall efficiency gains to the organization as a result of competition. Ultimately, therefore, Birkinshaw retained an economic model of these dynamics and also avoided stepping too far beyond the boundaries of the firm into issues of social and economic power.

Westney on the other hand did begin to make these steps. Her edited collection with Ghoshal *Organization Theory and the Multinational Corporation* derived from a conference held in INSEAD in 1989 although the book itself was not published until 1993. It stands as the main effort during most of the 1990s to bring these two areas together. Its authors included firstly the main contributors to the emerging 'transnational' paradigm (Bartlett, Ghoshal, Doz, Hedlund), secondly some emerging organization theory scholars (Westney herself plus van Maanen and Kilduff) as well as representatives of other strands of theorizing (Egelhoff with his information-based contingency approach to the structure of MNEs (see also Egelhoff 1982; 1993); Hennart with his transaction cost approach and Kogut with his effort to link national contexts and international competition). The editors described their goal as a 'bridge-building enterprise':

> 'This book represents not closure . . . but only a beginning. Our hope is that the book will trigger reflection and debate in the organization theory and international management communities – that perhaps it will generate some collaboration across the two fields – but above all else that it will stimulate mutual interest and further research that can benefit both fields.' (Ghoshal and Westney 1993: 20)

Westney herself with her previous interests in the history and development of R&D in Japanese enterprises picked up the developing theoretical field of neo-institutionalism, deriving from DiMaggio and Powell as well as Scott, and Meyer and Rowan. She introduced the idea of isomorphism from this field into the analysis of multinationals arguing that 'the MNE operates in many institutional environments and provides a context in which the nature and strength of isomorphic pulls within and across fields can be analyzed'. She used this to argue that the home institutional environment of the MNE created a pressure on the firm to conform to certain patterns of behaviour and structure. Thus when the MNE extended its operation to other contexts it inevitably created a situation of tension between the isomorphic pull of the home environment and that of the host environment. In this way, Westney was able to transcend the notion that integration or responsiveness were managerial strategies and instead to locate them as fundamental tensions in the nature of the MNE itself (Westney, 1990, 1993; Westney and Zaheer, 2001).

These insights were developed later in the decade in a series of papers by Kostova *et al.* (Kostova, 1999; Kostova and Zaheer, 1999; Kostova and Roth, 2002). Kostova has argued that the multinational subsidiary is in a situation of 'institutional duality'. On the one hand, it is pressurized by the headquarters to adopt a particular set of practices derived from the home base of the firm; on the other hand, the subsidiary is pressurized by its host context to follow local practices. The subsidiary faces the question of which set of institutions are more important to it – those that make it legitimate within the multinational or those which legitimate it in its local context? The greater the 'institutional distance' between the home and host countries, the greater the difficulty for the HQ of successfully transferring practices from one to the other (Kostova and Roth, 2002; also Xu and Shenkar, 2002) and the more likely host influences will prevail. Kostova and Roth's findings are that 'both dimensions of practice adoption, implementation and internalization, vary across foreign subsidiaries as a result of two factors – the institutional environment in the host country and the relational context within the MNE' (Kostova and Roth, 2002: 227). By relational context is meant the degree of dependence, trust and identity between the subsidiary and the head office. In combination, institutional duality and the relational context produce four types of subsidiary response to head office initiatives – which they label as 'active', 'minimal', 'assent' and 'ceremonial' (p. 229).

Unlike Westney, Kostova was quite narrow and static in her analysis of institutions. Westney in her 1993 chapter used her knowledge of Japan and Japanese firms to show how there was ongoing adaptation and change in Japanese transplants. She resisted any temptation to resort to static indices of national culture derived from authors such as Hofstede and instead developed a very specific view of institutions and their historical evolution. She also emphasized the role of the state and politics and power in influencing isomorphic processes. Overall, Westney has sought to develop a view of multinationals which locates them in specific historical institutional contexts and looks at how over time they evolve and change as a result of organizational, institutional and economic pressures.

In her chapter in this book, Westney suggests that by drawing more systematically on developments in organization theory we can make the evolutionary model more explicit and stronger as a theoretical basis for understanding MNEs. Inspiration is drawn first from the work of Bruce Kogut and a few others that have examined variation and retention processes within the firm, building for example on Nelson and Winter's concept of routines. Second, a bridge is built between two very different empirical studies to present the MNE as an evolutionary system, with subsystems that co-evolve in interaction with each other and their differentiated environments.

Along with a small number of authors (such as Kogut (2001) and Guillen (2001)), Westney has pushed beyond the initial boundaries of international business scholarship into an analysis of MNEs which is much more sociological in conception, where the MNE is subject to external isomorphic pressures from distinctive institutional contexts and where managers and employees in different positions within the firm struggle to deal with the competing demands of the external market, the internal coordination processes and different institutional pressures.

Beyond the International Business Mainstream

Beyond this framework, there was relatively little interest in MNEs. The hopes of Ghoshal and Westney in 1993, that there would be more interaction between the different perspectives, tended to wither. Part of the problem was that international business analysis was given its intellectual rigour by its location within the Coasian framework. Although there were different perspectives, as has been discussed, the very labelling of them as 'eclectic' worked to devalue them from the point of view of economic theory. Similarly efforts to introduce neo-institutionalist theories which, at their heart, challenge efficiency logics, were always going to meet strong resistance in academic contexts where such logics are seen to predominate as an explanatory schema, which was how international business had increasingly positioned itself.

On the other hand, organization theory was equally uninterested in any rapprochement around the study of multinationals. Other than Westney herself it is hard to identify any of the main organization theory scholars of the time who took a serious interest in understanding the specific nature of multinationals. European organization theory was particularly parlous in this respect, a somewhat strange outcome given how diverse, innovative and open this field had become by the early 1990s. It was only gradually that this began to change. Partly this was stimulated by a growing sense that the arguments of Birkinshaw, Westney and others were actually creating new possibilities for organization theory that could meaningfully tackle the distinctiveness of MNEs. Partly, this was also stimulated by the ever growing importance of MNEs in public discourse about globalization and its impact on societies.[3]

However there were two specific developments which pushed this forward, particularly in the European context. The first was the effort to move industrial relations research in a more comparative direction, itself significantly stimulated by the project to create the European Community and the Single Market. The second was the renewed emphasis on institutional contexts or what became variously labelled as 'divergent capitalisms', 'varieties of capitalism', 'competing capitalisms'.

In relation to industrial relations, the discipline had become progressively more comparative over the 1980s and early 1990s (see e.g. Crouch, 1993; Streeck, 1992; Ferner and Hyman, 1998). There was a greater understanding of the differences between national systems of industrial relations. This was not just an academic development. It also linked strongly to debates in the EU concerning the development of the Single Market. If there was to be a Single Market covering the whole of the EU, ought there not to be a single social model that harmonized areas such as employment and industrial relations? Otherwise, it could be argued, employers will shift to contexts where labour is cheapest and least protected. The fall of the Berlin Wall and the opening up of Eastern and Central Europe increased concerns that employment would fall in the Western European countries and 'coercive comparisons' would be used to force unions in these countries to agree to a lessening of standards, conditions and rewards in order to avoid the loss of jobs to low wage and low social protection economies. The growing importance of China from the mid 1990s increased these arguments. Thus different industrial relations traditions affected how MNEs took decisions on location of production. Whilst EU policy developments were relatively limited, there were some which also raised the profile of industrial relations concerns. One of the most obvious was the EU initiative on European Works Councils which involved building on the German model of works councils in allowing employees within a multinational based in the EU to come together to discuss and be informed about the management strategy. In the US, the loss of manufacturing jobs in the 1980s and 1990s had similar effects. Protectionist arguments about building barriers to foreign goods, dismantling key provisions in the NAFTA agreements and generally supporting US manufacturing continue to be made, particularly at election time in US states where trade unions and working class Democratic politics remain strong. Thus the issue of how MNCs used different locations to reduce their wage costs led to debate about the role of national governments, international organizations such as the ILO and trade unions in managing the public social consequences of private economic action.

These developments led in a number of directions, many of which started to overlap with the concerns of Birkinshaw and others regarding the relations between subsidiaries and MNE headquarters. One area concerned the whole dynamic of bargaining and power within the MNE that occurred as senior managers and trade unions negotiated over new investments, closures and relocations. It was inevitable, given the origins of industrial relations scholarship in issues of power and conflict, that the central focus would be on what Edwards and Bélanger in their contribution to this book describe as 'the contested terrain'. In earlier work, Bélanger along with colleagues from different countries, had studied ABB. In that discussion, it was shown that the powers of employees and managers depended firstly on the institutional context in which the subsidiary was located and secondly on the power and autonomy of the subsidiary in relation to the headquarters. The authors made no assumptions about unified interests either at the level of the MNE as a whole or inside subsidiaries. Instead they sought to understand the conflicts which arose. Indeed this makes an interesting contrast to the image of ABB presented in the famous matrix case developed by Bartlett (Bartlett, Ghoshal and Birkinshaw, 2006) where the emphasis is on managerial problem solving with little regard to issues of national context or the role of labour. Edwards and Bélanger stress, however, the interdependence of the various actors. The 'contested terrain' is one in which compromises occur and both sides settle for a time at least for less than they might have wanted. As the balance of power shifts for whatever reason, the terrain becomes more contested again and new conflicts emerge and new compromises have to be forged.

These arguments soon became strongly intertwined with broader institutionalist analyses of how multinationals develop. The most obvious cross-over point has been the work of Ferner (e.g. Ferner and Edwards, 1995; Ferner and Varul, 1999) who, over a sustained period of time, has engaged in researching the impact of host and home country institutional contexts on how the industrial relations and human resource policies of multinationals develop. In his early work Ferner drew directly on the work of Whitley (2007, 1999), whose analysis of national business systems had sought to describe how institutions shape the strategy, structure and competitiveness of firms on international markets. Whitley's early work in turn tended to follow Hu's argument that multinationals are 'national firms with international operations'; in other words that multinationals sought to impose their own set of processes and structures on their subsidiaries. They were therefore little different from national firms. Gradually, however, both of these authors moved away from this and began to consider how institutional influences in the host contexts impacted on the multinational. Ferner and his colleagues studied this empirically in a study which culminated in a book on American Multinationals in Europe (Almond and Ferner, 2006). This book revealed the depth of micro-politics which occurred inside the MNEs as different groups struggled over resources. Whitley's interest in organization structure led him in a different direction to consider how multinationals sought to organize themselves across borders and whether it could be argued that they were developing a distinctive set of multinational capabilities (see e.g. the contribution of Whitley and others in Morgan *et al.*, 2001). In his chapter in this book, he meticulously considers how it is possible to identify the distinctive capabilities of multinationals that distinguish them from the capabilities generated inside firms located within specific national business systems. He argues that most multinationals are simply federations of national firms, leveraging skills and knowledge derived from these national contexts into different markets. Only a small number of managers in multinationals can be considered as transcending their national context and developing transnational skills. He is therefore sceptical about Bartlett and Ghoshal's notion of the transnational corporation (see also Whitley, 1999; 2007).

Loveridge also explores the MNE as comprised of multi-layered networks of relationships where the identities, aspirations and subsequent actions of both expatriate and indigenous managers can often differ and conflict. The agendas of individual decision-makers and the structure of inter-personal networks are not shaped solely by formal organizational goals, but by a more complex range of pressures than those proposed by functionalist and prescriptive analysis often found in the field of international business strategy. Loveridge examines the effects of organizational hierarchy and career expectations, formal education and tacit knowledge, and national and ethnic identity, in the shaping of intra-firm networks. These all underpin sociopolitical boundaries and support factional identities within interdependent transnational communities. More specifically, he suggests, they create obstacles to the information-exchange and recombination of ideas that support technological innovation and thereby competitive advantage. Innovation management is therefore presented as an on-going political process in which the ideologies of sub-groups intermediate in the interpretation and adjustment of strategic goals and actions across intra-firm networks.

A highly influential book in this debate has been Kristensen and Zeitlin (2005) *Local Players in Global Games*, which consists of a study of a single multinational, the dynamics of relations between its headquarters and three of its major subsidiaries. This book benefited from the depth of analysis which could be achieved by going into just one firm. It showed how micro-politics were developed and sustained by drawing on institutional resources in the wider social context. It linked this to issues of reform not just within the MNE but also in terms of reforming stock markets and reforming the monitoring of MNEs by various groups. Drawing together their interests in industrial relations, in history, in national institutional contexts and in changing levels of governance, the authors sought to connect the MNE to wider debates concerning the direction of social change. In the chapter by Morgan and Kristensen in this book, these themes are developed further. In particular, the authors emphasize that multinationals are searching for forms of cohesion and cooperation that can facilitate economic growth and development. However, these searches are undermined by different expectations about the purposes of the MNC. These differences are partly driven by different institutional contexts but they are also driven by different political and economic interests which reflect the growing significance of financial markets in determining the strategies and structures of multinationals. Financial markets undermine the ability of managers to provide what have been called 'credible commitments' to their employees. Credible commitments in this context refers to the ability of the MNC to provide careers, skills and income rewards to employees which encourages those employees to commit their skills and energy to the resolution of organizational problems. Morgan and Kristensen suggest that MNCs face a problem similar to that of any emerging society – how to create a structure of institutions which balances the interests of the different groups which belong to it in such a way that the groups are willing to put aside fundamental differences and instead concentrate on building not a zero-sum growth system but a growth system that increases benefits to all groups over the medium term. Drawing on historical analogies, the authors argue that it is only when this is achieved that societies enter into virtuous circles of growth rather than remaining trapped into vicious circles of conflict and instability. They argue that there is no inherent need to be pessimistic about such a future. Social and economic progress inevitably takes time but there is evidence that MNCs are gradually being reshaped towards credible commitments both by internal and external pressures.

Sharpe and Mir, however, take a different view. They see multinationals as central actors in a continued process of exploitation and unequal exchange. They focus on how MNCs sustain their power through connections to powerful states and powerful social actors in particular societies and use these connections to ensure that they are able to shift location to places where forms of surplus extraction are highest due to the weak power of labour and countervailing forces to the dominant groups. They take a broad view of the social responsibilities of MNCs and show how in their search for profit, MNCs push commodification processes into ever more private realms, such as through genetic modification and biotechnology. The struggles and conflicts within multinationals and between MNCs and social movements is, in their view, destined to grow stronger as these clashes become more intense.

Bringing Themes Together

What is striking is how much common ground has emerged over the last decade between scholars from different backgrounds. We now have a much more nuanced appreciation of the complexities of managing multinationals than was the case 10 years ago. We have the makings of a framework in which economic imperatives can be linked to organizational processes and these in turn can be understood by reference to the micro-politics that occur as groups spread across different institutional contexts as well as different sub-units and different functions. Clearly not everybody would agree that this common ground is there or indeed is useful in any way. The chapter which we have included by Mir and Sharpe, for example, takes a resolutely critical line on MNEs stretching back to a long tradition of radical social theory that has been renewed by the impact of globalization and the diverse movements of resistance which have emerged in and around MNEs in different countries in the last decade. Similarly in his chapter Alan Rugman dismisses national institutional effects and concentrates instead on markets and regions as the dominant frame of analysis. Many of the other contributions, however, do share similar concerns even if they express them in different ways. There is a shared interest in the internal dynamics of multinationals, and a search for explanations of how these internal dynamics are structured – what role is played by institutions, politics and power, market mechanisms and management control systems? How are these internal dynamics affected by the evolving external institutional context and the growth of new social movements that press onto the agenda issues of the environment, health and gender as well as older issues such as inequality and power? How do these processes affect innovation and competitive position? These questions raise the possibility of the field of MNEs consolidating more strongly across disciplinary boundaries that were previously rather impervious and drawing more explicitly on different traditions within the social sciences (see e.g. Henisz and Swaminathan, 2008; Jackson and Deeg, 2008). Of course, there are academic barriers to such a process as disciplines or subject areas such as those which exist in business schools tend to become their own self-enclosed communities with their own battles for power, prestige and reputation within themselves and also in relation to adjacent areas. However, there is real potential for increased dialogue on areas of common concern to the different disciplines.

Using This Book

One of our goals in this book is to provide a tool for those students and lecturers who want to create this dialogue, this single space. We have brought together many of the key voices that represent both the established and the emerging traditions in the study of MNEs. We have made them available in one book. We have sought to impose (loosely) a similar structure on chapters, asking authors to concentrate on developing their own distinctive approach and showing how it links to other literature as well as providing case vignettes which can be used as jumping off points for classroom discussion and debate. All the contributions presented here were written explicitly for this volume. This allowed us to create a common structure for each chapter, as well as a distinctive image of the MNE. Each chapter features an illustrative case study with related questions and a short list of recommended reading beyond the standard bibliography.

We have not sought to enclose the 'truth' about MNEs; to pin the MNE and eviscerate it looking for its inner essence. We believe that, at this stage, it is important to open things up rather than close them down – to invite people into the debate rather than to exclude them because they have not done (or read) x, y or z in advance. If the contributions are sufficiently stimulating, then we hope that readers will go on to extend their reading, back to some of the classics of the MNE literature as well as forward to some of the recent publications which may in 10 or 20 years themselves be seen as classics. In the meantime, test out the images; use them as ways to think about MNEs; relate them to your experience and to the reports which you see about

MNEs in newspapers, broadcasting media and on the internet. No doubt it will become clear that we have missed some crucial developments but then that is in the nature of the enterprise when one is trying to understand one of the most important influences on our social, political and economic life as is the case with the study of multinationals. Bon voyage!

References

Almond, P. and Ferner, A. (eds) (2006) *American Multinationals in Europe.* Oxford; Oxford University Press.

Anderson, S. and Cavanagh, J. (2000) *The Top 200: The Rise of Global Corporate Power.* Washington, DC: Institute for Policy Studies.

Baran, P. A. (1966) *Monopoly Capital.* London: Penguin.

Bartlett, C. A. and Ghoshal, S. (1989) *Managing Across Borders: The Transnational Solution.* London: Century Business.

Bartlett, C. A., Ghoshal, S. and Birkinshaw, J. (2006) *Transnational Management: Text and Cases: Text, Cases, and Readings in Cross-border Management.* McGraw-Hill Higher Education.

Birkinshaw, J. (1997) 'Entrepreneurship in Multinational Corporations: The Characteristics of Subsidiary Initiatives', *Strategic Management Journal*, 18: 207–29.

Birkinshaw, J. and Hood, N. (eds) (1998) *Multinational Corporate Evolution and Subsidiary Development.* London: Macmillan.

Buckley, P. and Casson, M. (1976) *The Future of the Multinational Enterprise.* London: Macmillan.

Burrell, G. and Morgan, G. (1978) *Sociological Paradigms and Organizational Analysis.* London: Heinemann.

Collinson, S. C. and Rugman, A. M. (2008) 'The Regional Nature of Japanese Multinational Business', *Journal of International Business Studies* (JIBS), 39: 2, 215–30, Palgrave Macmillan.

Collinson, S. C., Buckley, P., Dunning, J. and Yip, G. (2006) 'New Directions in International Business', in Fai, F.M. and Morgan, E.J. (eds) *Managerial Issues in International Business.* Basingstoke: Palgrave.

Crouch (1993) *Industrial Relations and European State Traditions.* Oxford: Clarendon Press.

Dunning, J. (1998) 'Reappraising the Eclectic Paradigm in an Age of Alliance Capitalism'. In M. Colombo. (ed.) *The Changing Boundaries of the Firm.* London: Routledge, 29–59.

Dunning, J. (2001) 'The Key Literature on IB Activities: 1960–2000'. In Rugman, A. M. and Brewer, T. (eds) *The Oxford Handbook of International Business.* Oxford: Oxford University Press, 36–68.

Dunning, J. (ed.) (2005) *Making Globalization Good.* Oxford: Oxford University Press.

Egelhoff, W. G. (1993) 'Information-Processing Theory and the Multinational Corporation'. In Ghoshal, S. and Westney, D. E. (eds) *Organization Theory and the Multinational.* London: Macmillan, 182–210.

Egelhoff, W. G. (1982) 'Strategy and Structure in Multinational Corporations: An Information Processing Approach', *Administrative Science Quarterly* 27: 435–58.

Ferner, A. and Edwards, P. (1995) 'Power and the Diffusion of Organizational Change Within Multinational Enterprises', *European Journal of Industrial Relations*, 1 (2): 229–57.

Ferner, A. and Hyman, R. (1998) *Changing Industrial Relations in Europe*. 2nd ed. Oxford; Blackwell.

Ferner, A. and Varul, M. (1999) *The German Way: German Multinationals and Human Resource Management*. London: Anglo-German Foundation for the Study of Industrial Society.

Ghoshal, S. and Westney, D. E. (eds) (1993) *Organization Theory and the Multinational*. London: Macmillan.

Giddens, A. (1992) *Modernity and Self Identity*. Cambridge: Polity Press.

Guillen, M. (2001) *The Limits of Convergence*. Princeton, NJ: Princeton University Press.

Gunder Frank, A. (1967) *Capitalism and Underdevelopment in Latin America: Historical Studies of Chile and Brazil*. New York: Monthly Review Press.

Hall, P. and Soskice, D. (2001) *Varieties of Capitalism*. Oxford: Oxford University Press.

Hedlund, G. (1986) 'The Hypermodern MNC – A Heterarchy?' *Human Resource Management*, 25 (1): 9–35.

Hedlund, G. (1999) 'The Intensity and extensity of Knowledge and the Multinational Corporation as a Nearly Recomposable System (NRS)', *Management International Review*, 1, special issue: 5–44.

Henisz, W. and Swaminathan, A. (2008) 'Institutions and International Business', *Journal of International Business Studies*, 39, 537–9.

Hennart, J.-F. (2001) 'Theories of the Multinational Enterprise'. In A. M. Rugman and T. Brewer. (eds) *The Oxford Handbook of International Business*. Oxford: Oxford University Press, 127–49,

Hirst, P. and Thompson, G. (1999) *Globalization in Question*. 2nd edn, Oxford: Polity Press.

Hymer, S. (1972) 'The Multinational Corporation and the Law of Uneven Development'. In Bhagwati, J. (ed.) *Economics in the World Order from the 1970s to the 1990s*. London: Collier-Macmillan, 113–40.

Jackson, G. and Deeg, R. (2008) 'Comparing Capitalisms: understanding institutional diversity and its implications for international business', *Journal of International Business Studies*, 39, 540–61.

Kogut, B. (2001) 'Methodological Contributions in International Business and the Direction of Academic Research Activity'. In Rugman, A. M. and Brewer, T. (eds) *The Oxford Handbook of International Business*. Oxford: Oxford University Press, 785–817.

Kostova, T. (1999) 'Transnational Transfer of Strategic Organizational Practices: A Contextual Perspective', *Academy of Management Review*, 24, 308–24.

Kostova, T. and Zaheer, S. (1999) 'Organizational Legitimacy under conditions of complexity: the case of the multinational enterprise', *Academy of Management Review*, 24, 64–81.

Kostova, T. and Roth, K. (2002) 'Adoption of Organizational Practice by Subsidiaries of Multinational Corporations: Institutional and Relational Effects', *Academy of Management Journal*, 45, 215–33.

Kristensen, P. H. and Zeitlin, J. (2005) *Local Players in Global Games. The Strategic Constitution of a Multinational Corporation*. Oxford: Oxford University Press.

Lyotard, J.-F. (1984) *The Postmodern Condition*. Minneapolis: University of Minnesota Press.

Morgan, G. (2006) *Images of Organization: updated edition*. London: Sage.

Morgan, G., Kristensen, P. H. and Whitley, R. (2001) *The Multinational Firm: Organizing Across National and Institutional Divides*. Oxford: Oxford University Press.

Nohria, N. and Ghoshal, S. (1997) *The Differentiated Network: Organizing Multinational Corporations for Value Creation*. San Francisco: Jossey Bass.

Poster, M. (ed.) (2001) *Jean Baudrillard: Selected Writings*. 2nd edn, Cambridge: Polity Press.

Radice, H. (ed.) (1975) *International Firms and Modern Imperialism*. London: Penguin.

Rugman, A. M. (2005) *The Regional Multinationals: MNEs and 'Global' Strategic Management*. Cambridge: Cambridge University Press.

Streeck, W. (1992) *Social Institutions and Economic Performance*. London: Sage.

Sullivan, D. P. and Daniels, J. D. (2004) 'Defining International Business Through its Research'. In Buckley, P. J. (ed.) (2004) *What is International Business?* Basingstoke: Palgrave Macmillan.

UNCTAD (2007) *The World Investment Report*, United Nations Conference on Trade and Development, New York and Geneva (http://unctad.org).

Vernon, R. (1966) 'International investment and international trade in the product cycle', *Quarterly Journal of Economics*, 80; 90–207.

Vernon, R. (1971) Sovereignty at Bay: the multinational spread of U.S. enterprises. London: Longman.

Westney, D. E. (1993) 'Country Patterns in R&D Organization: The United States and Japan'. In Kogut, B. (ed.) *Country Competitiveness*. Oxford: Oxford University Press, 36–53.

Westney, D. E. (1990) 'Internal and External Linkages in the MNC: the Case of R&D Subsidiaries in Japan'. In Bartlett, C., Doz, Y. and Hedlund, G. (eds) *Managing the Global Firm*. London: Routledge, 279–300.

Westney, D. E. and Zaheer, S. (2001) 'The Multinational Enterprise as an Organization'. In Rugman, A. M. and Brewer, T. (eds) *The Oxford Handbook of International Business*. Oxford: Oxford University Press, 349–79.

Whitley, R. (1999) *Divergent Capitalisms*. Oxford: Oxford University Press.

Whitley, R. (2007) *Business Systems and Organizational Capabilities*. Oxford: Oxford University Press.

Xu, D. and Shenkar, O. (2002) 'Institutional Distance and the Multinational Enterprise', *Academy of Management Review*, 27, 608–18.

NOTES

1. This divide has been noted by others. Sullivan and Daniels (2004), for example, characterize the two camps in international business research as 'scientific' and 'humanistic'.

2. Other authors had begun to develop similar ideas around this time. The Swedish author, Gunnar Hedlund (1986; 1999), represented the most creative European contribution to these new perspectives even if his work (partly due to his early death) never became as widely known as that of Bartlett and Ghoshal. The tension between integration and responsiveness (centralization/decentralization) was also explored in authors such as Doz.

3. Taking this a step further it might be argued that the very dichotomous nature of the academic debate over MNEs, a core theme in this introductory chapter, has made international business studies less relevant for (or less interesting to) the 'real world'. Failure to advance the academic debate, partly by developing more holistic, multidisciplinary approaches, may have further sidelined academic discussion in favour of highly stylized and simplistic media-driven images of MNEs. Academic studies, as a result may be less influential in the public and policy debates which are driven by the growing significance of MNEs in an increasingly globalized world (Collinson *et al.*, 2006).

Chapter 2 The Regional Dimension of Multinationals and the End of 'Varieties of Capitalism'

Alan Rugman and Alain Verbeke

Introduction

The empirical evidence is that the world's largest 500 multinational enterprises (MNEs) operate on an intra-regional basis rather than on a global one. This chapter re-examines recent data on this regional dimension of MNE activity. We then apply this logic to deconstruct the popular 'varieties of capitalism' approach to international political economy (IPE). We note that this type of IPE literature badly neglects MNEs and also that it confuses the alleged role of globalization (as a commonality) with the actual reality of regional activities. While the country level in the varieties of capitalism approach retains some validity, we demonstrate that this area of literature needs fundamental rethinking. In a world of MNEs and regional activity the varieties of capitalism offer out-of-date and misguided images.

The definition of a multinational enterprise (MNE) is that it produces and/or distributes products and/or services across national borders. These MNEs have repeatedly been identified as the drivers of globalization, (Yip, 2003). Yet, very few are 'global' firms, with a 'global' strategy, defined as the ability to sell the same products and/or services around the world in a homogeneous manner. Instead, nearly all the top world's largest firms exhibit aspects of heterogeneity and are regionally based in their home region of the 'triad' of North America, the EU or Asia. It follows that a firm can be internationally active across its home region market but not be global.

A large firm can have what appears to be an international integration strategy within its home region. This occurs if the firm's successful strategy includes selling the same products and/or services in the same manner within its home region of the

Images of the Multinational Firm Edited by Simon Collinson and Glenn Morgan
© 2009 John Wiley & Sons, Ltd

triad, allowing the firm to gain all the potential economies of scale and scope and/or differentiation advantages within its home region market.

If firms have exhausted their growth in their home region of the triad and still go into other regions, they then face a liability of foreignness and other additional risks by this global expansion. In other words, the advantages of standardization can be achieved within the home region of the triad, especially if the home region government pursues policies of an internal market such as social, cultural and political harmonization (as in the EU) or economic integration (as in NAFTA and Asia).

Furthermore, inter-block business is likely to be restricted by government-imposed barriers to entry. The EU and the United States are now fighting trade wars and are responsive to domestic business lobbies seeking shelter in the form of subsidies and/or protection, as in the case of the steel and agricultural sectors. There will remain cultural and political differences between members of the triad, but there will be fewer of these within each triad block. Increasingly, there will be European firms, North American firms and Asian firms. They will continue to have 70 % or more of their sales in their home region of the triad. There are only a handful of purely 'global' MNEs amongst the world's largest firms, (Rugman and Verbeke, 2004; Rugman, 2005). Globalization will remain a mirage in that regionalism will continue to dominate international business strategy.

Rugman (2000) developed evidence for this regional triad theme mainly at the aggregate level for the core triad of the United States, EU and Japan. The intra-regional trade and FDI across the 'broad' triad of North America (NAFTA), Europe and Asia (including Oceania) were also examined, and 20 cases of the regional strategies of multinationals were analysed.

Regional Multinationals

Rugman and Verbeke (2004) report that of the world's 500 largest firms, only nine can be classified as global whereas 320 of the 380 firms reporting regional sales have an average of 80 % of their sales in their home region. There are also some 36 bi-regional firms. These data are reclassified in Table 2.1. This lists the 380 firms by their home country. There are 169 from the United States, 66 from Japan and 119 from Europe. Europe, North America and Asia represent the 'triad' of economic activity which dominates international business (Rugman, 2000). The world's largest 500 firms account for over 90 % of the world's stock of foreign direct investment and about half of the world's trade. Despite evidence that most of them operate largely within their home regions (the 380 firms average 71 % home region sales) many of these MNEs state that they have a global strategy (Yip, 2003), (Govindarajan and Gupta, 2001). Before examining this issue, we examine the basic empirical evidence on the international business activities of the world's largest MNEs.

The average intra-regional sales of the US firms is 77.3 %; for the Japanese it is 74.7 %; and for the Europeans it is 62.8 %. Within the European group, the 27

Table 2.1 The world's largest 500 firms by country

Country	No. of Firms	Average Revenues (USD$bn)	Average intra-regional sales (%)*
United States	169	30.3	77.3
Japan	66	28.9	74.7
Germany	29	37.3	68.1
France	27	27.2	64.8
Britain	27	25.3	64.5
Canada	16	13.5	74.1
Switzerland	8	34.7	49.6
Italy	5	38.7	83.4
Australia	5	13.6	71.4
Sweden	5	16.4	54.3
Netherlands	5	42.1	39.1
European bi-national (*)	3	73.9	47.9
Norway	2	21.6	83.0
South Korea	2	26.3	71.2
Belgium	2	18.8	58.4
Finland	2	20.0	55.1
Spain	2	29.1	50.3
Taiwan	1	11.6	100.0
Luxembourg	1	13.0	95.0
Denmark	1	10.9	94.3
Brazil	1	24.5	88.0
Singapore	1	13.1	22.4
TOTAL	380	29.2	71.9

Data are for 2001.
Numbers might not add up due to rounding.
Average intra-regional sales are by the firm's size according to weighted revenues.
There are 120 firms in the world's largest 500 which report no data on regional sales.

British firms have intra-regional sales of 64.5 %. This suggests that the British (and European) firms may be somewhat less regionally based than US and Japanese firms. The British firms are in the mid range of European firms, with the most 'global' firms being the five from the Netherlands.

Table 2.2 reports the classifications of the 27 British MNEs, based on the Rugman and Verbeke (2004) and Rugman (2005) methodology. As with most of the world's other large firms, 19 of them are home region oriented. However, four are bi-regional and two are host region oriented (AstraZeneca and Wolseley) where these latter two firms have over 50 % of their sales in North America. The four bi-regionals are also big players in North America, in particular: BP, GlaxoSmithKline and Diageo. Yet many of the service-based firms are very home region-based: Tesco has 94 % of its

Table 2.2 The regional nature of UK multinational enterprises

500 Rank	Company	Revenues (US$/bn)	% intra-regional	North America % of total	Europe % of total	Asia Pacific % of total
Bi-regional						
4	BP	174.2	36.3	48.1	36.3	na
140	GlaxoSmithKline	29.5	28.6	49.2	28.6	na
262	Diageo	18.6	31.8	49.9	31.8	7.7
390	BAE Systems	13.0	38.1	32.3	38.1	2.7
Host Region Oriented						
301	AstraZeneca	16.5	32.0	52.8	32.0	5.2
487	Wolseley	10.4	28.7	66.3	28.7	na
Home Region Oriented						
114	Tesco	33.9	93.6	—	93.6	6.4
115	Royal Bank of Scotland	33.8	81.0	12.0	81.0	na
123	Vodafone	32.7	93.1	0.1	93.1	4.8
139	BT (q)	30.0	87.0	8.3	87.0	4.7
150	HBOS	27.8	92.1	na	92.1	na
154	Barclays	27.6	88.0	6.0	88.0	na
184	J. Sainsbury	24.6	83.3	16.7	83.3	—
206	Lloyds TSB Group	22.8	81.2	na	81.2	na
222	Royal & Sun Alliance	21.5	64.8	27.1	64.8	na

270	Centrica	18.2	93.8	6.2	93.8	na
280	Abbey National	17.8	99.5	0.5	99.5	—
314	Kingfisher (q)	16.1	98.3	0.8	98.3	0.6
409	Compass Group	12.6	67.6	32.4	67.6	—
418	Safeway	12.3	100.0	na	100.0	na
428	British Airways	11.9	64.8	18.6	64.8	na
439	Marks & Spencer	11.6	85.1	na	85.1	na
452	Corus Group	11.1	82.7	11.5	82.7	5.8
453	Old Mutual (q)	11.1	93.4	na	na	na
478	Alliance Unichem	10.5	100.0	na	100.0	na

Insufficient Information

271	British American Tobacco (q)	18.1	31.3	na	31.3	9.9
341	Anglo American	14.8	46.1	18.9	46.1	17.8
	Weighted Average	25.3	64.5			

Data are for 2001.
For further information on the data and definitions used please see the Appendix and company notes in Alan M. Rugman's *The Regional Multinationals* (Cambridge University Press, 2005).

sales in Europe; Vodafone has 93 %; Centrica has 94 %; Abbey National has 99.5 %; Kingfisher has 95 %; Safeway has 100 %, as does Alliance Unichem.

These data suggest that most large British service MNEs do most of their business within Britain and the EU. They are poor prospects for globalization. Why is this? What are the strategies, structures, processes and internal managerial factors that explain this lack of global sales? Are there any public policy factors such as government regulations that have an impact on these location-bound firms? But does it really matter when other large firms from Asia and North America are also very insular and home region-based?

Are there any industry effects that matter in explaining the competitiveness of British business? The preliminary answer is yes—there is a major difference between the manufacturing and service sectors, as can be seen in Table 2.3.

In Table 2.3, the 27 British MNEs fall into two categories, with only eight in manufacturing but 19 in services. The eight British manufacturing firms have lower intra-regional sales than the other European or world firms. This indicates that these eight British manufacturing MNEs are potentially more 'global' than other large firms. In contrast, in all but two of the service sectors, the British firms have higher intra-regional sales than the others. This indicates that these firms are much less global than others.

To conclude, preliminary analysis reports a relative lack of globalization in these large British firms. As these firms are often 'flagships', acting as the hubs of business clusters, it is likely that other businesses, especially small and medium-sized businesses, are even less global and more location bound, than frequently thought (Rugman and D'Cruz, 2000).

Evidence on Regional Multinationals

Rugman and Verbeke (2004) examined the triad/regional economic activity of the world's largest firms in the core triad of the United States, EU and Japan. In 2001, of the world's largest 500 firms, 428 were in these core triad regions, whereas back in 1981 it was 445. Over the last 20 years the trend has shown a decrease in the proportion of US firms, from 242 in 1981 to as few as 157 in 1991. The EU number is very consistent, being 141 for the old EEC members in 1981, but up to 155 for the enlarged EU in 1996, and down to 143 again by 2001.

Those 500 firms dominate international business. They account for over 90 % of the world's stock of FDI and nearly 50 % of the world trade. These firms are the 'unit of analysis' for research in international business. They are the key vehicles for both FDI and trade. Furthermore, research reveals that the majority of their sales, on average, are intra-regional, and for the great majority of them this intra-regional trade is concentrated in their home region of the triad. Very few of these 500 large firms actually have any significant presence in all three regions of the triad. (In fact only a handful, such as IBM, Coca Cola and LVMH qualify as 'global' firms.)

Table 2.3 The regional nature of British, European and world firms

Industry	Britain Average No. of intra-regional		Europe Average No. of intra-regional		World Average No. of intra-regional	
	Firms	Sales	Firms	Sales	Firms	Sales
Manufacturing						
Aerospace and Defence	1	38.1	2	42.7	11	66.3
Chemicals and Pharmaceuticals	2	29.8	7	37.6	18	56.5
Computer, Office and Electronics	0	na	6	49.4	36	56.2
Construction, Building Materials and Glass	0	na	5	60.6	11	73.5
Energy, Petroleum and Refining	1	36.3	7	53.8	31	66.0
Food, Drug and Tobacco	2	31.6	5	36.4	14	55.0
Motor Vehicle and Parts	0	na	8	54.4	29	60.6
Natural Resource Manufacturing	2	61.8	6	71.8	17	77.6
Other Manufacturing	0	na	5	54.0	13	57.8
Services						
Banks	5	87.4	23	75.4	40	78.3
Entertainment, Printing and Publishing	0	na	3	67.2	9	73.1
Merchandisers	6	92.4	15	75.5	63	87.9
Telecommunications and Utilities	3	91.0	11	82.8	27	87.6
Transportation Services	1	64.8	4	73.9	13	83.7
Other Financial Services	2	74.5	8	62.9	27	71.9
Other Services	2	50.0	4	51.5	21	75.8
TOTAL	27	64.5	119	62.8	380	71.9

Data are for 2001.
Numbers might not add up due to rounding.
Average intra-regional sales are by the firm's size according to weighted revenues.

Regional sales data were found for 380 firms, based on information in the annual reports and web pages. The 380 firms in Table 2.1 can then be classified according to those that are global, bi-regional and domestic. There are no data for 120 firms (most of which are entirely domestic) and incomplete data for 15 other firms. The main results are:

- home region oriented: of the top 500 firms, 320 have at least 50 % of their sales in their own region of the triad;
- bi-regional: only 25 of the 500 firms are bi-regional, with over 20 % of their sales in at least two parts of the triad plus less than 50 % of sales in their home region;
- host region oriented: 11 host region oriented firms have over 50 % of sales in a triad region other than their own;
- global: only nine of the top 500 MNEs are global, defined as having 20 % of sales or more in each of the three regions of the triad, but less than 50 % in any one region.

The intra-regional average sales for each group are:

80.3 % for the 320 home region oriented firms;
42.0 % for the 25 bi-regional MNEs;
30.9 % for the 11 host region ranked firms;
38.3 % for the nine global MNEs.

The average intra-regional sales for all 380 firms with available data are 71.9 %. These data confirm the analysis of Rugman (2000) on the myth of global strategy and the nature of triad-based business activity rather than globalization. These data also confirm the study of the 49 retail MNEs in the 500, in Rugman and Girod (2003). In that study only one retail MNE was found to be global, namely LVMH. This result is evident across all industry sectors except for electronics, which includes seven of the nine global firms in the set.

Rugman (2005) reports that there is no discernible trend towards either global branding or standardization. Only a few multinational brands, with Coca-Cola leading the way, are global. Even McDonald's is bi-regional, not global. In terms of the value chain, a few MNEs outsource offshore. Nike has 99 % of its production outside of the United States, almost all of it in South East Asia. Yet, its brand name drives sales on a regional basis: most of its sales are in North America and Europe.

International manufacturing is dominated by large MNEs in location-bound clusters. The best example is the automobile industry. The data on foreign sales of the world's largest automobile MNEs show that the majority of sales arose in their home regions. GM at 81 % and Ford at 61 % have most of their sales in North America. Similarly, BMW and VW have most of their sales in Europe. Assembly and production of vehicles, however, is generally carried out regionally in each market served.

The service sectors are even more regional. In retail, only one of the largest 49 retail firms was global—LVMH. In banking, all the companies had the vast majority of their assets in their home regions. Citigroup had 80 % of its assets in North America. Insurance is even more local. Even knowledge-intensive services industries are largely local. For example, professional service firms are embedded locally with partners largely immobile and their networks, at best, regionally based.

Most R&D undertaken by the world's largest 500 MNEs is in their back yards. Patents, for instance, are registered primarily in the home region. Active MNEs first attempt to register at the US Patent Office. To overcome regulatory barriers to marketing and distribution pharmaceutical R&D then spreads through separate national patents. Similarly, health care is not global but delivered locally, subject to local regulations. International markets, therefore, are not becoming homogenized. Only in a few sectors, such as consumer electronics, is a global strategy of economic integration viable.

It is possible that the upstream, 'back end', activities of the value chain are more globalized than the downstream 'front end' of sales. However, even there we find a picture of regionally based production clusters and networks similar to the automobile sector. Only in electronics is production likely to be globalized, as transportation costs are low relative to assembly. Otherwise, production in chemicals, resources and services is likely to be highly localized. In retailing, a few MNEs, such as Nike and Wal-Mart, source a significant part of their products from subcontractors in other regions; but, again, most production is localized in order to address national preferences.

All of this has major implications for business. Managers need to design regional strategies, not global ones. Only in a few sectors does a global strategy make sense. For most other sectors, strategies of national responsiveness are required. However, there is nothing to stop an MNE from pursuing an integration strategy within its home region. By this, a multinational will sell the same product or service in the same way across all the countries of its home region, allowing it to gain economies of scale. Only when an MNE exhausts the possibilities for growth in its home region, does it need to venture into other regions. In other words, all the advantages of global homogeneity can be achieved regionally, especially if the governments of that region pursue internal market policies such as social, cultural and political harmonization (as in the EU) or economic integration (as in NAFTA and in Asia).

In summary, recent research suggests that both globalization and the use of global strategy is a myth. Far from taking place in a single global market, most business activity by large firms takes place within regional blocks. Government regulations and cultural differences segment the world into the broad triad regions of North America, the EU and Asia-Pacific. Rival multinational enterprises from the triad compete for regional market share and so enhance economic efficiency. As a result, top managers now need to design triad-based regional strategies, not global ones. Markets across regions are not becoming homogenized, nor is there a trend towards globalization. Rather there is a trend, over the last quarter century, towards regionalization and increased intra-regional economic activity. Only in a few sectors, such as consumer electronics, is a global strategy of economic integration viable. For most other manufacturing (such as automobiles, chemicals, energy, etc.) and for all services (such as retail, banking, etc.) regional strategies are required. In this connection see the boxed case study on Microsoft, showing the danger of assuming a global system instead of a regionally regulated one.

Varieties of Capitalism and Multinational Enterprises

This section briefly reviews a number of recent insights on the 'varieties of capitalism' literature, as expressed by Hall and Soskice (2001). The modern political economy analysis of these varieties of capitalism argues that national institutional differences will not disappear in the long run, and may even greatly contribute to the national comparative advantage of specific industries. Each nation is characterized by a specific configuration of economic actors pursuing particular interests and by historically grown relationships among them.

This is a refinement of the concept of country-specific advantages (CSAs) used in the international business (IB) literature, e.g. Rugman and Verbeke (1990, 1992). However, Hall and Soskice (2001) and other writers in international political economy (IPE) fail to bridge to this IB literature as we do in this chapter. Indeed, this type of IPE literature appears to miss the basic point that MNEs now play a key role in the world economy and that they operate regionally. The presence of triad-based competition in many industries, with regional rivals from North America, the European Union and Japan (as discussed above), demonstrates that no single variety of capitalism is able to prevail. Instead, a regional approach is required.

In a strategic sense, the perceived presence of such varieties of capitalism poses a major challenge for most MNEs: these firms need to learn how to bridge the varieties of capitalism, and how to gain competitive advantage when faced with multiple, and to some extent contradictory, requirements imposed by national environments. We argue that MNEs should view varieties of capitalism not as constrained types of home CSAs but as both a constraint and an opportunity. Varieties of capitalism constitute a constraint as they limit the potential to gain benefits of 'integration', in particular as regards the transfer of micro-level best practices (not necessarily arising from the home CSAs) across borders. However, they also constitute an opportunity to learn from best practices in host countries, especially in the home region, to the extent that these practices can be 'internalized' and transferred inside the firm.

From a government perspective, the 'intrusion' of foreign CSAs in the national economy, again especially from other countries in the home triad region, may also lead to the identification of best practice approaches in the regulatory sphere. In other words, if it is accepted that particular institutions more effectively contribute to the development of specific types of firms or sectors (e.g. the impact of advanced accounting standards or specific venture capital rules on the development of fast growing, high technology firms) national governments may want to emulate successes achieved elsewhere. Indeed, complex sets of institutional elements may need to be replicated rather than using simple rules, and national adaptation may be required in order not to disturb broader, well-functioning institutions, for example in the sphere of corporate ownership and business organization.

The key starting point of recent work in IPE, on the institutional foundations of comparative advantage, is that important institutions vary across nations. These differences include both formal and informal rules, followed by individuals and organizations, in areas as diverse as corporate governance, labour market regulation and education and training. This work, inspired by North (1990), argues that institutions fundamentally affect the relationships among the key economic actors in society, including business firms, public agencies, organized labour, financial institutions etc.

The institutions themselves result from complex bargaining processes and coalition formation among various groups with specific interests. A variety of regulatory and political elements largely determine what constitutes efficient micro-level decision-making, e.g. in the finance area. LaPorta et al. (1998) and (1999) demonstrate this importance by focusing on the impact of legal regimes. One of their conclusions is that the Anglo-Saxon common law model (with substantial protection for minority investors) has been beneficial in the development of financial markets in those countries. However, the general legal regime is only one component of a country's institutional setting. It is critical to study the entire range of institutions that affects (and is affected by) the relationships among groups of economic actors with diverging interests.

In this context, a resource-based view of firm behaviour can be adopted. The ability of firms to develop and exploit competencies and capabilities is viewed as being largely determined by the quality of their relationships with internal and external stakeholders. This is a type of firm-specific advantage (FSA). More specifically, five areas of relationships are viewed as critical: corporate governance, vocational training and education, industrial relations, inter-firm relations (especially with suppliers and customers) and (intra-firm) human resources management (Hall and Soskice, 2001).

The institutions that shape the above relationships in a society are path-dependent, resulting from a particular historical trajectory of decisions and actions by the economic actors involved. In essence, as regards the governance issue, the key point is that each variety of capitalism is associated with a particular mix of coordination by markets, hierarchies and intermediate cooperative relationships. For example, this mix can influence the choice of capital structure, i.e. the relative importance of debt and equity. To a large extent, micro-level management decisions and actions are thus conditioned by collective institutions at the macro level, which encourage particular types of firm behaviour and discourage other types. Knetter (1989) is cited as an example: he found that UK and German firms exhibited different reaction patterns when faced with a similar appreciation in exchange rates. UK firms increased prices to maintain profitability, given that their access to capital in UK financial markets largely depends on sustained profitability. Their focus was on sustained access to resources available in free markets. In contrast, German firms reduced prices to maintain market share; in Germany access to capital is more independent of short-term financial performance, but maintaining market share is critical to achieve stable employment levels and good labour relations. The German firms' focus was therefore on co-specific assets, the return on which is conditioned by cooperation from relevant stakeholders operating in imperfect markets. The example above highlights the institutional complementarities both within the micro- or macro-level institutions, and between micro- and macro-level patterns in decisions and actions.

It is important to realize that individual firms have little direct control over these societal institutions and their evolution in time; rather, these institutions represent a set of opportunities and constraints with domestic firms being well positioned to take advantage of them in terms of competence and capability development and exploitation. No single set of institutions necessarily leads to superior economic performance (as measured by, e.g. economic growth rates and unemployment levels). It is precisely the complementarities among rules prevailing in the five domains mentioned above that lead to synergies and therefore to the potential for strong economic performance.

An important question regarding the sustainability of the present varieties of capitalism relates to the influence of 'globalization' forces. Unfortunately, Hall and Soskice (2001: 55) exhibit a basic lack of knowledge regarding modern international business research on globalization. They argue that the literature on globalization suggests a convergence toward an American-type capitalism, irrespective of the firms' origin. This has a focus on low labour unit costs with firms pressuring governments to reduce taxes and to deregulate the economy.

Hall and Soskice (2001) argue that their comparative institutional perspective fundamentally differs from the above view: firms differ across nations, other factors than low labour costs determine location, and most importantly, existing institutions in various countries could provide opportunities for firms engaged in institutional arbitrage. It is suggested that particular activities in the value chain may be located in those places where they can benefit most from specific sets of institutions (e.g. R&D facilities in appropriate knowledge clusters), thereby reinforcing rather than weakening existing institutions. As a result, only limited deregulation would occur in coordinated market economies such as Germany, in contrast to liberal market economies such as the United States.

The above description by Hall and Soskice (2001) of the alleged conventional view on globalization is incorrect, as demonstrated by Rugman and Verbeke's (2001a) synthesis of the international business literature on the location decisions of MNEs. Firms are not similar across nations but have substantially different administrative heritages, much in line with the empirical work of Bartlett and Ghoshal (1989). Cost elements, though important, are not the main driver of most foreign direct investment decisions: gaining market access and obtaining strategic assets are often much more critical considerations than cost reductions on basic production factors. Finally, the global economy is not moving toward a single optimal model: on the contrary, from a firm perspective, regional strategies and efforts to become insiders in host country clusters often require substantial isomorphic flexibility rather than an institutionalization approach (Van Den Bulcke and Verbeke, 2001; Rugman and Verbeke, 2001b). Hall and Soskice (2001) thus bring little new insight to the research table.

National Institutions and MNE Management

Substantial empirical evidence demonstrates that firms in different countries have different management approaches and that these differences are to some extent related to institutional variation, for example as regards financial practices, across countries, see Chui *et al.* (2002) and Mansi and Reeb (2002). Rajan and Zingales (1995, 1998) suggest a difference between market-based and relationship-based systems, much in line with Hall and Soskice's (2001) analysis that makes a distinction between liberal and coordinated market economies. The former are built on explicit, transparent contracts, which are enforceable in courts. In the latter, financiers who may be owners, lenders, suppliers or customers, benefit from institutionalized isolating mechanisms that allow substantial control over the firm. This control may take the form of regulation (as in the case of restrictions on hostile takeovers) or absence of transparency and lack of public disclosure of financial information. Here, long-term relationships and the associated reputation effects permit the financing system to function without extensive use of contracts or the guaranteed enforcement thereof by courts.

In terms of capital structure decisions, the differences between both systems are that the relationship-based approach permits 'inter-temporal cross-subsidization', i.e. a long-term rather than a short-term perspective on performance. This implies the acceptance of short-term losses if compensated by expected long-term gains.

Wald's (1999) and Booth *et al.*'s (2001) analyses demonstrate that capital structures and their determinants are not identical across countries. However, these studies also show that the varieties-of-capitalism approach, which builds on the fundamental distinction between liberal and coordinated market economies, contributes little to our understanding of what probably constitutes the single most important governance decision in business firms, namely the choice of capital structure. The Booth *et al.* (2001) study suggests the partial 'portability' of (effective) financial management decisions on capital structure across borders, even from developed countries to developing countries. Country-specific institutional factors remain critical but do not lend themselves to simple conceptual modelling that would permit a classification of countries in rather straightforward and easily understandable categories such as liberal market economies and coordinated market economies. In fact, regional integration and the related new regional institutions, especially as found in the EU and the NAFTA contexts, increasingly replace national modes of operation and national institutions, see Rugman and Verbeke (2005: ch. 23). Building upon the above elements, Figure 2.1 represents four different views on MNE management. The vertical axis makes a distinction between a weak and a strong impact of country-specific factors, especially national institutions, on MNE

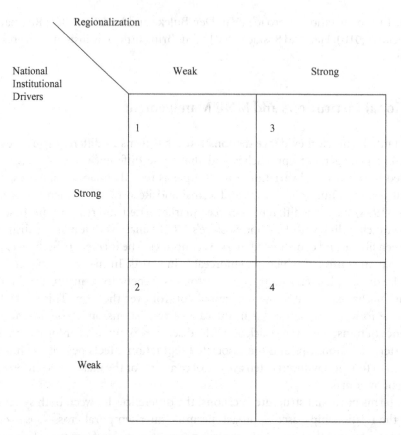

Figure 2.1   National institutional drivers and regionalization as determinants of MNE strategy

management whereas the horizontal axis distinguishes between weak and strong requirements imposed by regional, rather than national approaches to MNE strategy.

Quadrant 1 of Figure 2.1 reflects the varieties-of-capitalism approach: national institutions fundamentally determine MNE management. Here, any attempt to achieve regional integration would be squashed by the requirements to be nationally responsive to each variety of capitalism, represented by an individual country.

Quadrant 2 of Figure 2.1 represents the conventional view of MNE global strategic management. This view is exemplified in the financial management sphere by concepts such as the pecking-order hypothesis (Myers and Majluf, 1984) and various strands of the agency cost approach (Jensen and Meckling, 1976; Jensen, 1986; Stultz, 1990; Berger *et al.*, 1997), which are supposed to be universally applicable.

In quadrant 4 we depict the spread of regional integration, consistent with the data in the earlier sections of this chapter, at least as far as the home region is concerned. The efficiency considerations in this approach tend to eliminate historically grown, prevailing practices in individual nations, thereby leading to regional convergence in management approaches. If this convergence occurs only slowly it is primarily because of the entrenched positions of a number of economic actors in segmented markets that would incur substantial micro-level costs from moving toward a more efficient regional structure. The point is that national responsiveness becomes largely irrelevant when adopting this approach, and that higher regional integration at the firm level is an appropriate response to more regional commonality at the macro level.

Finally, quadrant 3 represents the approach adopted by most MNEs. These firms attempt to take advantage at the micro level of access to regional best practices and resources, sometimes available outside the home country, for example in the realm of financial or human resources that can be attracted by the firm, or in terms of access to favourable demand conditions, or to related and supplier industry conditions. Quadrant 3 implies the simultaneous focus on national responsiveness to each variety of capitalism, and, at the micro level, on the goal of achieving benefits of regional integration, especially through scale and scope economies in the home region.

Varieties of Capitalism and MNE Strategy

The above analysis has suggested that the varieties-of-capitalism approach suffers from a superficial understanding of the role of international business in the development of national institutions. We have established that both the heritage of national, institutional parameters and regional integration requirements need to be taken into account to explain micro-level MNE strategy. Now we consider the drivers that can improve the international competitiveness of a national economic system and the firms that operate in it.

It is surprising to observe that Hall and Soskice (2001) did not include in their study any serious analysis of MNE functioning. MNEs, defined as firms with value added operations in at least two countries, now dominate world trade and investment (Rugman and Collinson, 2006). The share of foreign MNEs in domestic manufacturing and service provision is increasing in all OECD countries, and in most countries these investments are primarily in high technology sectors (OECD, 2001). With such foreign involvement in domestic economies, foreign MNEs have a substantial impact on domestic governance structures, especially as regards finance, because of the mobility of capital and these firms' access to rather integrated capital markets, especially at the regional level.

Hall and Soskice's (2001) work conforms, from an institutionalist perspective, to Porter's (1990) diamond of national competitive advantage. Yet the latter has been discredited by conceptual and empirical research, (Rugman and Verbeke, 1998, 2001a; Davies and Ellis, 2000). Even the visual representation in 'diamond format' of their institutional framework seems to have been borrowed from Porter's (1990) diamond model. Porter's (1990) diamond approach argues that four elements, and the interactions among them, fundamentally determine the international competitiveness of specific industries: these four elements are factor conditions (with a focus on specialized, created factors such as skilled labour), demand conditions (with an

emphasis on market sophistication rather than size), related and supporting industries, and finally, strategy, structure and rivalry. The problem with Porter's diamond
is the assumption that competitive advantage is created at home in a first stage,
without involvement of foreign MNEs. Only in a second stage can firms expand
internationally, but always building upon their home base where all key strategic decisions are taken. Hall and Soskice (2001) make the same mistake: they also assume
that firms are fundamentally conditioned by home-country institutions, and that
they can tap only selectively into host-country diamonds to take advantage of these
countries' institutional strengths.

The reality is that many MNEs, especially those coming from small open
economies, need to take on board a 'double diamond' mindset to strategy from
the outset, with the second diamond reflecting access to resources available in a
home region beyond the home country (Rugman and D'Cruz, 1993; Van Den Bulcke and Verbeke, 2001). For example, most managers of large Canadian exporting
firms and MNEs pay equal attention to the Canadian and the United States' diamond determinants, given that the United States market is 10 times larger than the
Canadian one. The same holds in the EU where, for example, firms from Belgium
need to emulate behaviour viewed as legitimate in countries such as France, Germany, the UK and the Netherlands. It could be argued that these firms still face a
substantial 'liability of foreignness' as compared to insiders in these larger markets.
In other words, paying attention to foreign diamond determinants does not in itself
confer the same competitive advantages benefiting insiders in large nations. However, foreign direct investment allows the MNEs to bridge institutional differences
and to become insiders in foreign nations, especially in the home region.

Hall and Soskice's (2001) analysis would suggest that inefficiencies in relationship-
based economic systems would lead to the co-evolution of the various affected
institutions toward adapting to the new external environment. In fact, a much more
effective instrument to achieve such adaptation is to allow the entry of foreign MNEs
who can bring with them regional (not necessarily home country) best practices,
thereby facilitating changes in formal regulation, in selective policy interventions
and, most importantly, in the cognitive and strategic perceptions of the domestic
economic actors affected. Such foreign entry may thus be instrumental to realizing
the intentional strategic upgrading/re-engineering of national institutions.

In Figure 2.2, the varieties-of-capitalism approach is positioned in quadrant 2:
strategic interactions among interested economic actors operating in domestic networks lead to the co-evolution of various relevant institutions, including governance
mechanisms, when exogenous opportunities and threats demand change. The international character of MNEs, whether domestic or foreign ones, is not viewed
as a critical driver of institutional change, indeed, MNEs are often ignored in this
approach.

In contrast, Porter's (1990) diamond framework, which is positioned in quadrant 1 assumes the possibility of an intentional strategic upgrading of home country diamond components. It also argues that the domestic institutions that guide
the interactions among these components can be upgraded, for example through

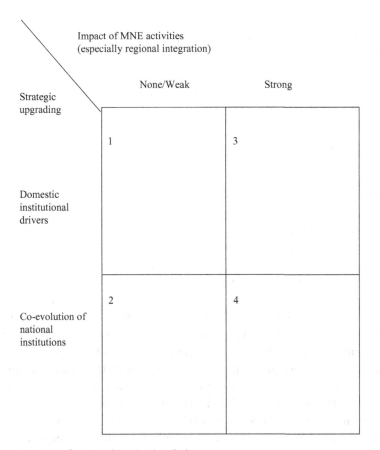

Figure 2.2   Drivers of national institutional change

business–government cooperation to advance the skill levels of specialized workers. Yet even in Porter's model MNEs do not perform an important role in the upgrading process; rather it is exports by an industry with an above average home country share that determines international competitiveness.

Quadrant 4 represents the opposite of Porter's (1990) approach, namely an institutional competition scenario: region-wide (e.g. the EU), national or sub-national governments (and their related agencies) try to attract (or repel) foreign direct investment. The latter is viewed as the most efficient instrument to achieve rapid economic upgrading, and to overcome the inertia prevailing in national institutions. In quadrant 4 the MNE is an agent of change. To some extent this is characteristic of the situation in the EU and in NAFTA. In these triad/regional blocks, state-level and national agencies are generally attempting to attract massive entries by foreign MNEs to stimulate economic growth and diversification. This occurs within a zero-sum game context, with the total level of FDI in each region being largely fixed. However, at times the agencies can reverse the regional institutions to repel MNEs – see the Microsoft case at the end of this chapter.

Finally, quadrant 3 represents a more balanced approach. It recognizes the major role played by inward and outward investment in domestic cluster upgrading, especially when this investment comes from the home region (Rugman and Verbeke, 1990, 1998; Van Den Bulcke and Verbeke, 2001), but also the need for domestic actors to design a coherent development program. Such a program should focus on attracting and developing regional best practices as a response to business needs rather than merely emulating a foreign system of institutions that would largely neglect the existing domestic institutional heritage and would therefore likely fail.

Conclusions

This chapter on the implications of regionalism and the varieties-of-capitalism approach for MNEs leads to five important conclusions.

First, the focus on national institutions, and the interactions among them, should be welcomed, even in a world system dominated by intra-regional business activity. MNE management is not conducted in an institutional vacuum, nor is it dominated by universally accepted 'global' practices; for example, the choice of capital structure varies across countries. More importantly, clear links exist between regional management systems and the economic growth of particular MNEs.

Second, there are two key difficulties associated with the varieties-of-capitalism approach. The first is the lack of clarity regarding the relevant set of institutions to consider. Hall and Soskice (2001) identify five types of key institutions, but some scholars focus on the legal system, others on the development of banking and financial markets and still others on cultural factors. If the relevant set of institutions cannot somehow be determined *ex ante*, everything can be explained *ex post* by 'institutions'. The use of ad hoc models without predictive ability and, more importantly, without a clearly articulated set of independent variables to explain phenomena, such as differences in capital structures among nations and firms, will do little to advance scientific knowledge in this domain.

Third, the absence of attention to MNEs and international business activities in general, in the varieties-of-capitalism approach, is a major shortcoming. How can IPE scholars make simplistic and even misinformed statements on the so-called 'conventional views on globalization' when they completely neglect all the relevant literature that has been written in this area for at least the past 30 years, for example, as synthesized in Rugman and Verbeke (1998, 2004).

Fourth, all firms build on a particular administrative heritage of interacting with domestic institutions, but they also need to take on board the regional institutions that are relevant, especially in the EU and NAFTA. This is not a plea in favour of emulating triad-based capitalism, but a prescription to adopt best MNE practices, irrespective of their geographic origin, as a complement to practices arising from the firm's national administrative heritage.

Fifth, national governments and related public agencies would be ill advised to rely on the natural co-evolution of domestic institutions as the key driver for adaptation to regionalization requirements. If institutional change is to benefit society at large, other elements are required than interactions among self-interested economic actors that would follow game-theory prescriptions. Effective leadership is needed to recognize the reality of regional business and the triad. Effective leadership requires clear choices by public policymakers to emulate regional best practices. It also implies acknowledging the major role that MNEs, both domestic and foreign ones, can play in this change process.

CASE STUDY: MICROSOFT

Microsoft Case Shows the World is not Global

The dispute between Microsoft and the European Commission demonstrates that globalization does not exist. Microsoft is a company that has ridden the wave of worldwide internet access and software applications. Yet, it has run into a brick wall in Brussels. There the EU Directorate General for Competition and State Aid (DG Comp) has imposed large fines for breaking its competition rules. In March 2004, the DG Comp ruled that Microsoft is abusing its dominant market position with its Windows operating system. Now the DG Comp is threatening to impose large daily fines because it says Microsoft is failing to comply with that ruling.

This case illustrates that even the world's most successful internet-based software company does not have unrestricted global market access for its products. Instead, the world is divided into a 'triad' with strong barriers for entry into the key regional markets of the EU, North America and the Asia Pacific. Microsoft is simply the latest large multinational enterprise to misread the world market place. Today, business activity is organized mainly within each region of the triad, not globally. For US firms, going to a foreign triad market in Europe and Asia is fraught with peril.

Rugman in *The Regional Multinationals* (2005) shows that the world's 500 largest firms, on average, sell 72% of their goods and services in their home region. Very few firms are truly global, defined as selling a significant percent of their products in each triad region. For example, the world's largest firm, Wal-Mart, has 94% of its sales in North America. Unfortunately, Microsoft does not reveal the geographic dispersion of its sales, but it is likely that a majority of them are also in North America. Firms like Wal-Mart and Microsoft need to understand that a business model developed for North America will need to be adapted when going to Europe and Asia.

In the case of Microsoft the key difference is in the way that the EU regulatory system operates. In Europe competition policy can be used as a barrier to entry. An individual firm (in this case, Sun Microsystems) can signal an EU-wide investigation. In this process the deck is stacked against the foreign firm. In 2001 General Electric also made a similar mistake in its acquisition of Honeywell which was disallowed by the EU.

While the United States has somewhat similar anti-trust provisions, the application of these is more business friendly than in Europe. Microsoft was able to settle its anti-trust case with the Bush Administration, but it has consistently failed to do so with the EU. The regulatory climate in Europe is harsher than in North America. Multinational firms like Microsoft which assume free trade, worldwide market entry, and the other attributes of globalization are learning expensive lessons. In addition to differences in regulatory standards across the triad, there are major cultural, social and political differences that deny globalization.

In terms of regulatory differences anti-trust is but one of an array of market entry barriers. Even worse are anti-dumping and countervailing duty laws which are used to keep out foreign rivals. The United States itself administers its anti-dumping and countervailing duty laws in favour of the home team. In March 2006, on security grounds, the US Congress overturned the executive branch decision to allow Dubai Ports International to acquire the US ports owned by P & O, a British firm. The Europeans perceive that the US commitment to free trade is weak; this is stiffening their spine with regard to Microsoft. The end result is typical triad-based economic warfare, where market entry is denied by the local bureaucrats and politicians.

While the US system is transparent, the EU investigation of unfair trade law cases, as well as anti-trust, can be opaque and self serving. The EU bureaucrats have continued the case against Microsoft even after Sun Microsystems and other business rivals in Europe, like Novell and RealNetworks, have settled their disputes. So now we have the EU, as an institution, fighting a foreign multinational. Not exactly a flat world.

In terms of our framework in this chapter, the Microsoft case can be summarized as follows. In Figure 2.1, the regional level of anti-trust regulations confronting Microsoft is an example of quadrant 4 policies, rather than the quadrant 1 varieties-of-capitalism approach. In terms of Figure 2.2, again we find no support for a variety-of-capitalism quadrant 2 approach in the EU's administration of anti-trust policy. Rather, Microsoft is positioned in quadrant 4 where there are triad-based regulations not only to attract MNEs but also designed to monitor and repel MNEs.

The lessons of the Microsoft case are the following. First, globalization is a myth; instead world business is conducted mainly on an intra-regional basis. Second, it is unlikely that the regulatory standards across the triad will be harmonized; thus, multinationals must be prepared to adapt their business models when they enter foreign regions of the triad. Third, even in high-tech areas such as software internet applications, the technology does not guarantee worldwide market access. The world is not flat; rather, there are strong regional fault lines.

Questions

1. How does European competition policy act as a barrier to entry, preventing foreign firms from leveraging their advantages in the European market?
2. Why do regional and national governments protect their domestic markets, rather than allow free trade?
3. What are the main strategic and organizational lessons here for Microsoft, in terms of its global ambitions?

Further Reading

Hall, P. A. and Soskice, D. (2001) *Varieties of Capitalism: The Institutional Foundations of Comparative Advantage*. Oxford: Oxford University Press.

Rugman, A. M. (2000) *The End of Globalization*. London: Random House Business Books.

Rugman, A. M. (2005) *The Regional Multinationals: MNEs and 'Global' Strategic Management*. Cambridge, New York: Cambridge University Press.

Rugman, A. M. and Verbeke, A. (2004) 'A perspective on regional and global strategies of multinational enterprises', *Journal of International Business Studies*, 35 (1): 3–18.

Rugman, A. M. and Verbeke, A. (2005) *Analysis of Multinational Strategic Management*. Cheltenham: E. Elgar.

References

Bartlett, C. A. and Ghoshal, S. (1989) *Managing Across Borders: The Transnational Solution*. Boston, Massachusetts: Harvard Business School Press.

Berger, P., Ofek, E. and Yermack, D. (1997) 'Managerial entrenchment and capital structure decisions', *Journal of Finance*, 50: 1411–30.

Booth, L., Aivazian, V., Demirguc-Kunt, A. and Maksimovic, V. (2001) 'Capital structures in developing countries', *Journal of Finance*, 56: 87–130.

Chui, A. C. W., Lloyd, A. E. and Kwok, C. C. Y. (2002) 'The determination of capital structure: is national culture a missing piece to the puzzle?' *Journal of International Business Studies*, 33 (1): 99–127.

Davies, H. and Ellis, P. (2000) 'Porter's competitive advantage of nations: time for the final judgement', *Journal of Management Studies*, 37 (8): 1189–213.

Govindarajan, V. and Gupta, A. (2001) *The Quest for Global Dominance*. San Francisco: Jossey-Bass.

Hall, P. A. and Soskice, D. (2001) *Varieties of Capitalism: The Institutional Foundations of Comparative Advantage*. Oxford: Oxford University Press.

Jensen, M. C. (1986) 'Agency costs of free cash flow, corporate finance and takeovers', *American Economic Review*, 76: 323–39.

Jensen, M. and Meckling, W. (1976) 'Theory of the firm: Managerial behaviour, agency costs and ownership structure', *Journal of Financial Economics*, 3: 305–60.

Knetter, M. (1989) 'Price discrimination by US and German exporters', *American Economic Review*, 79 (1): 198–210.

Laporta, R., Lopez de Silanes, F. and Shleifer, A. (1999) 'Corporate ownership around the world', *Journal of Finance*, 54 (2): 471–517.

Laporta, R., Lopez de Silanes, F., Shleifer, A. and Vishny, R. (1998) 'Law and finance', *The Journal of Political Economy*, 106: 1113–55.

Mansi, S. A. and Reeb, D. M. (2002) 'Corporate international activity and debt financing', *Journal of International Business Studies*, 33 (1): 129–47.

Myers, S. C. and Majluf, N. S. (1984) 'Corporate financing and investment decisions when firms have information that investors do not have', *Journal of Financial Economics*, 13: 187–221.

North, D. C. (1990) *Institutions, Institutional change and Economic Performance*. New York: Cambridge University Press.

OECD, (2001) *Measuring Globalisation: The Role of Multinationals in OECD Economies.* Paris: OECD.

Porter, M. E. (1990) *Competitive Advantage of Nations.* New York: The Free Press.

Rajan, R. G., and Zingales, L. (1995) 'Is there an optimal capital structure? Some evidence from international data', *The Journal of Finance,* 50: 1421–60.

Rajan, R. G., and Zingales, L. (1998) 'Financial Dependence and Growth', *American Economic Review,* 88: 559–86.

Rugman, A. M. (2000) *The End of Globalization.* London: Random House Business Books.

Rugman, A. M. (2005) *The Regional Multinationals: MNEs and 'Global' Strategic Management.* Cambridge, New York: Cambridge University Press.

Rugman, A. M. and Collinson, S. (2006) *International Business.* 4th edn, London: FT Prentice Hall.

Rugman, A. M. and D'Cruz, J. (1993) 'The double diamond', *Management International Review.* Special Issue 33: 17–39.

Rugman, A. M. and D'Cruz, J. (2000) *Multinationals as Flagship Firms: Regional Business Networks.* Oxford: Oxford University Press.

Rugman, A. M. and Girod, S. (2003) 'Retail multinationals and globalization: The evidence is regional', *European Management Journal* 21 (1), February: 24–37.

Rugman, A. M. and Verbeke, A. (1990) *Global Corporate Strategy and Trade Policy.* London and New York: Routledge.

Rugman, A. M. and Verbeke, A. (1992) 'A Note on the Transnational Solution and the Transaction Cost Theory of Multinational Strategic Management,' (with Alain Verbeke), *Journal of International Business Studies,* 23 (4): 761–72.

Rugman, A. M. and Verbeke, A. (1998) 'Multinational enterprises and public policy', *Journal of International Business Studies,* 29 (1): 115–36.

Rugman, A. M. and Verbeke, A. (2001a) 'Location, Competitiveness, and the Multinational Enterprise'. In A. M. Rugman and T. L. Brewer (eds) *The Oxford Handbook of International Business.* New York: Oxford University Press: 150–80.

Rugman, A. M. and Verbeke, A. (2001b) 'Subsidiary specific advantage in multinational enterprises', *Strategic Management Journal,* 22: 237–50.

Rugman, A. M. and Verbeke, A. (2004) 'A perspective on regional and global strategies of multinational enterprises', *Journal of International Business Studies,* 35 (1): 3–18.

Rugman, A. M. and Verbeke, A. (2005) *Analysis of Multinational Strategic Management.* Cheltenham: E. Elgar.

Stultz, R. (1990) 'Managerial discretion and optimal financing policies', *Journal of Financial Economics,* 26: 3–27.

Van Den Bulcke, D. and Verbeke, A. (2001) *Globalisation and the Small Open Economy.* Cheltenham: E. Elgar, 241.

Wald, J. K. (1999) 'How firm characteristics affect capital structure: An International Comparison', *Journal of Financial Research,* 22: 161–87.

Yip, G. S. (2003) *Total Global Strategy II.* Upper Saddle River, New Jersey: Prentice Hall.

Chapter 3   The Innovative Multinational Firm: The Dispersion of Creativity, and its Implications for the Firm and for World Development

John Cantwell and Yanli Zhang

Introduction: The Emergence of the Innovative Multinational Firm and Attempts to Reconfigure Earlier Images of the Multinational in Response

The image of the multinational corporation (MNC) as an innovative and networked firm is one that has emerged as a result of changes to the MNC as an organization, and changes in the environment in which it operates, over the past 30 years or so. The traditional MNC, from which the innovative MNC has evolved, generally arranged innovative activity in accordance with a relatively simple hierarchical structure within the firm. That is, the most original competence-creating activity was undertaken by the parent company in its home country, while subsidiaries were confined essentially to competence-exploiting forms of innovation, of the kind needed to adapt established products to local markets or established processes to local production conditions (Cantwell, 1995). As a result of the co-evolution of subsidiaries, of MNC corporate groups, and the environments in which they operate, in the innovative MNC competence-creating activities are more widely dispersed across the international network of the MNC. It is far more common for individual subsidiaries to undertake competence-creating lines of activity, usually in association with some product mandate or some similar specialized and acknowledged responsibility on behalf of their MNC group (Birkinshaw, Hood and Jonsson, 1998). In the most pronounced cases of such subsidiary level development, subsidiaries are recognized as centres of excellence for some key area of expertise on behalf of their respective MNC groups (Frost, Birkinshaw and Ensign, 2002).

Images of the Multinational Firm   Edited by Simon Collinson and Glenn Morgan
© 2009 John Wiley & Sons, Ltd

The geographical dispersion of competence-creating activities in the MNC over the past 30 years or so has five sets of implications that are explored here. The first is the shift towards more decentralized modes of governance within the MNC. Second, innovation, knowledge and the generation of new capabilities have themselves become more central to more recent MNC activities, and so the role of the firm as an organizational device for learning, and of knowledge as a locus for control within the MNC, have become more critical. Third, since innovation is in part location-specific as well as firm-specific, the MNC has come increasingly to draw upon a diversified locational portfolio of capabilities. Fourth, subsidiaries that have evolved competence-creating activities have needed to become more locally embedded in their own immediate environments, and so the interaction of MNCs with the development of regions has become more important both for MNCs and for local areas. Fifth, while development continues to be uneven across geographical space, the fragmentation of production and modularization of technologies have created new opportunities for countries catching up technologically, and they have resulted in more complex links between 'centre and periphery' via the activities of MNCs.

Before proceeding further, it may be helpful to elaborate briefly on the third and fourth of these themes, in terms of what is meant by innovation here. Following the perspective adopted in the literatures on national and regional systems of innovation (by those such as Freeman, 1987; Nelson, 1993; Breschi and Lissoni, 2001; Cooke, 2001), innovation is regarded as the introduction of products or processes that are new to the context of the location, and not necessarily new to the world as a whole. Thus, in this framework innovation is not defined relative to (best practice at) some notional world technology frontier. Innovation consists essentially of a continuous process of problem-solving in and around production (Rosenberg, 1982), and so relies upon learning of a localized kind (Nelson and Winter, 1982). At the level of countries or national systems, at earlier stages of development innovation may rely mainly on basic capabilities and simpler forms of knowledge, while with more mature development innovation requires more sophisticated capabilities and more complex kinds of knowledge, the generation of which draws upon a wider dispersion of prior knowledge sources. Hence, in the latter case of higher grade capabilities, MNCs and regional areas have tended to become steadily more interdependent in their mutual development. Locally embedded subsidiaries rely on their relationships with other local actors in regions that have some specialized fields of knowledge and expertise which are characteristic of the region, while in turn these local actors rely on the international networks of MNCs whose subsidiaries are situated locally for various complementary fields of knowledge that are not part of the specialization of the region.

The image or vision of the MNC as a system of more widely geographically distributed innovation is quite closely connected to the perspective of the MNC as a differentiated network (Nohria and Ghoshal, 1997). In the concept of a differentiated network, the structure of headquarters-subsidiary relationships (the degree of MNC group centralization versus subsidiary autonomy) is differentiated to fit the context of each subsidiary. Subsidiary-MNC group integration may rely somewhat more or less upon shared values and interpersonal networking, as it does upon hierarchical control or formalized rules. This bears some relationship to David's (1994) explanation of the role of historical experience in forming mutually consistent expectations that facilitate coordination without the need to rely perpetually on centralized direction (or to follow rules). However, Nohria and Ghoshal chose to sharply contrast their differentiated network with the notion of a pure undifferentiated hierarchy, as a unidirectional administrative mechanism functioning in the simple form of centralized MNC group power running from the parent company downwards, like in the traditional archetype of the MNC, as opposed to allowing for the possibility that subsidiary centres of excellence may themselves constitute further nodes of power or hierarchy within the MNC group. Their idea of a differentiated network is thus also treated in connection with its erosion of the dominance of hierarchy as an organizational device for coordination within the MNC, and not for the interactions of the MNC with geographical and locational hierarchies beyond the firm itself, which are a central feature of our discussion here.

Another concept related to the innovative MNC is that of the N-form corporation (Hedlund, 1994), which might also have stood for a networked form of enterprise, but was originally described as a new or novelty form of organization designed to improve knowledge management within the firm. The similarity with the image of the innovative MNC is that the N-form corporation is described as being a creation-oriented, recombinatorial and experimental organization. However, the various characteristics said to be associated with the N-form as an ideal type range wider than the treatment of innovation in the firm. Moreover, the N-form is argued to be especially representative of Japanese companies as opposed to Western firms, and while this decentralized and networked form of governance that relies more on lateral than on vertical communication may be true of their respective domestic structures, we will argue below that it is Western rather than Japanese MNCs that have evolved further towards international networks for innovation.

If the image of the innovative MNC has some parallels with that of the differentiated network or the N-form corporation, it can be contrasted with the image provided by Stephen Hymer based upon the traditional MNC as it once had stood in the 1960s and early 1970s, and on Hymer's forecast of the enhancement of his earlier image towards a more extreme state of singular hierarchy. Hymer was one of the key pioneers of the field of international business. In addition to his major contribution, which addressed the question of why national firms become MNCs, he also dealt with many other globalization and development-related issues. One of his key ideas in this area is his law of uneven development, discussed in the essay 'The Multinational Corporation and the Law of Uneven Development' (Hymer, 1972 and reprinted in Hymer, 1975). In this essay, Hymer had been asked to look ahead 30 years or so into the future, from around 1970 to 2000, and to do so he extrapolated from certain then contemporary trends and perspectives on the MNC, and predicted that MNCs would reinforce and perpetuate patterns of uneven development in the world.

Of course, what was then the future has now become the past, and we know now how MNCs have developed since 1970. So, with the benefit of hindsight, we can re-evaluate Hymer's speculations on what was for him then the future. Moreover, we can also take into consideration how MNCs have evolved and changed over time, partly as a reflection of the newer trends and perspectives that have emerged since then, some of which were not readily predictable by Hymer in the early 1970s. The emergence of the innovative MNC is very different from the traditional MNC described by Hymer in this regard, and so we discuss here how the MNC has evolved in a different direction than Hymer had expected from an extrapolation of the trends that he had observed through to around 1970, and how although the issue of locational hierarchies remains relevant, it does so for somewhat different reasons than those he had outlined. Indeed, the changes to international business since Hymer's time moved the MNC itself far enough away from his original image that any discussion of that image as a powerful and tightly centrally controlled hierarchy receded in the 1980s and for most of the 1990s.

However, the newly emerged innovative MNC has more recently encountered constraints upon its full achievement, and the difficulties in moving towards a more fully globally integrated firm have been noted by a growing number of scholars since the mid-1990s. Sölvell and Zander (1998) stress the role of the isolating mechanisms that may be associated with the greater local embeddedness of subsidiaries, and with a greater degree of subsidiary autonomy, such that the international diffusion of knowledge within the MNC may remain limited. Power struggles and intersubsidiary competition within the MNC may act as a further constraint on the willingness to share knowledge. Zander and Sölvell (2002) argue that a continuing dominance of competence-exploiting activities within the MNC suggest that cross-border innovation efforts continue to be small relative to the overall system of innovation within the MNC. Yamin and Forsgren (2006) have gone so far as to suggest that in line with Hymer's earlier focus on power within the MNC, the parent companies of MNCs have reacted to the trend towards increasing subsidiary authority by seeking to reduce the federative nature of multinationality. The outcome of this process, they contend, is that most MNCs have remained regional rather than global in their strategy and structure, as shown by Rugman (2005).

While Yamin and Forsgren have partially reintroduced Hymer's earlier image of the MNC in their interpretation of Rugman's evidence of regional MNCs, the fuller reappearance of Hymer's image has been central in works associated with the new anti-global movement, and in the re-emergence of radical critiques of the MNC in the early years of the new century (Ghauri and Buckley, 2002). Representatives of the current anti-global movement believe as did Hymer that MNCs help to perpetuate the existing international division of labour across countries, and so therefore they exploit the location-specific resources of less developed countries for their own ends. In an argument certainly reminiscent of Hymer, Klein (2000) perceives MNCs as firms with the strength of market power needed to push up the prices of branded necessary consumption goods such as drugs, while forcing down the prices of raw materials such as primary commodities and wages in less developed countries. Her argument relies on a conventional product-based view of the comparative advantage of countries in trade, and of firms capable of wielding high degrees of market power across national boundaries. (For a critique of the notions that MNCs pay lower wages in less developed countries and that globalization heralds a 'race to the bottom' across countries, see Graham (2000).) In Hertz's (2002) restatement of Hymer's claim that power comes to be increasingly concentrated in the head offices of MNCs, the losers are governments and political authorities that are believed to have ceded their power to MNCs through the constraints that they have allowed to be imposed upon themselves by multilateral organizations such as the WTO. In this case the less developed countries are said again to have lost especially through the adoption of inequitable trade rules (that suit MNCs).

Thus, in what follows we compare the changes that have led to the emergence of the innovative MNC with Hymer's earlier counter-image, an alternative vision which as we have just noted has far from entirely gone away, even though times have changed. The remainder of this chapter is divided into five sections. In Section 1, we revisit the traditional MNC of the early 1970s from which the innovative MNC has evolved. Thus, we briefly review Hymer's earlier law of uneven development, and how it was that he arrived at his conclusion based upon a stylized model of the traditional MNC of that time, and of its interaction with the geographical spread of economic activity. In Section 2, we examine how the emergence of the innovative MNC has impacted upon geographical hierarchies of activity. We show that in the current world too, a pattern of uneven development and of a reinforcing role of MNCs in that process are consistent with much empirical evidence. However, in Section 3 we contend that the evolution of the innovative MNC has occurred through an experimental movement towards more widely geographically distributed value-creating centers, rather than through a carefully planned dispersion of competence-creating activities under the central control of a traditional hierarchy. Thus, the rationale for the interaction of MNC centers with geographical hierarchies is different from and more complicated than that provided by Hymer, and the differences reflect the way in which MNCs have changed since Hymer's time. Uneven development is thus more due to bottom-up subsidiary evolution and complex processes of interaction between MNCs and the varying conditions of individual localities, rather than coming at the behest of a sole source of centralized control in MNC headquarters. In Section 4, we examine further the co-evolution of the innovative MNC with its environment. As a result of the complex interchange between MNCs and location-specific advantages, and the greater flexibility provided by the fragmentation of production, the pattern of uneven development today is not as extreme or as self-perpetuating as Hymer had supposed. Section 5 concludes by developing the contention that although Hymer's image of the traditional MNC and locational hierarchy was based upon assumptions that have since been revealed to be inaccurate, a balanced evaluation of the evolution of the more recent innovative MNC needs to take into account the constraints upon the newer networked organizational form, which suggests that Hymer's rather dated perspective, while much eroded, is still far from redundant.

The Traditional Multinational Firm and Uneven Development According to Hymer

As outlined above, the traditional MNC, from which the innovative MNC has evolved, generally arranged innovative activity in accordance with a relatively simple hierarchical structure within the firm. Most competence-creating activity was confined to the parent company, and to key facilities in urban centers in the home country. In his law of uneven development, Hymer constructed a theory of the locational implications of the Chandler and Redlich (1961) scheme of corporate hierarchy in an MNC context. In what follows in this section, we explain what the Chandler-Redlich scheme and the accompanying location theory are, and how Hymer brought them together.

Chandler and Redlich's (1961) scheme illustrated the structure of corporate hierarchy. This scheme distinguishes between three levels of managerial activities. Level III, the lowest level, is concerned with managing the day-to-day operations of one unit of the enterprise. Level II is concerned with coordination functions, such as coordinating the managers of different functional areas, e.g. marketing, finance, or coordinating managers of different divisions in a multi-divisional firm. Level I, the job of top management, is concerned with overall corporate strategy, goal determination and planning.

According to Hymer (1972), location theory suggests that the higher the level of activities, the more geographically concentrated they need to be. Level III activities would become more widely dispersed across the world according to local markets, resources and the pattern of comparative advantage. Level II activities, because of their need for white-collar workers, communication systems and information, tend to be concentrated in large cities. Level I activities tend to be even more concentrated than Level II activities, for they must be located close to a major capital market, the media and government decision-takers, because of the need for face-to-face contact with key actors in these other categories at higher levels of decision-making.

Thus, applying his formulation of location theory to the Chandler-Redlich scheme in an MNC context, Hymer expected that MNCs, with their combination of organizational hierarchy and international spread, would tend to reproduce a hierarchical division of labor between geographical regions that corresponded to the vertical division of labor within the firm. MNCs would tend to centralize high-level decision-making occupations in a few key cities in the advanced countries, surrounded by a number of regional sub-capitals, and confine their facilities in much of the rest of the world to lower levels of activity, i.e. to the status of towns and villages in a new imperial system (Hymer, 1972).

Inferring from the microcosm to the macrocosm, Hymer believed that the centralization of control within the MNC would lead to centralization of control within the international economy. Thus, geographical specialization would come to reflect the hierarchy of MNC corporate decision-making. With the increasing dominance of MNCs in the international economy, Hymer was concerned that the existing elements of inequality and dependency would be reinforced and perpetuated and peripheral regions might become locked in permanently.

It is worth noting that there is an important technological aspect in Hymer's locational hierarchy adopted from the Chandler-Redlich scheme. In his article (Hymer, 1972) he talks about how higher level technological innovation and the R&D function tend to be geographically centralized. Following a similar line of reasoning to that found contemporaneously in Vernon's product life cycle model (Vernon, 1966, 1979), Hymer supposed that innovation is usually generated in a few major centers in the home country due to the local presence of high and sophisticated demand, and then 'it spreads, or trickles down to other groups' through a cycle of diffusion (Hymer, 1975: 51). In this context, as has been noted by Pitelis (1991, 2002), Hymer also predicted the trend of outsourcing of simpler activities, based on the argument that MNCs would pass out non-key functions to peripheral regions, but retain control at MNC headquarters over key functions such as new product development and the creation and use of 'intangible' assets (see Hymer, 1979).

In summary, Hymer's extrapolation from the early 1970s of a trend towards the reinforcement of uneven development was derived by applying a theory of location to the MNC as a highly centralized hierarchy across national borders. Therefore, by allocating different level activities to different locations, he contended that MNCs would tend to reinforce existing patterns of geographical inequality in the international economy, subjecting underdeveloped regions to continuing poverty.

The Interaction of the Innovative Multinational Firm with Geographical Hierarchies

More than 30 years later, Hymer's prediction of uneven development has turned out to parallel some aspects of the currently observed reality. It seems that Hymer's notion of a correspondence between MNC location decisions and the pattern of uneven development in the world economy is partly consistent with current evidence of locational hierarchies and their self-reinforcing tendencies due to the geographical location of technological development activities in the MNCs.

We can observe a pattern of uneven regional development today, that is akin to Hymer's prediction that the world would be divided into centers and peripheries at the global or cross-country level, but this form of modern locational hierarchy follows more from the nature of the progressive interaction between MNCs and locations, and need not necessarily imply that existing patterns of inequality will be perpetuated forever. Cantwell (1987) adapted Hymer's notion and suggested that higher grade and lower grade functions may become locationally separated, and this may give rise to a distinction between higher order and lower order regions. Cantwell and Iammarino (2001, 2003) have shown that cross-regional hierarchies exist within Europe, and that regional differentiation also exists within countries.

In parallel to Hymer's scheme, we can classify the current locational hierarchy into higher order regions (all-around centers of excellence), intermediate regions (specialized centers of excellence) and lower level regions (that have little innovative effort) in the locational hierarchy (Cantwell, Iammarino and Noonan, 2001). On a world level, we can also see that many of the lower level activities have been relocated to less developed countries, sometimes through subcontracting or outsourcing, such as call centers in India, or the manufacture of textiles, garments and toys in China.

The characteristics of a location determine its degree of attraction to the siting of MNC research activities and the types of research activities attracted, because of the different nature of spillovers available (Dicken, 1992; Cowling and Sugden, 1994; Cantwell and Piscitello, 2002). By allocating different types of innovation activities to regions of the most appropriate kind, the degree of geographical differentiation between regions is likely to be reinforced by MNC decisions, in parallel with Hymer's idea of uneven development (Bailey and Driffield, 2002). Consistent with the lack of attractiveness for MNC innovative activities of locations in which local capabilities have been as yet little built up, a recent study by Athreye and Cantwell (2007) has found that on average across countries inward foreign direct investment (FDI) since 1950 has not preceded the emergence of the earlier stages of innovation in countries catching up. Indeed, the increased geographical dispersion of competence-creating innovative efforts within the existing international networks of MNCs appears to have reinforced the position of the most established technology producing countries. However, the extension of such FDI networks to new locations that had already built up sufficient absorptive capacity in the form of basic capabilities, has on average facilitated the catch-up of countries in more sophisticated kinds of innovation since the early 1990s.

In higher order regions, which might also be termed all-around centers of excellence, there is the greatest extent of technological activity, and the greatest diversity in the industrial sources of innovation, which generates general purpose spillovers, and attracts many kinds of economic activities to an area. In such regions there is a greater scope for knowledge-based interactions among MNCs and indigenous firms, and these interactions are likely to further upgrade activities in these locations, broaden the scope of local technological capability and produce stable mechanisms of collective knowledge accumulation (Porter, 1990; Storper, 1992).

Intermediate regions, which might also be termed specialized centers, rely upon the presence of a wide range of technologically active firms within a given industry or sector, all in the same geographical area. MNCs are attracted to intermediate regions to benefit from local traditions of technological accumulation in a closely allied field to their own specialization, and the associated favorable network and institutional environment.

Lower order regions, in contrast, lack these favorable mechanisms of technological accumulation. Thus, lower order regions are more likely to be left without much innovative capacity, since to set a development process in motion for the first time is always a difficult task. Therefore, polarization is likely to result, between the higher order and intermediate regions on the one hand, and lower order regions on the other hand.

The Emergence and Evolution of the Innovative Multinational Firm

However, although Hymer's idea of the role for the MNC in the presence of locational hierarchies can in some respects be supported by empirical evidence, the rationale underlying the uneven development that we observe today is in most key respects different from that given by Hymer. This is partly due to changes in the character of the MNC, which has a more widely geographically distributed innovation system, and partly due to changes in the business environment. The uneven development that we observe today, and the role of MNCs within it, emanates more from the differentiation and marked variations in the extent of local initiatives as between individual subsidiaries, and a bottom-up evolution in the networks of MNCs, rather than from a purely top-down central administrative control in an organizational MNC hierarchy. Also, it derives from a process of dynamic interaction between many actors, and not just from some prior determination by one single actor.

In Hymer's early analysis, the MNC was conceptualized as a simple hierarchy and a pure central planner. Over 30 years later, we can now better appreciate that Hymer's particular interpretation of the MNC as a simple form of organizational hierarchy has become increasingly inaccurate and outdated. Today, although hierarchies have always remained present within the various administrative structures that have evolved for the organization of the firm, Hymer's relatively simple conceptualization of the MNC as a well defined singular and uniform hierarchy has become misleading, owing to a shift in management structures, the emergence of newer and less centralized hierarchical organizational forms and the dispersion of knowledge-creating activity. There is growing evidence of the transformation of MNC headquarters to include – inter alia – aspects of decentralization despite the retention of core central control (Ferlie and Pettigrew, 1996), which makes the MNC organizational forms of today a more complex, hybrid and distributed form of hierarchy rather than the simpler singular hierarchy visualized by Hymer.

Therefore, much of the subsequent literature, especially since 1985, has taken a different view, reflecting what has been changing in the organization of MNCs. In contemporary analysis, MNCs are more commonly conceptualized as integrated global networks, with multiple geographically distributed higher value-creating centers. This contemporary view of MNCs has been reflected in the notion of the networked firm or firms as networks in Håkanson (1993, 1995) and Kobrin (2001), and the notion of MNCs as organizational heterarchies rather than as simple hierarchies in Hedlund (1986, 1993).

At the same time, this revised conceptualization of MNC organization also reflects changes over time in perceptions of the firm as such. Hymer's theory of the firm is based upon an industrial organization perspective of the establishment of barriers to entry that confer market power. In this approach, the MNC provides an organizational means of constructing monopolistic or collusive positions to exploit elsewhere monopolistic advantages formed initially in the home country. However, more recently, the resource-based view or knowledge-based view in the strategic management literature (Penrose, 1959; Wernerfelt, 1984; Barney, 1991; Kogut and Zander, 1992, 1993; Pitelis, 2001) has provided popular currency for a competence-based or technological accumulation approach to the MNC (Cantwell, 1989). In the context of the competence-based approach, the firm or MNC is seen as an institution that constructs capabilities through internal learning processes, in interaction with other firms and institutions (Cantwell, 1991; Kay, 2000; Love, 1997). Such firm-specific advantages derive from creating new streams of value adding activity derived from innovation, and they tend to be pro- rather than anti-competitive.

At the same time, this also reflects a change over time in the primary issue of concern as the MNC has reached a more mature stage of development, from Hymer's original question of why firms go abroad in their early internationalization to today's issue of cross-border network management in established MNCs. MNCs nowadays are not just to be seen as 'conquering the world' through an exploitation of their home advantages, as reflected in Hymer's perception of firms that were embarking on the earliest stages of internationalization. Rather, when MNCs have reached a mature stage, MNC advantages can be argued to derive from a continuous process of innovation throughout an international network rather than from the exercise of power in some specific national or geographically segmented market. The competitive advantage of established or mature MNCs increasingly stems instead from their abilities to build and control a network of global flows of information, resources and people. This ability to create global networks, utilize geographically specialized resources and transfer knowledge between different knowledge-creating nodes, lies at the core of many current conceptualizations of the MNC (Cantwell and Mudambi, 2005; Håkanson, 1993, 1995).

Thus, the competence-based approach to the firm and the maturing of MNCs has led to a growing interest in the asset-seeking motive for FDI (Dunning, 1995, 1996; Cantwell, 1989; Dunning and McKaig-Berliner, 2002; Pearce, 1999a; Makino, Lau and Yeh, 2002; Wesson, 2005), and in the greater decentralization in the management of international R&D to capture 'home-base augmenting' benefits (Kümmerle, 1999a, 1999b). The changes in economic activity that have been observed over the last 30 years, such as the greater importance of knowledge as a key asset, the role of alliance capitalism and increased globalization or cross-border interconnectedness of activities, have encouraged and required MNCs to leverage and combine the local knowledge and technological strengths of different regions in the world. Therefore, the role of MNCs has substantially shifted from being an agent of technology transfer to a range of individual host countries to instead being one of an international initiator of technology creation. By drawing on innovations of various kinds, depending upon the conditions prevailing in the relevant local research centers, MNCs have developed more complex technological systems, and through accessing geographically differentiated streams of knowledge they have established an important new source of competitive advantage (Almeida, 1996; Dunning, 1996; Dunning and Wymbs, 1999; Fors and Zejan, 1996; Kümmerle, 1999a; Pearce, 1999b).

The evolution of organizational systems for cross-border knowledge exchange within the innovative MNC has carried with it an important implication for the potential inclusion of developing countries as locations for the siting of competence-creating activities. In the context of discussions such as those over TRIPS, it has been suggested that developing countries will remain unattractive hosts for competence-creating innovation unless they substantially tighten both their intellectual property regimes, and the mechanisms for enforcement. However, where technologies have become modularized and component knowledge is developed at more than one location, then the MNC itself provides an alternative institutional device for intellectual property protection (Zhao, 2006). Even if the component knowledge developed locally in a developing country leaks out, it is of little value to others without understanding how it fits into a broader system of knowledge. While this finding of the role of knowledge integration within the innovative MNC may apply more to some industries than others, there is evidence that it applies especially to the areas of electronics – computers and telecommunications – in China (Zhao, 2006).

In the environment of the MNC there has in any event been some shift towards the emergence of new technology producing countries, and a widening geographical spread of innovative effort. While it was true that the period 1970–90 was consistent with Hymer's expectations in the sense that there was a further rise in the degree of geographical concentration across countries in the most advanced technology development as measured by patenting, lower level kinds of innovation were already dispersing as measured by the total international licensing receipts of countries for intellectual property creation (Athreye and Cantwell, 2007). It seems that this latter trend has been strongly encouraged especially since the early 1980s by the rapid growth of arm's length markets for intellectual property trade, which has created an opportunity for the emergence of new players. Indeed, since 1992 the more sophisticated kinds of innovative effort have become more geographically dispersed across countries too (Athreye and Cantwell, 2007), which is the reverse of what Hymer might have anticipated (let alone modern anti-global writers). This shift in the international location of dynamism in the external environment of the MNC implies that even without any shift in the competitive advantages of MNCs and in their incentives to preserve integrated corporate structures, MNCs may have been required to internationally restructure their activity especially towards East Asia, and in part through subcontracting and inter-firm cooperation in those new locations (Teece, 2006).

The Co-Evolution of the Innovative Multinational Firm with its Environment

The notion that the geographical dispersion of technological development enhances innovation in the network of the MNC as a whole is founded on the belief that innovation is location-specific, and depends critically on the supply of skilled resources available in each subsidiary site (Cantwell, 1989). This runs counter to Hymer's and Vernon's view, which treats innovation as a demand-led process that depends primarily on home country market size and the presence of high income consumers, which perspective accorded with that of their contemporary Schmookler (1966), but has now been rather discredited as an over-simplification (Mowery and Rosenberg, 1979). In the technological accumulation approach, innovation is not just essentially created in the home country and then diffused abroad, but is rather created in multiple geographically dispersed centers of excellence and fed back into further innovation in other parts of the MNC corporate group. One implication is that different MNCs follow a variety of strategies with respect to the types of activity they locate in any given site, depending upon their existing corporate capabilities and hence the specialized nature of their absorptive capacity. Thus, the emergence of a locational hierarchy in any industry regulates the cross-MNC variety of patterns of technology sourcing or asset-seeking investments that are observed, for MNCs that emanate from home countries of differing status in the hierarchy (Cantwell and Janne, 1999).

Innovation is a firm-specific cumulative learning and problem-solving process, that interacts with both the growth of market demand and the supply of scientific and technological knowledge. It thus depends critically on the local organizational and institutional environment in which these operations are sited (Cantwell and Fai, 1999). The scientific and technological traditions of each country, the shared experience of its researchers and production engineers and the communication between them across companies, the nature of its educational system and its common business practices all contribute to the distinctiveness of the path of technology development undertaken in each location (Cantwell, 2000; Pavitt, 1987; Rosenberg, 1976). The peculiarities of foreign production conditions and demand have required leading MNCs historically to be present in munificent locations to access certain capabilities and develop innovations in certain fields (Cantwell, 1995).

The shift of competence-creating activities towards selected subsidiaries within MNCs tends to involve the development of new location bound firm-specific capabilities that draw upon the characteristics of innovation in the place in which they are sited, but it is still likely that at least some elements of the knowledge that is created in this fashion can be transferred or exchanged (after some suitable adaptation) with other parts of the MNC's international network elsewhere. Of course, Hymer's original argument depended upon the interaction between higher level activities in the MNC and the locational boundedness of the key resources required for higher grade development efforts. Yet there are increasingly multiple potential centers for innovation in an industry, and the streams of innovation for which they are responsible are locally differentiated. While the expansion of the international networks of MNCs to take in new locations contributes to the decentralization of innovative activities within the MNC and to the catch-up of newer technology producers, the restructuring of existing MNC networks for innovation tends to reinforce the position of longer established centers, at least initially (Athreye and Cantwell, 2007).

Since subsidiaries rely upon locally embedded resources in developing their capabilities, this has tended to increase the political power of subsidiaries within their respective MNC groups (Mudambi and Navarra, 2004). Therefore, the dispersion of knowledge and innovation implies a dispersion of control in the MNC network. In the current knowledge-based economy, in which knowledge has become the key asset, control comes increasingly from the possession of knowledge, and the ability to create new knowledge or access complementary knowledge. Control in MNCs is increasingly subject to elements of decentralization to specialized nodes of excellence because MNC headquarters often cannot fully understand the complexities of the knowledge-related activities of their subsidiaries (Prahalad, 1976; Prahalad and Doz, 1981). In addition, the MNC headquarters has to allow selected subsidiaries to evolve towards greater autonomy (and their own control over some subset of networks) for them to become competence-creating in their own right (Birkinshaw and Hood, 1998). For subsidiaries to develop their own independent competence-creating capabilities in turn demands that they become more embedded in their own localities (Birkinshaw, Hood and Jonsson, 1998; Andersson and Forsgren, 2000; Andersson, Forsgren and Holm, 2002), a process that must be initiated and managed locally, and which therefore implies a dispersal of concentrations of power within the MNC. As Pitelis (2002) noted, in Hymer's later work he also came to acknowledge that the power of MNCs (and of corporate control within the MNC) derives increasingly from a control over intangibles such as knowledge and technological capability (Hymer, 1979).

The decentralization of control in MNCs has given rise to a widening diversity of MNC organizational forms. Bartlett and Ghoshal (1989) identified the four types of MNC organizations – multidomestic, international, global and transnational – and the utility of this typology has been supported empirically (such as by Ghoshal and Nohria (1993) and Harzing (2000)). Thus, the MNC portrayed by Hymer is descriptive of only one type of MNC organization, which may be subsumed under the global type in Bartlett and Ghoshal's (1989) typology, in which the headquarters constitutes the singular highly central actor.

All these changes, when taken together – MNCs becoming more like global networks, the vigorous asset-seeking activities of MNCs, the dispersion of knowledge and innovation and the decentralization of control – have undermined the narrow formulation of hierarchy found in Hymer's analysis. As Tolentino (2002) noted, it is now misleading to still think of the MNC as a singular allocator of world wealth, conducting a unilateral flow of investment, income and capabilities from center to periphery in each firm. MNCs can impact upon world development in complex and multi-faceted ways, both beneficial and detrimental. When analyzing the effect of MNCs on development, we need a broader perspective and must be open to a variety of potential forces and interactions.

Therefore, although we certainly still observe uneven development in the world, we can envisage a future world outlook that need not be as gloomy as Hymer had painted it. It is not inevitable that the existing peripheral regions will be locked in to their current status forever. It is a rather more nuanced story. Higher level technological centers arise not purely through the parent-led decisions of MNC headquarters, but as a consequence of the interaction of many actors, including at a location level local economic dynamics, the regional innovation system, local and national government policies, and at a firm level subsidiary-driven initiatives. The new conditions regulating the quality of a location imply a stronger role for the state in sustaining the competitive advantage of a country and increasing its share of value added, through encouraging the most appropriate kinds of local technological specialization, depending upon the particular characteristics of local skills and institutions. Most notably, government can help attract foreign-owned research activity of a locally competence-creating kind by funding a strong science and educational base.

We have seen that MNCs through their FDI, joint venture, licensing and subcontracting activities may sometimes facilitate the narrowing of gaps between regions at different levels of development and permit 'catching up', as illustrated by the recent experience of developing countries such as China and India, and previously the four East Asian 'tigers'. MNCs have begun to allocate rather more R&D and higher level activities to selected developing countries, and knowledge-creating nodes are increasingly being dispersed through global production networks that include some developing (or formerly developing) countries (Hobday, 1995; Ernst, 2001; Zhao, 2006). The emergence of international MNC network strategies for innovation and an increasing fragmentation of production systems have opened up new opportunities for at least some developing countries to catch up (Ernst, 2002, 2005; Ernst and Kim, 2002). Peripheral regions have opportunities to evolve in a positive direction into higher level regions rather than being forever locked into a vicious cycle. Therefore, MNCs and international business linkages are on balance just as likely to have positive as negative effects upon individual locations, and offer a means of catching up even if they also sometimes tend to reinforce geographical inequality.

While openness to international trade and openness to learning affect the ability of indigenous actors to begin the processes of innovation in the earliest stages of development (Landes, 1998) – and that may include linkages with international business through modes such as subcontracting and technology licensing – MNCs are unlikely to be attracted to invest much through FDI until local infrastructure and absorptive capacity has reached some threshold level of location-specific advantage (Dunning, 1993; Lall, 2001). In such cases investment is likely to be restricted to resource-seeking FDI where natural resources are available, as in much of sub-Saharan Africa today. Yet once a process of local innovation and development has begun, the extension of FDI to these newer locations tends to facilitate upgrading towards more sophisticated kinds of technological development (Athreye and Cantwell, 2007).

Conclusion: The Impact of the Innovative Multinational Firm, and Constraints upon its Further Evolution

In conclusion, 30 years later, Hymer's concern about uneven development remains warranted; we can observe various patterns of geographical inequality between higher order regions and lower order regions. However, the major driving forces that lie behind locational hierarchies today have shifted from the simpler types of centralized hierarchy described by Hymer towards the forms associated with networked MNCs that have distributed centers of excellence. With the benefit of hindsight, Hymer's perspective upon MNC hierarchy represents an essentially US-centric and early post-war view of the nature of MNCs. Owing to this now rather obsolete perspective, his explanation of uneven development tended to be somewhat one-sided and thus became overly exaggerated.

However, this is not to deny the original contribution that Hymer made in perceiving the essential relationship between MNC activity and uneven development. Like all scholars, Hymer was inevitably limited by the historical context of his time. Hymer's conceptualization of the MNC as a simple unidirectional hierarchy was a reflection of the then contemporary trends in large firm strategy and structure, as captured in various discussions at that time. The rise of the large-scale modern corporation during the first two-thirds of the twentieth century effectively demonstrated the power and efficacy of hierarchy, notably described by Chandler (1977) as a 'visible hand' of coordination. This centrally hierarchical means of organizing enabled the formation of the modern corporation and allowed it to reap the benefits of economies of scale and scope (Chandler, 1962, 1990). As a consequence, most discussions at that time, including that of Hymer, emphasized or incorporated a vision of MNCs as relatively uniform organizational hierarchies (Brooke and Remmers, 1970; Buckley and Casson, 1976; Williamson, 1975).

On the other hand, we can also see that Hymer was also limited by his market power orientation. He tended to emphasize the monopoly attributes of large MNCs, his analysis touched by aspects of ideological beliefs, with varying degrees of accuracy (Pitelis, 2002). His key inference – that 'there is a correspondence principle relating centralization of control within the MNC to centralization within the international economy' (Hymer, 1975) – relied in part on his prediction that the world would be increasingly dominated by a diminishing number of MNCs (Hymer, 1975; Hymer and Rowthorne, 1970), that would over time become stronger and more monopolistic while nation states became weaker. Although it has been recently reflected in the perspectives of the anti-global movement (Hertz, 2002), this conceptualization has not matched reality, given the rise of large MNCs since 1970 from Japan, Korea, and now from China and other newer source countries in which the state is often far from weak (Graham, 2002). As a result, from the standpoint of the early twentieth century hierarchies and networks, Hymer's approach was overly simplistically linear, failed to appreciate sufficiently the complexities of the interactions between a wide variety of actors in the world and thereby tended to overstate its case.

Perhaps somewhat ironically, Hymer's model of linear organizational hierarchy, in which the highest quality activities are retained in the home base of the MNC, in many ways now offers a closer representation of the relatively newer Japanese-owned MNCs than it does of the longer established US-owned or European-owned MNCs. Relative to US MNCs, Japanese MNCs appear to be more limited in the scope of their transnational learning capabilities because of the much more tightly integrated domestic organizational and business system within which they are embedded in their own home country's national system of innovation (Lam, 2003). The explanation rests primarily upon an important institutional characteristic of Japan, namely the close domestic inter-firm networks associated with the conglomerate industry structure in Japan known as the keiretsu system (Gerlach, 1992). However, while the keiretsu networks had contributed a great deal in the past to the efficiency of Japan's export oriented sectors, they had also sheltered a less visible largely inefficient sector, thereby rendering Japan a dual economy (Ozawa, 2003; Porter, Takeuchi and Sakakibara, 2000). What is more, the more recent efforts of Japanese MNCs to internationalize R&D through outward FDI and use it to help diversify their technological base have been inevitably constrained by their strong domestic inter-firm networks (Cantwell and Zhang, 2006). Thus, the Japanese example actually provides further evidence of the limited usefulness of Hymer's model of an overly rigidly centralized hierarchy in the current state of evolution of the modern MNC.

In the (further) development of the innovative MNC the critical issue is the need to establish a suitable balance between the needs of local responsiveness on the part of subsidiaries, and the needs of global integration of the MNC group as a whole (Doz, Bartlett and Prahalad, 1981; Prahalad and Doz, 1987). If this delicate balance is tilted too far one way or the other then the international network for innovation of the MNC becomes severely constrained. The limitations on the capacity of Japanese MNCs to shift in the direction of international networks for innovation owe precisely to the overly strong nature of embedded internal network connections, and the tightness of knowledge sharing routines between central R&D facilities and subsidiaries located elsewhere (Collinson and Wilson, 2006). Yet equally, if local traditions and connections with other local actors at the subsidiary level are overly strong, and if the geographical composition of subsidiary competence-creating efforts and the personnel involved in them shift significantly over time, strict limits may be placed upon the ability of the MNC group to sustain global integration through the creation of shared values and interpersonal networks (Morgan, 2001).

These are the current challenges facing the continued development of the innovative MNC. Yet it is this image of the MNC as a device for drawing upon dispersed sources of creativity and learning across borders that has emerged as a result of changes in the MNC and its environment since the early 1970s. This image can be contrasted with those earlier images of the MNC as a static efficiency maximizing and closely centrally coordinated device, or the MNC as a device for sustaining positions of market power across disparate operations, which have been inherited from the past. These latter perspectives continue to remain relevant, and they can in some ways be thought of as summarizing the various constraints that still lie in the way of the further fulfillment of the innovative MNC.

CASE STUDY: THE EVOLUTION OF ASEA INTO AN INNOVATIVE MNC IN ABB

Prior to its merger with the Swiss company Brown Boveri in 1987, the Swedish firm ASEA had seen the foreign share of its technological development activity rise only gradually from about 5 % in the 1920s through to slightly over 10 % just before the merger. In the newly merged firm 50 % of technological activity was located outside Sweden, with R&D operations in the other major centers of Switzerland, Germany and the US being of similar size. Historically, the home base in Sweden had been almost entirely responsible for the technological diversification (the diversification in the competence base) of ASEA. In ABB foreign-located facilities came to account for over half of the fields of technology creation of the MNC group. While efforts in the core fields of technological development of the group were duplicated across all facilities, specialized complementary capabilities arose in each major ABB center. Thus, in certain specific fields of technology in each case, the Swedish, Swiss, German, US or Japanese parts of ABB respectively were responsible for 100 % of the technological capabilities of the group.

Source: Zander (2002).

Questions

The following questions relate to the issues discussed in this chapter and can be answered partly by referring to the ABB case. In some cases further research is required to provide a complete answer, but the relevant issues are highlighted in this chapter.

1. When it occurs, what drives the evolution of local subsidiary innovation from the competence-exploiting kind (essentially adaptive of competences that already exist in the MNC corporate group) to the competence-creating kind (creating new areas of competence for the MNC corporate group)?
2. Why has the wave of M&As since the 1990s helped to give a major impetus to the geographical differentiation of innovation within MNCs?
3. What changes in the world environment, and in some emerging market economies in particular, have stimulated the evolution of the innovative MNC?
4. What have been the main impacts of the evolution of the innovative MNC on host countries and regions?

Further Reading

Note these are extracted from the list of References below, where the full citation is located.

The following articles can be considered milestones in the literature; each provides new insights (at the time of publication) into the empirical processes and theoretical explanations described in this chapter: Andersson *et al.* (2002), Athreye and Cantwell (2007), Birkinshaw *et al.* (1998), Cantwell and Mudambi (2005), Collinson and Wilson (2006), Dunning and Wymbs (1999), Ernst and Kim (2002),

Frost *et al.* (2002), Hedlund (1986), Kogut and Zander (1993), Kuemmerle (1999), Nohria and Ghoshal (1997), Pearce (1999b), Tolentino (2002), Zander (2002), Zhao (2006).

References

Almeida, P. (1996) Knowledge Sourcing by Foreign Multinationals: Patent Citation Analysis in the US Semiconductor Industry. *Strategic Management Journal*, 17 (Special Issue) 155–65.

Andersson, U. and Forsgren, M. (2000) 'In Search of Centre of Excellence: Network Embed-dedness and Subsidiary Roles in Multinational Corporations', *Management International Review*, 40(4): 329–50.

Andersson, U., Forsgren, M. and Holm, U. (2002) 'The Strategic Impact of External Networks: Subsidiary Performance and Competence Development in the Multinational Corporation', *Strategic Management Journal*, 23: 979–96.

Athreye, S. and Cantwell, J. A. (2007) 'Creating Competition? Globalisation and the Emergence of New Technology Producers', *Research Policy*, 36(2), 209–26.

Bailey, D. and Driffield, N. (2002) 'Hymer and Uneven Development Revisited: Foreign Direct Investment and Regional Inequalities', *Contributions to Political Economy*, 21: 55–68.

Barney, J. B. (1991) 'Firm Resources and Sustained Competitive Advantage', *Journal of Management*, 17: 99–120.

Bartlett, C. A. and Ghoshal, S. (1989) *Managing across Borders – The Transnational Solution.* Century Business: London.

Birkinshaw, J. M. and Hood, N. (1998) 'Multinational Subsidiary Evolution: Capability and Charter Change in Foreign-Owned Subsidiary Companies', *Academy of Management Review*, 23(4): 773–95.

Birkinshaw, J. M., Hood, N., and Jonsson, S. (1998) 'Building Firm-Specific Advantages in Multinational Corporations: The Role of Subsidiary Initiative', *Strategic Management Journal*, 19: 221–41.

Breschi, S. and Lissoni, F. (2001) 'Knowledge Spillovers and Innovation Systems: A Critical Survey', *Industrial and Corporate Change*, 10(4): 975–1005.

Brooke, M. and Remmers, H. (1970) *The Strategy of Multinational Enterprise: Organization and Finance.* London: Longman.

Buckley, P. J. and Casson, M. C. (1976) *The Future of the Multinational Enterprise.* London: Macmillan.

Cantwell, J. A. (1987) 'The Reorganisation of European Industries after Integration: Selected Evidence on the Role of Multinational Enterprise Activities', *Journal of Common Market Studies*, 26 (2): 127–51.

Cantwell, J. A. (1989) *Technological Innovation and Multinational Corporations.* Oxford: Basil Blackwell.

Cantwell, J. A. (1991) 'The Theory of Technological Competence and Its Application to International Production'. In D. G. McFetridge (ed.) *Foreign Investment, Technology and Growth.* Calgary: University of Calgary Press.

Cantwell, J. A. (1995) 'The Globalization of Technology: What Remains of the Product Cycle Model?' *Cambridge Journal of Economics*, 19(1): 155–74.

Cantwell, J. A. (2000) 'Technological Lock-in of Large Firms since the Interwar Period', *European Review of Economic History*, 4(2): 147–74.

Cantwell, J. A. and Fai, F. M. (1999) 'Firms as the Source of Innovation and Growth: The Evolution of Technological Competence', *Journal of Evolutionary Economics*, 9(3): 331–66.

Cantwell, J. A. and Iammarino, S. (2001) 'EU Regions and Multinational Corporations: Change, Stability and Strengthening of Technological Comparative Advantages', *Industrial and Corporate Change*, 10(4): 1007–37.

Cantwell, J. A. and Iammarino, S. (2003) *Multinational Corporations and European Regional Systems of Innovation*. London and New York: Routledge.

Cantwell, J. A., Iammarino, S. and Noonan, C. A. (2001) 'Sticky Places in Slippery Space – the Location of Innovation by MNCs in the European Regions'. In N. Pain (ed.) *Inward Investment, Technological Change and Growth: The Impact of MNCs on the UK Economy*. London and New York: Palgrave Macmillan.

Cantwell, J. A. and Janne, O. E. M. (1999) 'Technological Globalisation and Innovative Centres: The Role of Corporate Technological Leadership and Locational Hierarchy', *Research Policy*, 28(2–3): 119–44.

Cantwell, J. A. and Mudambi, R. (2005) 'MNE Competence-Creating Subsidiary Mandates', *Strategic Management Journal*, 26(12): 1109–28.

Cantwell, J. A. and Piscitello, L. (2002) 'The Location of Technological Activities of MNCs in European Regions: The Role of Spillovers and Local Competencies', *Journal of International Management*, 8(1): 69–96.

Cantwell, J. A. and Zhang, Y. (2006). 'Why is R&D Internationalization in Japanese Firms So Low? A Path-Dependent Explanation', *Asian Business and Management*, 5(2): 249–69.

Chandler, A. D. (1962) *Strategy and Structure: Chapters in the History of the Industrial Enterprise*. Cambridge, MA: MIT Press.

Chandler, A. D. (1977) *The Visible Hand: The Managerial Revolution in American Business*. Cambridge, MA: Belknap Press.

Chandler, A. D. (1990) *Scale and Scope: The Dynamics of Industrial Capitalism*. Cambridge, MA: Harvard University Press.

Chandler, A. D. and Redlich, F. (1961) 'Recent Developments in American Business Administration and Their Conceptualization', *Business History Review*, 35(1): 1–27.

Collinson, S. and Wilson, D. C. (2006) 'Inertia in Japanese Organizations: Knowledge Management Routines and Failure to Innovate', *Organization Studies*, 27(9): 1359–87.

Cooke, P. (2001) 'Regional Innovation Systems, Clusters, and the Knowledge Economy', *Industrial and Corporate Change*, 10(4): 945–74.

Cowling, K. and Sugden, R. (1994) *Beyond Capitalism*. London: Frances Pinter.

David, P. A. (1994) 'Why are Institutions the "Carriers of History"? Path Dependence and the Evolution of Conventions, Organisations and Institutions', *Structural Change and Economic Dynamics*, 4: 205–20.

Dicken, P. (1992) *Global Shift: Industrial change in a Turbulent World*. London: Paul Chapman.

Doz, Y. L., Bartlett, C. A. and Prahalad, C. K. (1981) 'Global Competitive Pressures vs. Host Country Demands: Managing Tensions in Multinational Corporations', *California Management Review*, 23(3): 63–74.

Dunning, J. H. (1993) *Multinational Enterprises and the Global Economy*. Wokingham: Addison Wesley.

Dunning, J. H. (1995) 'Reappraising the Eclectic Paradigm in an Age of Alliance Capitalism', *Journal of International Business Studies*, 26(3): 461–91.

Dunning, J. H. (1996) 'The Geographic Sources of the Competitiveness of Firms: Some Results of a New Survey', *Transnational Corporations*, 5: 1–29.

Dunning, J. H. and McKaig-Berliner, A. (2002) 'The Geographical Sources of Competitiveness: The Professional Business Service Industry', *Transnational Corporations*, 11(3): 1–38.

Dunning, J. H. and Wymbs, C. (1999) 'The Geographical Sourcing of Technology-Based Assets by Multinational Enterprise'. In D. Archibugi, J. Howells & J. Michie (eds) *Innovation Policy in a Global Economy*. Cambridge and New York: Cambridge University Press.

Ernst, D. (2001) 'Small Firms Competing in Globalised High-Tech Industries: The Co-Evolution of Domestic and International Knowledge Linkages in Taiwan's Computer Industry'. In P. Guerrieri, S. Iammarino and C. Pietrobelli (eds) *The Global Challenge to Industrial Districts: SMEs in Italy and Taiwan*. Cheltenham: Edward Elgar.

Ernst, D. (2002) 'Global Production Networks and the Changing Geography of Innovation Systems: Implications for Developing Countries', *Economics of Innovation and New Technology*, 11(6), 497–523.

Ernst, D. (2005) 'Complexity and Internationalisation of Innovation – Why is Chip Design Moving to East Asia?' *International Journal of Innovation Management*, 9(1), 47–73.

Ernst, D. and Kim, L. (2002) 'Global Production Networks, Knowledge Diffusion and Local Capability Formation', *Research Policy*, 31(8/9), 1417–29.

Ferlie, E. and Pettegrew, A. (1996) 'The Nature and Transformation of Corporate Headquarters: A Review of Recent Literature and a Research Agenda', *Journal of Management Studies*, 33(4): 495–523.

Fors, G. and Zejan, M. (1996) 'Overseas R&D by Multinationals in Foreign Centres of Excellence'. Industrial Institute for Economics and Social Research Working Paper, No. 458.

Freeman, C. (1987) *Technology Policy and Economic Performance: Lessons from Japan*. London: Frances Pinter.

Frost, T. S., Birkinshaw, J. M. and Ensign, P. C. (2002) 'Centers of Excellence in Multinational Corporations', *Strategic Management Journal*, 23(11): 997–1018.

Gerlach, M. (1992) *Alliance Capitalism: The Social Organization of Japanese Business*. Berkeley: University of California Press.

Ghauri, P. N. and Buckley, P. J. (2002) 'Globalisation and the End of Competition: A Critical Review of Rent-Seeking Multinationals'. In V. Havila, M. Forsgren and H. Håkanson (eds) *Critical Perspectives on Internationalisation*. Oxford: Pergamon.

Ghoshal, S. and Nohria, N. (1993) 'Horses for Courses: Organizational Forms for Multinational Corporations', *Sloan Management Review*, 34: 23–35.

Graham, E. M. (2000) *Fighting the Wrong Enemy: Antiglobal Activists and Multinational Enterprises*. Washington DC: Institute for International Economics.

Graham, E. M. (2002) 'The Contributions of Stephen Hymer: One View', *Contributions to Political Economy*, 21: 9–26.

Håkanson, H. and Johanson, J. (1993) 'The Network as a Governance Structure: Interfirm Cooperation Beyond Markets and Hierarchies'. In G. Grabher (ed.) *The Embedded Firm: The Socioeconomics of Industrial Networks*. London and New York: Routledge.

Håkanson, H. and Snehota, I. (eds) (1995) *Developing Relationships in Business Networks*. London and New York: Routledge.

Harzing, A.-W. (2000) 'An Empirical Analysis and Extension of the Bartlett and Ghoshal Typology of Multinational Companies', *Journal of International Business Studies*, 31(1): 101–20.

Hedlund, G. (1986) 'The Hypermodern MNC: A Heterarchy?' *Human Resource Management*, 25: 9–35.

Hedlund, G. (1993) 'Assumptions of Hierarchy and Heterarchy, with Application to the Management of the Multinational Corporation'. In S. Ghoshal and D. E. Westney. (eds) *Organization Theory and the Multinational Corporation*. London: Macmillan.

Hedlund, G. (1994) 'A Model of Knowledge Management and the N-Form Corporation', *Strategic Management Journal*, 15 (Special Issue): 73–90.

Hertz, N. (2002) *The Silent Takeover: Global Capitalism and the Death of Democracy*. London: Random House.

Hobday, M. (1995) *Innovation in East Asia: The Challenge to Japan*. Aldershot: Edward Elgar.

Hymer, S. (1972) 'The Multinational Corporation and the Law of Uneven Development'. In J. Bhagwati. (ed.) *Economics and World Order from the 1970s to the 1990s*. Collier-Macmillan.

Hymer, S. (1975) 'The Multinational Corporation and the Law of Uneven Development'. In H. Radice. (ed.) *International Firms and Modern Imperialism*. Harmondsworth: Penguin Books.

Hymer, S. (1979) *The Multinational Corporation*. Cambridge and New York: Cambridge University Press.

Hymer, S. and Rowthorn, R. (1970) 'Multinational Corporations and International Oligopoly: The Non-American Challenge'. In C. P. Kindleberger. (ed.) *The International Corporation*. Cambridge, MA: MIT Press.

Kay, N. (2000) 'The Resource-Based Approach to Multinational Enterprise'. In C. N. Pitelis and R. Sugden (eds) *The Nature of the Transnational Firm*. New York: Routledge.

Klein, N. (2000) *No Logo: Taking Aim at the Brand Bullies*. New York: Picador.

Kobrin, S. J. (2001) 'Sovereignty @ Bay: Globalisation, Multinational Enterprise, and the International Political System'. In A. M. Rugman and T. L. Brewer. (eds) *The Oxford Handbook of International Business*. New York: Oxford University Press.

Kogut, B. and Zander, U. (1992) 'Knowledge of the Firm, Combinative Capabilities, and the Replication of Technology', *Organization Science*, 3: 383–97.

Kogut, B. and Zander, U. (1993) 'Knowledge of the Firm and the Evolutionary Theory of the Multinational Corporation', *Journal of International Business Studies*, 24(4): 625–45.

Kümmerle, W. (1999a) 'The Drivers of Foreign Direct Investment into Research and Development: An Empirical Investigation', *Journal of International Business Studies*, 30(1): 1–24.

Kümmerle, W. (1999b) 'Foreign Direct Investment in Industrial Research in the Pharmaceutical and Electronic Industries – Results from a Survey of Multinational Firms', *Research Policy*, 28(2–3): 179–193.

Lall, S. (2001) *Competitiveness, Technology and Skills*. Cheltenham: Edward Elgar.

Lam, A. (2003) 'Organizational Learning in Multinationals: R&D Networks of Japanese and US MNEs in the UK', *Journal of Management Studies*, 40(3): 673–703.

Landes, D. S. (1998) *The Wealth and Poverty of Nations: Why Some are So Rich and Some So Poor*. New York: W. W. Norton.

Love, J. H. (1997) 'The Transaction Cost Theory of the (Multinational) Firm: A Note', *Journal of Institutional and Theoretical Economics*, 153: 674–81.

Makino, S., Lau, C.-M. and Yeh, R.-S. (2002) 'Asset Exploitation versus Asset Seeking: Implications for Location Choice of Foreign Direct Investment from Newly Industrialised Economies', *Journal of International Business Studies*, 33(3): 403–21.

Morgan, G. (2001) 'The Multinational Firm: Organizing Across Institutional and National Divides'. In G. Morgan, P. H. Kristensen and R. Whitley (eds) *The Multinational Firm: Organizing Across Institutional and National Divides*. Oxford and New York: Oxford University Press.

Mowery, D. C. and Rosenberg, N. (1979) 'The Influence of Market Demand Upon Innovation: A Critical Review of Some Recent Empirical Studies', *Research Policy*, 8: 102–53.

Mudambi, R. and Navarra, P. (2004) 'Is Knowledge Power? Knowledge Flows, Subsidiary Power and Rent Seeking within MNCs', *Journal of International Business Studies*, 35: 385–406.

Nelson, R. R. (ed.) (1993) *National Innovation Systems*. Oxford and New York: Oxford University Press.

Nelson, R. R. and Winter, S. G. (1982) *An Evolutionary Theory of Economic Change*. Cambridge, MA: Harvard University Press.

Nohria, N. and Ghoshal, S. (1997) *The Differentiated Network: Organizing Multinational Corporations for Value Creation*. San Francisco: Jossey-Bass.

Ozawa, T. (2003) 'Japan in an Institutional Quagmire: International Business to the Rescue?' *Journal of International Management*, 9(3): 219–35.

Pavitt, K. L. R. (1987) 'International Patterns of Technological Accumulation'. In J. E. Vahne. (ed.) *Strategies in Global Competition*. London: Croom Helm Ltd.

Pearce, R. D. (1999a) 'The Evolution of Technology in Multinational Enterprises: The Role of Creative Subsidiaries', *International Business Review*, 8: 125–48.

Pearce, R. D. (1999b) 'Decentralized R&D and Strategic Competitiveness: Globalized Approaches to Generation and Use of Technology in Multinational Enterprises', *Research Policy*, 28 (2–3): 157–78.

Penrose, E. (1959) *The Theory of the Growth of the Firm*. Oxford and New York: Oxford University Press.

Pitelis, C. (1991) *Market and Non-Market Hierarchies*. Cambridge, MA: Blackwell.

Pitelis, C. (2001) 'The Resource-Based Theory of the Transnational Corporation: Conceptual and Empirical Issues', *Global Business and Economics Review*, 3(1): 20–43.

Pitelis, C. (2002) 'Stephen Hymer: Life and the Political Economy of Multinational Corporate Capital', *Contributions to Political Economy*, 21: 9–26.

Porter, M. E. (1990) *The Competitive Advantage of Nations*. New York: Free Press.

Porter, M. E., Takeuchi, H. and Sakakibara, M. (2000) *Can Japan Compete?* Basingstoke: Palgrave Macmillan.

Prahalad, C. K. (1976) 'Strategic Choices in Diversified MNCs', *Harvard Business Review*, (July–August): 67–78.

Prahalad, C. K. and Doz, Y. L. (1981) 'An Approach to Strategic Control in MNCs', *Sloan Management Review* (Summer): 5–13.

Prahalad, C. K. and Doz, Y. L. (1987) *The Multinational Mission: Balancing Local Demands and Global Vision*. New York: The Free Press.

Rosenberg, N. (1976) *Perspectives on Technology*. Cambridge and New York: Cambridge University Press.

Rosenberg, N. (1982) *Inside the Black Box: Technology and Economics*. Cambridge and New York: Cambridge University Press.

Rugman, A. M. (2005) *The Regional Multinationals: MNEs and 'Global' Strategic Management.* Cambridge and New York: Cambridge University Press.

Schmookler, J. (1966). *Inventions and Economic Growth.* Cambridge, MA: Harvard University Press.

Sölvell, Ö. and Zander, I. (1998) 'International Diffusion of Knowledge: Isolating Mechanisms and the Role of the MNE'. In A. D. Chandler, P. Hagström and Ö. Sölvell (eds) *The Dynamic Firm: The Role of Technology, Strategy, Organization, and Regions.* Oxford and New York: Oxford University Press.

Storper, M. (1992) 'The Limits to Globalisation: Technology Districts and International Trade', *Economic Geography,* 68(60–93).

Teece, D. J. (2006) 'Reflections on the Hymer Thesis and the Multinational Enterprise', *International Business Review,* 15: 124–39.

Tolentino, P. E. E. (2002) 'Hierarchical Pyramids and Heterarchical Networks: Organizational Strategies and Structures of Multinational Corporations and Its Impact on World Development', *Contributions to Political Economy,* 21: 69–90.

Vernon, R. (1966) 'International Investment and International Trade in the Product Cycle', *Quarterly Journal of Economics,* 82(2): 190–207.

Vernon, R. (1979) 'The Product Cycle Hypothesis in a New International Environment', *Oxford Bulletin of Economics and Statistics,* 41(4): 255–67.

Wernerfelt, B. (1984) 'A Resource-Based View of the Firm', *Strategic Management Journal,* 5: 171–80.

Wesson, T. (2005) *Foreign Direct Investment and Competitive Advantage.* Cheltenham: Edward Elgar.

Williamson, O. E. (1975) *Markets and Hierarchies: Analysis and Antitrust Implications.* New York: Free Press.

Yamin, M. and Forsgren, M. (2006) 'Hymer's Analysis of the Multinational Organization: Power Retention and the Demise of the Federative MNE', *International Business Review,* 15: 166–79.

Zander, I. (2002) 'The Formation of International Innovation Networks in the Multinational Corporation: An Evolutionary Perspective', *Industrial and Corporate Change,* 11(2): 327–53.

Zander, I. and Sölvell, Ö. (2002) 'The Phantom Multinational'. In V. Havila, M. Forsgren and H. Håkanson (eds) *Critical Perspectives on Internationalisation.* Oxford: Pergamon.

Zhao, M. (2006) 'Conducting R&D in Countries with Weak Intellectual Property Rights Protection', *Management Science,* 52(8): 1185–99.

Chapter 4 The Multinational Firm as the Major Global Promoter of Economic Development

Simon Collinson

Introduction

Multinational enterprises (MNEs) not only develop and change in response to their external competitive environment, they significantly shape this environment. Until recently international business and management studies have focused on the first of these propositions but largely ignored the second. This chapter examines one form of MNE influence, presenting an image of the global firm as a key contributor of the innovative capabilities of host region firms in developing countries and therefore an important *positive* force for economic growth and social development in countries around the world. It also argues that MNEs usually perform this role unwittingly and often unwillingly. Whether harmful or beneficial, many of the effects of MNE activity are 'unintended'.

This image of the MNE not only challenges common public perceptions of large, global firms as the main protagonists of global inequalities it also challenges aspects of traditional international business theory.[1] In doing so it echoes Dunning and Sarianna in this volume and others, such as Kogut (2005), who point to the large gap in mainstream international business studies regarding the *effects* of MNEs.[2] The dominant focus of the field has been on the *determinants* of MNE behaviour and the factors which influence their performance. Foreign direct investment (FDI) is seen from the perspective of a rational profit-seeking entity, looking to exploit or augment internal assets in specific locations. But much of FDI has the effect of augmenting local assets and capabilities in recipient countries and this interactive, reciprocal effect needs to be better understood.

Images of the Multinational Firm   Edited by Simon Collinson and Glenn Morgan
© 2009 John Wiley & Sons, Ltd

So this imbalance in the focus of international business studies is one important rationale for this chapter. Another is the need to account for some of the 'new realities of globalization'. MNEs dominate the production of new technology and investment in R&D and innovation globally. Moreover they are a key driver, not only of the global distribution of new products and services, but also the dissemination of productive technologies, expertise, innovation capabilities and effective managerial processes. The past has been dominated by a Western view of the MNE partly because advanced industrial economies were home to almost all MNEs. FDI flows were largely 'one-way' and innovation, new products, services and technologies originated predominantly from these economies. The growing relevance of countries outside of the OECD, as recipients and sources of FDI, as homes to emerging MNEs and the locus of innovation, means these countries are an increasingly important part of the global multinational network.

In part the chapter takes a stakeholder perspective, examining the local effects of MNEs because the actions of these firms affect a wide variety of interest groups. But it is also relevant for MNE managers to understand the dynamic interplay between their actions and the contexts in which they operate. From the perspective of the profit-maximizer the knock-on effects can be both positive, such as: building necessary local skills and capabilities to support efficient subsidiary operations; developing local suppliers or infrastructure to support localization of inputs; shaping a favourable regulatory environment by lobbying policymakers. Or they can be 'negative', such as: helping competitors through all of the above activities or even breeding local competitors by introducing new technologies and capabilities.

The chapter begins by briefly summarizing some of the competing theories of economic development which international business scholars have tended to ignore. The following section outlines areas which show a clear coincidence of interests between MNE investment priorities and the development objectives of emerging and developing countries. Although uneven and often unequal, reciprocal relationships between MNEs and governments in such countries consist of a mutually beneficial give-and-take. Evidence of this reciprocity is presented in the form of data and a range of prior studies at the macro and micro levels. There is a specific focus here on how MNEs (unwittingly) support the development of technological capabilities in the host country, which subsequently allows local firms to move up industry value chains and compete in the global economy.

Finally, we examine some of the new realities of MNE activities, including the significant rise of FDI into developing countries and the shift towards high technology and R&D investments as well as intangible assets in knowledge-based businesses. These changes mean that the spill-over effects that promote indigenous development are even greater. GM's investments in China, and the subsequent rise of particular Chinese auto firms features as a case study to illustrate these patterns. The chapter concludes with a discussion of how this particular image of the MNE contrasts popular public perceptions and has not been sufficiently addressed in mainstream international business studies.

Competing Theories of Economic Development

As a precursor to understanding the MNE contribution to economic growth we need to briefly examine some of the major theories developed to explain national or regional economic development. What follows is a summary which we will build from later when we return to consider the role of MNEs.

For some time economic growth theories were firmly grounded in neo-classical economics and focused on the accumulation of physical capital as the primary driver of economic development. 'Modernist' theories of development characterized by Rostow's linear growth stages dominated and improvements in social welfare were seen to automatically follow through 'trickle-down' of surplus wealth. This consensus was replaced partly by the rise of the neo-Marxist dependency theorists in the 1960s, including the influential work of the Economic Commission for Latin America (ECLA), which called for a de-linking of Third World countries from exploitative trade relations with the West (Frank, 1969; Cardoso and Faletto, 1979). This left-wing consensus was in turn challenged by empirical changes, particularly the rapid growth of the so-called Asian Newly-Industrial Countries (NICs) of Hong Kong, Singapore, Taiwan and South Korea which stemmed directly from an *increased* participation in the global economy.[3]

A substantial rise in inward and outward trade and foreign direct investment (FDI) was a key driver of economic growth and subsequent social and political change in these countries. The expansion of FDI from MNEs played a central role and was the focus of a number of industry and firm-level studies of technical change and the transfer of indigenous technological capabilities, as described later in this chapter.

Development economists have used the contrasting examples of South Korea and Sudan. Both showed very similar, low levels of per capita GDP in the 1960s, before South Korea began its 'take-off' phase. By 2005 Sudanese GDP per capita remained at the LDC ('less-developed country') level of $2100 whilst South Korea had reached over $23 000, not far off the European Union average of $29 000.

Empirical studies in the 1960s and 1970s that tried to explain such growth rates using the accepted economists' relationship between inputs of capital and labour and productivity growth failed to account for the observed increases in productivity in these emerging economies. However, so-called 'residual' factors, such as investment in education, skills, health, research and development and 'national systems of innovation' as well as transfers of knowledge and capabilities were increasingly seen from then onwards to be central to improved competitiveness (Chenery *et al.*, 1986; Ducharme, 1998). Knowledge and capabilities and the channels by which they are transferred or learnt by individuals, organizations, industries and nations gradually became a central focus of development studies.

A number of theories evolved in order to open up the 'black box' of these residual factors and develop a better understanding of the nature and effects of intangible investment on economic growth. Human capital theory focused on the educational and training characteristics of individuals as productive assets. This extends from micro-level studies within specific production systems (such as manufacturing plants) to national education systems. Investment in the latter has been shown to provide positive externalities in the sense that it promotes the efficient acquisition and transmission of knowledge (now sometimes termed absorptive capacity) (Arrow, 1962; Fransman and King, 1984; Griliches, 1988; Bell and Pavitt, 1997).

Technical change and innovation theories focused on scientific and technological activity as an endogenous factor of economic growth, rather than a 'residual'. Early work led to the current recognition that innovation is a key element of competitive strategy at the firm level and a key element of national competitiveness and growth at the national level. Some built on the original studies of well-known economists such as Adam Smith, David Ricardo and Karl Marx, all of whom recognized the importance of technical change as a factor of economic growth.

Although it was not central to neo-classical economics studies many, such as Solow (1957), did consider the impact of technological change. Industrial economists, such as Griliches (1957), Arrow, (1962) and Scherer (1982) were closer to the emerging Schumpeterian evolutionary approach to understanding its effects and importance. Evolutionary theory and endogenous growth theory are together seen by many as 'new growth theories' underpinning current economic development studies. The latter is a direct descendent of neo-classical economics but goes much further in modelling and analysing technical change and knowledge accumulation as the main source of change and growth in competitive environments (Ducharme, 1998; Barro and Sala-I-Martin, 1995). Knowledge is seen to encompass human and organizational capital and embodied technology (physical capital) as primary sources of technical change. But many such approaches remain strongly wedded to modelling production functions in a linear way and are criticised for being empirically static.

Schumpeterian and other evolutionary approaches by contrast have attempted to account for the complex, dynamic, context-specific and path-dependent characteristics of innovation processes and technological change (Dosi et al., 1988). At the macro level studies have examined long-waves and paradigm shifts and at the micro level examined the routines which affect firm capabilities and behaviour (Nelson and Winter, 1982). Both forms of new growth theory are developing a better understanding of knowledge-based economies where intangible assets are the dominant contributors to economic activity and growth (Foray, 2006).

This brings us to the role of MNEs as a key source of technology and technological capabilities. The international expansion paths of MNEs provide the channels for many of the growth opportunities for developing countries.

A Coincidence of Interests: The Multinational Firm as a Contributor to Development

Theories that attempt to explain and predict the patterns, processes and practices of internationalization lie at the heart of international business studies. Foreign direct investment is driven by the search by firms for new markets and new inputs, including raw materials and resources, technologies or cheap labour and provides the main measure of internationalization. Different country markets are more or less attractive, depending on their country-specific advantages (Rugman, Collinson and Hodgetts, 2006), including the size and growth rates of their markets and the availability and price of the above kinds of inputs. How MNEs evolve in response to the changing global patterns of location-specific attractiveness and the structural and strategic challenges that arise from the interplay between the firm and its multiple environments, is central to the field.

Whilst this is a sensible focus for the IB field, as argued in other chapters of this book and in recent debates that discuss the future of the field (Buckley, 2005; Collinson et al., 2006), it has evolved to become rather one-sided. Investment locations are seen solely as the source of particular kinds of resources, assets or market opportunities and/or in terms of the adaptation challenges they represent for investing firms. A more dynamic, interactive approach which considers the exchange, interaction and evolving inter-relationships between organization and location is proposed, in support of a number of more recent studies that have begun to examine firm and location in tandem.

What Does Everyone Want?

Development economists have also long been interested in the attractiveness of particular locations for MNE investment. Others have shared this interest, including policymakers responsible for promoting growth in their own regions around the world. These constituencies are less interested in MNEs per se and more interested in what they can bring to a region. This is because MNEs bring capital investment, employment, new technology and a range of value-adding capabilities which support a variety of local development objectives. These are what national and provincial governments want from inward-investors.

Figure 4.1 summarizes the main interests of both national governments and MNEs. The development agendas of most developed, newly industrialized and under-developed countries around the world are remarkably similar. Governments want (right column) capital investment and local multiplier effects; employment, preferably in high-wage sectors to boost local consumption and generate demand-led growth; foreign exchange inputs to offset debt and currency instability; and technology and capability transfer to improve the ability of local firms to move up the value chain. To achieve their objectives policymakers have to build on a set of local endowments (both inherited/lower order and advanced/higher order, using Michael Porter's terminology) or country-specific advantages (CSAs, in Alan Rugman's terminology; Rugman, Collinson and Hodgetts (2006)) to improve the attractiveness of their region vis-à-vis competing regions and increase their bargaining power with MNEs. These are listed in the middle column.

The left column in Figure 4.1 summarizes the main kinds of investment objectives for MNEs. This is a simple re-working of existing categories which tend to be used to

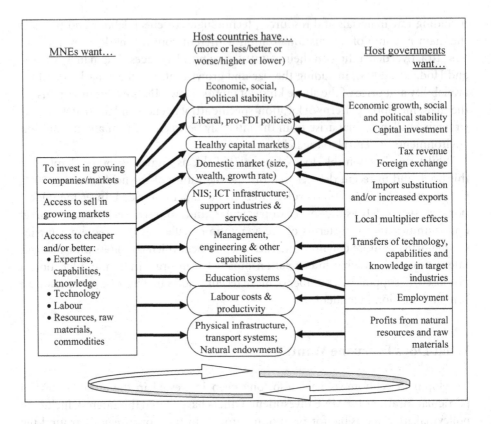

MNEs want...

Host countries have...
(more or less/better or
worse/higher or lower)

Host governments
want...

Economic, social,
political stability

Liberal, pro-FDI policies

Healthy capital markets

To invest in growing
companies/markets

Domestic market (size,
wealth, growth rate)

Access to sell in
growing markets

NIS; ICT infrastructure;
support industries &
services

Access to cheaper
and/or better:
• Expertise,
  capabilities,
  knowledge
• Technology
• Labour
• Resources, raw
  materials,
  commodities

Management,
engineering & other
capabilities

Education systems

Labour costs &
productivity

Physical infrastructure,
transport systems;
Natural endowments

Economic growth, social
and political stability
Capital investment

Tax revenue
Foreign exchange

Import substitution
and/or increased exports

Local multiplier effects

Transfers of technology,
capabilities and
knowledge in target
industries

Employment

Profits from natural
resources and raw
materials

NIS = National Innovation System

ICT = Information and communication technology

Figure 4.1   FDI drivers: MNE objectives, host country attractiveness and host government objectives
Source: FDI drivers figure adapted from Rugman, Collinson and Hodgetts (2006); pp. 385, fig. 13.4

classify the FDI motivations of MNEs: 'natural resource seeking', 'efficiency seeking', 'market seeking' and 'knowledge seeking' (Pearce, 2006). MNEs will (more or less intelligently) weigh up attractiveness, costs and risks, sometimes using a structured country risk analysis, before choosing where to locate FDI and which mode of entry to adopt. So, whilst this is a novel way of framing the agendas of MNEs and governments, and builds on prior research (Collinson, 1992), the individual points it contains are not particularly new. Dunning (2006) presents a variation on this theme and lists some antecedents.

Despite this common agenda, CSAs and the related investment attractiveness of countries or regions vary markedly, and this significantly influences which locations experience growth and which do not. Much of sub-Saharan Africa, except South Africa but including abovementioned Sudan, is unattractive to MNEs. Countries here have weak CSAs, including small, low-growth markets, poor infrastructure, under-resourced education systems and political instability. Governments here are not in a position to bargain effectively with MNEs to target particular kinds of inward investment or impose their national development agendas. China and other large, growing markets are in a much stronger position because of their attractiveness.

Past studies have tended to focus on economic variables, such as labour costs or per capita GDP, within this mix of factors, mainly because they are more easily quantified. More recently scholars closer to the centre of international business studies have highlighted the institutional factors that influence both attractiveness and growth prospects (Dunning and Sarianna in this volume; Henisz, 2004, 2000). This also points to an interesting, but little-explored interface between the 'varieties of capitalism' approaches (Whitely chapter in this book) and development economists.

On the other side of the equation to CSAs, in Figure 4.1, firm-specific advantages (FSAs) such as brands, patented technologies, financial power and unique management capabilities enhance the bargaining power of MNEs. When there are no competitors with the equivalent internalized advantages governments find it more difficult to play off firms against each other. FSA exclusivity provides greater bargaining power for MNEs, reducing the ability of country governments to force their own agenda when negotiating over FDI. Kobrin (1987) has used the terms 'power resources' and 'constraints' to refer to factors that determine the respective bargaining power of MNEs and host country governments when FDI is being considered.

Figure 4.1 depicts a widely accepted, static analysis of the general drivers of FDI at one period in time. A dynamic approach requires some consideration of processes, flows and change over time.

Reciprocity: A Two-Way Exchange

Figure 4.2 takes a process-oriented view to outline the main ways in which MNEs contribute to growth and development in the countries where they invest. As you would expect from the discussion above, economists of various kinds have tended to focus on capital inputs and employment effects, whilst a different range of studies have examined flows of technology, capability and knowledge. But more recently scholars have begun to explore the respective complementarities and contradictions of these two kinds of approaches (Cantwell and Janne, 2000).

As outlined above, countries with good CSAs or better endowments are relatively more attractive to MNEs. These are listed in the top part of Figure 4.2, matching those in the central column in Figure 4.1. Government policies play a mediating role, influencing attractiveness through both direct means, such as taxation and legislation affecting inward investment, and indirect means, such as employment legislation, which affects wage rates or labour skills, or by supporting particular science and technology infrastructure initiatives, for example.

The three inward flows of capital, technology and capability and employment in Figure 4.2 have each been the subject of some scrutiny, although they are usually

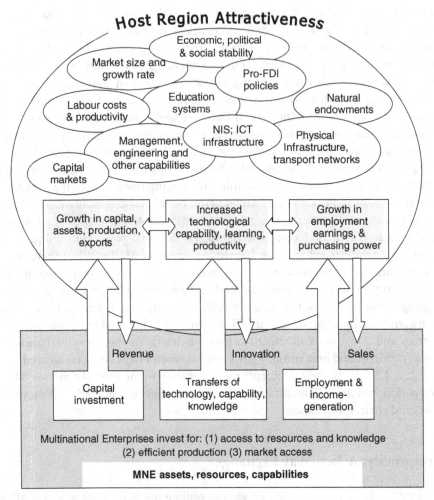

Host Region Attractiveness

- Economic, political & social stability
- Market size and growth rate
- Pro-FDI policies
- Labour costs & productivity
- Education systems
- Natural endowments
- NIS; ICT infrastructure
- Management, engineering and other capabilities
- Physical Infrastructure, transport networks
- Capital markets

Growth in capital, assets, production, exports

Increased technological capability, learning, productivity

Growth in employment earnings, & purchasing power

Revenue

Innovation

Sales

Capital investment

Transfers of technology, capability, knowledge

Employment & income-generation

Multinational Enterprises invest for: (1) access to resources and knowledge (2) efficient production (3) market access

MNE assets, resources, capabilities

Figure 4.2 Emerging economies and MNEs: the growth cycle

considered separately, rather than in combination. Firms commit to FDI with the expectation of positive net financial benefits over a specified period of time. Capital investment and local employment are direct effects of FDI, but vary substantially depending on the form and scale of the investment. Alongside FDI multinational firms engage in a wide range of activities to reduce risk and improve their return on investment. This includes infrastructure development, technology transfer and personnel training, as well as the development of local joint-venture partners, suppliers and supporting industries, and government lobbying. Although designed to safeguard and/or promote the interests of the investing MNE these activities all have an effect on the host country. Here we argue that this impact over time is normally beneficial, rather than detrimental to the development interests of the host country.

Capital investment and employment have fairly straightforward effects. FDI inflows into developing countries have increased markedly over the past decade, reaching $379 billion in 2006 (UNCTAD, 2007). These non-speculative investment flows support industry development and infrastructure construction as well as creating a multiplier effect benefiting local suppliers and a range of local service firms, from contract maintenance and cleaning firms to restaurants. MNEs in developing countries and in South East Europe and the CIS directly employed an estimated 7.4 million workers and generated more than $500 billion in value added outside their home countries in 2005 (UNCTAD, 2006), so the multiplier effects are known to be much more significant.

But in terms of enhancing the indigenous capacity of developing countries to drive their own economic growth, the central 'pipeline' in Figure 4.2, depicting the transfer of technology, capability and productive knowledge, is of critical importance. These represent channels for local learning. In addition to other local and international sources these provide the means by which indigenous firms learn to innovate, add value to products and services, grow market shares and appropriate the surplus profit to benefit local (rather than foreign) owners. This is a major driver of reduced dependency and indigenous development and the evidence for this is reviewed later in this chapter.

All of the channels represented in Figure 4.2 are reciprocal, two-way interactions. For the investing MNE 'outflows' of capital investment lead to 'inflows' of revenues and profits, as long as the FDI is successful. Investments in training and technology help develop local sources of innovation. Local expertise and knowledge in the host economy becomes a resource for the rest of the firm, as depicted in Nohria and Ghoshal's (1997) 'local-for-global' pattern of innovation. Finally, MNEs can improve their productivity and products and services by employing cheaper and/or better local employees. Moreover, as MNEs increase employment and boost local incomes directly or indirectly, through multiplier effects they help grow their own markets.

The Invisible Hand: Unintended Consequences of the Multinational Firm

As outlined in the previous section there is a coincidence of interests when the effects of FDI are beneficial for both the MNE and the recipient nation. These effects may be intended, as outlined earlier in Figures 4.1 and 4.2, where the MNE fulfils its strategic aims by gaining access to new markets or new resources in return for capital investment, employment and technology transfer all of which also support local development objectives. But they may also be unintended and beneficial, such as when, for example MNE employment has the effect of improving local incomes and therefore increasing demand which results in a rise in the MNE's own local product sales. This 'virtuous cycle of demand-led growth' is more apparent for consumer products companies, where increases in both disposable incomes and local sales of consumer products in emerging markets are jointly driven by the multiplier effect from inward investment. Large volumes of manufacturing FDI have a significant effect on employment and income generation, thus building the markets which MNEs sell to.

The effects of FDI can work against the MNE itself in unintended ways. For example, when such firms invest in production plants abroad they very often invest to develop supplier industries and related infrastructure which can benefit both foreign and local competitors. These 'free-rider' or externality effects can represent a form of subsidy. Other unintended side-effects include the loss of IPR and intangible assets, either via local joint ventures and alliances or through the loss of trained personnel, who may join (or start up) local competitors. Such leakage and spill-over effects have been studied at the macro-economic level (Crespo and Fontoura, 2007; Aitken, Hanson and Harrison, 1997) and are increasingly recognized at the firm level (Collinson, Sullivan-Taylor and Wang, 2007; Lyles and Easterby-Smith, 2003; Patibandla and Petersen, 2002). In more mainstream international business studies international joint ventures have been a strong focus of attention in this regard (Dhanaraj et al., 2004; Lane, Salk and Lyles, 2001).

In some respects MNEs breed their future competitors by unintentionally providing access to assets, technologies, capabilities and knowledge that enable them to add value, to innovate and to compete better (see the case study at the end of the chapter).

There are, therefore, a range of outcomes from FDI when examined in terms of the strategic intentions of the investing MNE, the resulting effects on the competitive position of the investing MNE, and the presence or absence of a coincidence of interests between the MNE and the host economy. Investment outcomes may be intended or unintended and beneficial or detrimental to either or both firm and host country.

Mainstream international business theory has not examined these unintended consequences of FDI to any great extent. Scholars have preferred to stick to rational agency approaches focusing on the appropriateness of different strategies for different contexts and the reasons for the success or failure of such strategies, rather than the additional externalities that affect other interest groups. The paradox that self-interest underpins the collective benefits of societies and economies is not new, however. It features in a range of studies, connecting work by authors such as Axelrod (1984) back to the early writings of Adam Smith on the 'invisible hand'. The former used game theoretic approaches to examine the unintended consequences of cooperation driven by self-interest. The latter would suggest that by investing in developing countries for private profit MNEs 'promote an end which was no part of their intention'.

We argue here that such unintended consequences should be of concern to MNE managers and shareholders, not just to host countries, development economists and social welfare interest groups. A dynamic approach to strategic thinking should encompass the entire range of effects that firms have on their competitive environment. Managers need to take account of the interactive effects of FDI in order to continuously adapt and survive. Again, this is not a discussion about what MNEs *should* do as part of the 'moral imperative' of global capitalism, it is about what they are already doing without necessarily intending to or recognizing, and about taking this into account in their strategic thinking.[4]

The Evidence

Evidence that points to the existence and impact of the kinds of processes shown in Figure 4.2 comes from a range of sources and levels of analysis. Observers have adopted different theoretical approaches and methodologies and examined different types of empirical data. This presents some important challenges, including the need to connect micro, meso and macro levels of analysis.

At the macro level there has long been a healthy debate on the relationship between inward FDI flows and economic growth based around aggregate panel data. The consensus amongst these, mainly econometric, tests, most of which focus on developing countries, is that there is a strong positive relationship between FDI and growth (De Mello, 1997, 1999; Nair-Reichert and Weinhold, 2001). This is also confirmed in recent studies exploring the sources of China's rapid economic growth (Liu and Burridge, 2002; Yao, 2006). But there are significant differences in the strength and nature of the relationship that depend on specific country conditions (Chowdhury and Mavrotas, 2006).

Such studies also highlight the importance of institutional openness and human capital as mediating factors (Oliva and Rivera-Batiz, 2002; Li and Liu, 2005). This complements the recent emphasis of some mainstream international business scholars, including John Dunning, on institutions (in this volume). Other scholars have highlighted the importance of national institutions and governance systems for much longer (Richard Whitely in this volume). Balasubramanyam has linked macro-level econometric approaches which look for patterns of economic growth and mainstream international business, building on the work of A. S. Bhalla (Balasubramanyam, Salisu and Sapsford, 1996).

Panel studies also highlight the role of inward FDI in promoting technology transfer and improved indigenous technological capabilities. This leads directly or indirectly to productivity improvements and product and process innovation capabilities in local firms, as highlighted in Figure 4.2. As mentioned above, the focus on technology transfer and local innovation capabilities goes back to the search for factors that would explain the unexplained residual in economists' productivity growth models. National systems of innovation research became a focus for this research, as an alternative to mainstream economic approaches and econometric models (Dosi et al., 1988).[5] Such macro-level studies connect with industry-level and firm-level studies of technology transfer, technological capability and learning (Freeman, 1987; Fransman and King, 1984; Fransman, 1986a; Collinson, 1992; Huay and Hui, 2006).[6]

Other studies have examined the connection between FDI and growth at the industry level. Research into the sources of competitive advantage in capital goods industries took centre stage for a time, because of its role as a support industry for manufacturing (Fransman, 1986b; Kaplinksy, 1990). But a wide range of studies from food and drink (Collinson, 1992) to semiconductors (Mathews and Cho, 2000) and electronics (Ernst, 2006) illustrate a connection between industry-specific FDI and the evolution of local industry capabilities. Moreover, innovation studies some time ago identified a 'leapfrogging effect' in some industries, superseding ideas based around linear technology 'catch-up' models (Perez and Soete, 1988; Hobday, 1994). Legacy systems and established infrastructures create inertia in developed economies in industries such as energy, utilities, telecoms and IT. The current jump to digital communications and mobile telephony in China, skipping analogue and land-line infrastructures, is an example of advantageous leapfrogging.

Target industries that are identified as central to the economic development plans of national governments (for import-substitution and/or export-promotion) will be the focus of specific FDI legislation to promote local learning. A large number of studies have linked such policies with the success of the Asian NICs (newly-industrializing countries, including Singapore, South Korea, Taiwan and Hong Kong) in the 1970s and 1980s (Dahlman, Ross-Larson and Westphal, 1985; Kaplinsky and Cooper, 1989; Hobday, 1995; Lall, 1992, 2003).

When we examine evidence of this connection at the level of the individual firm, the role of MNEs is central. First because they are the primary source of FDI globally, and second because they are regarded as being distinctive from other firms for their role in international technology transfer or diffusion (Cantwell and Mudambi, 2005). Again, much of the focus of international business studies is on the activities of MNEs as acquirers of resources, technology and capability, via local subsidiaries (Powell, 1998; Papanastassiou and Pearce, 1999; Pearce, 1999, 2006; Frost, 2001; Manolopoulos et al., 2005). But it is increasingly acknowledged that FDI can serve as a 'vehicle for carrying tacit knowledge as well as assisting enterprises at the frontiers of world technological learning' (Liu and Wang, 2003: 945).

There has been some focus on the local recipient firm, sometimes described in the context of newly industrializing and emerging markets as a 'latecomer firm'. Mathews and Cho (2000) provide a clear example in their in-depth study of the semiconductor industry in East Asia. Latecomer firms like Samsung and LG Semicon in South Korea, TSMC and TI-Acer in Taiwan and Tech Semiconductor in Singapore entered the global value chain by packaging imported chips. This was the low value-added, labour-intensive end of the value chain, where cheap local labour provided the means for local firms to enter the industry. Their goal, partly supported by government initiatives, was to move up the value chain to front-end wafer fabrication, mask production and eventually design and R&D. They managed this to such an extent that by the mid-1990s Samsung, LG, Hyundai and SMT were amongst the leading firms in the industry. MNE FDI, combined with strong government policies promoting local industry development, were key factors in this development. FDI from firms like Fairchild, Signetics, KMI, Motorola, Toshiba and Sanyo in the late 1960s and early 1970s, for example, led to the establishment of nine US-owned and seven Japanese-owned semiconductor facilities in South Korea (Mathews and Cho, 2000: 113).

The New Realities of FDI by Multinational Firms

There are a number of important empirical trends that heighten the significance of the dynamic, reciprocal relationship between MNEs and the regions in which they invest. Two are particularly important to the argument put forward here: (1) the changing global distribution of FDI from MNEs, particularly the increased FDI flowing into developing countries; (2) the changing substance of FDI, including more R&D FDI and, in line with the changing global economy, FDI that is based around knowledge and capabilities rather than physical and fixed assets where the boundaries of ownership are easier to maintain.

First, we know that the economic scope and geographic spread of MNEs is large and expanding. According to UNCTAD's World Investment Report (UNCTAD, 2007) there were an estimated 78 000 parent companies with over 780 000 foreign affiliates in 2006. These foreign affiliates employed about 73 million workers globally and generated about $4.5 trillion in value added. But more specifically, FDI is now the largest source of external finance for developing countries and has increased substantially in recent years; by a further 57 % in 2004 and 22 % in 2005 (UNCTAD, 2006). Africa experienced a rise of 78 % to record inflows of $32 billion in 2005, suggesting it is finally becoming more attractive to investors.

Developing countries' inward stock of FDI now amounts to about one third of their GDP, compared to just 10 % in 1980. Over half of the abovementioned foreign affiliates of the world's MNEs are now located in developing countries. Asia and China in particular continue to dominate as recipients of these investments.

So, overall we have seen an increase in the volume of FDI which, if we accept the basic proposition in Figure 4.2, will lead to a range of positive effects for developing countries. Moving to point 2 above, there is a marked shift away from investment in physical assets towards investment in intangible, knowledge-based assets. This follows the general pattern of change in the global economy where value increasingly equates to the knowledge embodied in products and services and stems from the integrated efforts of knowledgeable experts, rather than fixed assets or material inputs as the primary source competitive advantage (UNCTAD, 2007; Leydesdorff, 2006; MERIT, 2000; OECD, 1996).[7]

This change arguably means that ownership boundaries around the key sources of competitive advantage are more permeable, or less amenable to protection and control by MNEs. That is, knowledge, expertise and capabilities 'flow' between firms more easily than tangible assets such as land, plant and equipment, 'labour' and capital. They are less tangible, less easy to 'price' and less easily confined using the contractual and legal boundaries of ownership. This is seen as a challenge to some long-standing frameworks which adopt a neo-classical economics view placing an emphasis on ownership and market pricing mechanisms, such as John Dunning's OLI framework.

The general shift in the sources of added value, combined with the growing volume of FDI flows to developing countries therefore means that international flows of knowledge and capability via MNEs become even more significant as a contributor to economic development. What used to be seen as a residual element in economists' calculations of total factor productivity (TFP) growth (Chenery *et al.*, 1986) is now central to economic growth (Foray, 2006; Dosi *et al.*, 1988).

A more specific example of this pattern of change is the globalization of R&D. MNEs, which are responsible for a large share of global R&D, are distributing their R&D activities increasingly widely around the world. The R&D expenditure of foreign affiliates worldwide increased from $30 billion to $67 billion (that is from 10 % to 16 % of global business R&D) between 1993 and 2002 (UNCTAD, 2005). A particularly significant increase occurred in developing countries with the share of foreign affiliates in business R&D in the developing world rising to 18 % in 2002 from 2 % in 1996.

This has been noted by international business scholars, but again the emphasis is on the changing rationale and strategic priorities for MNEs, rather than a consideration of local effects. Shorter product life cycles, changing technologies and the need to cut costs in new product development are pushing firms to offshore existing R&D in different parts of the world (EIU, 2004). This is something initially commented on by observers such as Cantwell and Janne (1999) and Kuemmerle (1999), examining FDI, joint ventures and non-equity alliances. MNEs are increasingly seen as differentiated 'learning' networks for integrating geographically distributed knowledge and expertise to add value to products and services in global markets.

Again it is widely acknowledged that R&D-related FDI can directly benefit economic growth by stimulating, through the R&D activity undertaken by MNE affiliates, technological efficiency and technological change in the recipient country (UNCTAD, 2005). Host economies can also derive benefits from MNEs' R&D units through subcontracting and sponsorship of research in local universities; licensing technologies for by-products to local firms; counteracting the brain-drain and attracting skilled people from abroad; contributing indirectly to upgrading technologies as innovations emerge and consumption patterns change. A well-developed national innovation system (NIS); a 'network of institutions in the public and private sectors whose activities and interactions initiate, import, modify and diffuse new technologies' (Freeman, 1987) facilitates these processes.

Although the question of whether knowledge and skills can be separated from their original organization environment is central to the debate on the spill-over impact of MNEs, the need to hire and train local research staff combined with the mobility of these staff means that MNE R&D investments clearly have a knock-on effect on the host economy. Ancillary organization linkages, with consultancies, universities, government departments and training firms also drive a strong, high-technology multiplier effect in the local economy.

As indicated by Cantwell, in this volume and elsewhere, MNEs are moving from being commodity traders and manufacturers in search of cheap labour locations to being capability and knowledge brokers. A key difference lies in the relative immobility of sources of commodities and of cheap labour, where location advantages can be exploited solely by the MNE as a broker profiting from the cost differentials of different locations, compared to capabilities and knowledge, which are themselves not just transferred, but multiplied. Moreover, to reiterate the central theme of this chapter, this is not a simple one-way interaction. MNEs do not solely 'tap' into a static portfolio of knowledge resources. There is a dynamic interplay between MNEs in the process of accessing local assets and the development of these assets.

Discussion

This chapter presents an image of the MNE as a beneficial force in developing countries. Although it does not precisely describe the 'give and take' between firms and national economies it supports the view that MNEs make a positive contribution. They may be exploitative and self-interested but their investments have beneficial (intended and unintended) consequences. They (often unwittingly) play a significant part in developing local industry and promoting a growth cycle that improves the economic and social conditions far more than any flows of funds from governments or charities. We should acknowledge, however, first that some flows and effects of FDI are more beneficial than others and, second, some countries benefit far more than others. Many countries do not seem to be attracting MNE investment and/or reaping its benefits. This is the on-going challenge for development economists and policymakers: to engage MNEs more effectively in relationships that support the least-developed regions of the world.[8]

If we accept that MNEs are playing a pivotal role in the development of indigenous capabilities and the associated economic growth in *some* countries this is still counter to many prevailing views. This image of the MNE is at odds with common public perception and is at best peripheral to the central concerns of mainstream international business studies. Yet this is one of the most significant issues of our time.

Relieving this myopia, on the part of IB studies and scholars that have long examined the nature of MNEs, requires a change in theoretical and methodological approach as well as focus. This includes changing from a 'markets and hierarchies' perspective (Williamson, 1975; Coase, 1937; and others) which artificially separates the firm and its environment, to one which also considers interactions and interdependencies between organization and location more fully. Capabilities co-evolve in relationships and networks that incorporate and benefit both MNEs and local organizations in a synergistic way. A theory centred on the reciprocity between the MNE and its investment environment is perhaps required.

Associated with this is a need to complement an 'inside-out' view of the MNE, from the perspective of managers surviving in an external competitive environment, with one that considers the dynamic interplay between the MNE and the various contexts (places) in which it operates, influences and is influenced by. This also suggests more attention be paid to the interactions between micro-level processes and macro-level effects and vice versa. Some form of unified framework that combines micro-level and macro-level analyses is also called for by Dunning and Sarianna in this volume. They see a need for explicit analysis of the interdependence between micro and macro levels, to better understand both the learning patterns and strategic behaviour of the MNE and its effects on home and host countries.

Emerging and developing countries could be seen as important 'selection' and 'retention' environments (to use Eleanor Westney's terminology in this volume), rather than as passive recipients. Technology, processes, practices, capabilities and knowledge are selected and retained by indigenous firms during their interaction with MNEs; these can improve their innovative capacity, helping them move up the value chain and enhance their profitability. A sustained effect, across a large number of local firms, has an aggregate effect at the macro-economic level. A better understanding of the micro-level processes that underpin the positive effects of MNEs and FDI should lead the way to more intelligent interventions on the part of policymakers, managers and the public to improve on these positive effects. This may also work as a counter-balance to the current focus on the negative effects.

It seems likely that, as physical assets and resources give way to knowledge assets and capabilities as the foundations for competitive advantage, at the national and firm level, this relationship between MNEs and developing countries will also change. The attractiveness of specific locations for MNEs increasingly stems from the innovation potential that comes from combining these kinds of local endowments with the firm's own endowments held in other locations. But such intangible assets 'flow more easily' and are less easy to control, arguably giving rise to the potential for more significant levels of spill-over to local firms. Ownership of knowledge or expertise is less easy to assert and provides a less robust boundary around the value-adding attributes of the firm than ownership of manufacturing plants, technology hardware and perhaps unskilled labour.

These changes also represent challenges to the long-standing mainstream theories and frameworks of international business which are underpinned by concepts such as ownership, internalization and transactions costs. They also tend to assume, under the common principle of economic rationality, that strategic intent and effect are synonymous. This leads mainstream international business studies to overlook the significance of the unintended consequences of firm behaviour. In this case technology and capability spill-overs may be equally or more important as intended international technology transfer and training activities. MNEs may not be conscious agents of development but their positive effects on the economic growth and subsequent social benefits of development are significant and worthy of more attention.[9] Although these final points go well beyond the scope of this chapter, the new realities outlined here do seem to call for a substantial re-thinking of existing paradigms and frameworks and perhaps images of the MNE.

CASE STUDY: GM IN CHINA: DEVELOPING LOCAL CAPABILITIES (AND BREEDING FUTURE COMPETITORS?)

China became a net exporter of cars for the first time in 2005, with a major proportion going to other developing markets. Given that the country only began the process of market liberalization in the early 1980s this is a remarkable achievement. Moreover it appears that Western car firms have played an important role in the development of China's indigenous car industry.

GM, the world's largest vehicle manufacturer, entered China through a range of joint ventures (JVs) starting in 1992. This was long after the earliest entrant, VW, which began a JV with government-owned Shanghai Automotive Industry Corporation (SAIC) in 1984, followed by a second with the First Automotive Works (FAW) in 1991. VW, the only foreign entrant allowed into the market for some time, controlled over 56% of the market by 1998 before its dominance declined.

As a government-enforced condition of entry into China GM had initially invested in technology transfer and local training projects as a precursor to establishing manufacturing operations through a $1.6 billion joint venture with SAIC in 1997. Further JVs with Jinbei in 1998 and Luizhou Wuling in 2001 reaped rewards by 2003 as sales revenues and profits from the China market grew. By 2004 GM had around 10 000 employees in China, six JVs with investments amounting to $2 billion and two wholly-owned foreign enterprises, producing 530 000 vehicles.

GM reached a 10% market share to challenge VW as the latter's share declined. But both GM and VW faced growing competition from new foreign entrants after the 2001 WTO deregulation rulings began to take effect. Ford, Honda, Toyota, Hyundai and Suzuki all entered the market in the early to mid-2000s. More significantly, local car makers started to come into their own around this time.

Local Learning

Looking back over the brief history of the Chinese auto industry we can see it has rapidly moved up the value chain in a way reminiscent of the Indian software industry. Low cost advantages gained through cheap labour, available land and capital (in China mostly from the government) have been increasingly complemented by capabilities in design, engineering, manufacturing, marketing and management. Chinese firms have developed their ability to innovate, improving both products (making safer, more reliable and attractively designed cars with new features) and manufacturing processes (resulting in plant-level efficiency and better quality products).

How have they learnt to innovate? The evidence suggests that Western multinational firms engaged in alliances and joint ventures with local Chinese firms have been a significant source of these value-adding capabilities. In many cases knowledge and expertise is transferred intentionally, as part of the joint-venture agreement. GM, for example, joined with SAIC in 1997 to build the Pan Asia Technical Automotive Centre (PATAC) to train Chinese engineers to design new cars for GM and other car companies. Chinese managers at PATAC were also trained in production improvement processes through visits to manufacturing plants in North America. This arrangement, like many others, was a condition of GM's entry into China, negotiated by the Chinese government. Since its establishment PATAC has created a number of local designs including the Qilin, the first concept car built by Chinese engineers and designers for the China market. It has also re-designed or modified a range of Buick models, including the Sail, Regal, Excelle and Royaum for China. Of its 1100 employees, 35 % with masters and/or doctorate degrees, most receive special training at GM engineering and design centres abroad.

This is similar to FAW (First Automotive Works), now the largest producer in China, which has JVs with Mazda and Toyota, as well as VW. Nanjing Motors, on the other hand, chose to buy out rather than ally with MG Rover in July 2005 and subsequently moved all its production operations from the UK West Midlands to Nanjing, China. The government-owned company now produces and sells a range of MG and Rover (re-branded 'Roewe') cars in the domestic market and abroad.

Chinese firms have developed their own capabilities in new product design, manu-facturing technology, process management, R&D, sales and servicing, by learning from the above kinds of alliances and JVs, through collaborative agreements with foreign firms. But certain assets, including brands or technologies, and expertise have also been transferred 'unintentionally' through 'spill-over' effects and theft of intellectual property (IP). In 2002, for example, a successful local firm Chery launched its QQ model to face accusations from GM that it was a near-replica of the Matiz, later sold in China as the Chevrolet Spark with a price tag of $4600, $1000 more than the QQ. GM filed suit in December 2004 but the QQ continued to sell well, recording sales of over 61 000 units in the first seven months of 2005 compared to the Spark's 16 000 units. More recently they reached an undisclosed settlement and Chery continues to sell the QQ. This is not an isolated case with Toyota and Honda also suing Geely, another local firm, over branding and design infringements.

GM and the other foreign car companies have faced very different 'local rules-of-the-game' as well as regulatory restrictions and a weak legal infrastructure for safeguarding against IPR theft. National and provincial governments in China have targeted the auto industry as a key to future economic development and support local firms with financing, regulatory advantages and by using their influence over foreign direct investment (FDI) contracts. But we could also say that local firms have learnt fast, partly through their interaction with foreign multinationals, allowing them to move quickly beyond their low-cost advantage to develop innovative capabilities to compete globally. Multinationals that have rushed in to capture the growing domestic Chinese market as well as tap into China's cheap labour advantage have played a central role in developing China's own auto industry.

Questions

1. What made China attractive to GM; why did the firm invest there? What did the Chinese Government and State-owned enterprises (SOEs) want from GM? Does the story fit parts of the framework outlined in Figure 4.1 above?
2. What kinds of impact has GM had on the Chinese auto industry? Do these fit some of the effects described in the growth cycle framework in Figure 4.2 above?
3. Describe some of the main channels and mechanisms through which local firms have learnt from MNEs in the Chinese auto industry.
4. What impact do you think the development of the Chinese auto industry will have on (a) China, and (b) the global auto industry?

Further Reading

In addition to these sources the case is based on the author's own research, reported in Collinson, Sullivan-Taylor and Wang (2007).

Cadieux, D. and Conklin, D. (2004) *GM in China*, Richard Ivey School of Business Case studies, European Case Clearing House, Cranfield, UK (http://www.ecch.com/).

Chaurasia, S. and Madhav, T. P. (2004) *GM in China*, ICFAI Business School Case Study Development Centre, European Case Clearing House, Cranfield, UK (http://www.ecch.com/).

Chawla, T. (2005) *Volkswagen and General Motors in China*, ICFAI Business School Case Study Development Centre, European Case Clearing House, Cranfield, UK (http://www.ecch.com/).

Economist (2007) 'The world's big carmakers have unwittingly created a new Chinese rival,' *The Economist*, 24 February, London.

Ng, L. Fung-Yee and Chyau Tuan, C. (2005) ' Industry technology performance of manufacturing FDI: micro-level evidence from joint ventures in China', *International Journal of Technology Management*, Vol. 32 Issue 3/4, 246–63 (http://www.gmchina.com/english/).

References

Aitken, B., Hanson, G. and Harrison, A. (1997) 'Foreign Investment, Export Behavior, and Spillovers', *Journal of International Economics*, 43: 103–32.

Arrow, K. J. (1962) 'The Economic Implication of Learning by Doing', *Review of Economic Studies*, 29, June, 155–73.

Axelrod, R. (1984) *The Evolution of Cooperation*. New York, Basic Books.

Balasubramanyam, V. N., Salisu, M. and Sapsford, D. (1996) 'Foreign direct investment and growth in EP and IS countries', *Economic Journal*, Vol. 106, 92–105.

Barro, R. J. and Sala-I-Martin, X. (1995), *Economic Growth, Advanced Series in Economics*. New York: McGraw-Hill.

Bell, M. and Pavitt, K. (1992) 'Accumulating Technology Capability in Developing Countries', *World Bank Economic Review*, Summer, 257–81.

Bell, M. and Pavitt, K. (1997) 'Technological Accumulation and Industrial Growth: Contrasts between Developed and Developing Countries'. In D. Archibugi and J. Michie (eds)

Technology, Globalisation and Economic Performance. Cambridge: Cambridge University Press.

Berger, P. L. (1963) *Invitation to Sociology: A Humanistic Perspective*. New York: Anchor.

Bhagwati, J. (2005) *In Defense of Globalization*. Oxford: Oxford University Press.

Cantwell, J. and Janne, O. (1999) 'Technological globalisation and innovative centres: The role of corporate technological leadership and locational hierarchy', *Research Policy*, 28: 119–44.

Buckley, P. J. (ed.) (2005) *What is International Business?* New York: Palgrave Macmillan.

Cantwell, J. A. and Mudambi, R. (2005) MNE competence-creating subsidiary mandates. *Strategic Management Journal*, 26(12): 1109–1128.

Cantwell, J. and Janne, O. (2000) 'The role of multinational corporations and national states in the globalisation of innovatory capacity: The European perspective', *Technology Analysis and Strategic Management*, 12 (2): 243–62.

Cardoso, F. H. and Faletto, E. (1979) *Dependency and Development in Latin America*. Los Angeles: University of California Press.

Chenery, H. B., Robinson, S. and Syrquin, M. (1986) *Industrialization and Growth: A Comparative Study*, New York: Oxford University Press.

Chowdhury, A. and Mavrotas, G. (2006) 'FDI and Growth: What Causes What?' *World Economy*, Oxford: Blackwell Publishing Limited.

Coase, R .H. (1937) 'The Nature of the Firm', *Economica*, 4: 386–405.

Collinson, S. C. (1992) 'Constraints on the Transfer of Manufacturing Technology: A British-Kenyan Comparison', *Science, Technology and Development*, Vol. 11, No. 2, 113–43, London: Frank Cass.

Collinson, S. C., Sullivan-Taylor, B. and Wang, J. L. (2007) *Adapting to the China Challenge: Lessons from Experienced Multinationals*, Advanced Institute of Management (AIM) Research Executive Briefing, London (http://www.aimresearch.org/publications/adaptingtochina.pdf).

Collinson, S. C., Buckley, P., Dunning, J. and Yip, G. (2006) 'New Directions in International Business'. In F. M. Fai and E. J. Morgan (eds) *Managerial Issues in International Business*. Basingstoke, Palgrave Macmillan.

Crespo, N. and Fontoura, M. P. (2007) 'Determinant Factors of FDI Spillovers – What Do We Really Know?' *World Development*, 35, 3, 410–25.

Dahlman, C., Ross-Larson, B. and Westphal, L. (1985) '*Managing Technological Development: Lessons from the Newly Industrializing Countries*', The World Bank, Washington DC.

De Mello, L. R. (1997) 'Foreign direct investment in developing countries and growth: a selective survey', *Journal of Development Studies*, Vol. 34 Issue 1, 1–34.

De Mello, L. R. (1999) 'Foreign direct investment led growth: evidence from time series and panel data', *Oxford Economic Papers*, Vol. 51, 133–51.

Dhanaraj, C., Lyles, M., Steensma, H. K. and Tihanyi, L. (2004) 'Managing tacit and implicit knowledge transfer in IJVs: The role of relational embeddedness and the impact on performance', *Journal of International Business Studies*, 35 (5), 456–8.

Dosi, G., *et al.* (1988) *Technical Change and Economic Theory*. London: Pinter Publishers.

Dunning, J. H. (2006) 'Towards a new paradigm of development: implications for the determinants of international business activity', *Transnational Corporations*, 15, 1, 183–228.

Dunning, J. H. (ed.) (2003) *Making Globalization Good: the Moral Challenges of Global Capitalism*. Oxford: Oxford University Press.

Ducharme, L.-M. (1998) *Measuring Intangible Investment*, Statistics Canada, OECD, Paris.

Economist (2004) 'Scattering the seeds of invention: The globalisation of research and development', Economist Intelligence Unit *(EIU)*, London (http://graphics.eiu.com/files/ad_pdfs/RnD_GLOBILISATION_WHITEPAPER.pdf).

Ernst, D. (2006) 'Searching for a new role in East Asian regionalisation – Japanese production networks in the electronics industry'. In Katzenstein, P. J. and Shiraishi, T. *Beyond Japan: The Dynamics of East Asian Regionalism*, Cornell University Press.

Ernst, D., Ganiatsos, T. and Mytelka, L. (1998) *Technological Capabilities and Export Success in Asia: Lessons from East Asia*. London: Routledge.

Foray. D. (2006) *The Economics of Knowledge*. Boston: MIT Press.

Frank, A. G. (1969) *Capitalism and Underdevelopment in Latin America*. New York: The Free Press.

Fransman, M. (1986a) *Technology and Economic Development*, Brighton: Wheatsheaf Books Ltd.

Fransman, M. (1986b) 'International Competitiveness, Technical Change, and the State: The Machine Tool Industry in Taiwan and Japan', *World Development*, Vol. 14, No. 11, November.

Fransman, M. and King, K. (1984) *Technological Capability in the Third World*, New York: Palgrave Macmillan.

Freeman, C. (1987) *Technology and Economic Performance: Lessons from Japan*. London: Pinter.

Freeman, O. L. (1981) *The multinational company: Instrument for world growth*. New York: Praeger.

Frost, T. S. (2001) The geographic sources of foreign subsidiaries' innovations, *Strategic Management Journal* 22(2): 101–123.

Griliches, Z. (1988) *Technology, Education and Productivity*. London: Basil Blackwell.

Henisz, W. J. (2000) 'The Institutional Environment for Multinational Investment', *Journal of Law, Economics and Organization*, 16 (2): 334–64.

Henisz, W. J. (2004) 'The Institutional Environment for International Business'. In Buckley, P. J. (ed.), *What is International Business?* New York: Palgrave.

Hobday, M. (1994) 'Technological learning in Singapore: a test case of leapfrogging', *Journal of Development Studies*, Vol. 30 831–58.

Hobday, M. (1995) *Innovation in East Asia: the challenge to Japan*. Aldershot: Elgar.

Huay, L. and Hui B. T. (2006) 'Technology Transfer, FDI and Economic Growth in the ASEAN Region', *Journal of the Asia Pacific Economy*, Vol. 11 Issue 4, 394–410.

Kaplinsky, R. (1990), *The Economies of Small: Appropriate Technology in a Changing World*. London: IT Publications.

Kaplinsky, R. and Cooper, C. (eds) (1989) *Technology and Development in the Third Industrial Revolution*. Frank Cass & Co.

Kim, L. (1997) *Imitation to Innovation: the Dynamics of Korea's Technological Learning*. Cambridge, MA: Harvard Business School Press.

Kobrin, S. (1987) Testing the Bargaining Hypothesis in the Manufacturing Sector in Developing Countries, *International Organization*, 57 (Autumn), 609–638.

Kogut (2005) 'Defining International Business through its Research'. In Buckley, P. J. (Ed.) (2005) *What is International Business?* New York: Palgrave Macmillan.

Kuemmerle, W. (1999) 'Foreign direct investment in industrial research in the pharmaceutical and electronics industries – results from a survey of multinational firms', *Research Policy* 28 (2–3): 179–93.

Lall, S. (1992) 'Technological capabilities and industrialization', *World Development* 20, No. 2 165–86.

Lall, S. (2003) *Foreign Direct Investment, Technology Development, and Competitiveness: Issues and Evidence*, World Bank Institute Working Paper, Washington, DC, USA.

Lane, P. J., Salk, J. E. and Lyles, M. A. (2001) 'Absorptive capacity, learning and performance in international joint ventures', *Strategic Management Journal* 22, 1139–61.

Leydesdorff, L. (2006) *The Knowledge-Based Economy: Modelled, Measured, Simulated.* Boca Rota, FL: Universal Publishers.

Li, X. and Liu, X. (2005) 'Foreign Direct Investment and Economic Growth: An Increasingly Endogenous Relationship', *World Development*, Vol. 33 Issue 3, 393–407.

Liu, X. and Wang, C. (2003) 'Does foreign direct investment facilitate technological progress? Evidence from Chinese industries', *Research Policy* 32: 945–53.

Liu, X., Burridge, P. and Sinclair, P. J. N. (2002) 'Relationships between economic growth, foreign direct investment and trade: evidence from China', *Applied Economics*, 34, 1433–40, Taylor & Francis Ltd.

Lyles, M. A. and Easterby-Smith, M. (2003) 'Organizational learning and knowledge management: Agendas for future research'. In M. Easterby-Smith and M. Lyles. (eds) *Blackwell Handbook of Organizational Learning and Knowledge Management.* Oxford: Blackwell, 639–52.

Manolopoulos, D., Papanastassiou, M. and Pearce, R. (2005) Technology sourcing in multinational enterprises and the roles of subsidiaries: an empirical investigation, *International Business Review*, 14(3): 249–267.

Mathews, J. A. and Cho, D. S. (2000) *Tiger Technology: The Creation of a Semiconductor Industry in East Asia.* Cambridge: Cambridge University Press.

MERIT (2000) *Innovation policy in a knowledge-based economy* (http://cordis.europa.eu/innovation-policy/studies/gen_study4.htm).

Nair-Reichert, U. and Weinhold, D. (2001) 'Causality Tests for Cross-Country Panels: a New Look at FDI and Economic Growth in Developing Countries', *Oxford Bulletin of Economics & Statistics*, Vol. 63 Issue 2, 153, 19p.

Nelson, R. R. and Winter, S. G. (1982) *An evolutionary theory of economic change.* London: Bellknap Press.

Nohria, N. and Ghoshal, S. (1997) *The differentiated network: organizing MNCs for value creation*, San Francisco: Jossey-Bass.

OECD (1996) *The Knowledge Based Economy*, Organisation for Economic Cooperation and Development, Paris (http://www.oecd.org/dataoecd/51/8/1913021.pdf).

Oliva, M.-A. and Rivera-Batiz, L. (2002) 'Political Institutions, Capital Flows and Developing Country Growth: an Empirical Investigation', *Review of Development Economics*, Vol. 6, 248–62.

Papanastassiou, M. and Pearce, R. (1999) *Multinationals, Technology and National Competitiveness.* Cheltenham: Edward Elgar.

Patibandla, M. and Petersen, B. (2002) 'The Role of Transnational Corporations in the Evolution of a High-Tech Industry: The Case of India's Software Industry', *World Development*, 30, 9, 1561–77.

Pearce, R. D. (1999) 'Decentralised R&D and strategic competitiveness: Globalised approaches to generation and use of technology in multinational enterprises (MNEs)', *Research Policy*, 28: 157–78.

Pearce, R. D. (2006) 'Globalization and development: An international business strategy approach', *Transnational Corporations*, 15, 1, 39–74.

Perez, C. and Soete, L. (1988) 'Catching up in technology: entry barriers and windows of opportunity', in G. Dosi *et al. Technical Change and Economic Theory.* London: Pinter Publishers.

Powell, W. W. (1998) Learning from Collaboration: Knowledge and Networks in the Biotechnology and Pharmaceutical Industries, *California Management Review*, 40(3): 228–240.

Rugman, A. M., Collinson, S. C. and Hodgetts, R. (2006) *International Business.* 4th edn, Harlow: FT Prentice Hall.

Scherer, F. M. (1982) 'Demand-pull and technological innovation: Schmookler revisited', *Journal of Industrial Economics*, 30: 225–37.

Smith, A. *An Inquiry into the Nature and Causes of the Wealth of Nations* (Vol. IV of the 1976 Glasgow Edition of Adam Smith's works).

Solow, R. M. (1957) 'Technical change and the aggregate production.' *Review of Economics and Statistics*, 39, 312–20.

Stiglitz, J. E. (2003) *Globalization and Its Discontents.* New York: W. W. Norton & Company.

UNCTAD (2005) *World Investment Report: Transnational Corporations and the Internationalization of R&D*, United Nations Conference on Trade and Development, Geneva.

UNCTAD (2006) *World Investment Report: FDI from Developing and Transition Economies: Implications for Development*, United Nations Conference on Trade and Development, Geneva.

UNCTAD (2007) *World Investment Report: Transnational Corporations, Extractive Industries and Development*, United Nations Conference on Trade and Development, Geneva.

Williamson, O. E. (1975) *Markets and Hierarchies: Analysis and antitrust implications.* New York: The Free Press.

Wolf, M. (2004) *Why Globalization Works.* Yale University Press.

Yao, S. (2006) 'On economic growth, FDI and exports in China', *Applied Economics*, Vol. 38 Issue 3, 339–51.

NOTES

1. As regards public perception, a common, but largely unspecified view is that MNEs promote as well as exploit global inequalities in their role as the main agents and beneficiaries of globalization. A number of populist books by respected economists challenged this view (Bhagwati, 2005; Wolf, 2004; Stiglitz, 2003). These writers herald the beneficial effects of globalization in general, but fail to explain the key role of MNEs or explain the firm-level processes that underlie the effects they describe.

2. In Peter Buckley's book entitled *What is International Business*, Bruce Kogut's 'damning critique of the literature of international business of recent years' focuses on his view that it has 'lost its engagement with the real world'. In particular he states that the 'effects on development of multinational corporations' is one of the important questions that are largely absent from IB journals (Kogut, 2005: 66).

3. Balsubramanyam (1985), one of the most influential bridge-builders linking international trade theory, development economics and theories about MNEs, described development

theories as 'colourful and fluid' because of this lively contest between left- and right-wing theorists. This work has been effectively developed by Pearce (2006) amongst others.

4. Adam Smith also provided useful advice for those looking to promote a 'moral imperative' amongst MNEs (Dunning, 2003): 'We address ourselves not to their humanity but to their self-love, and never talk to them of our necessities but of their advantages' (Smith, 1776).

5. Freeman observed this positive function of MNEs some time ago, commenting: 'MNEs take technology to poorer countries; they are the equivalent of workhorses for the World' (Freeman, 1981: 13–14).

6. The term 'technological capability' is used here to refer to the ability to make effective use of technological knowledge in efforts to assimilate, use, adapt and change existing technologies. It also enables one to create new technologies and to develop new products and processes in response to a changing economic environment. This is developed from the definition used by Bell and Pavitt (1992, 1997), Ernst *et al.* (1998), Fransman (1986a) and Kim (1997).

7. Empirical studies in OECD countries have also shown that investment in complementary assets and capabilities has outgrown that related to the gross formation of fixed capital (Ducharme, 1998).

8. The implications for economic development policy are well-rehearsed (UNCTAD, 2006; Lall, 2003, 1992).

9. There are parallels here with Max Weber's well-known connection between the religious and cultural values of Protestants and the patterns of wealth accumulation and investment that facilitated the industrial revolution (the 'spirit of capitalism'). In fact Weber's central point is often misunderstood. It was not the intention of Calvinists to build capitalist systems; this was an unintended outcome of their actions (Berger, 1963).

Chapter 5 The Multinational Firm as a Creator, Fashioner and Respondent to Institutional Change

John H. Dunning and Sarianna M. Lundan

Introduction

The contemporary international business and management literature views the MNE as a creator, coordinator and cross-border transferor of a bundle of resources and competences. These resources and competencies typically include financial capital, technology, managerial and organizational skills and the abilities to search out and effectively exploit markets. While most of the literature related to the costs and benefits of accessing or transferring these assets and/or the intermediate products arising from them, has been concerned with *hard* technology and R&D capacity, more recently, scholars have begun to appreciate that no less important to the success of MNEs is their willingness and ability to access and transfer and/or adapt *soft* technology and, in particular, organizational structures and work practices.

In this chapter, we present a conceptual framework that specifically incorporates the content and quality of institutions into mainstream thinking about the motives and effects of MNE activity. Such institutions, we shall argue, may affect the host countries in ways that can be good or bad, but without explicitly identifying this component of the package of assets transferred by the MNE, it is unlikely that much attention would be paid to such effects. Consequently, we believe that gaining an understanding of the institutional dimension of the behaviour and actions of MNEs will not only lead to an improved analysis of the MNE *qua* MNE, but will also better enable us to evaluate how MNE activity may influence national institutions, and by doing so, the economic and social goals of countries.

Images of the Multinational Firm   Edited by Simon Collinson and Glenn Morgan
© 2009 John Wiley & Sons, Ltd

While the international business literature has dealt with institutional issues in the past, and is increasingly doing so now, the fact that the discussion has drawn on very different sources has prevented any successful integration of the firm-level analysis with the national level analysis. While this approach has allowed some progress to be made in understanding the *determinants* of MNE behaviour, we do not think it has been so successful in illuminating the *effects* of MNE activity. We believe that a unified framework that combines micro-level and macro-level analyses, and explicitly considers the interdependence between the two, would help to bring about not only a better understanding of the learning patterns and strategic behaviour of the MNE per se, but also of its effects on the home and host countries. We would further assert that the eclectic or OLI paradigm (Dunning, 2004; Dunning and Lundan, 2008), on account of its holistic nature, is well-suited for this purpose.

We begin this chapter by a brief discussion on why we believe the role of institutions has attracted the attention of business scholars over the past two decades. We then present our definition of institutions and institutional change, which draws substantially on the work of Douglass North (1990, 2005), and analyse each of the three components of the OLI paradigm to articulate how an institutional dimension could be incorporated into the analysis. We shall pay particular attention to the institutional component of the ownership (O) advantages of MNEs, and use a case describing a recent cross-border acquisition to illustrate the process of institutional evolution.

Why Focus on Institutions?

Why have institutions become the subject of increasing attention by IB scholars over the past two or three decades? We would argue that the reasons lie both in our changing conception of the MNE as an organizational entity, and in the dramatic developments in the global economic and political landscape.

Throughout its history, most economic theory of the determinants of IB activity has been asset-based, whether these assets were owned, accessed or organized by the MNE. However, in the past two or three decades, the composition and significance of competitiveness-enhancing assets has changed, as the unique resources and capabilities available to firms have become more knowledge and information-intensive (Dunning, 2004). At the same time, their geographic sourcing and deployment have become more widely spread. This has led to an increased importance of the MNE as an organizer and coordinator of international economic activity, and consequently the motives, values and norms that shape and condition MNE decision-making. It has also raised the awareness of the various constituents of the global economy of the varied role played by institutions in different countries in affecting the wealth-creating process.

We see the MNE as a coordinated system of value-added activities, the structure of which is determined by the hierarchical costs of production, the market costs of exchange, and the interdependence of production and exchange relations (Dunning, 2003). Our conception is similar to that of Madhok (2002), who considers three kinds of factors, namely the governance structure, transaction and resource attributes of firms, to explain their functions and boundaries. Since different combinations of attributes are possible – indeed likely – firms do not necessarily organize similar transactions in the same way, and in this sense, transaction costs are unique to the firm. For example, while for one firm, an inter-firm collaborative arrangement might make economic sense, for another, the same agreement might be prohibitively costly in terms of its monitoring costs. Thus the ownership-specific (O) advantages of a firm affect how particular resources and competences are created, accessed or deployed. Finally, different combinations of governance structure, transaction costs and resource attributes, are essential to an understanding of why the value of assets and competencies that the firm does not own, but to which it can gain access, differs between firms, depending on their stock of wealth-creating assets and their path-dependent development.

It is particularly in connection with strategic asset-seeking FDI, which has grown greatly in importance over the past three decades, that the distinction between the exploitation of the existing competitive advantages of firms, and the augmentation of these advantages comes into focus. Strategic asset-seeking investments often have value that is dependent on the other assets owned, controlled or accessed by the MNE, and on the extent to which it can successfully learn from these, and/or coordinate these within its system of global activities. Such systemic capabilities thus make the acquisition of a given asset more valuable to one firm than to another. However, much of the existing analysis of IB scholars gives relatively little attention either to the quality of intra or inter-firm relationships, or to the incentive mechanisms – i.e. institutions both internal and external to the firm – that underpin the accessing, creation and usage of a firm's resources and capabilities.

In addition to the changing boundaries of the firm, another factor increasing the importance of institutional factors at the firm-level is the increased importance of locational 'stickiness' in our contemporary global economy. Globalization has resulted in an increase in the number of locations where value-added activity can take place. This presents more options to MNEs both to exploit locationally bound or sticky assets wherever they may be sited, whether contractually or through direct investment, and, at the same time, to engage in footloose investment to benefit from cost savings in the production of commodities that do not draw on locationally bound resources. Institutions at the national level affect the value adding opportunities open to firms, including those associated with agglomerative or clustering economies (Enright, 2000). While for some kinds of activities, such as simple parts assembly, a firm is often able to choose among multiple locations; for knowledge exploiting and learning activities the number of alternative sites may be small or equal to one. This makes it imperative to understand both how macro- or national level institutions might affect the value adding opportunities of firms, and how the actions of firms might affect the content and significance of these institutions over time.

Defining Institutions

The definition of institutions we have adopted draws on the work of Douglass North (1990, 1994, 2005) who, perhaps more than any other scholar, has advanced our understanding on institutions at the macro level. North defines institutions as formal rules (e.g. constitutions, laws and regulations) and informal constraints (norms of behaviour, conventions and self-imposed codes of conduct). Institutions (and their enforcement mechanisms) set the 'rules of the game', which organizations, in pursuit of their own creative and resource allocative goals, must follow. An institutional system is complete only when both formal and informal institutions are taken into account.

Like Adam Smith, North has a clearly articulated theory of human nature that underpins his analysis.[1] His is a model based on the cognitive limitations and non-rational behaviour of individuals in times of uncertainty, and the consequent influence both informal and formal institutions may have on their motivations and actions. People devise and implement institutions that are effective in meeting their own particular objectives, and that economize on their need to process information. However, there is no guarantee that the institutions so devised are efficient from an economic perspective, or even desirable from a societal perspective. Institutional change is a path-dependent process, and there are frequently considerable transaction costs in changing the existing structure of resource creation, coordination and usage, as both individuals and organizations tend to embrace such changes with great caution. Furthermore, any set of institutions is always a combination of elements that both promote and hinder economic efficiency and innovatory activity. Consequently, even in countries where efficient institutions tend to outnumber inefficient ones, institutional change is never guaranteed to produce the kinds of results it is intended to do. Partly the reason for this is what North (2005: 19) calls the non-ergodic nature of much of the contemporary world, which means that uncertainty is extremely difficult to measure or deal with, let alone overcome, by reference to past events, information and intentions. This poses particular challenges for countries with predominantly undeveloped institutions, as institutional change is even less likely to bring about the intended results.

What then accounts for the dynamics of institutional change? The conventional economic response is to attribute such changes to a restructuring of relative prices. The fundamental economic condition of scarcity leads to competition, which acts as an incentive to learn and to devise better institutions. But this does not account for all of institutional change, and according to North, the primary reason seems in fact to lie in the role of the informal rather than formal institutions. Such a 'bottom-up' theory of institutional change implies that anything that is likely to influence or substitute for individual decision-making, such as education and belief systems, are likely to affect the choice of institutions and consequently the path of economic growth.

In its emphasis on culture as the method by which beliefs, values and norms are transmitted through generations and across space, North's argument is, of course, reminiscent of Weber's (1920) analysis of the connection between the Protestant work ethic and the growth of capitalism, as well as that of other studies linking the role of national culture to economic growth (Casson and Godley, 2000; Gray, 1996; Jones, 1995). However, of these, North is the only one to offer a general and complete theory that connects the motives, intentions and actions of micro-level actors – be they individuals or firms – to patterns of economic growth at the macro level, without being specific to time or place. Among international business scholars, the work of Mark Casson (1982, 1997a, 1997b) on the influence of national culture on economic growth comes closest to North's ideas, if not to his methodology. Casson looks specifically at the role of trust versus formal monitoring procedures in influencing entrepreneurial activity, but approaches this from a more strictly rational action perspective. Although not explicitly inspired by North, this work shares the same 'bottom-up' logic by building a theory of international business activity that rests on the intentions and information processing of the individual entrepreneur.[2]

We argue that there is no reason why this kind of institutional reasoning should not be extended to analysing the motivations and behaviour of the MNE. This kind of reasoning would embrace the rules and norms that govern relationships within the firm, and those between the firm and its external stakeholders, including its suppliers, customers and community groups. In our understanding, institutions are, by their nature, restrictive in that they close off courses of action that otherwise would be available, by making them excessively costly, or depriving them of value. At the same time, many institutions do not simply impose constraints on the actions of firms; they may also affect the cognition of managers and condition the possible behavioural paths an MNE might pursue.[3] Importantly, we also believe that in some circumstances MNEs may have the ability to alter the formal or informal incentive structures that affect their actions.

Conceived in this way, the design and implementation of incentive structures and enforcement mechanisms affect all three parts of the eclectic paradigm. The most direct link is between the burgeoning literature in economics of the importance of institutions in explaining national level economic growth, and the location-based (L) advantages in the OLI paradigm. The internalization factor (I) is already institutional at the micro level, although it largely confines its attention to comparing the efficiency of different forms of organizing transactions, and does not counter the possibility of non-rational behaviour by firms in a non-ergodic world. Of the three components of the OLI paradigm, the ownership-specific advantages are the most difficult, as well as the most critical, to deal with.[4] The O-advantages require us to examine the extent to which it is possible to describe institutions (formal and informal) at the level of the firm, and the advantages derived from them (Oi), and then to distinguish these from the asset (Oa) and transaction (Ot)-based advantages identified in the received literature (e.g. Dunning (2004)). Finally, all three factors will need to be considered in a dynamic setting, where, for example, the Oa and Oi in time 't' influence both I, or mode of entry, and the L advantages of alternative locations, in time 't+1'.

Ownership-specific Advantages and Institutions

Types of Ownership-specific Advantages

The asset-based advantages (Oa) of the MNE include the know-how related to production management, organizational systems, innovatory capacity, organization of work, and so on.[5] Consequently, one way to deal with institutions within the OLI paradigm would be to subsume them under Oa as another form of organizational know-how.[6] While there are reasons to recommend this approach, parsimony being a primary one, we do not believe it is adequate to deal with the issues posed here. Thus while incentive structures, both internal and external to the firm, may affect the extent to which and the way in which particular inputs are converted into particular outputs, we believe that they are not just another form of 'soft' technology.

Although they share many similarities, an important difference between techno-logical assets (whether 'hard' or 'soft'), and institutional advantages, has to do with the origins of Oa and Oi. While some components of Oi are reflected in firm-specific norms, values and enforcement mechanisms – sometimes labelled 'corporate culture' – others are also strongly influenced by the customs and belief systems external to the firm, particularly the human environment in which the MNE operates.[7] The development of both Oa and Oi advantages is also subject to changes in the demands of the marketplace. While these may be directly related to the quantity and quality of the products or services being marketed, they may also be influenced by shifts in values or perceptions, which may or may not directly relate to the range of products or services the firm is offering.[8] For basically the same reasons, we think that institutional variables should be kept separately from those traditionally embraced in the resource-based view (RBV) of the firm.[9]

While the asset advantages (Oa) of a firm can be enhanced and regenerated, for example by technological innovation, we currently know very little of the mechanism by which a firm might add to, or restructure, its institutional advantages. Indeed, Nelson (2005) puts great weight on the argument that while progress in 'hard' technology boils down to developing adequate isolating mechanisms (e.g. physical technology protected from vibration or dust) that allow for a scientific approach to assessing the efficiency of production functions, the contents of the human environ-ment are much more difficult to isolate or evaluate. North (2005) agrees when he asserts that changes in the human environment are much more difficult to predict than those in the physical environment as they involve non-ergodic uncertainties.

Why Do Institutional Advantages Matter?

One way in which firms today are challenged to reveal their institutional and cultural underpinnings is reflected in the increasing monitoring and reporting on corpo-rate social responsibility (CSR) to meet external demands. From an institutional perspective, one would expect that financially successful firms would have both the resources and the coordinating mechanisms (Oa and Ot) as well as the motivation (Oi) to behave in a way consistent with societal interests. Stakeholders present firms with a range of often conflicting demands, but we would suggest that a firm with strong institutional assets (Oi) is likely to have a better sense of what is and what is not consistent with its own resources, capabilities and social objectives. While integrating CSR issues into every aspect of how a business is run is likely to yield the best performance both economically and socially, the more the issues of social responsibility become entangled with business strategy, the less tractable and transparent they are likely to become to outside observers. This again makes it imperative to investigate what kinds of intentions and belief systems underlie and influence Oi.

In addition to making a difference in how Oa and Oi advantages are developed and employed within the firm, Oi advantages are of growing importance in understanding the effects of MNE activity from a home or host country perspective. Like all forms of technology transfer, the transfer of Oa and Oi includes both intentional transfer of practices and institutions, as well as unintentional 'spillage' to other firms. Although innovation in a social (as opposed to technological) context is difficult, and there are limits to how far best practices can be copied and absorbed, MNEs are unique in engaging in such cross-border transfers on a continuous basis. If we accept that different institutions can be functionally equivalent, the numerous transfers that take place within the internal and external MNE network provide a robust context for experimentation and the creation of new institutions.[10]

Neoclassical economists assumed single motivations and goals of firms and of the incentive mechanisms directed to achieving these goals. Moreover, in conditions of perfect competition, there is no strategic choice, no uncertainty, and no ability to earn economic rents. Today's global economy is different with the goals of economic activity becoming more multifaceted, with stakeholder capitalism partly replacing shareholder capitalism, with the role of non-market actors becoming more prominent, and uncertainty, volatility and complexity leading to imperfect markets and a widening choice. Hence the motivating forces influencing the conduct of firms towards the creation, absorption and deployment of resources and capabilities (and the rewards emanating from them), have become critical in determining a firm's success. While in extant theories, Oi advantages may well be built into Oa and Ot, we believe that, because of the characteristics of our contemporary human environment, there is merit in separating the Oi advantages, and considering them as an influencing factor on the ways in which firms access or create new assets, or utilize more effectively their existing resources, capabilities and markets.

What are these institutional advantages? Essentially, they comprise that part of the governance structure of a firm which underpins the wealth-creating process, and which is unique to that firm. At any given moment of time, such a governance structure comprises a galaxy of both internally generated and externally imposed incentives, regulations and norms (and the response of the firm to these), each of which may affect all areas of managerial decision-taking, the attitudes and behaviour of the firm's stakeholders, and of how each of these relates to that of other economic and political actors in the wealth-creating process. Such a governance structure may be formal or informal (in the Northian sense), and be backed up by the firm's own enforcement mechanisms.

The composition and strength of the Oi advantages of firms is likely to be strongly contextual. In particular, it is likely to reflect the character of the macro-institutional infrastructure of the country or countries in which they operate. The extent and ways in which the internal incentive structure of MNEs, or potential MNEs, of a particular nationality take on board these institutions, and adapt them to their own particular requirements, is likely to be an important ingredient of the content and quality of the former's unique and sustainable resources and capabilities. For example, an ethnocentric approach to the institutional management of an MNE's foreign affiliates, which are located in very different cultural or political regimes from that of the investing country, is less likely to generate Oi advantages, than that of a geocentric approach which externalizes the distinctive incentive structures of an MNE most useful for organizing its cross-border operations.

The institutional portfolio of MNEs is also likely to vary according to the kind of value activities carried out by them and their affiliates, and the *raison d'être* for them. Thus the 'rules of the game' and enforcement mechanisms to stimulate cost effective innovatory activities – particularly where the latter are jointly undertaken with another firm – are likely to be very different from those underpinning the conduct of both home and foreign-based personnel managers in their human resource strategies, or those of purchasing managers in setting standards for the employment practices and safety procedures of their subcontractors, or those of marketing managers in ensuring acceptable quality control procedures from their local distributors.

With respect to the motives for MNE activity, it seems likely that some kinds of asset augmenting FDI are designed to gain access to and learn from not only foreign-based resources, capabilities and markets, but firm or country-specific institutions. In particular this is likely to be the case where the economic structure and business and social culture in the home and host countries is markedly different. Adaptations to the home-based Oi assets of market-seeking MNEs – and particularly of those with the least experience of foreign markets – may also need to take account of differences in consumer preferences and behaviour; while the incentive structures underpinning efficiency-seeking FDI – particularly in (and between) low labour cost developing countries – may require modifying because of the different expectations, requirements and values of individual workers and/or labour unions. Lastly, the reconciliation of country specific institutional differences is likely to play a less significant role in the case of natural resource or capital-intensive MNEs which involve relatively few and fairly straightforward production processes and transactions, than in that of knowledge intensive manufacturing or service MNEs, which operate within a dynamic technology environment and complex networks of human interaction.

CASE STUDY: CREATING CROSS-BORDER INSTITUTIONAL HYBRIDS: LENOVO AND IBM

Lenovo was founded in 1984 under the auspices of the Chinese Academy of Sciences, when scientists were given seed capital to look for commercial applications for the research conducted at the Academy. Although Legend, as the company was called at the time, operated independently of the government, the Academy held a majority ownership stake throughout most of its existence, and even after the deal with IBM, it holds 27 % of the company. In the late 1980s, Legend applied for a licence to produce PCs in China, but was refused. Subsequently the company opened a subsidiary in Hong Kong, and eventually expanded its business by distributing PCs and peripherals of foreign manufacturers like IBM and Hewlett-Packard in mainland China.

In 1997, Legend became the first Chinese company to implement an enterprise resource planning system from SAP to ensure that the company had a technological platform equal to its foreign rivals. By the late 1990s, Legend had become the best-selling PC brand in China with 20 % of the Chinese market. This was attributed to a combination of operational efficiency, and PCs designed specifically for the Chinese market. In 2001, the distribution side of the business was spun off, and in 2003 the company changed its name from Legend to Lenovo, with the aid of branding consultants.

The acquisition of IBM's PC division in December 2004 for $1.75 billion transformed Lenovo from a company selling exclusively in China, to a multinational enterprise with 60 % of its sales outside of China. Part of the acquisition price was paid in Lenovo stock, giving IBM a 13 % share in the company. Before the deal, Lenovo was the ninth largest PC company globally, while IBM was the third. The combined company remains in third place, behind Dell and Hewlett-Packard, and ahead of Acer and Fujitsu-Siemens. Almost a year after the merger, the stock of Lenovo had gained about 25 % on the Hong Kong exchange.

Prior to the deal, Lenovo was an entrepreneurial company with one core product and one core market, where the employees had an average age of 28. The IBM PC unit, by contrast, was part of a multidivisional MNE with a global reach. Nonetheless, the message from Yang Yuanqing and Steve Ward, the chairman and CEO respectively, was that this was neither a takeover nor a reverse takeover, but the creation of a new company, which required reinventing how work gets done. This is in stark contrast to other acquisitions in the industry, such as that of Compaq by Hewlett-Packard, where the integration process was speeded up by making explicit choices on one side or the other regarding processes that were to be kept or discarded.

On the operational side, the benefits of the merger were expected to include lower component costs through consolidated procurement and the integration of supply chains. However, in addition to this, in strategic asset-seeking acquisitions, the ac-quirer is looking to gain both hard and soft technology, as well as the institutional resources and capabilities of the target firm. In terms of hard technology, the strengths of IBM and Lenovo can be seen as complementary. IBM embodies industrial design targeted at the corporate market, and focuses on innovation that is mostly hidden from view, including features that make the machines more reliable and cheaper to run. Lenovo, by contrast, has focused on adapting PCs for different types of home use. As regards soft technology, IBM brings considerable operational excellence to the deal. According to a former IBM executive who is now a VP of strategy at Lenovo: 'We have outstanding processes to make things happen, measure them and keep them on task. We don't miss dates.'

The culture at Lenovo is strongly influenced by its 41-year-old chairman, who has a strong preference for clarity and precision. Employees are required to clock in and clock out, and turning up late for meetings is forbidden. However, clarity and precision do not just apply to employees and their timekeeping. Lenovo is unusually explicit about what it expects of executives, employees, suppliers and business partners. For example, when foreign PC companies developed a reputation for squeezing the margins of distributors when the market took a downturn, Lenovo stuck to its rules, which clearly outlined responsibilities on both sides. This behaviour earned the company considerable loyalty among the distributors.

Lenovo has also absorbed management influences from abroad at arm's length. The company uses a performance assessment tool, made popular by Jack Welch of GE, which requires managers to classify their employees as high achievers, solid perform-ers or underperformers. This system, which is not universally accepted even in the individualistic context of the United States, is in strong contrast to the prevailing attitudes in China. While the company says that it will not impose its idiosyncratic work practices on its international workforce, some concerns regarding its manage-ment practices have been raised. For example, in Germany, Lenovo faced a shortage of employees when many former IBM employees chose to leave the company, and in Japan Lenovo admits to having had to 'over-manage' to achieve compliance.

Based on a series of articles in the *Financial Times*, 9–11 November 2005.

The Lenovo and IBM case illustrates the case of the Chinese computer maker Lenovo and its acquisition of IBM's PC business. When compared either to the traditional networks of Chinese entrepreneurs prominent in Hong Kong, Singapore or Malaysia, or the so-called dragon multinationals such as Acer, the strategy of acquisition adopted by Lenovo is quite unusual. The traditional Chinese networks are based on relationships between family members and other trusted insiders, which have enabled the firms to remain flexible, while attaining a considerable size (Yeung, 2002). By contrast, the dragons of South East Asia have grown to achieve global scale, not through FDI, but through a network of alliances and contractual relationships (Mathews, 2002).

Lenovo is also unusual in terms of its eclectic mix of a Chinese cultural back-ground, imported management principles and technology, strong rules-based val-ues imposed by a visionary CEO, and the ambition to create entirely new ways of conducting business by absorbing the considerable institutional legacy of a major foreign MNE. Whether the creation of this institutional hybrid will affect Lenovo's future performance in positive or negative terms is an empirical question. Cross-border international business activity makes systems of norms and values interact in ways that promotes the creation of new institutional forms, and out of these may emerge more effective ways to set incentives, or by contrast, they may sow the seeds of future conflict.

The global economy connects growing numbers of people and organizations from countries with different institutional legacies with each other as consumers and producers, and MNES are important facilitators of this process. Consequently, we believe that the way in which the MNE adapts internally to institutional differences will be increasingly important for its long-term competitiveness. For example, the particularism and paternalism associated with Chinese family firms (see e.g. Redding (2001)), while perfectly functional in its cultural context, stands in opposition to those US and European firms, that emphasize the importance of transparency, equality and diversity, not just as means to reach better organizational effectiveness, but as a reflection of wider societal norms. Institutional hybrids that can effectively bridge organizations from different institutional contexts can lower the costs of transacting, but achieving this in the social (human) environment, rather than in the physical (technological) environment, as has been customary, is likely to prove challenging.

Empirical Evidence of Institutional Advantages

Thus Oi advantages are important because they influence the motivation and conduct of firms, and consequently the way in which Oa and Ot advantages are deployed. But what evidence is there in the literature of the importance of Oi advantages? Since the latter have not been considered separately from different forms of technology and other O-specific assets, it is not possible to assess this directly. Nonetheless, three examples can be found. These are to do first with the transfer of organizational practices (Oi transferred along Oa), second where Oi advantages influence I (entry mode or degree of internalization, discussed in a subsequent section), and third where Oi influence or are influenced by L-specific advantages. As regards the transfer of organizational practices, historical examples include the introduction of the M-form from the US to Europe in the 1920s and 1930s (Chandler, 1990), the transfer of US management models and incentive structures from the US to Europe in the 1950s and 60s (Kipping and Bjarnar, 1998; Zeitlin and Herrigel, 2000), and the transplantation of Japanese work practices and quality control procedures into the US and Europe in the 1980s.[11] It deserves to be noted that whereas European firms were fairly quick to introduce the mass production methods in automotive and other industries in the early twentieth century, it took them much longer to adopt the multidivisional (or M-form) organization (Kogut, c05+bib+0050). The transaction costs of overcoming the rigidities of ingrained tradition and business practices are considerably higher than those of replacing 'hard' technology or introducing new products. This, indeed, is one of the reasons why we believe that Oi advantages need to be considered as advantages in their own right.

With increasing global activity by MNEs, a more diverse range of standards is being transferred by MNEs through their affiliate networks.[12] These can include standards for quality management processes, such as ISO 9000 (Guler, Guillén, and Macpherson, 2002), or environmental management processes, such as EMAS and ISO 14000 (Christmann and Taylor, 2001). Indirectly, this also includes the transfer of regulatory standards, such as elementally chlorine free (ECF) pulping from Scandinavia to the United States (Lundan, 2004), or the diffusion of the arm's length standard of transfer pricing within North America (Eden, Dacin and Wan, 2001). Institutional transfer can also involve the cross-border transmission of employment practices, such as the 'one union' system imposed by Japanese MNEs on their affiliates in the UK in the 1980s (Dunning, 1986; Oliver and Wilkinson, 1988), and in the adoption (and adaptation) of workforce diversity policies in some UK affiliates of US MNEs (Ferner, Almond and Colling, 2005). Other institutional changes not solely attributable to MNEs, but often influenced by them, are the importation of an anti-union culture centred on individual achievement and individual rewards, as well as challenges to traditional work–life balance, resulting in a more atomistic (less communitarian) society (Guillén, 2000; Peoples and Sugden, 2000).

Instances where the Oi advantages of MNEs are both influenced by the institutional L advantages of home (or host) countries, as well as contributing to them, can be found in the extensive discussion of the role of social capital affecting the product profiles and strategies of MNEs (e.g. Kostova and Roth (2003)), as well in the discussion on the 'born globals' and the accelerated internationalization of small (technology intensive) firms (e.g. Yli-Renko et al. (2001)).

Locational Factors[13]

Within the field of economics, institutional analysis has risen to prominence in recent years. Particularly interesting have been the analyses, in fields as diverse as economic history, public choice, sociology, international political economy and international economics, on the importance of institutions and good governance for economic efficiency and growth.[14] The national level institutions are more readily identifiable (though not always easily measurable) than their firm-specific equivalents, and thus ample evidence exists of the importance of institutions in a static sense, or comparative static sense, though little has been written on the role of MNEs in affecting these institutions.[15]

We believe that institutions and the values and belief systems underpinning them are playing an increasingly important role in the L attractions of countries in a world in which many Oa advantages, are becoming increasingly available, and can be more easily transferred between countries than in the past. Whether the Oa of MNEs can be successfully absorbed or built upon by the transferring entities rests essentially on the content and quality of L-specific institutions, particularly as the goals of countries have widened to embrace environmental, security and other 'quality of life' concerns (Dunning, 2006). While some country-specific institutions are directed specifically to encouraging inward or outward FDI, others are more general, but nonetheless critical to the success of MNE activity. We would argue that globalization is compelling a re-examination of both the formal and informal institutional infrastructure of different home and host economies, not least because its form and content is becoming an L advantage (or disadvantage) in its own right. As Pournarakis and Varsakelis (2004: 89) have put it, the quality of national institutions 'render a country attractive for TNCs beyond market size, its productive endowments and internationalization'.

Like the Oi advantages of firms, the institutionally related location advantages of countries (Li) are likely to be highly situational, and to differ considerably both between developed and developing countries, and among them. As an example of the latter, over most of the 1970s, 1980s and early 1990s, the incentive structures and enforcement mechanisms of most East Asian countries were much more conducive to promoting the creation and usage of their resources, capabilities and markets, and to advancing their development goals than those of most Latin American and virtually all sub-Saharan African countries. The balance between top-down and bottom-up incentive structures, and that between obligatory and voluntary enforcement mechanisms, is also likely to be a strongly country-specific Li variable.

Of course, there are many other country-specific characteristics determining the content of Li advantages. These include the openness of a country, and the extent to which it is engaged in cross-border commerce involving different countries (cf. Singapore with Ghana); the extent to which it is multicultural and tolerant of different belief systems (cf. Malaysia with Iran), its stage of economic and social development (which may affect the quality of its supportive institutional infrastructure (cf. Pakistan with Korea)); the institutional demands of its particular industrial structure (cf. Saudi Arabia with Hong Kong); its size (cf. Sri Lanka with Indonesia); its culture towards wealth creation and entrepreneurship (cf. Taiwan with North Korea); the extent and seriousness of its social unrest or dysfunction (cf. Colombia with Chile); and perhaps most important of all, the extent of democracy, and freedom of action allowed to the main wealth creators in society (cf. the contemporary situation in Vietnam and Cambodia with that of the 1980s, or that of Zimbabwe with Botswana in 2005). If nothing else, these examples show (a) how important the institutional component of a country's locational advantage is; (b) how sophisticated and complex the composition and quality of its various components are, and (c) how much, and why, institutional distance may vary between particular home and host countries.[16]

What then is the evidence that institutions, both formal and informal, affect either a country's ability to attract FDI, or the benefits it can derive from it? On the latter question there is, as yet, little evidence available, but on the first issue cross-sectional studies on the effects of good and bad governance have generally confirmed that countries with a good governance structure attract the most FDI (Globerman and Shapiro, 2002; Henisz, 2000; Stein and Daude, 2001), while other research has demonstrated that strong property rights protection generally has a marked positive effect on the flows of FDI (Li and Resnick, 2003). Panel studies, which enable an analysis of the time dimension, have also begun to analyse the effects of changes in the institutional structure, such as in the tightening of an IPR regime, and of how this affects the investment decisions of MNEs (Branstetter, Fisman and Foley, 2005;

Smarzynska Javorcik, 2004). Several studies (e.g. Bevan, Estrin and Meyer (2003), Grosse and Trevino (2005) and Dunning (2005)) have also shown that the upgrading of institutions in the transition economies of Central and Eastern Europe has led to more FDI in these economies. Other available evidence would also seem to confirm that bad governance (endemic corruption, poor environmental protection) repels rather than attracts inbound FDI (Habib and Zurawicki, 2002; OECD, 1999; Wei, 2000).[17]

Internalization

The internalization factor (I) of the OLI paradigm explains the firm's propensity to internalize market failure. As we have already stated, a great deal of the received wisdom on I is directly or indirectly institutional in its approach. This is because it is directed at identifying and evaluating the costs and benefits of alternative modes of exploiting and accessing O-specific advantages, however these are determined. For example, the extent of opportunism and moral hazard is determined by the quality and effectiveness of non-market (internal) versus (external) market institutions.

As we indicated in the beginning of this chapter, embracing an institutional perspective has led us to consider the MNE as a system of value-added activities and transactions of both inter- and intra-firm nature. The question then becomes, under what conditions is it best to engage in intra-firm or inter-firm value-added activities and transactions? Here we believe that institutions play an important part in determining the complementarity or substitutability of the different operational modes. Different modes of coordination simply represent different usages made of two fundamentally different mechanisms, viz. coordination by prices over the market and coordination by behaviour constraints within the hierarchy. Neither of these modes by themselves will be able to solve all problems of coordination, and both are subject to diminishing returns in use (Hennart, 2001).

Furthermore, while transaction costs economics can determine what kinds of markets are most likely to be internalized, it cannot indicate what types of firms will internalize what kind of market failure. Our contention is that to answer the latter question requires an explanation that rests on both the Oa and Oi of a firm. Rather than equate ownership with internalization, we now understand it to reflect the sum total of the make-or-buy decisions made by the firm. The MNE is thus best considered as a collection of value adding activities, both internal and external to the ownership boundary of the firm, that are controlled and managed by it. The costs of motivating the decision-taking agents within the firm, even if lower than the costs of transacting in the market place, are dependent on the incentive structures and enforcement mechanisms devised and implemented by the firm, and thus the formal and informal institutions therein. Under any form of relational contracting, whether market-related or undertaken within the hierarchy of a firm, the incentive structures matter to the successful execution of the contract.

How do Oi advantages then influence I advantages? At the one extreme (e.g. in some kinds of asset-seeking FDI) the incentive structures of the investing company or country may be totally inappropriate for it to impose on its foreign affiliates. The choice then is either to adapt its home-based (or global) incentive structures, or to engage in some kind of partnership with a local firm, so that the (other) O advantages transferred and combined with the resources of the partner firm may be effectively deployed. The latter organizational form is likely to be most prevalent in cases of firms investing in countries with very different business cultures and/or belief systems (e.g. Iran and Germany) or between those at different stages of development (e.g. Australia and Sri Lanka). At the same time, if the incentive structures of the investing firm reflect those which are likely to be eventually embraced by the host countries (as now seems to be happening in the case of UK and German FDI in the Baltic States and in Croatia and Slovenia), then the transactions and coordination of value added activity, at least in the initial stages of its FDI in an unfamiliar country, are more likely to be internalized.

However, as with any form of foreign involvement, much will depend on the host government's attitude and policy towards the non-resident ownership of its indigenous assets. On the one hand, the liberalization of markets in the 1990s and the increasing integration of many developing countries into the global economy e.g. via efficiency-seeking FDI, is leading to a harmonization of intra-firm incentive structures. On the other, the increasing attention now being paid to all aspects of corporate social responsibility has encouraged some developing countries to renew their earlier attempts to ensure that the conduct and performance of foreign affiliates promotes their particular economic and social needs and objectives. Inter alia, these include the encouragement of foreign affiliates to abide by the formal and informal institutional mores of the host countries, and to respect the values and belief systems underpinning them. The response of many MNEs is to conclude non-equity business relationships, e.g. in the subcontracting of the early stage manufacturing process in the electronics and textile industries, and in transference of call centres from several developed to developing countries, notably to India.

In the international business literature, there have been a number of studies confirming that the institutional content and quality in the host country may affect the mode of entry of the MNE. Several studies, in particular, have recognized the importance of institutions in fostering the development of East Asian economies (Kasper, 1998), and their role in influencing both inward and outward foreign direct investment (Mathews, 2006; Peng and Delios, 2006). Other research has examined the choice of entry mode related to institutional quality in Central and Eastern Europe and Vietnam (Meyer, 2001; Meyer and Nguyen, 2005), as well as in the EU (Brouthers, 2002). Delios and Henisz (2003) have considered the effects of both organizational capabilities as well as public and private expropriation hazards on the entry mode choice of Japanese MNEs. Moving away from measures of psychic distance, Yiu and Makino (2002) have applied the concept of institutional distance to explain the choice of entry mode in a cross-section of countries. At the firm level, other scholars have examined the effects of imitation on the mode of entry (Chang and Rosenzweig, 2001; Davis, Desai and Francis, 2000; Guillén, 2003; Lu, 2002).

We would make one final, but, we believe important, point. Most of the research on the internalization of markets assumes that firms behave in an economically rational way, and in so far as it is considered at all, are able to combat, or at least minimize, uncertainty. However, in a non-ergodic world, and one in which firms pursue multiple changing interests and engage in unfamiliar cultural domains, the efficiency-based transaction cost model may need some modification. In such situations, in order to promote the kind of institutions it believes will best protect or enhance its dynamic Oa and Ot advantages, and minimize the adverse effects of change, firms may need to consider a variety of non-economic (and in that sense, non-rational) elements. But this is largely unexplored territory to internalization scholars!

Conclusion

In some ways, aspects of institutional analysis have been present in the existing theories of IB for a long time. However, for the reasons we have outlined in this chapter, we feel that it would be fruitful for future scholarship to clearly separate the institutional effects from other influences on the activities and strategies of MNEs. This is partly to do with an increasing need to accommodate stakeholder considerations in addition to shareholder interests, but it is not limited to issues of social performance. Indeed, an institutional view makes no presumptions about whether the institutions that develop are beneficial or not, or whether new institutions will develop at all. Our contention is that formal institutions cannot be studied apart from the motivations and belief systems that underlie them. Static comparisons of institutional forms have ignored the fact that functionally equivalent institutions can take on many different forms, while it is the underlying informal institutions that are likely to determine the outcomes in the long run. We have also argued that in a dynamic, complex and volatile global economy, the role of both firm and location-specific institutions in reducing the transaction costs of cross-border, value-added and exchange activities is becoming more important.

We believe that conceiving of the bundle transferred by MNEs as consisting not just of financial capital and technology, but including institutional advantages as well, will be critical to improving our understanding of what determines the ability and willingness of the MNE to transfer knowledge across borders, and the ability and willingness of the firms and individuals in the host country to appropriate this knowledge. Cross-border business activity provides many opportunities for the creation and exploitation of new institutional forms. While not all such hybrids will be successful, new institutions embodying norms and values, e.g. from developed and developing economies, entrepreneurial and established firms, or individualist and collective cultures, are likely become increasingly common. So, indeed, are the challenges being posed by the multiple goals of firms and governments that increasingly incorporate diverse non-economic objectives. Consequently, the cross-border activities of firms deserve to be studied not just in terms of the different product–market combinations they bring under one system of governance, but also in terms of the informal institutions they embody. From a managerial point of view, there is potential for efficiency gains or losses from the introduction of new institutional forms. From a policy point of view, the hybrids introduced by domestic and foreign MNEs are likely to play an important role in influencing the dynamics of institutional change at the national level.

Questions

1. The system of incentives and norms that prevailed at Lenovo prior to the deal with IBM was itself a hybrid. To what extent was this hybrid typical or representative of other Chinese firms?
2. What was Lenovo looking for in its deal with IBM? To what extent is it likely to receive what it sought?
3. What are the main difficulties in integrating the institutional structure of Lenovo with that of IBM? To what extent are the difficulties specific to these two firms?
4. Under what conditions is the institutional hybrid created by Lenovo and IBM likely to provide a source of sustainable competitive advantage?

Further Reading

For institutions in general

North, D. C. (2005) *Understanding the Process of Economic Change*. Princeton, NJ: Princeton University Press.
Williamson, O. E. (2000) 'The New Institutional Economics: Taking Stock, Looking Ahead', *Journal of Economic Literature*, 38(3), 595.

For institutions and international business
(a) Theory and analysis

Dunning, J. H. (2006) 'Towards a new paradigm of development: Implications for the determinants of international business activity', *Transnational Corporations*, 15(2).
Maitland, E. and Nicholas, E. (2003) 'New institutional economics: An organizing framework for OLI'. In J. Cantwell and R. Narula (eds) *International business and the eclectic paradigm*. London and New York: Routledge, 47–73.
Mudambi, R. and Navarra, P. (2002) 'Institutions and international business: a theoretical overview', *International Business Review*, 11(6), 635.
Rondinelli, D. A. and Behrman, J. N. (2000) 'The institutional imperatives of globalization', *Global Focus*, 12(1), 65–78.

(b) Empirical work

Bevan, A., Estrin, S. and Meyer, K. E. (2003) 'Foreign investment location and institutional development in transition economies', *International Business Review*, 13(1), 43–64.

Guillén, M. F. (2003) 'Experience, imitation, and the sequence of foreign entry: wholly owned and joint-venture manufacturing by South Korean firms and business groups in China, 1987–1995', *Journal of International Business Studies*, 34(2), 185.

Meyer, K. E. and Nguyen, H. V. (2005) 'Foreign Investment Strategies and Sub-national Institutions in Emerging Markets: Evidence from Vietnam', *Journal of Management Studies*, 42(1), 63–93.

References

Bevan, A., Estrin, S. and Meyer, K. E. (2003) 'Foreign investment location and institutional development in transition economies', *International Business Review*, 13(1), 43–64.

Branstetter, L., Fisman, R. and Foley, C. F. (2005) 'Do stronger intellectual property rights increase international technology transfer? Empirical evidence from U.S. firm-level data': NBER Working Paper 11516.

Brewer, T. L. and Lundan, S. M. (2006) 'Environmental policy and institutional transparency in Europe'. In L. Oxelheim (ed.), *Corporate and Institutional Transparency for Economic Growth in Europe*. Oxford: Elsevier, 93–116.

Brouthers, K. D. (2002) 'Institutional, Cultural and Transaction Cost Influences on Entry Mode Choice and Performance', *Journal of International Business Studies*, 33(2), 203.

Campos, E., Lien, D. and Pradhan, S. (1999) 'The impact of corruption on investment: Predictability matters', *World Development*, 27(6), 1059–67.

Casson, M. (1982) *The entrepreneur: An economic theory*. Oxford: Martin Robertson.

Casson, M. (1997a) *Information and Organization: A new perspective on the theory of the firm*. Oxford and New York: Oxford University Press, Clarendon Press.

Casson, M. (1997b) 'Institutional economics and business history: A way forward?' *Business History*, 39(4), 151.

Casson, M. and Godley, A. (eds) (2000) *Cultural Factors in Economic Growth*. Heidelberg and New York: Springer.

Casson, M. and Lundan, S. M. (1999) 'Explaining international differences in economic institutions: A critique of the "national business system" as an analytical tool', *International Studies of Management & Organization*, 29(2), 25–42.

Chandler, A. D. (1990) *Scale and Scope: The Dynamics of Industrial Capitalism*. Cambridge, MA: Harvard/Belknap.

Chang, S.-J., and Rosenzweig, P. M. (2001) 'The choice of entry mode in sequential foreign direct investment', *Strategic Management Journal*, 22(8), 747.

Christmann, P. and Taylor, G. (2001) 'Globalization and the Environment: Determinants of Firm Self-Regulation in China', *Journal of International Business Studies*, 32(3), 439.

Davis, P. S., Desai, A. B. and Francis, J. D. (2000) 'Mode of International Entry: An Isomorphism Perspective', *Journal of International Business Studies*, 31(2), 239.

Delios, A. and Henisz, W. J. (2003) 'Policy uncertainty and the sequence of entry by Japanese firms, 1980–1998', *Journal of International Business Studies*, 34(3), 227–41.

Dunning, J. H. (1986) *Japanese Participation in British Industry*. London: Croom Helm.

Dunning, J. H. (2003) 'Some antecedents of internalization theory', *Journal of International Business Studies*, 34(1), 108.

Dunning, J. H. (2004) 'An evolving paradigm of the economic determinants of international business activity'. In J. L. C. Cheng and M. A. Hitt. (eds) *Managing Multinationals in a Knowledge Economy: Economics, culture, and human resources*, Vol. 15, Amsterdam: Elsevier, 3–27.

Dunning, J. H. (2005) 'Institutional reform, foreign direct investment and European transition economies'. In R. Grosse. (ed.) *International Business and Government Relations in the 21st Century*. Cambridge: Cambridge University Press.

Dunning, J. H. (2006) 'Towards a new paradigm of development: Implications for the determinants of international business activity', *Transnational Corporations*, 15(2).

Dunning, J. H. and Lundan, S. M. (2008) *Multinational Enterprises and the Global Economy*. 2nd edn. Cheltenham: Edward Elgar.

Eden, L., Dacin, M. T. and Wan, W. P. (2001) 'Standards across borders: Crossborder diffusion of the arm's length standard in North America', *Accounting, Organizations & Society*, 26(1), 1.

Enright, M. J. (2000) 'Regional Clusters and Multinational Enterprises', *International Studies of Management & Organization*, 30(2), 114–39.

Ferner, A., Almond, P. and Colling, T. (2005) 'Institutional theory and the cross-national transfer of employment policy: the case of "workforce diversity" in US multinationals', *Journal of International Business Studies*, 36(3), 304–21.

Glaeser, E. L., Porta, R. L., Lopez-de-Silanes, F. and Shleifer, A. (2004) 'Do Institutions Cause Growth?: National Bureau of Economic Research, Inc.', NBER Working Papers: 10568.

Globerman, S. and Shapiro, D. (2002) 'Global Foreign Direct Investment Flows: The Role of Governance Infrastructure', *World Development*, 30(11), 1899.

Gray, H. P. (1996) 'Culture and economic performance: Policy as an intervening variable', *Journal of Comparative Economics*, 23(3), 278.

Grosse, R. and Trevino, L. J. (2005) 'New institutional economics and FDI location in Central and Eastern Europe', *Management International Review*, 45(2), 123–45.

Guillén, M. F. (2000) 'Organized labor's images of multinational enterprise: Divergent foreign investment ideologies in Argentina, South Korea, and Spain', *Industrial & Labor Relations Review*, 53(3), 419.

Guillén, M. F. (2003) 'Experience, imitation, and the sequence of foreign entry: wholly owned and joint-venture manufacturing by South Korean firms and business groups in China, 1987-1995', *Journal of International Business Studies*, 34(2), 185.

Guler, I., Guillén, M. F. and Macpherson, J. M. (2002) 'Global competition, institutions, and the diffusion of organizational practices: The international spread of ISO9000 quality certificates', *Administrative Science Quarterly*, 47, 207–32.

Habib, M. and Zurawicki, L. (2002) 'Corruption and foreign direct investment', *Journal of International Business Studies*, 33(2), 291–307.

Henisz, W. J. (2000) 'The institutional environment for multinational investment', *Journal of Law, Economics & Organization*, 16(2), 334–64.

Hennart, J.-F. (2001) 'Theories of the multinational enterprise'. In A. M. Rugman and T. L. Brewer. (eds) *Oxford Handbook of International Business*. Oxford: Oxford University Press, 127–49.

Hoffman, A. J. (1997) *From Heresy to Dogma: An institutional history of corporate environmentalism*. San Francisco: The New Lexington Press.

Jensen, R. and Szulanski, G. (2004) 'Stickiness and the adaptation of organizational practices in cross-border knowledge transfers', *Journal of International Business Studies*, 35(6), 508–23.

Jones, E. L. (1995) 'Culture and its Relationship to Economic Change', *Journal of Institutional and Theoretical Economics*, 151(2), 269–85.

Kasper, W. (1998) 'Rapid development in East Asia: Institutional evolution and backlogs', *Malaysian Journal of Economic Studies*, XXXV(1 & 2), 45–66.

Kaufmann, D., Kraay, A. and Mastruzzi, M. (2005) 'Governance Matters IV: Governance Indicators for 1996–2004', World Bank Policy Research Working Paper Series No. 3630, The World Bank.

Kipping, M. and Bjarnar, O. (eds) (1998) *The Americanisation of European Business: The Marshall Plan and the Transfer of US Management Models*. London: Routledge.

Kogut, B. (1990) The permeability of borders and the speed of learning among countries, *Globalization of Firms and the Competitiveness of Nations*, Crafoord Lectures. Lund: University of Lund.

Kostova, T. and Roth, K. (2003) 'Social capital in multinational corporations and a micro-macro model of its formation', *Academy of Management Review*, 28(2), 297.

Li, Q. and Resnick, A. (2003) 'Reversal of Fortunes: Democratic Institutions and Foreign Direct Inflows to Developing Countries', *International Organization*, 57(1), 175–211.

Lu, J. W. (2002) 'Intra- and Inter-organizational Imitative Behavior: Institutional Influences on Japanese Firms' Entry Mode Choice', *Journal of International Business Studies*, 33(1), 19.

Lundan, S. M. (2004) 'Multinationals, NGOs and regulation: Greenpeace and the global phase-out of chlorine bleaching'. In S. M. Lundan. (ed.) *Multinationals, Environment and Global Competition*. Oxford: JAI (Elsevier), 147–70.

Madhok, A. (2002) 'Reassessing the Fundamentals and Beyond: Ronald Coase, the Transaction Cost and Resource-based Theories of the Firm and the Institutional Structure of Production', *Strategic Management Journal*, 23(6), 535.

Mathews, J. (2006) 'Dragon multinationals: New players in 21st century globalization', *Asia Pacific Journal of Management*, 23(1), 5–27.

Mathews, J. A. (2002) *Dragon Multinational: A New Model for Global Growth*. Oxford: Oxford University Press.

Meyer, K. E. (2001) 'Institutions, Transaction Costs, and Entry Mode Choice in Eastern Europe', *Journal of International Business Studies*, 32(2), 357–67.

Meyer, K. E. and Nguyen, H. V. (2005) 'Foreign Investment Strategies and Sub-national Institutions in Emerging Markets: Evidence from Vietnam', *Journal of Management Studies*, 42(1), 63–93.

Nelson, R. R. (2002) 'Bringing institutions into evolutionary growth theory', *Journal of Evolutionary Economics*, 12(1/2), 17.

Nelson, R. R. (2005) 'Evolutionary Social Science and Universal Darwinism'. Columbia University: mimeo.

Noorderhaven, N. G. and Harzing, A.-W. (2003) 'The "Country-of-origin Effect" in Multinational Corporations: Sources, Mechanisms and Moderating Conditions', *Management International Review*, 43(2), 47–66.

North, D. C. (1990) *Institutions, Institutional Change and Economic Performance*. Cambridge: Cambridge University Press.

North, D. C. (1994) 'Economic performance through time', *American Economic Review*, 84(3), 359.

North, D. C. (2005) *Understanding the Process of Economic Change*. Princeton, NJ: Princeton University Press.

OECD. (1999) *Foreign Direct Investment and the Environment*. Paris: OECD.

Oliver, C. (1991) 'Strategic responses to institutional processes', *Academy of Management Review*, 16(1), 145.

Oliver, C. (1997) 'Sustainable competitive advantage: combining institutional and resource-based views', *Strategic Management Journal*, 18(9), 697–713.

Oliver, N. and Wilkinson, B. (1988) *The Japanization of British Industry*. Oxford: Basil Blackwell.

Ozawa, T. (2003) 'Japan's network capitalism in evolution'. In J. H. Dunning and G. Boyd. (eds) *Alliance Capitalism and Corporate Management*. Cheltenham, UK: Edward Elgar.

Ozawa, T. (2005) *Institutions, Industrial Upgrading and Economic Performance in Japan*. Cheltenham, UK: Edward Elgar.

Peng, M. W. (2001) 'The resource-based view and international business', *Journal of Management*, 27(6), 803.

Peng, M. W. and Delios, A. (2006) 'What determines the scope of the firm over time and around the world? An Asia Pacific perspective', *Asia Pacific Journal of Management*, 23(4).

Peoples, J. and Sugden, R. (2000) 'Divide and rule by transnational corporations'. In C. Pitelis and R. Sugden. (eds) *The Nature of the Transnational Firm*. London and New York: Routledge.

Pournarakis, M. and Varsakelis, N. C. (2004) 'Institutions, Internationalization and FDI: The Case of Economies in Transition', *Transnational Corporations*, 13(2), 77–94.

Redding, G. (2001) 'The smaller economies of Pacific Asia and their business systems'. In A. M. Rugman and T. Brewer. (eds) *The Oxford Handbook of International Business*. Oxford: Oxford University Press, 760–84.

Rodrik, D., Subramanian, A. and Trebbi, F. (2002) 'Institutions Rule: The Primacy of Institutions over Geography and Integration in Economic Development: National Bureau of Economic Research', NBER Working Papers: 9305.

Smarzynska Javorcik, B. (2004) 'The Composition of Foreign Direct Investment and Protection of Intellectual Property Rights: Evidence from Transition Economies', *European Economic Review*, 48(1), 39–62.

Smith, A. (1790) *The Theory of Moral Sentiments*. Cambridge: Cambridge University Press.

Stein, E. and Daude, C. (2001) 'Institutions, Integration and the Location of Foreign Direct Investment: Inter-American Development Bank'. New Horisons of Foreign Direct Investment, OECD Global Forum on International Investment, Paris, France 2002.

von Hippel, E. and von Krogh, G. (2003) 'Open Source Software and the "Private-Collective" Innovation Model: Issues for Organization Science', *Organization Science*, 14(2), 209–23.

Weber, M. (1920) *The Protestant Ethic and the Spirit of Capitalism*. New York: Scribner & Sons.

Wei, S.-J. (2000) 'How Taxing Is Corruption on International Investors?' *Review of Economics & Statistics*, 82(1), 1.

Yeung, H. W.-C. (2002) *Entrepreneurship and the Internationalisation of Asian Firms: An institutional perspective*. Cheltenham, UK and Northampton, MA: Edward Elgar.

Yiu, D. and Makino, S. (2002) 'The Choice Between Joint Venture and Wholly Owned Subsidiary: An Institutional Perspective', *Organization Science*, 13(6), 667.

Yli-Renko, H., Autio, E. and Sapienza, H. J. (2001) 'Social capital, knowledge acquisition, and knowledge exploitation in young technology-based firms', *Strategic Management Journal*, 22(6/7), 587.

Zeitlin, J. and Herrigel, G. (eds) (2000) *Americanization and its Limits*. Oxford: Oxford University Press.

Zysman, J. (2004) 'Creating value in a digital era: How do wealthy nations stay wealthy?' University of California, Berkeley: BRIE Working Paper 165.

NOTES

1. Adam Smith's underlying theory of human nature is articulated in his *Theory of Moral Sentiments* (1790).
2. See also Casson and Lundan (1999) for a critique of the top-down approach of comparative institutional studies. Instead of explaining how national level institutions constrain or enable economic activity, they suggest a bottom-up approach centred on explaining differences in the institutions encouraging entrepreneurship.
3. Nelson (2002) uses the metaphor of a makeshift road across a swamp. While the road restricts where one can travel on the swamp, focusing on this restriction is to miss the point of the possibilities created by the existence of a road.
4. These advantages reflect those firm-specific advantages (FSAs) identified by Alan Rugman and Alain Verbeke (in this volume) which specifically arise from the (nationality of) ownership of the firm.
5. Elsewhere we refer to these as resource, capability or market (RCM) exploiting advantages (Dunning, 2006).
6. The transactional (Ot) advantages arising from the economies of common governance are essentially unaffected by the inclusion of the Oi.
7. Noorderhaven and Harzing (2003) define the country-of-origin effect in MNEs as the tacit beliefs and implicit values of key decision-makers.
8. A recent ideological shift that has directly affected the products and services of firms is the open source movement, which has emphasized the value of maintaining a 'knowledge commons' to encourage innovation (von Hippel and von Krogh, 2003). This has contrasted with the strategies of many large ICT and pharmaceutical firms, which have focused on extending the boundaries of private knowledge through extensions to IPR law. See also Hoffman (1997) on the changing attitudes concerning environmental issues in the chemical industry.
9. For earlier attempts to do just this, see Oliver (1991, 1997). More recently, Peng (2001: 821) has argued that the RBV needs to pay more attention to the 'rich insights of institutional theory'.
10. Both Zysman (2004) and Nelson (2005) provide arguments that highlight the importance (and difficulty) of conscious experimentation to achieving growth in an increasingly uncertain environment.
11. See Ozawa (2005: 206) on how US MNEs have contributed to the institutional transformation ongoing in Japan. In his words 'foreign multinationals which are now eagerly welcomed in Japan to revitalise its corporate business sector are serving as renovators that can remodel Japan's inner set of institutions more closely in accordance with the norms of the outer set'. See also Ozawa (2003).
12. This is not to suggest that the process of intra-firm transfer is either easy or predictable. See e.g. Jensen and Szulanski (2004).
13. These are basically similar to those designated by Rugman and Verbeke (in this volume) as country-specific advantages (CSAs). However, in our connotation, location embraces a spatial dimension which may be smaller or larger than a particular country.
14. One could argue, as Nelson (2002) does, that while classical economics was both evolutionary and institutional, neoclassical economics has been neither, and thus the current trend represents a return to old themes.

15. Foremost among these have been the attempts of World Bank scholars to identify and evaluate governance indicators of institutional robustness (or its absence!). See, for example Kaufmann, Kraay and Mastruzzi (2005), who identify six dimensions of governance, viz. voice and accountability, political instability and violence, government effectiveness, regulatory quality, rule of law ad control of corruption.

16. Rodrik, Subramanian and Trebbi (2002) set out to compare three rival sets of determinants of economic growth, composed of geographical measures (climate, natural resources, disease burden and transportation costs), the role of economic openness and international trade and the role of institutions (property rights, the rule of law and social infrastructure). The authors come to the conclusion that institutions 'trump' everything else. In other words, once institutional quality is controlled for, economic integration through trade has no direct effect on income, and geography has at best weak effects. Other scholars emphasize the fundamental role of human capital in economic growth, arguing that the upgrading of human capital (through education) enables growth, which in turn enables institutional upgrading (Glaeser, Porta, Lopez-de-Silanes and Shleifer, 2004).

17. Campos, Lien and Pradhan (1999) found that in addition to levels of corruption, the *unpredictability* of corruption matters for investors based on survey responses, while Brewer and Lundan (2006) evaluated the extent to which *transparency* at different levels of environmental policymaking in the EU affects firm behaviour and the costs of compliance.

Chapter 6 The Multinational Firm as an Evolutionary System

D. Eleanor Westney

Introduction

One of the most pervasive images of the multinational firm sees it as an extended se-lection regime, selecting certain locations, modes of internationalization, subsidiary roles, structures and processes – even people – and discarding others on its path to greater scale, scope, and cross-border integration. Some portrayals of the MNE give a positive focus to this image: the MNE introduces and maintains organizational patterns and management techniques that are more advanced than those developed by local evolutionary processes, thereby acting as a change agent in less developed contexts and speeding up the evolution of the local environment as well as of its own subsidiary (Thorelli, 1966; Ohmae, 1990; Kwok and Tadesse, 2006).[1] Many critics of the MNE, in contrast, see it as the organizational equivalent of an invasive species, sucking scarce resources away from local organizations and imposing alien patterns on its local operations and on its suppliers, customers, and even regulators, thereby eroding the resilience and variety of the local organizational ecology and its local subunits (for example, Korten, 1998; Klein, 2000).

Both images portray the MNE as a coherent system. The image of the MNE as a unit in a larger evolutionary system or set of evolutionary systems (country-level, regional, global) that shape its organization and its activities has long been a familiar presence in the debates over the nature and impact of the MNE. Images of MNEs as powerful actors in a larger evolutionary system have also emerged, especially in studies of the impact of foreign direct investment on host societies. The image of the MNE as itself an evolutionary system has been less explicit but equally influential. With its subunits embedded to varying degrees in an array of different local environments, the MNE has in the past two decades increasingly been portrayed as cultivating internal variation and innovations, reducing that variety by selecting the most promising

Images of the Multinational Firm   Edited by Simon Collinson and Glenn Morgan
© 2009 John Wiley & Sons, Ltd

and successful, and disseminating and retaining selected innovations and processes across its subunits over time. Each MNC subsidiary is portrayed as trying to be an 'insider in two systems,' coping with potentially competing selection pressures from the external local environment and the internal MNC system (Westney 1988, 1993; Rosenzweig and Singh, 1991; Kostova and Roth, 2002).

Much of this work has taken an evolutionary model for granted and has focused on understanding what is happening in MNE organization rather than on developing or testing an explicit model. Making the evolutionary model of the MNE more explicit, examining the assumptions on which it is grounded, and drawing more systematically on recent developments in organization theory can provide a stronger theoretical anchor for MNE research, help to find an effective balance between the drive to understand what is happening in the complex organizational world of the MNE and the need to explain why it is happening, and may even integrate apparently unrelated areas of study in past and current research on the MNE.

Evolutionary Perspectives on Organizations

The fundamental feature of evolutionary theories is the basic assumption that change in organizations takes place through processes of variation, selection and retention in a bounded system (though the boundaries may be fuzzy and mutable). Over the last three decades, much evolutionary theory has focused on external systems above the individual organization that shape its structure and activities: the population, the community, the institutional field. However, a considerable amount of work has also examined the organization itself as a bounded evolutionary system in which change is shaped by internal variation, selection and retention processes, which may interact with the external environment processes but do not necessarily mirror them.

Evolutionary perspectives in organization studies come in many variants, in large part because, in the words of Howard Aldrich: 'Evolutionary models are not causal, in the sense that they do not specify the engines driving variation, selection, and retention' (Aldrich, 1999: 42). It is precisely the specification of the 'engines' that differentiates the major theories of organizational change, and the fierce debates that have roiled Organization Theory have focused primarily on selection processes: in particular, what is being selected (for example, organizational forms, subunits, transactions, routines) and what the criteria for selection are (for example, efficiency, legitimacy, political interests). Fundamentally, however, virtually all theories of organizational change, from the many stage models of Organization Development (starting with Lewin, 1947)[2] to Transaction Cost Analysis and institutional theory, build implicitly or explicitly on the evolutionary framework of variation, selection and retention (Aldrich, 1999: ch. 3; Greve, 2002). A recent review of evolutionary theory went so far as to assert that 'evolutionary arguments are uncontroversial in organization theory and do not need to be presented polemically' (Greve, 2002: 568).

This may be true in much of organization theory; however, the popular imagery associated with evolutionary models in the social sciences in general, which is the legacy of the Social Darwinism of a century ago, is anything but uncontroversial (Aldrich, 1999: 21). That imagery has cast a shadow over the evolutionary perspectives in organization studies, although most recent contributions have worked hard to dispel it. In particular, two powerful images cling to evolutionary models, however explicitly they are repudiated. One is the image of the deterministic 'survival of the fittest'—the 'fittest' being selected by an inevitable, unerring and impersonal force. The other is of inevitable upward progress and improvement (an image etched in memory, perhaps, by the evolutionary tree of life presented in so many high school classes, depicting the progress through the millennia from the single-celled organism to the triumphant emergence of *homo sapiens*).

Several significant developments in evolutionary perspectives in organization studies challenge the relevance of this imagery to the work now being done on organizations. One development is the widespread recognition that evolutionary processes occur at multiple levels, and that therefore evolutionary theories need not – indeed should not – assert that any one particular level alone has primacy in explaining outcomes.[3] Evolutionary perspectives today recognize several system levels at which all three basic evolutionary processes occur: the larger systems composed of many organizations (populations, communities, institutional fields, ecologies, markets); the organization itself; and the nested levels within organizations (see for example the chapters on evolution by Warglien, Amburgey and Singh, and Greve in Baum's 2002 *Blackwell Companion to Organizations*). As the organizational theories at each level have expanded their research scope, there is growing recognition that a major challenge for organization studies is to examine how evolutionary processes at these different levels interact (Warglien, 2002). There is little empirical basis for the assumption that evolutionary processes at each level mirror those above them – although this assumption is made all too often. Multiple interacting levels of evolutionary processes make simple deterministic models of evolution impossible to sustain; as Marshall Meyer pointedly observed: 'What people adapt to within organizations may be very different from what organizations adapt to in environments' (1991: 110). Those who have studied MNCs from the subsidiary viewpoint would hasten to agree.

The recognition of interacting levels of evolutionary processes that do not simply replicate processes at other levels underlies the growing popularity of the concept of 'co-evolution': evolutionary processes at one system level both influence and are influenced by processes at another level. Joel Baum and Jitendra Singh have advocated the value of co-evolution for addressing

'. . . organizational problems that share the stylized structure in which an organization (or a group of organizations) responds to elements in its environment (or another organization), and the environment, in turn, changes in response to the focal organization's actions. Such patterns may exist in the domains of public policy and regulation, technological innovation, and mutual competition, to name but a few'. (Baum and Singh, 1994b: 399)

Their list of relevant domains coincides remarkably with some of the core concerns of studies of the MNC.

In addition, there is growing recognition that even on a single level of analysis, there may well be multiple 'engines' of evolutionary processes – and most importantly, of selection, which has been the focus of most of the organization-environment models. Population ecology, for example, has focused on resource efficiency as the principal criterion for selection, institutional theory on legitimacy, and resource dependence and political economy approaches on power and interests. More and more theorists, however, have been willing to concede that rather than selection being determined by a single 'engine', all three – resource efficiency, legitimacy and interests – coexist as valid, often simultaneous, and sometimes competing selection criteria (Carroll, 1988; Nelson, 1993; Amburgey and Singh, 2002).

Greater attention to the interactions of evolutionary processes across levels, co-evolution, and the co-existence of multiple evolutionary drivers has become more pronounced at all levels of analysis. One consequence is the recognition of the prevalence of 'weak selection' in organizational evolution (Nelson, 1993: 112; Amburgey and Singh, 2002). Strong selection means that 'species'– organizations or organizational patterns – that do not fit the selection criteria are 'selected out' and eliminated (the stance of early population ecology). Weak selection, in contrast, means that organizations that do not fit the selection criteria can learn and adapt, a process that itself can lead to further variation, or that although they suffer disadvantages in acquiring resources compared to their better adapted competitors, they continue to survive. Within the organization, weak selection means that certain organizational patterns may not be positively selected, but are not actively selected out. They continue to survive, often in protected niches within the organization, and are therefore available as variations to which the organization may turn when conditions change.

At the organizational level, still another development separates today's evolutionary models from the deterministic imagery of Social Darwinism: growing attention to the processes of variation and retention, as well as a more detailed look at selection processes. In work on evolution at the macro level (meaning the interactions between organizations and environments), the primary focus of attention has been on selection, particularly on selection outcomes and selection criteria, while both variation and retention have been neglected (Greve, 2002). Variation in particular has received little attention and is often quickly dismissed as a random process not susceptible to systematic study (Nelson, 1993: 114; Greve, 2002: 558). Analysing a multi-unit organization such as the MNE as an evolutionary system, however, immediately makes variation a process that is both more interesting theoretically and more amenable to empirical analysis. The study of innovation in organizations, for example, can quickly be assimilated to the 'variation-selection-retention' framework, and many of the key research questions in this literature address variation processes: which actors (individuals and subunits) within an organization originate new products or processes? How do these variations get developed? How much variation occurs within an organization before selection processes winnow out and 'select for' one variation over another (see for example the work on the 'ambidextrous organization' that manages to maintain two internal selection regimes, one for exploitation and one for exploration)[4] ?

Robert Burgelman's work on strategy proposes a useful framing for discussions of intra-organizational variation when he distinguishes between 'autonomous' and 'induced' strategic processes. The first type of process is driven by subunits or individual managers within the organization; it does not fit the organization's recognized 'strategy' and introduces variation into the organization (Burgelman, 1990: 167). The second, 'induced', strategic process, is driven by top management, in line with the organizational strategy, and while it may introduce variations in products and processes, Burgelman does not define this as variation, since the 'selection targets' in his evolutionary model are strategies, not products and processes. This basic distinction between autonomous and induced variation processes has long been used implicitly in studies of innovation in the MNE, and this is discussed further in the following section. Indeed the relationship between the two is integral to studies of innovation in MNEs, where subsidiary initiatives that expand local capabilities can either continue as 'autonomous' processes or be identified by the HQ as a corporate resource – for example, as a 'centre of excellence' – in which further innovation is 'induced' and funded by HQ (see Frost et al., 2002).

This raises the issue of how to frame selection processes within an organization. At the macro-organizational level, the analysis of selection processes has focused on selection outcomes (for example, organizational founding and death rates and density in population ecology, diffusion or rejection of organizational patterns in institutional theory), and on selection criteria (such as efficiency, legitimacy or serving the interests of powerful social actors). When the level of analysis shifts to the individual organization, however, selection is harder to portray as an impersonal force, and analysts pay more attention to selection agents: that is, which social actors are doing the selecting. Researchers are also confronted with a wider array of potential selection targets. Nelson and Winter (1982) and Howard Aldrich (1999) are among the many evolutionary theorists who focus on 'routines and competences' as the key units for analysis, but a wider array of organizational features is amenable to evolutionary analysis as targets of selection processes: for example, strategies, product and process innovations, change initiatives, subunits, linking mechanisms, even individuals. These four aspects of the selection process (criteria, outcomes, agents and targets) can be termed the organization's selection regime.

Retention processes have suffered less from neglect in macro-organizational theory than variation – although some models do take them for granted as implicit in the selection process (e.g. Nelson, 1993). After all, if what has been selected by the environment is not retained in the organizations operating in that environment, how would one know that selection had taken place? Early versions of population ecology went so far as to assert that selection is the only way 'fit' organizational forms are maintained in a population (Hannan and Freeman, 1977). Today, most macro-organizational theorists agree that organizational patterns are also retained in a community, field or population by the emulation of more successful organizations by less successful ones, through adaptation and learning. These processes have become central to the study of retention.[5]

Despite some attempts to identify the organizational equivalent of genes in biological organisms,[6] evolutionary models in organization studies at all levels have recognized that retention is much more problematic in social systems than in biology. Macro-organizational theorists acknowledge that, while some retention processes may involve collective action within the population or field (for example, agreement on standards or regulations), most retention processes operate within the individual organization. At this intra-organizational level, several approaches not widely associated with evolutionary models address the issue of retention of organizational patterns over time, including the literatures on culture and socialization, organizational learning and capabilities.

What March (1994) has called 'the evolution of evolution' has made the evolutionary model an increasingly helpful paradigm in the analysis of change in large complex organizational systems. And the scale, scope and complexity of the MNE make it a prime candidate for analysis as an evolutionary system. As writers of international business textbooks are much given to pointing out, the annual sales of many of the world's major MNEs exceed the GDP of many of the countries in which they operate (see, for example, Bartlett *et al.*, 2004: 4). Many more MNEs that don't make the Global Fortune 500 list cover a considerable range of countries and businesses, and constitute complex systems by any definition. Moreover, the analysis of change over time has been at the heart of studies of the MNE, beginning with the internationalization process itself, and including such core topics of research as changing modes of international operations, changing structures and modes of coordination and control, and changing subsidiary roles and capabilities. An evolutionary perspective underlies much of the analysis of the MNE.

Evolutionary Perspectives on MNEs

The amount of theory and research in the study of MNEs that is explicitly associated with evolutionary models is not large. The longest lived models associated with an evolutionary perspective are the stage models of the development of the MNE over time (see Westney and Zaheer, 2001 for a more detailed discussion). The early models (e.g. Perlmutter, 1969 on changing mind-sets; Johansen and Vahlne, 1977 on the incremental processes of internationalization; Stopford and Wells, 1972 and Daniels *et al.*, 1984 on organization designs) and some later ones (e.g. Contractor *et al.*, 2003) located the drivers of change within the MNE itself, and saw expanding international reach and experience as the principal force moving the organization from one stage to the next. The models of the 1980s, still widely used today, saw the external environment as driving the change from stage to stage (Bartlett and Ghoshal, 1989; Prahalad and Doz, 1987). One feature that the models shared, however, was a linear model of evolution, from less to more advanced, a framing that the evolutionary theorists in the 1990s were increasingly concerned to disavow (see March, 1993; Aldrich, 1999, ch. 2).

However, the economic models of the MNE that have dominated the IB field have been implicitly rather than explicitly evolutionary. They have focused on two elements of the selection regime: selection criteria and selection targets. Indeed, they have focused on a single selection criterion, efficiency: in the words of Jean-Francois Hennart: 'An MNE will expand abroad (will organize interdependencies through hierarchy, i.e. through employment contracts) when it can organize interdependencies between agents in different countries more efficiently than markets' (Hennart, 2001: 136). The selection targets that these theories address have steadily expanded over time, from locations and functions like manufacturing to R&D, alliances and business networks, but the efficiency criterion remains constant. The selection agents are, usually implicitly, top managers (indeed, a recent test of economic versus experience theories of internationalization by Buckley et al. (2007) made this assumption explicit). Selection outcomes, the fourth element of the selection regime, have tended to assume strong selection: categorical variables such as entry/non-entry into specific locations, or choice of mode (either/or on joint ventures versus wholly-owned subsidiaries) are the most common focus of inquiry. Variation and retention have received less systematic attention. Variation seems largely to be external (opportunities and threats in the environment). Retention has received more attention in Transaction Cost analyses than from other variants of these economic theories, and has focused on incentives and monitoring as the key retention processes.

This paradigm has produced a large body of very informative research over the past four decades, but it is not without its critics. One critic has been Bruce Kogut, who has produced a significant body of work that takes an explicitly evolutionary approach to the MNE. It may be worth noting that Kogut's work with Udo Zander (Zander and Kogut, 1993, 1995) stands as one of the few IB research contributions cited by organization theorists working on the evolutionary paradigm.[7] Kogut has built on Nelson and Winter's framing from *An Evolutionary Theory of Economic Change* (1982), which identified competences as the key target of selection processes, and routines and work processes as the key mechanisms for retention within the firm. Kogut's critique of standard theories of the MNE (e.g. 1993) provides an example of how an evolutionary framing can help in comparing different theories. Kogut is especially critical of those analyses based on a Transaction Cost model (that it is itself an evolutionary model is not always recognized by its proponents), and sees them as inadequate on several counts. First, they pay far too little attention to innovation, which Kogut treats as the central manifestation of variation in the MNE. He also takes issue with the identification in Transaction Cost models of the key criterion of selection as efficiency; for Kogut, it is (or should be) the enhancement of competitive capabilities. Finally, and perhaps most important, he challenges the TCM focus on incentives and monitoring as the key retention processes within organizations; for Kogut, those keys are routines and embedded knowledge. Kogut gives the processes of retention much more attention than they often receive in studies of change in the MNE, defining retention in Aldrich's terms: 'Retention occurs when selected variations are preserved, duplicated, or otherwise reproduced so that the selected activities are repeated on future occasions or the selected structures appear again in future generations' (Aldrich, 1999: 30). For Kogut, the MNE's retention processes, which shape its capacity to extend its organizational systems across borders, become a critically important element of his model.

In general, however, most of the work on the MNE has tended to follow the pattern that Henrich Greve identified as widespread in organization studies in general:

> 'Organizational scholars incorporate evolutionary arguments into other theoretical perspectives, which have given evolutionary theory a position of being used frequently in a subsidiary role but rarely as a main theory.' (Greve, 2002: 568)

Evolutionary 'arguments', in the sense of providing underlying assumptions, have been pervasive in the study of MNE organization. The fundamental questions about the MNE as an organization can be framed as 'who does what, where, why, and how does that change over time?' The first three variables – who (which subunits), what (activities), and where (locations) – are at any single point in time the outcomes of evolutionary processes of variation, selection and retention. And the why can be seen as the selection criteria used by the MNE system and subsystems, and as requiring analysis of the interaction between the MNE system and its internal subsystems on the one hand and with its external environment on the other, especially on selection processes.

That the implicit use of an evolutionary perspective on the MNE has so often centred on selection may well be due to the fact that internal variation is often taken for granted in MNE studies, not because it is seen as random, as it has been in macro-level studies, but because it is usually seen as an inherent attribute of the MNE given its multiple locations, which provide exposure to varied environmental stimuli. Indeed, of all kinds of organization, the MNE seems most prone to generating internal variations. The potential competitive advantage of the MNE's internal variety has become a truism in the IB field: internal variety provides stimuli and resources for innovation, and gives the MNE resilience in the face of changes in the external environment.[8] One of the apparent paradoxes of the MNE is that in order to take advantage of its internal variety, its management spends considerable attention and effort trying to reduce it, being exhorted by consultants and academics alike to disseminate 'best practice' throughout the organization – that is, to select the most successful variations and select out existing variants to replace them with the more successful. Many empirical studies of the MNE, however, when translated into an evolutionary framing, share the problem of much of the empirical organizational research that implicitly rather than explicitly uses this approach: they carefully collect data on what they identify as selection outcomes, but provide few detailed examinations of how selection processes actually operate within the MNE.

There are, fortunately, notable exceptions. Two richly detailed empirical studies, undertaken over a decade apart, provide two quite different pictures of the evolutionary processes inside the large diversified MNE: Bartlett and Ghoshal's *Managing Across Borders* (1989), and Peer Hull Kristensen and Jonathan Zeitlin's *Local Players in Global Games* (2005). While neither adopted an explicitly evolutionary model, both studies can be readily mapped onto an evolutionary framework. Much extremely valuable information is lost in doing so, but both the ubiquity and the utility of evolutionary models in the study of the MNE are illuminated by such mapping.

The two studies have much in common, in terms of focus. The variations on which both studies concentrate are product and process innovations and the distinctive subsidiary capabilities that nourish them within the MNE. Both identify the MNE subsidiary as a locus of innovation, and examine whether a particular subsidiary innovation is 'selected' and picked up in the larger MNE system, and how – and whether – the innovations are sustained ('retained') in that larger system. Both also see variations in subsidiary capabilities as a key resource for the MNE system. Both devote considerable attention to the processes by which subsidiary capabilities are recognized and fostered ('selected') in the larger MNE system, and the processes by which they can be deliberately undercut ('selected out') or eroded inadvertently ('not retained'). Finally, both provide detailed analysis of the interactions between the variation, selection and retention patterns of the corporate headquarters and those of the subsidiaries, providing insights onto one of the core challenges in contemporary evolutionary: understanding 'how processes at different levels relate to each other' (Warglien, 2002: 104).

Chris Bartlett and Sumantra Ghoshal's nine-company analysis, presented in their book and in numerous journal articles in the late 1980s and early 1990s, is probably the most influential and widely referenced study of the MNE ever published. Both authors were anchored in the fields of international business and strategy, and in the Preface to their book they set out clearly what drove them to undertake such an extensive study, involving interviews in nine companies in three industries, between 1984 and 1986:

'Our objective was to gain a rich understanding of the organizational and administrative tasks facing managers in companies with worldwide operations in a time of major environmental change ... More specifically, we hoped to reach some understanding of the organizational characteristics required to manage in the emerging environment. And finally, we wanted to extract some guidance on how companies might develop and manage such characteristics.' (Bartlett and Ghoshal 1989: x[9])

The underlying framework of evolutionary thinking is obvious from this statement: MNE organizations face a changing external environment, which has altered the selection pressures on the MNE, and MNE managers can, with guidance, alter the evolutionary processes within their organization to cope more effectively with those pressures.

The Kristensen and Zeitlin study is much more recent, and it has yet to have the impact it deserves in the IB community, perhaps not only because it is so recent but also because the authors are sociologists whose previous (and considerable) body of research has not been in the IB field but has focused on 'the historical development, internal dynamics, and innovative capabilities of industrial districts or regional clusters organized around flexibly specialized networks of small and medium-sized firms' (Kristensen and Zeitlin, 2005: xiii). They were drawn to their research on three plants in a single MNE (APV, the world's largest producer of food and drink processing systems) serendipitously, discovering at a conference that each had an interest in one of the plants that had been acquired by a British MNE, APV, which had through acquisitions become the world's largest firm in food and drink processing systems.[10] As they say in their book: 'this was too good an opportunity to pass up' (p. xvi), and from early 1995 until the parent firm was acquired by another, larger MNE in 1997, they conducted further field studies in those two plants, a third plant in the UK, and the corporate headquarters.

Kristensen and Zeitlin were themselves very much aware of the Bartlett and Ghoshal model of the transnational as the next stage of evolution of the MNE. Moreover, they found that the executives at APV headquarters were also aware of it and tried to adopt many of the steps that those authors had recommended to guide MNEs toward the transnational model. APV did not, however, succeed in getting the anticipated outcomes from those efforts. Both because of their observations of APV and because of their shared backgrounds in the study of the embedding of firms in local clusters,[11] Kristensen and Zeitlin framed the issues that anchored their study very differently from Bartlett and Ghoshal:

> 'What happens when a number of previously autonomous firms from different countries, each with their own historically constituted identities, routines, and capabilities, come together inside a single multinational company (MNC)? And what happens when each of the participants in this new global game, including top management at the corporate headquarters, starts to play by the rules of their national business system, mobilizing local allies and resources to defend and advance their position within the MNC? Can a unified cooperative game be established that positively advances the development of the multi-national as a whole, and if so, through what organizational mechanisms? Or may misunderstandings and the unintended consequences of strategic inter-action among the players lead instead to endemic conflict and disintegration?' (2005: xiii)

Kristensen and Zeitlin's 'new global game' was not the external global competition within industries that the term customarily invokes; instead, it referred to the MNE's internal evolutionary system. Transposed into evolutionary terminology, their ques-tions asked what happens when several organizations, each of which has developed its own processes of variation, selection and retention that have co-evolved with its distinctive environment, are incorporated into a larger organizational system that attempts to impose an overall selection regime on them. Kristensen and Zeitlin raised the possibility of two different outcomes. If an emergent evolutionary system develops that accommodates a variety of internal subsystems and allows positive interactions across them, the MNE can flourish; if the different systems compete and no coherent system of selection and retention emerges, the MNE will not survive. It will, presumably, be 'selected out' by the larger environment.

The subsidiary was a critically important level of analysis in both studies. What was signified by the term 'subsidiary', however, differed significantly. Bartlett and Ghoshal explicitly defined their primary unit of analysis as the 'national subsidiary';[12] for Kristensen and Zeitlin, it was the manufacturing plant and its co-located engineering organization. The difference was due partly to the difference in orientation of the researchers, but more importantly to changes in the MNE that occurred between the mid-1980s, when Bartlett and Ghoshal conducted their fieldwork, and the latter half of the 1990s, when Kristensen and Zeitlin did theirs.

The national subsidiary had tended to be the dominant organizational (or in the terminology of this approach, evolutionary) subunit within MNEs until well into the 1980s. In 1980, for example, a study of MNE subsidiaries in Brazil took the country subsidiary form for granted, and reported that 'whether by design or by almost subconscious evolution, the structures of most subsidiaries in our survey reflected a mirror image, reduced in size, of the parent company' (Hulbert and Brandt, 1980: 27). By the mid-1980s, however, many diversified MNEs had adopted global business divisions. Indeed in five of the nine companies in the Bartlett-Ghoshal study, their research focused on one division among several in the company (in Matsushita, Philips, NEC, General Electric and ITT), although this was not explicitly acknowledged in their text. This created some ambiguity about whether they were focusing on that part of the 'national subsidiary' that covered a certain division's product line, or whether the MNE had incorporated different subsidiaries for each major division. If the latter was the case, one can certainly find some justification for their ignoring the distinction: these were very large business divisions covering an extensive array of products, and they tended to have as their second-order design parameter the country unit, so the researchers felt justified in continuing to employ the term 'national subsidiary'. This created, however, some ambiguity in their discussion of the 'Headquarters' role, which in some instances seemed to refer to the division headquarters, and in some to the corporate headquarters.

For an explicitly evolutionary approach, these distinctions cannot be set aside so easily: the business divisions constitute another set of evolutionary subsystems within the MNE system, whose interactions with that larger system are potentially problematic. Bartlett and Ghoshal did address this issue, in their own way, and their approach is theoretically most interesting. For them, the national subsidiary was only one of three subsystems below the corporate level; business and function were the others. Business, geography/country, and function are the classic dimensions of organizational structure, but Bartlett and Ghoshal saw them not as structures but as 'perspectives' and as organizational roles that shaped managers' decision criteria and induced them to favour certain outcomes over others. In other words, the three dimensions are not simply design parameters but entail strong cultural and political aspects that drive behaviours.

This portrayal actually fits neatly onto a model of three evolutionary subsystems. Each 'dimension' – geography, business and function – fosters a distinctive kind of variation: geographic management encourages variations stimulated by local, 'country by country' (1989: 157) opportunities; business management, variations that reduce costs; functional management, variations that expand expertise and extend functional capabilities. Each constitutes a distinctive selection regime, with the managers of the organizational subunits in charge of each dimension (business units managers, country managers, functional managers) acting as the selection agents. Bartlett and Ghoshal clearly identified the selection criterion for each with a particular selection criterion of the external environment: business with efficiency, geography with local responsiveness, and function with expertise and knowledge-sharing. Each therefore embodies within the MNE a selection regime whose key selection criterion matches one of the environmental forces that Bartlett and Ghoshal portrayed as driving the change to the transnational model.

This explains, at least in part, their strong resistance to identifying a structural solution for the transnational, which they saw as facing all three environmental pressures simultaneously. No single dimension of the organization could therefore be allowed to dominate the others consistently. The corporate executives who are the selection agents for the system as a whole should therefore have as their critical selection criterion a balancing of the three internal regimes over time and across issues, to enable the MNE system as a whole to succeed in the external environment. Whether a particular variation was selected out, selected for, or allowed to continue as a variation with just enough resources to survive was seen as shaped by the inter-actions between the corporate system and the business, geographic, and functional subsystems.

By the time Kristensen and Zeitlin embarked on their multi-subsidiary study, however, the 'subsidiary' had been fragmented by the widespread elimination of the national subsidiaries in favour of smaller, more focused units. Julian Birkinshaw has described this pattern as follows:

'Most MNEs have moved towards some variant of the global business unit structure in their international operations, and a corresponding dilution in the power and responsibilities of the country manager. The result is that the national subsidiary no longer exists in most developed countries. Instead, there is a series of discrete value-adding activities (a sales operation, a manufacturing plant, an R&D centre), each of which reports through its own business unit or functional line.' (Birkinshaw, 2001: 381)

By 2001, Birkinshaw defined the subsidiary on which MNE research should focus as 'a discrete value-adding activity outside the home country, in other words at a level below the national subsidiary' (Birkinshaw, 2001: 381).

One of the first MNEs to move toward this disaggregated model was ABB (see accompanying case). It kept the country subsidiary as a formal structure, but the operating unit that formed the fundamental building block of the organization was the 'discrete value-adding activity . . . below the national subsidiary', usually centred on a production site, which reported to a global business manager as well as to the country manager. Ironically, given that in the early 1990s, Bartlett and Ghoshal presented ABB as the MNE that was the closest approximation to the transnational ideal type in their experience, the influence of the country manager waned from the mid-1990s on, and the much-vaunted balance of business, geography and function eroded. The geographic side of the matrix was formally weakened in 1998, and eliminated in a further reorganization in 2001.

The pursuit of efficiency was a major factor in this change in many MNEs, but so too was the effort of MNE top management to eliminate the power of the country managers to block corporate change initiatives, which top management believed were necessitated by the external competitive environment. Lew Gerstner of IBM articulated the perception of many CEOs in the early 1990s when he describes what he found on arriving at IBM as CEO in 1993 as 'powerful geographic fiefdoms with duplicate infrastructure in each country' (Gerstner, 2002: 42), and describes his subsequent actions as 'I declared war on the geographic fiefdoms' (p. 86). An explicitly evolutionary framing of the structural change to disaggregated focused subunits might be as follows: MNE top management (the primary selection agents of the corporate system) came to believe that shifts in the external competitive environment demanded internal changes to improve the fit between the MNE organization and that environment. The changes they selected at the corporate/system level were being blocked ('selected out') by a powerful subsystem, the national subsidiaries, and so the corporate selection regime selected out the national subsidiaries. It thereby eliminated this subsystem level within the MNE, and focused instead on what had been the lower level subsystems of the 'discrete value-adding activities (a sales operation, a manufacturing plant, an R&D centre)' (Birkinshaw, 2001: 381, quoted above). The corporate selection agents (top management) expected to be able to align the selection regimes at this subsystem level more quickly with the selection processes of the HQ, because the smaller, more focused units were less buffered from HQ influence. They controlled fewer resources, and had less individual power and influence, and less visibility at the national level in their local environments. This change in the structure of the MNE subsystems also facilitated the absorption of acquired companies, which, whatever their formal structure, could relatively quickly be disaggregated into focused operating units. This structure also made it much easier to sell non-core businesses. Both processes were increasingly common in MNEs during the 1990s, and it is no accident that the company that was one of the pioneers of the new model, ABB, was itself the product of a cross-border merger and expanded rapidly internationally through acquisition.

Another significant difference between the subsidiaries of the Bartlett and Ghoshal study of those of the later Kristensen and Zeitlin work was that Bartlett and Ghoshal had taken it for granted that the national subsidiaries in their study had developed organically over time, within the parent company. The MNE studied by Kristensen and Zeitlin, in contrast, had expanded by acquisition, usually by buying plants from companies that were selling off non-core businesses. All three of the plants in their study had been founded in the last quarter of the nineteenth century and had undergone several changes of ownership before being acquired by APV (the Wisconsin plant in 1973, the Danish plant in 1985 and the UK plant in 1989). When Bartlett and Ghoshal's book was published in 1989, their companies represented the dominant mode of organization and expansion of the MNE of the time. When Kristensen and Zeitlin published their study in 2005, after the world had witnessed a decade of accelerating cross-border M&A, APV was arguably the more representative model of the MNE.

Interestingly enough, Bartlett and Ghoshal published a revised second edition of *Managing Across Borders* in 1998, which had two new chapters that incorporated material from their studies of ABB, Electrolux and GE in the intervening decade. Even though all three companies had exemplified the shift from national to focused subsidiaries and to international expansion by M&A instead of organic growth, neither of the chapters explicitly referred to these developments. Instead, in the first of the new chapters they elaborated on the roles of the country, business and functional managers, and they strengthened their insistence on the HQ need to balance their influence, thereby reinforcing their identification of three evolutionary subsystems. The other new chapter described three additional processes (rationalization, revitalization and regeneration) to be managed by the corporate managers, each of which could be viewed as an evolutionary process of variation, selection and retention. This may have been their mode of acknowledging the increased complexity of the 1990s MNE.

This left unanswered whether they continued to view the subsidiary as embodying the selection criterion of local responsiveness. However, elements of the research on APV suggest that they might well have done so with some reason. Kristensen and Zeitlin suggested that the MNE that has grown by acquisition faces problems that differ considerably from those of the MNEs studied by Bartlett and Ghoshal:

> 'When the HQ managers at APV introduced the new managerial principles advocated by Bartlett and Ghoshal, these could not be seen as an incremental reform of a pre-existing system. They represented instead a radical transformation of many distinct local systems, which had very different effects in different parts of the MNC ... many different administrative heritages and forms of coordination of which its top managers had little knowledge.' (Kristensen and Zeitlin, 2005: 193)

This suggests that, in removing the country organization level, corporate management had not necessarily increased their capacity for re-aligning the evolutionary processes of the subsidiaries.

Kristensen and Zeitlin's vivid analyses of the distinctive processes of these acquired units provide further reasons why, in APV, larger numbers of smaller and more focused subsidiaries below the country level did not make it easier for corporate HQ to align the locally differentiated evolutionary processes of these subsystems with its own evolutionary processes. Kristensen and Zeitlin identify most of these factors with the selection regime at HQ rather than the subsystem. The larger number of subsidiaries, widely dispersed geographically, made it difficult for the selection agents at HQ to understand the capabilities and selection processes of each of them well, a problem exacerbated in APV (as in many MNEs today) by the relatively brief length of any assignment of high-potential managers sent to the subsidiaries on their route to the corporate offices (see ch. 9 in Kristensen and Zeitlin for a detailed discussion). In addition, the environmental signals with which HQ managers were trying to align the corporate selection regime had the features recognized by current evolutionary theory: multiple selection criteria, changing short-term salience of those criteria and weak signals. Although the financial organizations in the environment applied strong pressure to APV to deliver greater profitability, those demands were as much for likely future profits as for immediate profits, and the announcement of new programmes and the replacement of corporate leaders with new faces at the top were read as signals of improving prospects for profitability and rewarded with a rise in the share price. This led to rapidly changing and inconsistent targets and criteria in the corporate selection regime, which, in Kristensen and Zeitlin's portrayal, combined with the relatively uninformed selection agents, led to arbitrary targets and unanticipated outcomes, when the selection regime actually achieved an outcome in the face of resistance from the subsidiaries.

The analysis of product and process innovations (variation) in the two studies reinforces the contrast between Bartlett and Ghoshal's image of the corporate HQ carefully guiding the evolutionary processes in the MNE and Kristensen and Zeitlin's portrayal of APV, where 'the HQ of the MNC as an absentee owner intervenes blindly in this [innovation] process, and risks destroying its own assets' (2005: 241). Bartlett and Ghoshal identify four types of innovation processes: local-for-local (when a subsidiary innovates for a local market), central-for-local (when the corporate level function innovates for adoption throughout the MNE subsystems), locally-leveraged (when a local-for-local innovation is selected by the HQ for adoption throughout the MNE subsystems) and globally-linked (when the corporate level initiates an innovation process whose activities are distributed across several subsidiaries). Bartlett and Ghoshal assert that all four types should be fostered within the MNE, but see the latter two as distinctively 'transnational'. To adopt Burgelman's categories, the first and third are 'autonomous' and the second and fourth 'induced'.

In APV, the variations induced by top management provided Kristensen and Zeitlin with failure cases, not success stories. The successful innovations they present were overwhelmingly dominated by subsidiary initiatives ('autonomous processes'), some 'local-for-local', in the Bartlett-Ghoshal categories, but some 'local-for-global', where the innovations were selected for wider adoption not by the HQ but by other subsidiaries. Innovations were not induced by the corporate HQ, or at least not effectively induced.[13] When the attempt was made, subsidiaries circumvented its efforts and captured the initiative, often winning *ex post* endorsement from the corporate HQ. This suggests that to Albert Hirschman's classic list of responses to hierarchical fiat – exit, voice and loyalty – we need to add a fourth: subversion.

Both studies focus on selection processes regarding one other variation: subsidiary roles. Bartlett and Ghoshal make the allocation of differentiated subsidiary roles one of the central functions of the corporate level. In evolutionary terms, variations arise in all subsidiaries, but in some, those variations have value for others in the system, and corporate management fosters variations in those subsidiaries by allocating them a 'Strategic Leader' role, based on one internal factor (the organizational capabilities of the unit) and one external (the 'strategic importance of the environment', presumably as calibrated by the corporate selection agents). In other subsidiaries, where both the capabilities of the subsidiary and the importance of the environment are low, their capacity to generate and sustain variations is deliberately constrained (the 'Implementer' role) by giving them very few resources and limiting the range of their activities. 'Contributors' are allowed to foster variations in a narrowly defined range, because their organizational capabilities are significant although the importance of their environment is not. And 'Black Holes' lack the capacity to generate variations, because the organizational units are small relative to the significance of their environments, and the corporate level tries to enhance their capabilities as quickly as possible. Of course, the evaluation of the subsidiary capabilities and the 'strategic importance of the environment' are selection criteria defined by corporate HQ (or by the consultants they hire to do it for them), and are open to contestation by the subsidiaries themselves (an issue not specifically addressed by Bartlett and Ghoshal, but further developed in Birkinshaw and Hood (1998a, 1998b) and in chapters in Morgan et al., 2001).

According to Kristensen and Zeitlin, APV corporate HQ tried to pursue this variation-fostering and variation-constraining role, but unsuccessfully. The problems were two-fold: its lack of understanding of the organizational capabilities of the subsidiaries meant that it misallocated roles; and the capabilities of the designated Strategic Leader subsidiaries were eroded by the allocation of their scarce human resources to support other subsidiaries in the system. The HQ did indeed act in a variation-constraining role, but that was an unintended consequence of certain selection processes, such as across-the-board cuts in head count that resulted in the dismissal of valuable, newly trained younger workers, and the selling off of profitable product lines that had synergies with the technical capabilities of certain local subsidiaries but fell outside the current list of 'core businesses' at the HQ level.

In summary, these two studies portray the evolutionary system of the MNE very differently, although neither is a conventional 'nested' hierarchical model of layers of subsystems under an overarching corporate system. For Bartlett and Ghoshal, the corporate system does indeed provide the dominant system-level selection regime, but under it are three parallel subsystems – business, geography/country and function – whose different variation, selection and retention processes are kept in balance by the corporate evolutionary processes. Kristensen and Zeitlin's image seems at first to be the more conventional HQ/corporate system level above a subsidiary subsystem level – but in fact their portrayal is the more radical. They portray the HQ not as the global arbiter of the subordinate systems but a separate subsystem embedded in its own local environment, London's financial centre, with a selection regime strongly shaped by that environment. It is the subsidiary, not the HQ, that in their model is trying to balance the competing selection regimes of business, geography and function – the subsidiary, which is local but not 'national', and which is more narrowly focused on a particular set of functions (in the case of their three research sites, on manufacturing and engineering). The system level, in this model, is not defined by the corporate level but by the emergent 'interactive game' among subsidiaries, which is beginning to constitute a network-level evolutionary system. It is not completely clear who the selection agents at this level are, but the account suggests that they are the middle-level managers in charge of the numerous business units focused on one line of products.

Bartlett and Ghoshal asserted that one of the hallmarks of the transnational is that the home country operations cease to be identified with the corporate headquarters and instead come to be considered as simply one subsidiary among many. Kristensen and Zeitlin suggest that, at least in some MNEs, the corporate headquarters itself may come to be considered as one unit in the interacting network that constitutes the MNE system.

Conclusion

Analysing the MNE as an evolutionary system involves looking closely at its internal subsystems. As some scholars have pointed out, treating the MNE as a unitary system does not do justice to the complexity of the MNE, nor does it facilitate understanding the dynamics of change in the MNE over time (see for example Morgan, 2001). Seeing the MNE in terms of evolutionary system and subsystems that co-evolve in interaction with each other, as well as with their differentiated environments, is one approach to addressing this complexity.

Identifying the system level of the MNE with its headquarters and the subsystem level with the subsidiaries may seem an obvious approach to developing an evolutionary model. After all, the terms 'HQ' and 'subsidiary' have been used across four decades of MNE research, even though, as we have seen, the boundaries of the 'subsidiary' have changed dramatically over that period, to the point that changing the terminology from 'subsidiary' to 'operating unit' might be preferable (although this removes the useful implication that the subunit is a legally distinct entity in a jurisdiction outside the home country, which is the case for the MNE). Moreover, the MNE headquarters has actively tried to shape the evolutionary processes of the MNE as a coherent system, from its creation of 'miniature replicas' of its home country operations in other countries in the first decades of post-war MNE expansion, through the resort to business divisions in the 1980s, the fragmentation of country subsidiaries in the 1990s, to the campaigns in so many contemporary MNEs to present a 'one company' image to the external environment. Today, we are increasingly seeing an organization design in which the MNE corporate 'executive team' includes executives representing businesses, regions and functions, presiding over organizational subsystems whose interactions at the subsidiary level are opaque to the outsider (and perhaps to some insiders). Each of these shifts can be seen as an effort by the corporate HQ to align the evolutionary processes of its subsidiaries more closely with its own.

However, it is far from clear that these efforts were successful. The relatively small number of empirical studies from the subsidiary viewpoint (e.g. Belanger *et al.*, 1998 and of course Kristensen and Zeitlin, 2005) suggest that there are widely varying degrees of alignment between subsidiary and corporate evolutionary processes. So too do the repeated efforts at the corporate level in many MNEs to change structures and mandate shared processes. The apparently restless pursuit of new change initiatives by MNE executives over the last two decades may owe as much to frustration with their inability to shape the variation, selection and retention processes of their geographically dispersed operating units as to an infatuation with staying abreast of management fads and fashions.

An important issue highlighted by the Kristensen and Zeitlin study is the extent to which operating units regard the corporate-level evolutionary processes as legitimate, especially the selection processes. This is not as constant as a narrow definition of hierarchy as conferring the uncontested right of fiat on the top level of an organization might assume. Kristensen and Zeitlin invoke Chester Barnard's concept of a 'zone of indifference' – the area in which the decisions of the manager are unquestioned by subordinates – to suggest that this area is problematic within MNEs. Subsidiary-level acceptance of corporate selection processes may vary considerably across MNEs (for example, those built through a rapid series of acquisitions may be less likely to accept changes in the HQ selection regime), across subsidiaries (for example, US subunits have tended to be particularly recalcitrant for non-US MNEs), and within any given MNE over time (for example, a corporate-level crisis may erode the legitimacy of previously strong HQ selection regimes, precisely at a point in time where the environment is pressing the MNE to respond quickly).

What might this lack of HQ internal legitimacy mean, in terms of the evolutionary model? The most obvious implication is that selection criteria would differ significantly between the subsidiary and the corporate level. Other implications are that efforts at strong selection at the corporate level become weak selection at the subsidiary level (often through 'ritual isomorphism' and simulated compliance), and that retention processes for corporate selections are weak. Systematic study of changes in the extent of subsidiary-level adoption of corporate initiatives over time and across initiatives might be very illuminating in terms of understanding the shifting patterns of interaction between corporate and subsidiary evolutionary processes.

A related area of inquiry stems from the recognition that the misalignment of the corporate and subsidiary evolutionary processes may benefit the system as a whole. A very different kind of 'zone of indifference' from that defined by Barnard is the fact that corporate selection regimes cannot and do not target all variations at the subsidiary level. Even though the corporate selection targets may be quite extensive, subsidiaries can and do become adept at identifying activities that contribute to their capabilities development that will be overlooked by – be 'under the radar' of – the corporate selection agents. Identifying the areas where variations arise at the subsidiary level that are ignored by the corporate selection regime provides another window for studying the co-evolution of system and subsystem in the MNE.

However, a further complication in aligning corporate and subsidiary evolutionary processes in MNEs is that they are not simply the hierarchically 'nested' systems portrayed in most theoretical models. Potentially, business, function and geography are parallel evolutionary subsystems situated below the corporate level (but represented in the corporate selection regime). These three dimensions constitute distinctive subsystems to the extent that they are embodied in organizational structures above the subsidiary level, which is the case for most but not all MNEs. A separate functional reporting structure (for example, R&D/technology development, manufacturing or Human Resources), which reports to the corporate level, has selection agents in positions of some authority and a distinctive set of criteria and targets. The outcomes of the functional selection regime may be considerably weaker than those of business or geography in an organizational structure that gives the subsidiary a direct reporting line to a business or region and a 'dotted line' to the functional organization, but it is unlikely to be inconsequential. Conceivably, an MNE could be organized with a purely business structure, such that the functions are contained entirely within the subsidiary, with no 'superstructure' of function or geography above that level. In that case, function and geography become subsystems of the subsidiary but not of the MNE as a whole. This would probably make the alignment of corporate and subsidiary evolutionary processes even more problematic, because the subsidiary processes would involve a 'balancing' (to use Bartlett and Ghoshal's phrase) across the three dimensions that has no analogue at the corporate level, which would be business-driven.

The evolutionary perspective reasserts the importance of organizational structure, which, although a continuous concern for MNE executives, has fallen somewhat out of favour as a focus of research in the international business field. Business, function and geography are not simply design parameters; the organizational structures in which they are embodied constitute evolutionary subsystems, with distinctive processes of variation, selection and retention that co-evolve with the corporate and subsidiary processes. Obviously, evolutionary models do not readily accommodate relatively simple causal models. The interactions between system and subsystems and across subsystems are emergent, and often indeterminate. Howard Aldrich has pointed out that:

'One of the most difficult principles of the evolutionary approach for social scientists to accept is the indeterminacy of outcomes ... Persons impatient with indeterminacy and unsympathetic to an evolutionary perspective often commit a retrospective fallacy, viewing earlier events as though they were controlled by their subsequent outcomes. At the time of the events' occurrence, however, many other outcomes were equally probable.'

Building evolutionary models of the MNE puts high value on the kinds of detailed case studies exemplified by those of Bartlett and Ghoshal and Kristensen and Zeitlin. It also values close observation over time: compare the rich insights into the Danish plant in Kristensen and Zeitlin, which cover over a decade of fieldwork and enable the researchers to interpret the retrospective stories of the participants, with the entirely retrospective accounts (however valuable) collected by Bartlett and Ghoshal. This is not to dismiss the great value of the Bartlett and Ghoshal case studies: their accounts are infinitely more revealing than the regression analyses based on their survey of 66 MNEs that helped them make their work known in numerous journal articles. In the last decade, more of this kind of case study work has emerged in Europe (see for example Bélanger et al., 1999; Jones 2003; Morgan et al., 2001), but it is a kind of research not currently favoured by the leading journals so highly regarded by the current selection regimes in academia. Academic researchers have their own evolutionary systems to worry about.

An evolutionary perspective provides both models and metaphors, and the latter are much more widely used than the former, though the former are potentially more valuable. As a metaphor in organization studies, 'evolutionary' should, based on current theory, invoke images of change processes that are path-dependent but not path-determined. Evolutionary models provide frameworks for systematic analysis of processes that are complex, multi-level and emergent. Both are invaluable resources in the study of the MNE.

CASE STUDY: ABB

'ABB...is, in our view, one of the best examples of a transnational company.' (Bartlett and Ghoshal, 1998: xii)

On 17 August 1987, Asea (a Swedish-based electrical engineering company) and Brown Boveri (BBC, one of its major competitors, based in Switzerland) announced a merger, creating ABB (Asea Brown Boveri), the largest European company in its industry. The companies shared certain features: both prided themselves on their strong engineering, and most managers had technical backgrounds. They differed in recent business performance, however: Asea, under its dynamic CEO, Percy Barnevik, had expanded rapidly and profits had tripled since he took over in 1980; BBC's sales were falling and it was barely profitable. Moreover, Asea had a Business Unit structure; BBC had a geographic structure with strong country organizations. One of the principal features of the new ABB was a business/geography matrix.

One of the first steps taken by the new top management was the radical reduction of the company headquarters. Within a few months, the headcount at corporate HQ in Zurich went from over 1300 professional staff to just over 100. Another crucial step was the design of a company-wide information system, called ABACUS, which collected monthly performance data from each unit, put it into a standard currency (US dollars), and compiled the data for HQ managers. Today, such systems are common, but in the early years of ABB, it gave top management a distinctive tool for monitoring the performance of the decentralized units.

The key unit of ABB's organization was the local operating company, called a *Business Unit* (BU). Much smaller than either the old BUs of Asea or the country subsidiary companies of the old BBC, the BU focused on a single business and market, incorporating both manufacturing and sales and marketing functions. ABB was among the first MNEs to move to such small, highly focused subsidiaries. In 1988, ABB had 800 BUs; by 1991, acquisitions expanded it to 1100. The average size of the BU was about 200 employees, with about $50 million in annual revenues. ABB factories, on which the BUs were centred, tended in most of its businesses to be smaller than those of its leading competitors. ABB's strategy was to concentrate on radically reducing costs in each site, reducing throughput times, maximizing design and production flexibility and focusing on local customer needs.

The heads of the BU had CEO-style responsibilities for operations, including investments below a certain level. They reported to two bosses: the Business Area Manager and the Country Manager. The Business Area (BA) manager was responsible for the worldwide strategy and performance of a business. BA management tasks included co-ordinating technology development, deciding on internal transfer prices, transferring expertise within the BA (disseminating internal 'best practice'), capturing economies of scale in purchasing and, perhaps most important, allocation of export markets to BUs. The country managers had profit-and-loss responsibilities for all ABB activities within their country. Their tasks were to realize the potential synergies across the various local ABB BUs, to present a 'local face' for major projects within that country, to provide the legal and political infrastructure for operations and to make sure that the local political and social environment was understood and considered appropriately in business area decisions.

Performance evaluations of the BU presidents were conducted by both the BA head and the country manager. Often these collided, and then the unit had to decide how to balance the potentially conflicting criteria. One of the key features of ABB's matrix was that, in contrast to many matrix structures where many positions have dual reporting responsibilities, ABB simplified its matrix so that only the top manager in each unit lived in the matrix world.

For the early years of the 1990s, ABB's organization was widely admired and envied, and held up as a model of the transnational and indeed of twenty-first century organization (the archetype of Barnevik's vision of a company that was simultaneously 'local and global, big and small, centralized and decentralized'). However, changes in the industry by the mid-1990s were straining the system. The privatization of utilities, the growing competition from increasingly capable local and global competitors and increasing demands from customers for integrated systems rather than components all meant that the pressures for efficiency and cross-border coordination were rising, and the value customers placed on local presence was decreasing. The BUs resisted the erosion of their autonomy, and it could be time-consuming and challenging to get them to cooperate in producing the complex integrated systems that customers were increasingly demanding. As margins became squeezed unit managers spent more and more time arguing about internal transfer prices, delaying the preparation of bids for contracts and giving ABB the reputation of being slow to deliver. ABB tried to expand its operations in the low-cost, fast-growing markets of Asia, using employees from its most capable established units to train local Asian managers, but such efforts strained the resources of those units, the 'lean management' of which was a significant factor in their high performance. Adding to the problems, the Asian financial crisis of 1997 cut deeply into the emerging markets on which ABB was relying for its growth.

In 2001, a new CEO called in a team of consultants and announced that ABB was going to change to a Front–Back structure, which had been developed by some IT companies and was widely hailed as the latest in organization design. However, the stock market crash of 2001, precipitated by crises in the IT world, added to ABB's woes, and its effects were exacerbated by the high levels of debt the company was carrying from its acquisitions, from the asbestos liabilities that came with its US acquisitions and from an outcry over discoveries of what had been (by European standards) an extremely lavish retirement package conferred on Barnevik and his successor. The new CEO lasted less than two years, and the new design was jettisoned by his replacement in favour of a simpler structure of two large business divisions. Some of the smaller units were also consolidated into larger subsidiaries. A third division, made up of ABB's businesses in the oil and gas sector, was groomed for a sell-off, to help reduce the company's debt. There seemed to be little sign of the Barnevik-era 'transnational' in what the business press increasingly referred to as 'ABB, the troubled Swedish-Swiss engineering company'.[14]

Questions

1. How would you explain the resistance of the BUs to pressures for greater integration from both the external environment and the internal BA in the latter half of the 1990s, in evolutionary terms?

2. The third dimension of Bartlett and Ghoshal's model, in addition to business and geography, is function. How do you see this evolutionary dimension being incorporated into Barnevik's model?

3. ABB under Barnevik was widely portrayed as the epitome of the twenty-first century transnational, effectively balancing business, function, and geography. By the early twenty-first century, however, the organizational structure that was credited with doing this so well had been abandoned. What external selection processes might account for this? How important were internal selection processes? To what extent can the function-oriented back end/customer-oriented front end structure be seen as an equally effective way of balancing the three subsystems?

4. What challenges might you foresee when corporate headquarters re-structured to impose a new selection regime on the subsystems (the division into the front–back structure).

Further Reading

For evolutionary theory

Aldrich, H. (1999) *Organizations Evolving.* London: Sage Publications.

This provides the best single-volume discussion of evolutionary models in the study of organizations.

Baum, J. A. C. (ed.) (2002) *The Blackwell Companion to Organizations.* Oxford: Blackwell
  Publishers.

The three chapters on the evolutionary perspective in this volume provide insight into how the models differ at three levels of analysis: the intra-organizational (by Massimo Warglien), organizational (by Terry Amburgey and Jitendra Singh) and inter-organizational (Henrich Greve).

For evolutionary models in the study of the MNE

Delacroix, J. (1993) 'The European Subsidiaries of American Multinationals: an Exercise in
  Ecological Analysis'. In S. Ghoshal and D. E. Westney (eds) *Organization Theory and the
  Multinational Corporation.* Basingstoke: Macmillan Press, 105–35.

This chapter provides an excellent example of the application of population ecology, one of the most widely used evolutionary models in the study of organizations, to MNEs operating in Europe from 1903 to 1974.

Kogut, B. (1993) 'Learning, or the importance of being inert: Country imprinting and
  international competition'. In S. Ghoshal and D. E. Westney (eds) *Organization Theory
  and the Multinational Corporation.* Basingstoke: Macmillan Press, 136–54.
Kogut, B. (1995) 'An Evolutionary Perspective on the Multinational Corporation'. In D. Nigh
  and B. Toyne (eds) *International Business Inquiry: An Emerging Vision.* Columbus, SC: USC
  Press.
Zander, U. and Kogut, B. (1993) 'Knowledge of the firm and the evolutionary theory of the
  multinational corporation', *Journal of International Business Studies* 24: 625–45.
Zander, U. and Kogut, B. (1995) 'Knowledge and the speed of transfer and imitation of
  organizational capabilities: An empirical test'. *Organization Science* 6: 76–92.

Bruce Kogut's work is one of the most significant bodies of work taking an explicitly evolutionary theory-based approach to the MNE, employing the Nelson and Winter evolutionary framing.

Westney, D. E. and Zaheer, S. (2001) 'The Multinational Corporation as an Organization'. In
  A. M. Rugman and T. L. Brewer (eds) *Handbook of International Business.* Oxford: Oxford
  University Press, 349–79.

This chapter provides an overview of organizational analyses of the MNE, examining the emphasis that different theories place on internal and external drivers of change.

Additional empirical studies

Belanger, J., Berggren, C., Björkman, T. and Köhler, C. (eds) (1998) *Being Local Worldwide: ABB and the Challenge of Global Management*. Ithaca: Cornell University Press.

Kogut, B. (ed.) (1993) *Country Competitiveness: Technology and the Organization of Work*. Oxford: Oxford University Press.

Morgan, G., Kristensen, P.H. and Whitley, R. (eds) (2001) *The Multinational Firm: Organizing across Institutional and National Divides*. Oxford: Oxford University Press.

References

Aldrich, H. (1999) *Organizations Evolving*. London: Sage Publications.

Amburgey, T. L. and Singh, J. V. (2002) 'Organizational Evolution'. In J. A. C. Baum (ed.) *The Blackwell Companion to Organizations*. Oxford: Blackwell Publishers, pp. 327–43.

Bartlett, C. A. (1995) 'ABB's Relays Business: Building and Managing a Global Matrix', Harvard Business School case #9-394-016, revised January 7, 1995.

Bartlett, C. A. and Ghoshal, S. (1989). *Managing Across Borders: The Transnational Solution*. Boston, MA: Harvard Business School Press.

Bartlett, C. A. and Ghoshal, S. (1998) *Managing Across Borders: The Transnational Solution*. 2nd edn, Boston, MA: Harvard Business School Press.

Bartlett, C. A., Ghoshal, S. and Birkinshaw, J. (2004) *Transnational Management: Text, Cases, and Readings in Cross-Border Management*. 4th edn, New York: McGraw-Hill/Irwin.

Baum, J. A. C. (ed.) (2002) *The Blackwell Companion to Organizations*. Oxford: Blackwell Publishers.

Baum, J. A. C. and Singh, J. (eds) (1994a) *Evolutionary Dynamics of Organizations*. Oxford: Oxford University Press, 39–49.

Baum, J. A. C. and Singh, J. (1994b) 'Organization-Environment Co-evolution'. In J. A. C. Baum and J. Singh (eds) *Evolutionary Dynamics of Organizations*. Oxford: Oxford University Press, 379–401.

Bélanger, J., Berggren, C., Björkman, T., and Köhler, C. (eds) (1999) *Being Local Worldwide: ABB and the Challenge of Global Management*. Ithaca: Cornell University Press.

Birkinshaw, J. and Hood, N. (1998a) *Multinational Corporate Evolution and Subsidiary Development*. London: Macmillan.

Birkinshaw, J. and Hood, N. (1998b) 'Multinational subsidiary evolution: capability and charter change in foreign-owned subsidiary companies', *Academy of Management Review* 23-4, 773–96.

Birkinshaw, J. (2001) 'Strategy and Management in MNE Subsidiaries'. In A. M. Rugman and T. L. Brewer (eds) *Handbook of International Business*. Oxford: Oxford University Press, 380–401.

Black, J. S. and Gregersen, H. B (2002) *Leading Strategic Change: Breaking through the brain barrier*. Upper Saddle River, NJ: Financial Times Prentice Hall.

Buckley, P. J., Devinney, T. M. and Louviere, J. L. (2007) 'Do managers behave the way theory suggests? A choice-theoretic examination of foreign direct investment location decision-making', *Journal of International Business Studies*, 38-7: 1069–94.

Burgelman, R. A. (1990) 'Strategy-making and organizational ecology: A conceptual integration'. In J. V. Singh (ed.) *Organizational Evolution: New Directions*. Newbury Park: Sage Publications, 164–81.

Burgelman, R. A. (1991) 'Intraorganizational ecology of strategy making and organizational adaptation: Theory and field research', *Organization Science* 2-3, 239–62.

Carroll, G. (1988) 'Organizational ecology in theoretical perspective'. In G. R. Carroll. (ed.) *Ecological Models of Organizations*. Cambridge, MA: Ballinger, 1–6.

Collinson, S. and Wilson, D. C. (2006) 'Inertia in Japanese Organizations: Knowledge Management Routines and Failure to Innovate', *Organization Studies*, Vol. 27 No. 9: 1359–87.

Contractor, F. J., Kundu, S.K. and Hsu, C. (2003) 'A Three-Stage Theory of International Expansion: The Link Between Multinationality and Performance In The Service Sector', *Journal of International Business Studies*, Vol. 34, No. 1: 5–18.

Daniels, J. D., Pitts, R.A. and Tretter, M. J. (1984) 'Strategy and Structure of U.S. Multinationals: An exploratory study', *Academy of Management Journal*, 27-2: 292–307.

Delacroix, J. (1993). 'The European Subsidiaries of American Multinationals: an Exercise in Ecological Analysis'. In S. Ghoshal and D. E. Westney. (eds) *Organization Theory and the Multinational Corporation*. Basingstoke: Macmillan Press, 105–35.

Frost, T. S., Birkinshaw, J. M. and Ensign, P. C. (2002) 'Centers of Excellence in Multinational Corporations', *Strategic Management Journal*, 23 (11), 997–1018.

Gerstner, L. V. Jr. (2002) *Who Says Elephants Can't Dance? Inside IBM's Historic Turnaround*. New York: Harper Business.

Ghoshal, S. and Bartlett, C. A. (1998) *The Individualized Corporation*. London: Heinemann.

Greve, H. (2002) Interorganizational Evolution. In J. A. C. Baum. (ed.) *The Blackwell Companion to Organizations*. Oxford: Blackwell Publishers, 557–78.

Hannan, M. T. and Freeman, J. (1977) 'The population ecology of organizations', *American Journal of Sociology*, 82: 929–64.

Hennart, J.-F. (2001) 'Theories of the Multinational Enterprise'. In A. M. Rugman and T. L. Brewer. (eds) *Handbook of International Business*. Oxford: Oxford University Press, 127–49.

Hood, N. and Young, S. (eds) (1999) *The Globalization of Multinational Activity and Economic Development*. London: Macmillan.

Hulbert, J. M. and Brandt, W. K. (1980) *Managing the Multinational Subsidiary*, New York: Holt, Rinehart, and Winston.

Jain, S. C. and Vachani, S. (eds) (2005) *Multinational Corporations and Global Poverty Reduction*. Cheltenham, UK: Edward Elgar Publishing.

Johanson, J. and Vahlne, J.-E. (1977) 'The Internationalization Process of the Firm: A Model of Knowledge Development and Increasing Foreign Market Commitments', *Journal of International Business Studies*, 8-1: 23–32.

Jones, A. (2003) *Management Consultancy and Banking in an Era of Globalization*. Basingstoke, UK: Palgrave Macmillan.

Klein, N. (2000) *No Logo*. New York: Picador.

Kogut, B. (1993) 'Learning, or the importance of being inert: Country Imprinting and international competition'. In S. Ghoshal and D. E. Westney. (eds) *Organization Theory and the Multinational Corporation*. Basingstoke: Macmillan Press, 136–54.

Kogut, B. (1995) 'An Evolutionary Perspective on the Multinational Corporation'. In D. Nigh and B. Toyne. (eds) *International Business Inquiry: An Emerging Vision*. Columbus, SC: USC Press.

Korten, D. C. (1998) *When Corporations Rule the World*. West Hartford, CT: Kumarian Press.

Kostova, T. and Roth, K. (2002) 'Adoption of an Organizational Practice by the Subsidiaries of the MNC: Institutional and Relational Effects', *Academy of Management Journal*, 45-1: 215–33.

Kristensen, P.H. and Zeitlin, J. (2005) *Local Players in Global Games: The Strategic Constitution of a Multinational Corporation*, Oxford: Oxford University Press.

Kwok, C. C. Y. and Tadesse, S. (2006) 'The MNC as an agent of change for host-country institutions: FDI and corruption', *Journal of International Business Studies*, 37-6: 767–85.

Lewin, K. (1947) 'Frontiers in Group Dynamics – Concept, Method, and Reality in Social Science: Social Equilibria and Social Change', *Human Relations*, Vol. 1: 5–41.

March, J. G. (1991) 'Exploitation and exploration in organizational learning', *Organization Science*, 2-1: 71–87.

March, J. G. (1994) 'The Evolution of Evolution'. In J. A. C. Baum and J. Singh. (eds) *Evolutionary Dynamics of Organizations*. Oxford: Oxford University Press, 39–49.

McKelvey, B. (1982) *Organizational Systematics: Taxonomy, Evolution, Classification*. Berkeley, CA: University of California Press.

Meyer, M. W. (1991) 'Turning evolution inside the organization'. In J. A. C. Baum and J. V. Singh. (eds) *Evolutionary Dynamics of Organizations*. New York: Oxford University Press, 109–16.

Morgan, G., Kristensen, P. H. and Whitley, R. (eds) (2001) *The Multinational Firm: Organizing across institutional and national divides*. Oxford: Oxford University Press.

Nelson, R. R. (1993a) 'Evolutionary theorizing about economic change'. In N. Smelser and R. Swedberg. (eds) *Handbook of Economic Sociology*. Princeton: Princeton University Press, 108–36.

Nelson, R. R. (ed.) (1993b) *National Innovation Systems: A Comparative Analysis*. Oxford: Oxford University Press.

Nelson, R. and Winter, S. (1982) *An Evolutionary Theory of Economic Change*. Cambridge, MA: Harvard University Press.

Ohmae, K. (1990) *The Borderless World: Power and Strategy in the Interlinked Global Economy*. New York: Harper Collins.

Perlmutter, H. (1969) 'The tortuous evolution of the multinational corporation', *Columbia Journal of World Business*, 5 (1), 9–18.

Powell, W. W. and Smith-Doerr, L. (1993) 'Networks and economic life'. In N. J. Smelser and R. Swedberg. (eds) *The Handbook of Sociology*. Princeton: Princeton University Press, 368–402.

Prahalad, C. K., and Doz, Y. (1987) *The Multinational Mission: Balancing Local Demands and Global Vision*. New York: The Free Press.

Roberts, J. (2004) *The Modern Firm: Organizational design for performance and growth*. Oxford: Oxford University Press.

Rosenzweig, P. and Singh, J. (1991) 'Organizational Environments and the Multinational Enterprise', *Academy of Management Review*, 16-2: 340–61.

Sidhu, J. S., Commandeur, H. R. and Volberda, H. W. (1991) 'The Multifaceted Nature of Exploration and Exploitation: Value of Supply, Demand, and Spatial Search for Innovation', *Organization Science*, 18-1: 20–38.

Smith, W. K. and Tushman, M. L. (2005) 'Managing Strategic Contradictions: A top management model for managing innovation streams', *Organization Science*, 16-5: 522–36.

Stopford, J. M. and Wells, L. T., Jr. (1972) *Managing the Multinational Enterprise: Organization of the Firm and Ownership of the Subsidiaries*. New York: Basic Books.

Taylor, W. (1991) 'The Logic of Global Business: An Interview with ABB's Percy Barnevik', *Harvard Business Review*, (March–April), 90–104.

Thorelli, H. (1966) 'The Multinational Corporation as a change agent', *Southern Journal of Business*, 1-3: 1–9.

Tushman, M. L. and O'Reilly, C. A. (1996) 'Ambidextrous organizations: Managing evolutionary and revolutionary change', *California Management Review*, 38-4: 8–30.

Warglien, M. (2002) 'Intraorganizational Evolution'. In J. A. C. Baum. (ed.) *The Blackwell Companion to Organizations*. Oxford: Blackwell Publishers, 98–118.

Westney, D. E. (1988) 'Isomorphism, Institutionalization and the Multinational Enterprise'. Paper presented at the Academy of International Business Annual Meetings, October. San Diego, California.

Westney, D. E. (1993) 'Institutionalization Theory and the Multinational Corporation'. In S. Ghoshal and D. E. Westney. (eds) *Organization Theory and the Multinational Corporation*. London: Macmillan, 53–76.

Westney, D. E. and Zaheer, S. (2001) 'The Multinational Corporation as an Organization'. In A. M. Rugman and T. L. Brewer. (eds) *Handbook of International Business*. Oxford: Oxford University Press, 349–79.

Zander, U. and Kogut, B. (1993) 'Knowledge of the firm and the evolutionary theory of the multinational corporation', *Journal of International Business Studies*, 24: 625–45.

Zander, U. and Kogut, B. (1995) 'Knowledge and the speed of transfer and imitation of organizational capabilities: An empirical test', *Organization Science*, 6: 76–92.

NOTES

1. See also the papers collected in Jain and Vachani (2006) and Hood and Young (1999).
2. Lewin's classic three-stage model of organizational change, 'Unfreezing-Change-Refreezing', has influenced countless change models down to the present day; see for example Black and Gregerson's articulation of the challenges of change as 'failing to see, failing to move, failing to finish' (2002).
3. Alfred Chandler famously distinguished between the 'invisible hand' of the external marketplace and the 'visible hand' of top management within the firm: both represent selection forces. The 1994 volume, *Evolutionary Dynamics of Organizations*, edited by Joel Baum and Jitendra Singh, organized its contributions by three levels of analysis: intra-organizational evolution, organizational evolution and population evolution.
4. This literature is too extensive to be cited comprehensively here, but two seminal pieces are March (1991) and Tushman and O'Reilly (1996); for recent discussions, see Smith and Tushman (2005) and Sidhu *et al.* (2007).
5. These processes also lead to patterns being retained long after changes in the environment make them subject to negative external selection pressures that are deflected by internal evolutionary dynamics (see the discussion in Collinson and Wilson, 2006).
6. Although metaphorical language of 'genes' and 'genetic code' in organizations has become increasingly widespread in business writing, there have been few serious attempts to build a direct parallel between organizations and the genetic code of biological organisms since Bill McKelvey's 1982 work on Dominant Competences, or 'comps'. In McKelvey's words, 'the comps play the same genotypic role as the genetic material of biological organisms' (1982: 197). McKelvey had few followers.
7. See for example the lengthy discussion of Zander and Kogut (1993, 1995) in Warglien's 2002 review of intra-organizational evolution, and Powell and Smith-Doerr's citation of Kogut *et al.* (1993) in their review chapter on networks in *The Handbook of Economic Sociology* (1993).

8. One of the most common examples of the resilience conferred by variation is the case of Xerox, which, when faced with competition from small copiers produced by Canon and other Japanese competitors was able to draw on products and designs from its Japanese subsidiary, Fuji-Xerox, to combat the 'invasion' of its home market (see Roberts (2004: 209–12)).
9. To forestall irritation on the part of editors and readers, the 'x' here is indeed the page number, not a place-holder for a page number to be named later.
10. At a 1993 conference on SMEs, Kristensen gave Zeitlin a research paper on local strategic initiatives in a Danish manufacturing plant that he had been studying for nearly a decade and that had been acquired in the late 1980s by a British manufacturing firm. Zeitlin had not only been studying the debates on British industrial performance but he had visited a plant in Wisconsin owned by the same firm.
11. Both authors are sociologists, and they describe their shared interests as 'the historical development, internal dynamics, and innovative capabilities of industrial districts or regional clusters organized around flexibly specialized networks of small and medium-sized firms' (Kristensen and Zeitlin, 2005: xiii). They came to the study of APV much more interested in understanding the effect of acquisition of locally-embedded firms into an MNE than in helping MNE executives to develop more effective management systems, although they end up making recommendations for the latter as well.
12. See their methodological appendix in the 1989 edition, especially pp. 217–20.
13. One factor in APV may be that, having grown by acquisition, it seemed that the company did not have a central technology development organization, at least not one large enough to figure in the narratives of the three plants. In this, it may be more 'typical' than the companies studied by Bartlett and Ghoshal: the 1990s saw an evisceration of corporate R&D in most large firms, and the outsourcing of much functional expertise.
14. This case is based on Bartlett (1995), Bélanger et al. (1998), Ghoshal and Bartlett (1997), Taylor (1991) and articles in the business press.

Chapter 7 The Multinational Firm as a Distinct Organizational Form

Richard Whitley

Introduction

Multinational companies (MNCs) coordinate and control operations in many different parts of the world through unified authority and ownership structures. They represent the extension of the visible hand of managerial hierarchies from national economies to supranational regional and worldwide ones, and have been seen by some as novel kinds of international learning systems and differentiated networks (Birkinshaw and Hood, 1998; Hedlund, 1993; Holm and Pedersen, 2000; Nohria and Ghoshal, 1997). By operating facilities in different kinds of environments, MNCs are in principle able to generate new knowledge and skills that differ from their more nationally specific competitors and become a distinct type of organization. Through integrating novel competences across subsidiaries, some MNCs transformed themselves into quite new kinds of 'transnational' corporations in the 1980s according to Bartlett and Ghoshal (1989).

However, it is questionable to what extent MNCs do constitute a new form of visible hand, as opposed to enabling firm-specific advantages and managerial practices developed in the domestic economy to be generalized across national borders. As Solvell and Zander (1998) and Zander and Solvell (2002) have pointed out, the ability of MNCs to do something qualitatively different from national firms is more often assumed than demonstrated (see also, Arvidsson (1999) and Szulanski (1996)). It remains unclear how they develop firm-specific capabilities that are distinctly transnational as opposed to being embedded in a particular local context. To become transnational organizations MNCs would have to develop distinctive organizational systems and processes that are the product of the international circulation of knowledge, ideas and people from different locations rather than being based on

Images of the Multinational Firm   Edited by Simon Collinson and Glenn Morgan
© 2009 John Wiley & Sons, Ltd

domestic practices. This is only likely to happen under particular, rather limited, conditions.

In general terms, MNCs are more likely to become distinctive kinds of organization when they locate major proportions of key assets and activities in quite different kinds of institutional contexts. This potentially exposes them to new approaches and routines for dealing with novel business partners and markets. In itself, however, this does not tell us much because MNCs vary in the extent to which they allow their foreign subsidiaries to adapt to local conventions and innovate in their procedures, products and services. Some, like Ford in England in the 1920s and 1930s, insist on their overseas units following domestic policies and practices (Tolliday, 2000), while others permit more diverse responses to different markets and patterns of economic organization, and a few actively encourage subsidiaries to experiment with new approaches, as perhaps is the case with some German MNCs in the Americas and central Europe in recent years (Lane, 2001).

Clearly, MNCs that simply export their domestic practices to foreign locations are unlikely to develop new knowledge and skills as a result of operating internationally. Such organizations remain predominantly national companies that extend their current systems and procedures to international operations. They cannot be considered to constitute a new organizational form if their subsidiaries remain dominated by home-based practices and personnel. Equally, the MNC that leaves its overseas subsidiaries to act autonomously in responding to local market demands will not become a distinct kind of organization. This latter pattern makes the MNC a loosely bound federation of 'national' firms and the MNC per se will not develop distinctively new kinds of collective competences.

For MNCs to become distinctive kinds of organizations as a result of operating across national borders, they have to 'learn from abroad' in the sense of incorporating novel ideas, skills and technologies from innovating subsidiaries in other parts of the organization. So, it is the combination of diversity of markets, employees, business partners and institutions with the systematic integration of organizational innovations within ownership-based boundaries that makes MNCs potentially significant different kinds of economic actors. Central to the successful integration of knowledge and skills from different subunits in MNCs, and so to their development of distinctive kinds of collective transnational capabilities, is the involvement of key employees in problem-solving on a continuing basis.

In general terms, collective organizational capabilities take time to build and typically involve relatively 'low powered' incentives to encourage employees to work together to deal with technical and organizational problems and to generate firm-specific knowledge. For a MNC to learn systematically from its operations in quite different environments in such a way as to generate novel transnational competences it has to encourage its employees and business partners in those environments to become committed to developing and improving such cross-national capabilities.

Two ways of generating such commitment are authority sharing and organizational careers (Whitley, 2003). By authority sharing I mean the delegation of considerable discretion over work performance and organization to skilled staff such that they become involved in problem-solving activities and are regarded as authoritative contributors to organizational issues. In general, the more employers are willing to involve employees in complex problem solving and encourage their participation in the collective development of organizational knowledge, the more likely they are to become committed to contributing their experience and learning.

Authority can be shared with a variety of groups inside the organization. The most centralized case occurs when authority is concentrated in the hands of the owners and closely associated top managers of the organization. Alternatively, authority can be shared with three other groups. The first consists of senior and middle managers, which in MNCs might include the heads of foreign subsidiaries and their top management teams. The second consists of 'professionals' or 'experts'. This implies more than simply utilizing the distinctive expertise of such groups; it also suggests giving them more authority to take action and shape the strategy and structure of the firm. The third group consists of skilled employees engaged in operating activities. This form of authority sharing primarily concerns work organization and allowing some autonomy to teams and work groups over how tasks are performed.

Establishing organizational careers also encourages employee commitment by rewarding continuing contributions to collective problem solving through long-term employment and promotion. They provide strong incentives for staff to work together in dealing with firm-specific issues and opportunities over substantial periods of time, rather than concentrating on enhancing their individual skills that may be more tradable on external labour markets. Firms that offer long-term careers for many groups of skilled staff are more likely to gain continuing employee investment in organization-specific knowledge and skills than are those that restrict careers to only a few staff and/or where such commitments lack credibility.

For organizational careers to generate firm-specific knowledge and skills in MNCs, they would have to be constructed internationally rather than nationally. Employees could be expected to be rewarded for contributions to collective problem-solving through promotion in the MNC, rather than in just a single part of the firm. Firms that offer long-term international careers for many groups of skilled staff are more likely to gain continuing employee investment in transnational organization-specific knowledge and skills than are those that restrict such careers to only a few staff and/or where such commitments lack credibility.

Differences in authority sharing and organizational careers between firms are strongly affected by the nature of the dominant institutions governing economic activities and relationships (Whitley, 1999, 2007). This chapter examines how these relationships influence the development of different kinds of MNCs by first showing how different institutional regimes can be expected to encourage different kinds of authority sharing and careers inside firms. Next, I consider what this means for the development of MNCs from different forms of capitalism. Emerging from this, the third part of the chapter identifies six types of MNCs, which have varying degrees of similarity to the transnational model. In conclusion, it is argued that only in very distinctive institutional circumstances is it likely that a transnational type of MNC may emerge.

Institutions, Authority-sharing and Careers

Particularly important features of societal institutions that affect levels of authority sharing and provision of organizational careers include: a) the overall reliability and efficacy of formal institutions such as the legal system, b) the role of the state in constraining short-term opportunism and supporting firm development, c) the extent and nature of risk sharing between banks, capital, markets and companies, d) the power of intermediary associations such as employers' groups and labour unions and, e) the efficacy of the skill formation system (Whitley, 2003, 2007). Combinations of these constitute four different institutional regimes that vary greatly in the degree to which they encourage authority sharing and long-term commitments between employers and employees: particularistic, arm's length, solidaristic collaborative, and segmented collaborative.

Particularistic institutional regimes, such as those found in many industrializing and post state-socialist societies, discourage extensive delegation and employer–employee commitment, primarily because of the low level of trust in the operation and predictability of formal institutions that characterises such societies (Whitley, 1999). This means that owners feel unable to rely on the legal system, accounting conventions and formal systems for assessing competence and ensuring contractual compliance in order to control the behaviour of customers, suppliers and employees in predictable ways. Consequently they tend not to delegate substantial amounts of authority to relative strangers with whom they do not have strong personal bonds. Additionally, in paternalist political cultures owners tend to consider employees as unqualified to exercise discretion. In these social systems, authority sharing is limited at all possible levels (managers, professionals and employees) and control is preferably kept within the family.

Arm's length institutional regimes, such as those found in many late twentieth century Anglophone countries, combine much greater trust in formal institutions with relatively few constraints on opportunistic behaviour by economic actors beyond the formal, legal framework governing market transactions. Corporate strategies are driven by large and liquid capital markets that facilitate hostile takeovers and encourage frequent restructurings to meet stock market demands. It is therefore difficult to provide credible long-term commitments to employees, who in turn are likely to be mobile on the external labour market, developing skills that are visible and saleable outside the firm. There is little authority sharing with employees engaged in operating activities since they are rarely regarded as long-term members of the organization.

The impact of these constraints on authority sharing with managers and professionals is, however, more complex. In order to manage such hierarchies, strong systems of financial and managerial control are embedded in processes, routines and rules. 'Management' as a particular activity, a particular legitimation system and a particular career system binds together large numbers of senior, middle and junior managers, particularly where this is based on a shared education, such as the MBA, and a shared knowledge base (reflected in newspapers, journals and the outputs of popular management texts as well as in the output and activity of consultants). There is therefore the potential for some authority sharing with other managers given that they will share similar orientations. Similarly, professional expertise may also be the basis for authority sharing in particular contexts.

Considering next more collaborative institutional regimes, these are characterized by stronger constraints on opportunistic behaviour by economic actors. They typically have promotional states that encourage firms to share risks, sometimes by providing direct support for new investments and/or technology development, and to work together to develop new industries and markets (Evans, 1994; Whitley, 2007). The more states encourage such collaborative development and sharing of technical and market risks, the more owners and managers are likely to share more authority between themselves and reduce risks of opportunistic behaviour. This provides a relatively stable basis for establishing organizational careers for skilled staff and investing in their training.

These kinds of societies also tend to have credit-based financial systems with relatively small and illiquid capital markets and considerable concentrations of shareholder control over large companies. The market for corporate control is limited here, especially if significant proportions of firms' shares are held by strategic investors and/or are effectively controlled by top managers, as is the case in many European countries (Barca and Becht, 2001) and Japan (Sheard, 1994). Such stability of ownership also encourages longer term employer–employee commitments, and indeed other long-term strategies. Strong business associations, particularly employers' associations, are also significant features of the business environment in these regimes that encourage employer–employee commitment, as Soskice (1999) has emphasized. As well as controlling opportunistic behaviour by member companies, and so encouraging longer term investments in technology and employees, such organizations restrict employee opportunism.

Two types of collaborative institutional regimes can be distinguished. Solidaristic collaborative regimes (e.g. Germany, Denmark, Finland) combine relatively strong labour unions, often organized around industries, with highly organized bargaining systems and strong public training systems. These skill formation systems usually involve collaboration between state agencies, employers and unions and develop highly valued standardized skills for a majority of the labour force that form the basis for strong occupational identities (Crouch et al., 1999; Marsden, 1999). Here, pride in one's publicly certified expertise is considerable, and encourages loyalty as much to horizontally defined occupational groups as to vertical authority hierarchies constituting firms. Such skills additionally facilitate mobility between companies and the institutionalization of active labour markets within particular occupational boundaries (Hinz, 1999).

However, in many continental European countries this mobility is restrained by strong employers' associations and centralised wage bargaining organized on a sectoral basis, as well as by legal constraints on unilateral employer actions. Together with barriers to firing staff in market downturns, and industry-wide barriers to hiring new skills from competitors, these factors mean that both firms and workers here have strong incentives to improve individual and collective skills within current technological trajectories and industry boundaries. Organizational careers are here encouraged by extensive employer–union collaboration within each industry that ties firms and workers into a common destiny.

Segmented collaborative societies, (e.g. post-war Japan) in contrast, have weaker unions that are often enterprise-based, mostly decentralized wage bargaining arrangements and largely privately organized skill formation systems. In these systems, the general educational system strongly selects children and young adults for different positions in the labour market through academic examinations, and the public training system is relatively poorly developed and/or low in prestige. Firms, especially larger ones, rely on the educational system to select and train workers in general competences that they can build upon during the course of a working lifetime.

Because the strong business associations characteristic of such societies restrict poaching and limit free riders' ability to appropriate skills developed by competitors, both employers and employees make considerable investments in collective competence development through organizational careers. Authority sharing in large firms in these kinds of collaborative institutional frameworks is considerable because both managers and workers are highly dependent on the growth of the firm, and jointly develop distinctive competitive capabilities. Such interdependence is, however, often lower in smaller firms where labour turnover is greater and skills less organization-specific.

The lack of strong horizontal occupational identities based on certified expertise in these kinds of societies facilitates job rotation across functional groups, as well as cooperation between them, so that innovation development and implementation are, in principle, faster and more effective than where functional boundaries are reinforced by publicly standardized skills. Expertise therefore becomes highly firm-specific in large companies in such economies as both managers and core workers invest in the long-term development and improvement of distinctive organizational capabilities.

In conclusion, owners of firms in particularistic systems are very unlikely to share authority with anybody who is not personally tied to them. Owners and managers in arm's length systems do not share authority with most employees but they do develop a division of labour that allows for some sharing of authority provided there are strong elements binding the actors (such as shared skill base, shared language and legitimation orders). Collaborative systems are built on sharing authority with skilled employees; professional and technical expertise is generally subsumed into that sharing, as is management.

Institutional Regimes, Cross-national Authority Sharing and Organizational Careers in MNCs

Turning now to consider how MNCs from these different institutional regimes are likely to encourage varying degrees of employee commitment, I first discuss the probable patterns of authority sharing and careers in MNCs from particularistic business environments. Since owners in these kinds of market economies are reluctant to share authority with employees in their domestic location because of unreliable formal institutions and an unpredictable political environment, they are equally unlikely to trust foreign employees a great deal or to delegate much discretion to them.

Equally, the common restriction of long-term career opportunities to relatives and others with whom family-like relationships have been developed in these frameworks suggests that few firms will offer organizational careers to foreign employees, even those who are fairly senior managers or highly skilled professionals. As a result, hardly any subsidiary staff are likely to become so committed to the parent company that they will invest their energies in improving firm-specific knowledge and skills on a medium to long-term basis. This means that enterprises from such environments are unlikely to develop strong international organizational capabilities, as distinct from those based on predominantly individual relationships and qualities.

In contrast, MNCs from arm's length institutional regimes that share authority with, and develop organizational careers for, managers and some professionals can be expected to delegate rather more discretion to those in charge of foreign subsidiaries where formal institutions are considered reliable. They may also involve foreign managers and professional staff in cross-national problem-solving teams when their specialist expertise is highly valued. This is especially likely when dealing with complex problems that require knowledge of different business environments, as in many professional service companies (Morgan and Quack, 2005).

Authority sharing with foreign professionals will here depend on the knowledge that managers of these MNCs have of their expertise and the reputation of national skill formation systems. Given the importance of technical knowledge and specialist skills in dealing with complex and uncertain tasks, domestic managers of MNCs are unlikely to share much authority with foreigners unless they are convinced that they are highly skilled and able to contribute to current problems. This will be greatly facilitated by skills being standardized through professional associations that operate in similar ways in different countries, and so is more straightforward between firms from arm's length economies that have flexible labour markets and similar institutional arrangements for developing high-level expertise, such as the USA and the UK.

In general, though, any such authority sharing by firms from arm's length economies is unlikely to extend much beyond professional staff and managers, given similar limitations at home. While their subsidiaries located in economies with strong collaborative institutions may develop greater levels of authority sharing with skilled workers, this seems likely to be limited to local operations given the arm's length nature of the parent MNC's domestic business environment. Similarly, few firms from these kinds of institutional frameworks are likely to make long-term career commitments to foreign employees, especially at the international level. Because commitments in general are short-term in such economies, most employers will not feel able to offer long-term cross-national organizational careers to more than a few senior foreign managers or professionals.

MNCs in collaborative market economies are embedded in a number of relatively long-term obligations with particular business partners, including skilled employees. Where such firms consider that their core capabilities are substantially derived from these long-term commitments and are highly specific to their home business environment, they will be reluctant to invest much in authority sharing with foreign staff where conditions are significantly different. The more MNCs see their distinctive competences as being generated by their domestic organization and its particular pattern of employment relations, the less they are likely to involve foreign staff from quite different environments in substantial international problem-solving activities. This seems to be the case for many Japanese MNCs (see e.g. Kopp, 1999: Pucik, 1999).

However, some companies from collaborative institutional frameworks have become more willing to delegate considerable discretion to foreign managers and professionals and to involve them extensively in international problem-solving teams as they seek to acquire new kinds of capabilities that their domestic business system appears unable to provide. In situations where the lock-ins encouraged by home economy institutions are seen to be inhibiting radical innovation and limiting growth, such MNCs may deliberately use foreign subsidiaries to try novel practices with different kinds of approaches and skills developed in societies with contrasting institutional frameworks, such as Japanese investments in UK and US biotechnology facilities (Kneller, 2003; Lam, 2003). Some German companies seem to have tried to do this in the 1990s, although such plans have not always been realised in practice, particularly in the car industry (Fleury and Salerno, 1998; Jurgens, 1998; Lane, 2001).

MNCs from solidaristic collaborative frameworks that organize careers and identities around specialist skills and activities may well find this kind of authority sharing and joint problem-solving with foreign employees easier to accomplish than do those from segmented ones whose internal labour markets are more structured around generalist competences. This is because their home and host economy professional staff are more likely to share a common cognitive framework and approach to problem understanding than are employees in MNCs where engineers and other highly educated employees are encouraged to become organizational generalists.

This contrast in ease of collaboration in dealing with cross-border problems will be especially marked when professionals from collaborative economies are working with those in arm's length ones, since these latter tend to be more specialized and focused on their professional identity rather than that of their current employer. We would expect, then, MNCs from solidaristic collaborative institutional frameworks to be more willing to share authority with managers and professionals in arm's length economies than those from segmented ones, and to be more effective in managing international problem-solving teams.

They may also be more willing to develop long-term career commitments to foreign staff because of a greater specialisation of organizational careers around professional expertise. However, for many MNCs from collaborative institutional frameworks, the importance of their considerable commitments to domestic skilled workers for the development of their firm-specific competences, and the lack of strong international institutions encouraging similar commitments to foreign staff, mean that extending long-term organizational careers abroad will be difficult, especially to workers in arm's length economies. Indeed, some may not wish to do so in order to increase their flexibility and ability to change competences in foreign subsidiaries at short notice. In effect, these kinds of MNCs develop contrasting employment relations in different environments in order to generate varied kinds of capabilities, as have perhaps some continental European investors in new technology firms in the USA.

MNCs from segmented collaborative institutional frameworks are particularly unlikely to establish credible long-term organizational careers for foreign employees since their distinctive organizational capabilities are often generated by generalist career structures that reward long-term contributions to the organization as a whole rather than those to particular specialisms. Weak professional identities and the highly firm-specific nature of careers and skills in such economies enable extensive rotation across functions and divisions facilitating organization-wide communication and learning. Incorporating foreign employees into such career structures is extremely difficult. As a result, many large Japanese firms have become noted for relatively limited career opportunities for foreign staff including managers, especially when they remain heavily dependent upon domestic customers as do most banks (Morgan et al., 2003; Sakai, 2000; Whitley et al., 2003).

These points suggest that firms from arm's length economies could find it easier to develop multinational career structures for key foreign managers and technical experts than do MNCs originating in collaborative ones because their competitive capabilities are not so closely tied to home economy employee involvement in joint problem-solving and knowledge development. Insofar, then, as the former companies do establish long-term organizational careers for key employees to gain their continuing commitment to organizational specific problem-solving and knowledge development, they may extend them to some senior staff in overseas subsidiaries to a greater extent than would firms from collaborative business environments.

International Authority Sharing, Careers and Capabilities of Six Types of MNC

From this analysis of cross-national authority sharing and organizational careers in MNCs from different institutional regimes, it is possible to identify six ideal types of MNC that combine varying degrees of these characteristics.

1. The Colonial MNC keeps key decision-making over resources, skills and knowledge production at home. Whether run as a highly centralized and personally controlled business from a particularistic institutional environment or a home-focused hierarchy from a more stable society, these kinds of MNCs function as national companies with foreign operations that are highly subservient to the head office. Consequently, their capabilities will be largely those developed domestically, with few if any new ones being generated from their cross-border activities. In some of these kinds of MNCs, career success is tied to the long-term cultivation of, and services for, large domestic customers.

CASE EXAMPLE 1: JAPANESE BANKS AND THEIR EXPATRIATE EMPLOYEES

In studies of Japanese banks, which had set up international operations in London in the 1980s, it was found that managers and other staff who work abroad outside Japan became regarded as second rate and less successful in promotion tournaments, as in a number of Japanese banks in the 1980s and 1990s (Sakai, 2000; Morgan et al., 2003). Knowledge and skills obtained from such assignments were not highly regarded and rarely impinged greatly on domestically developed capabilities. Employees who had quite high status positions in London, dealing with large international clients and Japanese embassy staff and engaging in trade and commercial activities in Europe, might find themselves assigned to traditional branch banking when they returned to Japan. From the bank's point of view, they wished to produce generalists who knew the bank's business as a whole rather than becoming specialist in a certain sort of activity such as international banking. International activities were very much peripheral to the banks' core activities in Japan and although a certain amount of learning about the operation of Western financial markets occurred, this was very limited.

British employees working in these banks rarely dealt with home-based customers. They lacked networks into the Japanese head office and were typically excluded from parent company-based organizational careers (Morgan et al., 2003). Consequently, foreign-based capabilities were poorly developed, except perhaps for some projects involving highly paid foreign experts, and rarely made any impact on the parent company. As international companies, then, they did not generate any distinctive kinds of collective competences that distinguish them from their domestic competitors.

2. Domestically dominated MNCs have some authority sharing with foreign managers over local issues but combined with few, if any, international careers for foreigners. Here, the home economy and employer are dominant, with overseas subsidiaries either seen as peripheral in terms of collective competences and learning, or else built upon the domestically developed recipe. These firms tend to view their foreign operations as extensions of their domestic ones, and careers in the worldwide organization are largely based on success in the domestic business. Foreign managers may be involved in developing local business strategies, as well as being entrusted with handling personnel matters, but this is often after they have fully imbibed the parent firm's philosophy and can be trusted to follow the x company's 'way'.

CASE EXAMPLE 2: JAPANESE MANUFACTURING MULTINATIONALS

In the case of many Japanese car assembly MNCs in Europe and the USA, the 'hard side' of the production system, i.e. equipment, technical processes and standard operating procedures, is often transferred as a standard package with little flexibility for local staff to alter specifications or practices, although other features are adapted to local circumstances (Abo, 1994; Botti, 1995; Brannen *et al.*, 1999; Kenney and Florida, 1993). Authority sharing with foreigners is often considerably circumscribed by expatriate 'coordinators' who are in daily contact with head office (Pil and MacDuffie, 1999). Although improvements to manufacturing processes in these companies derive from foreign operations as well as domestic ones, they are usually planned by engineers and managers in Japan on the basis of continuous feedback from overseas and home plants without much foreign involvement (Whitley *et al.*, 2003). Most managerial careers in these kinds of MNC remain predominantly national, or at most regional.

Furthermore, domestically based career success dominates foreign performance since the domestic operations remain the primary source of collective competence development and location of the key succession tournaments. Even when foreign production exceeds domestic output, and successful domestic careers increasingly include some foreign experience, long-term contribution to organizational problem-solving and success in the home economy usually remains more important than foreign success in such MNCs. As a result, foreign staff have limited incentives to invest in long-term MNC-specific knowledge and skill development, and are more likely to focus on demonstrating their expertise and effectiveness at a national or maybe regional level in ways that are externally visible. Japanese subsidiaries in the UK face the problem of retaining managerial staff once they have trained them up for two reasons.

Firstly those staff are likely to be frustrated at the ceiling to their ambition because key regional and head office roles are restricted to Japanese managers. Secondly, those staff become attractive employees for other firms because they will have absorbed a great deal of managerial know-how from their experience inside the Japanese firm. They will thus often be better trained and informed about modern production methods than their UK equivalents without this training. Where the firms poaching these employees are suppliers to Japanese firms, this 'insider' knowledge will be even more valuable.

Developing new and distinctive capabilities in foreign subsidiaries will not, then, be encouraged in domestically dominated MNCs, and any international competences they do generate will be highly dependent on those developed in their home economy. Strong coordinating and learning capabilities in these kinds of MNCs are more derived from their home economy than from their international operations as a whole, and so they are unlikely to develop separate transnational collective competences that are specific to the company as an international firm.

3. Managerially coordinated MNCs combine some authority sharing with foreign managers to deal with local needs and opportunities with the establishment of international careers for some foreign top managers. Commitments by leading subsidiary managers to such parent companies can thus be expected to be greater than in domestically dominated MNCs, and the creation of a more international managerial elite should help to develop distinctive routines for coordinating activities across national borders. However, the largely local focus of most subsidiary managers and

professionals, coupled with their lack of involvement in cross-national problem-solving in these kinds of firms limit the extent of international integration of knowledge and skills.

Most cross-national coordination, planning and innovation is accordingly based on home country routines and competences in these kinds of MNCs, with little input from foreign subsidiaries. However, the growth of a multinational managerial elite may encourage some cross-national learning as foreign managers become assimilated into the top management ranks and seek to build on their foreign experiences. This possibility will, though, be restricted by the strong pressures for conformity to the domestically dominated culture and domestically derived operating procedures. The opening of some senior MNC posts to foreign employees in these kinds of firm does not alter their largely ethnocentric nature, as Perlmutter (1969) emphasizes. Similarly, while the limited extent of authority sharing enables the top managers of such companies to restructure subsidiaries relatively easily and speedily, especially those in arm's length institutional regimes, the lack of involvement of most foreign employees in cross-national activities means that most organizational capabilities are more derived from domestic practices than from international ones.

The limited autonomy granted to some foreign subsidiaries in these kinds of MNC does, however, allow them to develop more varied approaches to some organizational issues at the local level. Employees in collaborative market economies, for example, may well be more loyal and committed to the success of their national organizational unit than to the parent company because there is only limited international authority sharing and long-term commitment. Equally, organizational careers and commitments for dealing with organizational problems will be more focused on the national or regional employer than the parent one. Problem-solving efforts and collaboration are accordingly more likely to be easier to manage within these units than internationally, and so collective coordinating and learning capabilities are more developed at the national level.

In contrast, employees of managerially coordinated MNCs in more arm's length market economies will limit their commitment to organization-specific problem-solving at both national and international levels, and so restrict the development of distinctive, continually improving employer-specific competences. However, formal coordination of generic skills nationally and internationally should be relatively straightforward in these subsidiaries, and flexibility in changing direction considerable. Skilled staff here are likely to prefer to work on project-based problem-solving activities that enhance and display technically specialised expertise and so managerial integration of such projects across national labour markets should not be too difficult. They will not be encouraged, though, to commit considerable time and energy to learning about, and contributing to, MNC-wide activities on a long-term basis, and thus building organization-specific capabilities.

The variety of organizational commitments in different subsidiaries of such MNCs, then, can be considerable, but at the worldwide level they are unlikely to develop firm-specific collective competences through long-term cooperative problem-solving and learning. Instead, the international managerial elite may well prefer to focus on refining formal coordination and control systems for realizing the benefits of integrating diverse national and regional capabilities, as well as dealing with international capital markets, suppliers and customers on a cross-national basis. A key 'global' organizational capability of such MNCs, then, may well be their ability to develop and implement standard routines and procedures for integrating diverse operations and competences located in different kinds of business environments, often building on those developed domestically.

4. Delegated professional MNCs share considerable authority with a number of foreign employees and delegate high levels of discretion to them, but limit the extent and scope of international careers. They mobilize managers and professionals from around the world to work on highly complex and often risky problems, as in, for instance, many business services, but are unable to offer long-term organizational commitments to most staff. This is often because they undertake highly uncertain activities that have unpredictable and risky outcomes, and so flexibility in developing and using skills is more important than the long-term development of organization-specific knowledge.

A major capability of such firms, then, is the capacity to create and direct cross-national project teams for specific, discrete problems with finite outcomes and clear performance criteria. International coordination is achieved primarily through such project teams that combine relatively standardized sets of expertise for dealing with particular, one-off problems. Long-term integration of activities and skills leading to the development of international organization-specific capabilities tends to be limited in such companies, especially their cross-national coordinating and learning capabilities. Although teams may contribute codified information to a central database, as in some consultancy firms, their short-term nature limits the extent to which the organization as a whole can build firm-specific knowledge internationally. Given the disparity of commitments, skills and capabilities between teams in different kinds of market economies, such MNCs may well experience considerable coordination difficulties and effectively decentralise decision-making to national subsidiaries to a high degree, as in franchise-based professional service organizations.

However, their flexibility and ability to mobilise highly skilled staff to work on complex and risky problems can enable them to develop strong international abilities to transform key assets and skills. Particularly where there are strong technical communities and fluid labour markets across national boundaries, these kinds of MNCs are able to adapt rapidly to changing circumstances and their capabilities for change can be expected to be considerable, as in some business service companies. This is less likely in highly regulated professional service firms where skills and technologies are more standardized and problem-solving is more a matter of applying current skills to particular client problems than inventing new technologies.

5. Delegated managerial MNCs combine considerable delegation of authority to managers and professionals in many foreign subsidiaries with international careers for senior subsidiary managers. These kinds of MNCs encourage foreign subsidiaries to develop distinctive capabilities that contribute to international strategies as well

as meeting local targets. By delegating considerable discretion to local managers and professionals they enable them to innovate and adapt to local conditions, and so generate varied capabilities at the local level. By also involving them in international teams to deal with more global issues they are able to draw upon these different backgrounds and expertise. The establishment of international managerial careers here should ensure that commitments to the long-term development of the parent MNC is greater than in delegated professional MNCs and integration of activities through managerial routines and controls correspondingly more developed.

CASE EXAMPLE 3: ABB

In the case of ABB in the 1990s, for instance, considerable local diversity in one division was combined with extensive use of benchmarking and imposition of common improvement programmes from the centre to upgrade process efficiencies and learn from the better performers (Bélanger et al., 1999). Here, a cadre of international managers was developed by rotating successful plant executives across countries and continents, and eventually to leading positions in global divisions. They transferred effective recipes and processes between subsidiaries and so were key components of the MNC's learning activities. Committed to the success of the parent company, these elite managers contributed to the development of its international knowledge and capabilities on a continuing, long-term basis.

The predominantly national nature of organizational careers for most foreign employees, however, means that their loyalties will be more focused on national labour markets than the parent company. This means that local institutional differences are likely to affect levels and foci of long term commitments such that significant variations can be expected between, say, R&D teams in the UK and Japan that affect cross-national organizational learning, as some Japanese pharmaceutical firms have found out (Methe and Penner-Hahn, 1999; Lam, 2003).

While the international coordination of technology development activities through project planning and regular communication may be relatively straightforward when problem-solving activities follow relatively predictable trajectories, it becomes more difficult as the importance of tacit knowledge increases and technical uncertainty grows (Cantwell, 2001). Long-term international cooperation to develop organization-specific knowledge and skills in situations of considerable uncertainty is obviously not easy to accomplish when labour market institutions in some countries discourage long-term organizational commitments – whether national or international – and key staff are as much concerned with enhancing their external reputations and generic skills as developing firm-specific knowledge.

6. Highly integrated MNCs develop organizational careers and commitments that dominate those within national and regional subsidiaries, and reward both managerial and professional employees who demonstrate success in dealing with

international problem-solving and commitment to the parent organization. As a result, these firms develop distinctive knowledge and skills at the international level and their organizational capabilities are transnational rather than national. In particular, complementary activities are here integrated across borders by technical experts, as well as by managers, whose loyalties and identities are as much focused on the MNC as a whole as on national subsidiaries or local labour markets. Technical careers are as international as senior managerial ones, and depend on internationally visible success in solving organization-specific problems cross-nationally.

Ambitious foreign professionals and managers in these kinds of MNCs seek to demonstrate their success cross-nationally in contributing to major parent company issues rather than focusing on enhancing their reputations in local labour markets. This should generate strong international coordinating and learning capabilities as professional and managerial elites compete in the transnational organizational labour market on the basis of their success in dealing with major MNC problems. Because international careers dominate purely national ones, complex and tacit knowledge is more likely to be transferred and built upon by technical experts across national units than in delegated managerial MNCs.

The more international nature of commitments and loyalties in highly integrated MNCs additionally encourages the development of customer-specific knowledge at the international level. The primacy of international careers and problem-solving in these MNCs means that any investments in dealing with customers' problems will be cross-national rather than national. Similarly, they are as likely to compete with other MNCs at the international level as nationally, and so collectively develop an international competitive system that can, in some industries such as oil exploration, refining and distribution, dominate local markets.

For firms to be able to make credible commitments to key members of their international labour force such that they are encouraged to invest in long-term, firm-specific problem-solving and knowledge development, they need to be large and stable enough to maintain employment over business cycles and to offer international promotion prospects that greatly exceed domestic ones. MNCs are only likely to want to develop distinctive transnational capabilities through such commitments when they have strong international coordination and learning needs that far outweigh national and regional market variations and labour costs considerations. These points suggest that the relatively few MNCs that do develop long-term international careers for key experts and managers will be in capital-intensive industries with systemic technologies and worldwide markets for standardised products dominated by a few vertically integrated companies, such as the oil extraction, refining and distribution industry.

The primacy of international careers and commitments in such companies suggests that they may be more difficult to establish in collaborative economies than in arm's length ones because domestic organizational loyalties and authority sharing are greater in the former societies. Separating a relatively small group of highly trained employees for international careers from local colleagues, and rewarding cross-national competence development more than focusing on nationally specific issues is likely to be more difficult in these kinds of market economy. In contrast, because arm's length institutional regimes discourage high levels of employer–employee interdependence with the bulk of the workforce, they may enable MNCs from such domestic economies to provide organizational careers for technical and managerial staff. Additionally, low levels of authority sharing with business partners in these kinds of societies enable MNCs to develop a variety of linkages with customers and suppliers on a worldwide basis without having to integrate these with home economy ones. Insofar, then, as companies are able to establish such integrated international organizations that generate distinctive cross-national capabilities, they are more likely to originate in arm's length economies than collaborative ones.

CASE EXAMPLE 4: OIL COMPANIES

The large international oil companies, particularly those which are based in Europe, i.e. BP and Shell, appear to share many of these characteristics of highly integrated MNCs. Authority over operations beyond the head office is shared with highly skilled professional engineers and managers. These groups are frequently recruited direct from university from across the globe and their skills are adapted and shaped to the requirements of the firm with multiple opportunities for training and development. Their broader abilities are closely monitored and their assignments across different locations, different tasks and different functions is carefully managed. For the individual, this means seeing their home and family life through the lens of the organization. It is a high commitment undertaking and in return there is an expectation of the individual and the family being well looked after.

Some of these employees are gradually identified as of senior management quality and their careers will be further scrutinised to give them opportunities to learn a range of skills across the firm's operations and its subsidiaries. Technical and managerial problems to do with oil discovery, extraction and refining have a certain commonality though the conditions under which these activities take place will vary hugely. Capacities to learn how to manage these settings will be acquired gradually through experience and learning. This requires that the firm is able to sustain these long-term commitments. Although the oil industry has become more uncertain in recent years, this does not seem to have undermined the ability of these large firms to retain a core group of employees.

Conclusions

This analysis of the organizational capabilities of MNCs in the light of differences in the institutional frameworks of home and host economies suggests a number of conclusions about their development of transnational competences. First, while many companies with major facilities in different countries may develop distinctive collective capabilities at the national and regional levels, by no means all of them do so internationally. Many companies are often reluctant to share authority with foreign managers and professionals or to offer them long-term organizational commitments. This means that their organizational capabilities as MNCs are little different from those of their domestic organization, together perhaps with those generated separately by some subsidiaries. The coordination of economic activities in different countries does not, then, necessarily produce distinctive cross-national collective capabilities. Only in particular circumstances do forms of transnational capabilities emerge.

Second, at the broad institutional level, the forces against the development of transnational capabilities are strong. Arm's length institutional frameworks, for example, encourage firms to develop the ability to manage varied kinds of businesses through managerial procedures and routines that do not involve the bulk of the workforce. This in turn leads MNCs from such backgrounds to extend these control and planning systems to operations in different countries, limiting any authority sharing and career commitments to senior managers and professionals. The kinds of international organizational capabilities that they develop are therefore likely to be quite similar to domestic ones. Similarly, MNCs from highly coordinated economies that have developed strong organizational learning capabilities through considerable authority sharing with, and career commitments to, many domestic employees are likely to restrict such commitments to foreign staff because the institutions that constrained opportunism in the home economy are often missing in their societies. This is particularly probable when long-term careers in the domestic organization are both highly firm-specific and general across specialisms, as in many MNCs from segmented collaborative regimes.

Additionally, the impact of host economy institutions governing skill formation and labour markets can affect the development of cross-national capabilities by varying in their standardization and certification of practical expertise, as well as in their control over employer and employee opportunism. In general, the more fluid are external labour markets in an economy, and the more standardized are skills through educational and/or professional development and certification, the more difficult it becomes to develop long-term employee commitment at both national and international levels. While such institutional arrangements do facilitate employers' ability to hire and fire staff with varied kinds of skills, and so rapidly transform their knowledge and expertise base, they limit employees' willingness to invest in developing firm-specific capabilities on a continuing basis.

On the other hand, this suggests, thirdly, that cross-national problem-solving and learning should be easier when skill boundaries, knowledge bases and organizational structures in different countries overlap and provide common languages for joint problem-solving. When they do, careers in both internal and external labour markets are likely to reward comparable kinds of technically specialized contributions and to facilitate the development of cross-national cooperation and learning. These kinds of expertise-based career structures are in turn encouraged by similar kinds of public skill formation and evaluation systems that generate social identities and loyalties around certified skills. Overall, the more varied are subsidiaries' environments and their organization of careers, especially the kinds of contributions and skills that they reward, the more difficult it is likely to be for MNCs to develop a common language for problem-solving and distinctive international learning capabilities.

Fourth, the few MNCs that do develop strong coordinating and learning capabilities across borders through long-term international employer–employee commitments are less likely than delegated professional MNCs to be able to reconfigure their skills and competences radically to deal with rapidly changing circumstances. This is because of their dependence on current employees' skills and their establishment of transnational integrating routines. Building and maintaining long-term firm-specific organizational capabilities at the international level usually involves considerable investments in cross-national procedures, routines and competences. These are unlikely to encourage rapid and radical transformation of key skills and technologies that would enable firms to move effectively into quite novel industries with discontinuous technological trajectories and markets.

Delegated professional MNCs, in contrast, are more flexible, especially when their major operations are in fluid external labour markets, but tend to limit the international coordination of knowledge and skill development to cross-national teams working on discrete, one-off problems (Morgan and Quack, 2005). They are therefore able to adjust relatively quickly to changing technologies and markets, particularly when there are highly organized markets for technical specialists, but key competences are as much individual and team-based as organizationally specific. International capabilities here involve coordinating teams of specialists across countries on a largely ad hoc opportunistic basis with little employer or employee commitment to organizational careers. Mobilizing and controlling such teams are here central organizational competences that depend on considerable knowledge of local labour markets and reputational networks, further encouraging authority sharing and delegation of operational control, as in many project-based firms in emerging industries (Grabher, 2002a, 2002b).

In conclusion, the idea that there is a distinctively transnational model of the MNC has been considerably overstated. Institutional factors mean that most MNCs do not share significant amounts of decision-making authority across national borders nor do they develop global careers that could facilitate extensive and long-term collaborative learning across countries. Only under very limited circumstances does this become possible and even here the extent of it varies between companies.

Questions

In order to understand the relationship between MNCs and their development of distinctive sorts of competences through authority sharing and the development of organizational careers, you should look in detail at a number of examples of MNCs. Try to select MNCs with different national origins; also select firms in similar sectors so you can understand the effect that particular product and labour markets are having on the firm.

1. In the examples you have selected how does the national institutional origin affect the type of MNC that has developed?
2. Compare three firms from different contexts and see what differences there are in terms of:
   (a) The national origins of members of their top management teams
   (b) The sorts of careers pursued by these top managers, e.g. have they been predominantly within the one firm, within a single industry, within a single country.
3. Which of the companies you have looked at comes closest to a 'transnational' firm and why?

Further Reading

In-depth studies of companies which enable us to understand the dynamics discussed here are rare, as it is difficult to undertake global research about a multinational, particularly over a long period of time and where the focus is on the development of intangible assets and the careers of individuals. The following give some sense of the dynamics of these processes:

Almond, P. and Ferner, A. (eds) (2006) *American Multinationals in Europe*. Oxford: Oxford University Press.

Belanger, J., Berggren, C., Bjorkman, T. and Kohler, C. (eds) (1999) *Being Local Worldwide: ABB and the challenge of global management*. Ithaca, NY: Cornell University Press.

Geppert, M. and Williams, K. (2006) 'Global, National and Local Practices in Multinational Corporations', *International Journal of Human Resource Management*, 17, 49–69.

Kristensen, P. H. and Zeitlin, J. (2005) *Local Players in Global Games: The strategic constitution of a multinational corporation*. Oxford: Oxford University Press.

Lam, A. (2003) 'Managing Global R&D Networks and Transnational Organizational Learning: Japanese and US multinationals in the ICT and pharmaceutical industries', *Journal of Management Studies*, 40.3, 673–703.

Malnight, T. W. (1995) 'Globalization of an Ethnocentric Firm: An evolutionary perspective', *Strategic Management Journal*, 16, 119–41.

Morgan, G., Kelly, W., Sharpe, D. and Whitley, R. (2003) 'Global Managers and Japanese Multinationals: Internationalisation and management in Japanese financial institutions', *International Journal of Human Resource Management*, 14.3, 389–407.

Morgan, G. and Quack, S. (2005) 'Internationalisation and Capability Development in Professional Service Firms'. In G. Morgan, R. Whitley and E. Moen (eds) *Changing Capitalisms? Internationalisation, Institutional Change and Systems of Economic Organization*, Oxford: Oxford University Press, 277–311.

Sakai, J. (2000) *Japanese Bankers in the City of London*. London: Routledge.

Whitley, R., Morgan, G., Kelly, W. and Sharpe, D. (2003) 'The Changing Japanese MNC', *Journal of Management Studies*, 40, 639–68.

References

Abo, T. (ed.) (1994) *Hybrid Factories: The Japanese production system in the United States.* Oxford: Oxford University Press.

Arvidsson, N. (1999) *The Ignorant MNE: The role of perception gaps in knowledge management.* Stockholm: Stockholm School of Economics.

Barca, F. and Becht, M. (eds.) (2001) *The Control of Corporate Europe.* Oxford; Oxford University Press.

Bartlett, C. and Ghoshal, S. (1989) *Managing across Borders.* London: Century Books.

Beechler, S. L. and Bird, A. (eds) (1999) *Japanese Multinationals Abroad: Individual and organizational learning.* Oxford: Oxford University Press.

Bélanger, J., Berggren, C., Bjorkman, T. and Kohler, C. (eds) (1999) *Being Local Worldwide: ABB and the challenge of global management.* Ithaca, NY: Cornell University Press.

Birkinshaw, J. and Hood, N. (eds) (1998) *Multinational Corporate Evolution and Subsidiary Development.* London: Macmillan.

Botti, H. (1995) 'Misunderstandings: A Japanese Transplant in Italy Strives for Lean Production', *Organization,* 2, 55–86.

Brannen, M. Y., Liker, J. K. and Fruin, W. M. (1999) 'Recontextualization and Factory-to-Factory Knowledge Transfer from Japan to the United States: The case of NSK'. In J. K. Liker, W. M. Fruin and P. S. Adler (eds) *Remade in America: Transplanting and transforming Japanese management systems,* New York: Oxford University Press, 117–53.

Cantwell, J. (2001) 'Innovation and Information Technology in the MNE'. In A. Rugman and T. Brewer (eds) *The Oxford Handbook of International Business.* Oxford: Oxford University Press, 431–56.

Crouch, C., Finegold, D. and Sako, M. (1999) *Are Skills the Answer? The Political Economy of Skill Creation in Advanced Industrial Countries.* Oxford: Oxford University Press.

Evans, P. (1994) *Embedded Autonomy: States and Industrial Transformation.* Princeton, NJ; Princeton University Press.

Fleury, A. and Salerno, M. S. (1998) 'The Transfer and Hybridization of New Models of production in the Brazilian Automobile Industry'. In R. Boyer, E. Charron, U. Jurgens and S. Tolliday (eds) *Between Imitation and Innovation: The transfer and hybridization of productive models in the international automobile industry.* Oxford: Oxford University Press, 278–94.

Grabher, G. (2002a) 'Cool Projects, Boring Institutions: Temporary collaboration in social context', *Regional Studies,* 36, 204–14.

Grabher, G. (2002b) 'Fragile Sector, Robust Practices: Project ecologies in new media', *Environment and Planning,* A, 34, 1911–26.

Hedlund, G. (1993) 'Assumptions of Hierarchy and Heterarchy, with Applications to the management of the Multinational Corporation'. In S. Ghoshal and E. Westney (eds) *Organization Theory and the Multinational Corporation.* London: Macmillan, 211–36.

Hinz, T. (1999) 'Vocational training and Job Mobility in Comparative Perspective'. In P. D. Culpepper and D. Finegold (eds) *The German Skills Machine.* New York: Berghahn Books, 159–88.

Holm, U. and Pedersen, T. (eds) (2000) *The Emergence and Impact of MNC Centres of Excellence: A subsidiary perspective.* London: Macmillan.

Jurgens, U. (1998) 'Implanting Change: The role of "indigenous transplants" in transforming the German productive model'. In Robert Boyer *et al.* (eds) *Between Imitation and Innovation.* Oxford: Oxford University Press, 319–60.

Kenney, M. and Florida, R. (1993) *Beyond Mass Production*. Oxford: Oxford University Press.

Kneller, R. (2003) 'Autarkic Drug Discovery in Japanese Pharmaceutical Companies: Insights into national differences in industrial innovation', *Research Policy*, 32, 1805–27.

Kopp, R. (1999) 'The Rice-Paper Ceiling in Japanese Companies: Why It Exists and Persists'. In S. L. Beechler, and A. Bird (eds) *Japanese Multinationals Abroad: Individual and Organizational Learning*. New York: Oxford University Press, 107–28.

Lam, A. (2003) 'Managing Global R&D Networks and Transnational Organizational Learning: Japanese and US multinationals in the ICT and pharmaceutical industries', *Journal of Management Studies* 40.3, 673–703.

Lane, C. (2001) 'The Emergence of German Transnational Companies'. In G. Morgan, P. H. Kristensen and R. Whitley (eds) *The Multinational Firm*. Oxford: Oxford University Press, 69–96.

Malnight, T. W. (1995) 'Globalization of an Ethnocentric Firm: An evolutionary perspective', *Strategic Management Journal*, 16, 119–41.

Marsden, D. (1999) *A Theory of Employment Systems*. Oxford: Oxford University Press.

Methe, D. P. and Penner-Hahn, J. D. (1999) 'Globalization of Pharmaceutical Research and Development in Japanese Companies'. In S. L. Beechler and A. Bird (eds) *Japanese Multinationals Abroad: Individual and Organizational Learning*. Oxford: Oxford University Press, 191–210.

Morgan, G. and Quack, S. (2005) 'Internationalisation and Capability Development in Professional Service Firms'. In G. Morgan, R. Whitley and E. Moen (eds) *Changing Capitalisms? Internationalisation, Institutional Change and Systems of Economic Organization*. Oxford: Oxford University Press, 277–311.

Morgan, G., Kelly, W., Sharpe, D. and Whitley, R. (2003) ' Global Managers and Japanese Multinationals: Internationalisation and management in Japanese financial institutions', *International Journal of Human Resource Management*, 14.3, 389–407.

Nohria, N. and Ghoshal, S. (1997) *The Differentiated Network: Organizing multinational corporations for value creation*. San Francisco: Jossey-Bass.

Perlmutter, H. (1969) 'The Tortuous Evolution of the multinational corporation' *Columbia Journal of World Business*, 4, 9–18.

Pil, F. and MacDuffie, J. P. (1999) 'Transferring Competitive Advantage across Borders: A study of Japanese auto transplants in North America'. In J. K. Liker, W. M. Fruin and P. S. Adler (eds) *Remade in America: Transplanting and Transforming Japanese Management Systems*. New York : Oxford University Press, 39–74.

Pucik, V. (1999) 'When Performance Does Not Matter: Human resource management in Japanese-owned US affiliates'. In S. L. Beechler and A. Bird (eds) *Japanese Multinationals Abroad*. Oxford: Oxford University Press, 169–88.

Sakai, J. (2000) *Japanese Bankers in the City of London*. London: Routledge.

Sheard, P. (1994) 'Interlocking Shareholdings and Corporate Governance in Japan' In Aoki, M. and Dore, R. (eds.) *The Japanese Firm: The sources of competitive strength*. Oxford: Oxford University Press, 310–349.

Sölvell, O. and Zander, I. (1998) 'International Diffusion of Knowledge: Isolating mechanisms and the role of the MNE'. In A. D. Chandler, P. Hagstrom and O. Solvell (eds) *The Dynamic Firm: The role of technology, strategy, and regions*. Oxford: Oxford University Press, 402–16.

Soskice, D. (1999) 'Divergent Production Regimes: Coordinated and uncoordinated market economies in the 1980s and 1990s'. In Kitschelt, H., Lange, P., Marks, G. and Stephens,

J. (eds.) *Continuity and Change in Contemporary Capitalism*. Cambridge: Cambridge University Press, 101–134.

Szulanski, G. (1996) 'Exploring Internal Stickiness: Impediments to the transfer of best practices within the firm', *Strategic Management Journal*, 17, 27–44.

Tolliday, S. (2000) 'Transplanting the American Model? US Automobile Companies and the Transfer of Technology and Management to Britain, France, and Germany, 1928–1962'. In J. Zeitlin and G. Herrigel (eds) *Americanization and its Limits: Reworking US technology and management in post-war Europe and Japan*. Oxford: Oxford University Press, 76–119.

Whitley, R. (1999) *Divergent Capitalisms: The social structuring and change of business systems*. Oxford: Oxford University Press.

Whitley, R. (2003) 'The Institutional Structuring of Organizational Capabilities: The role of authority sharing and organizational careers', *Organization Studies*, 24, 667–95.

Whitley, R. (2007) *Business Systems and Organizational Capabilities*. Oxford: Oxford University Press.

Whitley, R., Morgan, G., Kelly, W. and Sharpe, D. (2003) 'The Changing Japanese MNC', *Journal of Management Studies*, 40, 639–68.

Zander, I. and Solvell, O. (2002) 'The Phantom Multinational'. In V. Havila, M. Forsgren and H. Hakansson (eds) *Critical Perspectives on Internationalisation*. Oxford: Pergamon, 81–106.

Chapter 8   Multinational Firms as Societies

Glenn Morgan and Peer Hull Kristensen

Introduction

In this chapter, we think about multinationals as being 'like' societies. We are not claiming that multinationals 'are' societies. We do not seek to scientifically prove that we have accessed the 'correct' image of a multinational and everybody else has got it wrong. We put this image forward in a book of 'images' with the intention of getting readers thinking again about how multinationals work and whether our particular image has any resonances with what we experience in the world of multinationals.

Before we proceed to our main arguments, however, we want to give an initial justification for fixing on this image of MNCs. Why use the image of MNCs as 'societies' in the first place? There are two reasons.

The first is that we need to grasp the fundamental influence which MNCs exercise over the lives of participants, localities and social systems generally. In their sheer size they are beginning to dwarf all but the largest societies in terms of the economic resources which they allocate. Although there are problems in making such comparisons, it has been argued that the largest multinationals are now larger than countries in terms of the economic resources they manage. Anderson and Cavanagh (2005), comparing company turnover and country GDP, for example, find that of the 100 largest economies in the world, 51 are corporations and only 49 are countries. They state that:

> 'Wal-Mart – the number 12 corporation – is bigger than 161 countries, including Israel, Poland, and Greece. Mitsubishi is larger than the fourth most populous nation on earth: Indonesia. General Motors is bigger than Denmark. Ford is bigger than South Africa. Toyota is bigger than Norway.'

The largest 100 MNCs accounted for 4.3 % of world GDP in 2000 and according to Anderson and Cavanagh the combined sales of the top 200 are around 28.3 % of

Images of the Multinational Firm   Edited by Simon Collinson and Glenn Morgan
© 2009 John Wiley & Sons, Ltd

world GDP which makes them bigger than the combined economies of all countries minus the biggest nine. The 2006 UNCTAD World Investment Report reported that there were 77 175 multinational parent companies in the world and 773 019 subsidiaries of these companies. In the same report, the top 20 non-financial multinationals ranked by assets in 2004 employed over 3.8 million people (WIR 2006: own calculations). The impact of MNCs on direct employment is, of course, magnified by the impact which they have indirectly through their contractors and subcontractors. In global terms, therefore, economic resources are organized significantly through and by multinationals. The fates of communities and individuals are intimately tied up with the investment, management and organization of multinationals. This influence gives them some of the power which previously we have associated with societies. Indeed this is explicitly discussed in many contexts where the rise of the multinationals and the decline of the nation state are seen as two sides of the same coin. In this sense, multinationals have become important from a political and social point of view as well as from an economic point of view. By examining the image of multinationals as societies, we are forced to recognize this and we are in effect responding to the broader debate of the role of multinationals in the modern world.

The second reason is that when we discuss the nature of societies, we are interested in social order, a process which involves beliefs, morals and values. Grand theorists such as Parsons (1964) saw societies as consisting of a series of functionally related areas – including its political subsystem, its economic subsystem, its cultural subsystem and its socialization subsystem. A society was both political and economic, social and moral, cultural and instrumental. If we say that multinationals are like societies, we do so because we want to say that they are not solely economic entities; they are much more complex with social, political, moral and ethical issues at stake. In what follows, we seek to demonstrate this in a particular way.

Our chapter proceeds in the following steps. Firstly we construct a very specific image of societies. Our focus is on the construction of social order and societies that characterizes the emergence of European nation states out of the feudal era into the era of liberal democracy. In keeping with our 'images' approach, we develop an image of this transition drawing on recent socio-historical overviews of this process. Secondly, we argue that multinationals are in some ways 'like' societies. In order to develop this argument, we draw on our discussion of the emergence of the European nation states, focusing in particular on how diverse centres of power and influence interact. The societal transition we discuss is characterized by the reconstruction of both hierarchical relationships (with the monarchy) and lateral relationships (with other feudal lords) and the creation of a new system where power and influence is balanced and 'constitutionalized'. Our basic reflection is that multinationals, particularly as discussed in the current period, are also like this in that they are reconstructing hierarchical and lateral relationships between centres of power and influence in order to produce a new network of power that is distinctive in its nature. In the third section, we focus particularly on this process of building a 'constitutional' order; what might be the gains of such an order, what are the civilizing forces and what might be the inhibiting factors? In this way, we suggest that some of the dynamics in and around multinationals might be perceived in a new light if we developed the image of MNCs as societies.

Societies Past and Present

A basic building block for our analysis is the nexus between face-to-face social relationships and social relationships conducted at a distance and how this nexus is reconfigured over time in terms of authority and power relations. Face-to-face social relationships can never be decoupled from broader relationships, e.g. shared languages and religions, patterns of trade and markets, systems of justice and authority. Societies consist first of all of mechanisms which cut across local contexts and bind face-to-face relationships into a larger whole – at the ideational level through religion, nationalism, socialism, communism etc. and at the level of social practice through systems of education, social welfare and justice, systems of taxation and systems of military service that are present at the local level but organized at a distance. Societies vary in terms of how this nexus is organized. The idea that power and authority over the local is embedded in a single sovereign is an outcome of the formation of states themselves in the period from the sixteenth century onwards in Western Europe. The parcellization of authority between different actors, constructed through religious hierarchies, through feudal hierarchies and through the creation of privileges for 'free cities' was common in Europe until the seventeenth century. European pre-modern societies were characterized by what seemed an almost impossible struggle to create a single principle of secular sovereignty within a bordered territory and to do away with the remnants of authority and ordering based on different principles.

This needed also to involve a fundamental transition in the nature of power. John Hall (1986) has described the 'capstone' form of power in pre-industrial societies where a central authority sits on top of local relationships which it deems as part of its estate. In contrast to modern states, territories were more loosely organized for two reasons. Firstly, in the European context, there were a variety of forms of authority which claimed overlapping forms of jurisdiction. The church, for example, claimed not just spiritual authority but also legal authority over certain forms of activities and certain territories. Some cities claimed rights of self-government derived in part from charters granted by kings, the church and other authorities such as the Holy Roman Empire. Other territories occupied an ambiguous position between competing claimants. Secondly, territories were loosely bounded according to familial alliances and warfare, and not necessarily geographical propinquity. Kingdoms and lesser forms of authority changed their shapes frequently as new alliances and new wars took place. Central forms of authority such as kings relied on the support of local lords who controlled localities to provide them with armies or forced levies for public works. The loyalty of the nobles was based on the ability of the king to extend territories and provide them with more land and thereby more wealth. The nobles extracted tax and labour from localities and dispensed forms of justice but did not engage more deeply with localities in terms of organizing agricultural production.

As Weber (1992) effectively illustrated, the result of this was that most pre-industrial societies were characterized firstly by wars of territorial expansion that depended on the mobilization of nobles and their feudal subjects by the king, and secondly by rebellions prompted by the attempts of nobles to increase control and surplus extraction over local contexts. The result was a cycle of war and peace with different authorities gaining and losing control and influence over territory that was loosely bounded and weakly policed.

It is of central interest to historical sociologists how European societies got out of this cycle. There are, of course, many competing explanations, but the one which is relevant for our discussion concerns the idea of what Elias (2000) calls a 'civilizing process'. For Elias, one of the important moments in social development occurs when actors with different interests decide they are no longer going to compete through physical force but are going to engage in a 'civilized' process of mutual constitution, competition and exchange (see also Hirschmann, 1997). This does not involve giving up interests but engaging them in a way which is structured and institutionalized. There are two phases to this process that can be broadly distinguished.

The first phase concerns a new form of relationship between the central power, the monarch and the powers at a distance – feudal lords. This phase is characterized by an increasing dependence on the central power of the dispersed powers. Elias labeled this the development of 'court-society' (Elias, 1983). The King assembled 'his' feudal lords in his presence and institutionalized a game by which he forced his vassals and rivals alike to compete for his favours. This involved the King drawing on resources which were not dependent on the feudal lords and thereby becoming increasingly powerful in his own right, a power which was symbolized by the creation of royal palaces and courts and the events and processes which occurred 'at court'. These resources involved new forms of taxation of as well as borrowing from the growing bourgeoisie of the towns and cities. In feudal times, royal courts had frequently moved around the country descending on nobles for extended periods of stay. Increasingly, however, the royal court became fixed in a single geographical location and lords were forced to attend the king rather than vice versa. Attendance was compulsory and expensive. Failure to be present meant loss of influence and through this a loss of wealth but being present also required wealth sufficient to keep a home in the country and in the town, often characterized by sumptuous luxury in the face of the extravagance of the court (which reached its height in Louis XIV's palace at Versailles).

This had two effects. Firstly, nobles sought to extract more from their lands, bearing down harder on the incomes and living standards of peasants. However, because there were limits to this and because the costs of court life were so high, many nobles became increasingly impoverished or found themselves facing low-level conflict in their domains. Success and position in the court, being favoured by the king, enabled them to avoid this impoverishment though it increased their dependence on the central authority.

Secondly, courts were also associated with the creation of new standards of behaviour and rules of manners and courtesy. Swords and other weapons become forms of ritual and dress rather than physical threats. Instead of relying on the lords to provide peasant armies of their vassals, the King relied upon taxation and borrowing to generate the income necessary to pay mercenaries and later a professional army such as that constructed in Prussia under Frederick the Great. Feudal lords 'demilitarized' in the sense that they no longer kept their own standing army, instead becoming frequently assimilated into the armies kept by kings.

This process created tensions in towns as well as in the countryside. Concentrating the feudal lords around the King created a vacuum of control in the countryside and parallel with the formation of these intensive courts Europe witnessed an increasing number of local conflicts, which often became transnationally linked around issues of religion but were also based in local circumstances (Te Brake, 1998). In the towns, rises in taxation and borrowing impacted on the growing bourgeoisie which increasingly became concerned itself to have a voice at court or some influence over the King leading to demands for parliaments, constitutions and the rule of law. Through the seventeenth century these forces ushered in civil and religious war across most of the European continent as well as in the British Isles. Thus although feudal power had been eroded and centralized monarchical power increased, this remained unstable, provoking scattered conflicts, religious wars and wars between states in Europe and elsewhere that undermined the stability of the emerging system.

It was this which prompted the move from this first phase of the centralizing of state power towards a second phase broadly associated with the development of the rule of law, the independence of the state from the monarchy, and the development of liberal institutions and civil society, a period which characterized the transitions of European societies through the eighteenth and nineteenth centuries. North and Weingast put forward a compelling argument that Europe began to first move out of this cycle in England following the Civil War, the regicide of Charles I, the Restoration of the Stuarts followed by the overthrow of James II and the Glorious Revolution of 1688 (North and Weingast, 1989). Religious strife associated with the issue of where power lay between the monarch and the Parliament threatened to undermine the growing wealth and economic activity of merchants and commercial intermediaries that were establishing themselves in the emergent maritime economy associated with the opening up of the Americas. The two parties (Parliament and the monarchy) recognized that if they did not reach agreement through suspending the wholesale pursuit of their own interests, they might end up destroying each other and thereby destroying the emerging economic prosperity that was benefiting both sides. The future could be bright if there was a solution to these conflicts. They therefore compromised and created a new institutional system, which allowed for a liberal form of the state to emerge that guaranteed private property and individual rights before the law, whilst not questioning the right of the monarchy to exist. For both parties this meant giving up 'maximalist' claims that previously might have been pursued, taming the 'passions' of kings and nobles for warfare and territorial expansion in favour of creating a system based on 'interests' and the pursuit of economic wealth (Hirschmann, 1997). They had to recognize that sometimes, things would happen which they would not like but they agreed to forego conflict on these points. They were creating an environment of 'credible commitments' in which the recognition that there were infinitely repeatable games and that the present had consequences for a future in which all the participants were going to have to repeat their actions required that conflict over fundamental issues should decline, and be replaced by bargaining and negotiation.

The emergence of capitalist organization and markets furthered these processes by reinforcing and developing sources of power that were market-based and not directly dependent on access to central political power. Thus capitalist relations, liberal ideas of property rights and later the rights of individuals together with the declining significance of the 'divine right of kings' gave rise in certain European countries to a new set of relationships between social actors. Later developments in what became the United States and in the turmoil arising from the French Revolution and the Napoleonic Wars reinforced the emergence of what became known as 'constitutional monarchies'. In many parts of Europe this was a process that lasted throughout the nineteenth century, becoming engulfed later in the development of democracy and the rise of working class politics, as well as in the rise of nationalism and new forms of authoritarian rule. Thus 'court society' evolves into 'liberal society', not in an automatic or painless way but through protracted struggles and conflicts.

What is important here is that this transition has an economic impact. Societies become more 'powerful' in economic terms as they make this transition because they gain a new set of capacities. Foucault illustrated this paradox in typically dramatic fashion with his contrast between the treatment of the regicide and the emergence of the prison and the category of 'criminal' (Foucault, 1979). The regicide is hung, drawn and quartered, his mutilated body displayed to the people, as an illustration of the awesome repressive power of the capstone state when it is provoked into action. But this power to punish, to create 'shock and awe' in subjects is a negative power, not what Foucault describes as 'productive power'. Productive or positive power is illustrated for Foucault through the way in which within a few decades the state is creating prisons where criminals are being categorized, measured and disciplined in order to turn them back into 'normal' citizens. Individuals are placed into networks of what Foucault refers to as the microphysics of power where discipline is not something exercised from outside over the body of the subject but is rather something by which the subject knows their own individuality and their own powers to reproduce or remake their subjectivity. The state engages in a reshaping of the subjectivity of the individual through expert power; the invisible acting on the invisible mind in contrast to the visible action of the state on the body of the regicide. Power becomes a motivating force, motivating the will for knowledge and the development of the human sciences with techniques of governmentality (Burchell, 1991). This in turn reshapes how subjects see themselves and act. This reshaping occurs on the basis of the state gaining what Mann (1986) terms 'infrastructural power' (in contrast to the capstone view of power). The 'infrastructural' view of the state emphasizes the capacity of the state to engage with and reorganize social relations at the local and individual level rather than simply sitting on top as a coercive power of punishment. The issue here concerns the growing capacity of the state to categorize, identify and exercise, to measure, grade and normalize, to educate, socialize and mould, to control, sanction and punish citizens, families, groups and the society as a whole. The modern state can do things that previous states and social orders could not do because it has shaped its population into disciplined subjects – so disciplined that they will walk into a hail of machine gun bullets in order to serve their country. Citizens are no longer recalcitrant social objects to be disciplined by physical force and coercion but are now willing participants in the development of power. Such a setting is powerful in a new way, enabling things to be organized and done in increasingly efficient systems where issues of consent and legitimacy have been broadly resolved and conflicts are confined to the interstices of society and do not threaten its fundamental basis. Competition between groups and individuals is fundamental but constitutionalized, ruled, orderly. It is of course the case that societies relate to this image in diverse ways and in many cases the power of the new form of state has been turned inwards and outwards to create totalitarian movements which threaten this liberal model. If the eighteenth and nineteenth centuries saw the gradual rise of the model, then the twentieth century was undoubtedly characterized by a set of world wars, hot and cold, which threatened to overwhelm it.

Nevertheless, the important things which we wish to emphasize in terms of the creation of societies and social order in the modern period are two-fold. Firstly, the creation of court society brought hierarchical and lateral relationships into a new form of order binding the lords and the monarch in a new more 'civilized' set of relationships where the 'conduct of conduct' in Foucault's terms was more strictly produced and monitored through rules of interaction. Competition through force of arms was replaced by competition over status and influence within the court society. Rivalries previously enacted on the battlefield were now played out in the intrigues and politics of the court where behaviour and appearance was strongly monitored. However, this did not resolve the broader problem of order but rather weakened some of the controls exercised by feudal lords over their populations, since they were now more focused on the centralized court than on their role in disciplining their subjects. Secondly, it was only when 'court society' itself was challenged and replaced by constitutions that applied the rule of law more broadly and developed institutional frameworks for representing a more diverse group of actors than those involved in the court that a new form of social order was created. This new form of order also retained competition between actors with different interests but placed them in the competition for social space according to new sets of rules. These rules bound all the actors together and civilized their competition for social space, pushing violence and armed conflict within the boundaries of the new social order to the periphery or into the relations with other states. Associated with this, the cooperative game facilitated a new form of power that is intensive rather than extensive, productive rather than coercive. It was this new form of power that enabled societies to move ahead towards an industrialized economy. If conflict had continued such a move could not have occurred; only because the actors were willing to 'civilize' themselves, were they then able to cooperate in building a new more productive society.

Multinationals, Constitutions and Social Order

The simple starting point for our analysis is that, like societies, multinationals consist of local socially embedded relations and a central power, which acts on localities at a distance. Drawing on our previous discussion, we examine three elements of this. Firstly, we look at how multinationals can be characterized as a new form of 'court society'. Secondly, we consider what this means for subsidiaries in terms of the goals which they pursue and how they act. Thirdly, we examine the forces which are conducive and those which are resistant to the development of a constitutionalization process.

Multinationals as 'Court Societies'

We begin from the assumption that over the last 20 years, multinationals have evolved in new directions. Broadly speaking this is represented by Barlett and Ghoshal's identification of a 'transnational' form (Bartlett and Ghoshal, 1991) though this was anticipated in Hedlund's concept of heterarchy (Hedlund, 1986, 1999) and reinforced in later analyses of network MNCs and more recently discussions of knowledge transfer in MNCs. Previous approaches to MNCs tended to see the nature of interactions inside the firm from two perspectives. The first perspective emphasized the way in which the expertise or resources of the head office were fed into subsidiaries. This was created in the home base and was then leveraged to create advantages in new and old markets. In the second perspective, MNCs were seen as federations of national companies where expertise and knowledge rested in the national context and the headquarters barely interfered with local practices. Both of these perspectives reflected an emphasis on territorial expansion which can be seen as analogous to that of the feudal era. New territories were conquered providing managers with opportunities for building their careers.

These perspectives appeared increasingly inadequate as barriers to trade and the flow of capital declined and multinationals took on new forms. Three developments in particular were important (see Westney and Zaheer (2001) for a summary of these developments). The first was that MNC subsidiaries took on roles that extended beyond either the host market in which they were based or the home market of their headquarters. They became increasingly responsible for activities across varying geographical scales – the region, the continent, the world etc. and not just the national market. MNCs were moving towards a more global organizational structure. The second development concerned the fact that a range of different activities could now become spread across subsidiary units, including research and development, sales and marketing, as well as production. The third development was that in order for this to happen, it was necessary for subsidiaries and headquarters to engage horizontally and vertically in much more intensive forms of knowledge management, knowledge transfer, the monitoring and assessment of performance levels and the coordination of processes and procedures. The transition to these two latter forms of MNC represents the development of the transnational model in the terminology of Bartlett and Ghoshal.

Within the literature of international business, this has led to a much greater focus on the complexities of the subsidiary/headquarters relationships and it is this which we consider in the rest of this section. Subsidiaries are no longer to be considered as passive recipients of an order created by the head office. On the contrary it is clear that subsidiaries could become active and develop their own strategies (Birkinshaw, 1997; Birkinshaw and Hood, 1998). Similarly these authors began to analyse how headquarters stimulated and shaped this process of subsidiary strategizing and in turn how subsidiaries interact with each other as well as with different head office functions. The MNC is not so much a system of dispersed and separated units as an interconnected web of relationships. To return to our metaphor what occurred was a shift from a dispersed and uncertain system of authority to the development of a 'court society' in which rules of behaviour and civilized competition were being developed. This court consists of senior headquarters managers and the managers of subsidiaries (and regional geographic/functional structures) engaging with each other under emergent rules of civilized behaviour, i.e. what is considered as a legitimate form of control and monitoring.

Birkinshaw (2000) identified the competition process in terms of the development of three different sorts of internal markets in which subsidiaries competed against each other.

- *Intermediate products or services*: competition with internal and external providers over the delivery of products or services to the next stage in the value chain (which could be an internal or external customer).
- *Charter*: Birkinshaw refers to this as 'most visible in cases of new investments – a new production plant, an R&D centre or a logistics centre. While new investments are almost always actively competed for ... existing charters are increasingly deemed to be mobile and therefore open to competition' (Birkinshaw, 2000: 119). He further states that this form of market is quite expensive because proposals have to be evaluated as well as being quite conflictual since the consequence of a loss of charter could be the closure of a subsidiary. Birkinshaw and Lingblad (2005) have examined the degree to which charters overlap in multiunit businesses. They distinguish two dimensions of this question. The first is the degree to which two units in the firm occupy or overlap in the same charter space. The second is the degree to which a unit's charter boundary is defined; is it closely defined and solid or is it fluid and consistent with managers having the freedom to move beyond their original boundaries to redefine a charter? What they suggest is that the greater the ambiguity and uncertainty in the environment, the more likely there is to be charter overlap and fluidity in the charter definition state.
- *Capability or practice*: this refers to the transfer of best practices between sites and is dependent on internal benchmarking processes. Birkinshaw states that this is not overtly 'competitive' but the consequences of such transfers may

be complex. On the one hand, a subsidiary that engages in transfer gains a reputation for its expertise in particular processes and this may give it a strong position in winning charters or positions in internal markets. On the other hand, the transfer process potentially dilutes this power by diffusing knowledge across to other subsidiaries. Thus competition exists but the rules of the game and how one wins such a competition and with what consequences are unclear.

The 'court society' of the MNC in the current era is defined by an increasingly rigorous application of the rules of the market to the allocation of resources and status to subsidiaries. Recent work has suggested that subsidiary managers recognize this and engage in positioning themselves in these processes. They become part of this 'court society'. They do this in a number of ways. The most important of these is to engage in their own initiatives and evolve their own strategies. Again Birkinshaw (2000: ch. 2) provided a useful typology of forms of initiative which could be undertaken:

- *Local market initiatives*: building and developing products, services and linkages in the host context.
- *Global market initiatives*: 'driven by unmet product or market needs among non-local suppliers and customers', subsidiaries may attempt to develop initiatives that have broader implications.
- *Internal market initiatives*: 'geared towards reconfiguring and rationalizing the activity system in the MNC', internal market initiatives are 'symptomatic of an overall shift towards geographical concentration by value-adding function in MNCs'.
- *Global-internal hybrid initiatives*: Birkinshaw states that 'the locus of the market opportunity is outside the subsidiary's home market. But like internal initiatives, the locus of *pursuit* is internal in that it involves convincing head office managers, not external customers' (ibid.: 28).

A crucial aspect of this process has been identified in further work. Ling *et al.* refer to this as 'issue-selling by subsidiary managers' (Ling *et al.*, 2005) whilst Bouquet and Birkinshaw discuss 'how foreign subsidiaries gain attention from corporate head-quarters' (Bouquet and Birkinshaw, 2008). Ling *et al.* define 'issue-selling' as the discretionary behaviour used to direct top management's attention toward or increase their understanding of, strategic issues. Their main concern is with developing Hofstede's cultural model to show that subsidiary managers from different cultural contexts will take different approaches to (a) selling issues to head office senior managers and (b) interpreting the ways in which head office wants issues to be sold to it. What is significant from our discussion of the MNC and 'court society' is that the authors emphasize the importance of the nature of communication between head office and subsidiary managers. The 'courtier' is concerned to make an impression on the king – to appear as a worthy courtier and to advance his/her interests against those of the other courtiers. The analysis of court society suggests that this is not just about building an economic case but about display, reputation, alliances within the court, and participating effectively in the language and games of the court. Being successful in this way brings resources to the subsidiary.

Bouquet and Birkinshaw develop a similar theme from a slightly different perspective. They are interested in the strategies that organizational units deploy to attract HQ attention as a 'key question becomes how they gain the necessary levels of HQ attention to deliver on their potential and contribute to the MNE's long-term success'. From their empirical studies, they argue that 'initiative taking and profile building constitute important drivers of HQ attention ... To be successful in shaping the perception that they are reliable, credible and trustworthy actors of the MNE organization, our findings suggest that subsidiaries will not only need to maintain a basic track-record of success, but also reaffirm their commitment to the parent's objectives and, then finally, take deliberate steps to manage impressions with powerbrokers at head office.' Clearly the courtiers have to prove their loyalty to the king; analogously so do the subsidiary managers have to prove their loyalty to the headquarters.

These processes, we would suggest, are highly analogous to the processes in the formation of 'court society'. As with 'court society', a new set of rules has emerged which more strictly demarcates what is acceptable behaviour, how this should be demonstrated, how it is to be monitored and with what effect. What were in previous types of multinationals, relatively informal, ambiguous and partial systems of control have now become much more clearly defined. Relations between the headquarters (the centre, the monarch) and the periphery (the subsidiaries, the feudal lords) are now organized in a new more systematic way. Central to this is a process of civilized competition between the peripheral actors under rules set in place by the headquarters. This is a competition over resources to expand positions in the internal market – for products and services, for charters and for reputation. Winning and losing these competitions has a fundamental impact on the future of the subsidiary. For this reason, subsidiaries and their managers have to be present in the court; they have to be visible; they have to sell their issues to senior managers and gain attention from them. If they are invisible, fail to develop a 'voice' in court or to take strategic initiatives, their future looks grim. They have to learn the rules of the court (and how to maximize their interests by bending and shaping rules); they have to play the games according to those rules and they have to be seen to do so. They cannot opt out of 'court life'. Thus the monarch (the senior managers of the MNC) controls and governs the system by increasing the dependence of the feudal lords (the subsidiary managers) on the resources allocated from the centre. In the process, a set of courtly rules about how to behave in these circumstances is constructed. These rules serve to differentiate this level in the system more clearly from the diverse rules that exist in subsidiaries where local institutional and cultural effects remain successful. In the following section, we draw on our previous analysis to look at how this disjunction impacts more widely.

The Dysfunctions of Court Society

In our analysis of court society, we noted that although highly elaborated rules of behaviour were developed to manage the conduct of those brought within the confines of the court, this did not resolve the problems or produce the sort of productive power which was eventually unleashed when the actors involved constitutionalized their relationships. On the contrary in some ways it exacerbated them. In our analysis of multinationals we want to suggest a similar set of problems. We want to focus on three of them in particular which we label the taxation problem, the social embeddedness problem and the conflict problem.

The Taxation Problem

Court societies are expensive. In the classic model of the emergence of European states, court societies are non-productive. Indeed they can be seen as parasitic, dependent for their existence on raising taxes from the subjects over which they rule. As courts become more elaborated, taxes increase in order to fund expenditure on the accoutrements of civilization such as buildings, travel, hospitality and conspicuous consumption of all sorts. The prestige and status of a country and its monarch may increase but at the expense of the subjects.

In our view, there are similar processes at work inside multinationals. Clearly this is a complex question and we do not want to exaggerate, just use analogical reasoning to point out similarities. It could, for example, be argued that on the contrary, in MNCs, there is an outward flow of FDI from the centre to the periphery that builds up the periphery, sometimes at the expense of the centre, given that payback calculations can go disastrously awry in times of uncertainty. Moreover, the headquarters does, as we have described, implement systems that improve the efficiency and coordination of the subsidiaries.

However, whatever the operational logics, it would be hard to deny that the purpose of the MNC setting up subsidiaries is ultimately to improve the capital accumulation processes of the MNC's head office. In itself, however, this is hardly news. What is perhaps more interesting is our argument that if we see the headquarters as a form of court in which complex codes of conduct are being elaborated and where competitive pressures over status, reputation and social position are being played out, then we can begin to understand part of why the pressure builds up that requires increasing the value generated out of the subsidiaries (putting to one side issues of financial markets and shareholder pressure to which we will return as an important issue in our final section). As Birkinshaw and others acknowledge, running internal markets is a highly expensive system. It builds into the MNC high levels of overhead. Although MNCs and other large firms frequently implement cost-cutting measures at their headquarters as well as in their subsidiaries, they cannot step back from developing further the basic model where the logic of running systems of conduct and performance monitoring requires a tax on the productive activities of subsidiaries.

It is the subsidiaries which are producing the value; as with any multi-unit business, the centre only survives because of the subsidiaries.

The model which we have been describing subjects each subsidiary and activity to increasing scrutiny in order to evaluate what it is contributing to the MNC as a whole. The whole panoply of accounting systems and information systems that now characterizes MNCs makes it almost impossible to escape the gaze of headquarters. With this gaze comes monitoring and control, setting targets and the process of discipline and punish. Failure to provide the appropriate tax level to the head office may lead to closure but well before that it can lead to restructuring and change. The MNC is a taxation society. Is it more or less of a taxation society than any other M-form business? Possibly not – but because of its geographical diversity, it is more difficult to successfully sell the legitimacy of the taxation to different subsidiaries across the world than it is to maintain such a logic within the confines of a single national system.

It is important to note that in this taxation logic, the managers of the subsidiaries themselves get increasingly sucked in. They have to play this game of increasing returns to the centre or the logic of the business dictates that they will be replaced by others more willing to engage in the game. As a result of managing these processes, subsidiary managers may well become disengaged from the subsidiary because their focus of attention and often their physical presence is elsewhere – at headquarters or traveling around the region or the world negotiating over targets, budgets, extensions to charters etc. These ritualized encounters of a global elite develop their own logic as well as their own need for funds from the pool of taxation being generated. The new court of the MNC is based on a global elite creating itself out of shared education, shared experiences of management and shared networks of alliances into management consultancies, advertising agencies, financial markets, accountancy and auditing firms and law firms, all of whom also extract their 'share' of value, their share of the taxation, from the productive activities of subsidiaries (Thrift, 2006).

The Social Embeddedness Problem

Multinationals have subsidiaries spread across different societies where patterns of employment, skill, collective bargaining, innovative potential, network structures are different. These subsidiaries are characterized by forms of local face-to-face interaction both within the firm and within various institutional contexts outside the firm – local training and research institutions, technology transfer institutions, local government and in some cases systems of local finance. Out of these interactions emerge particular forms of subsidiary identity and cohesion. Some are embedded in social systems where employees and managers negotiate and favour profit-sharing in one way or another; while others are embedded in societies with centralized authority and few rights for workers.

The literature on 'varieties of capitalism' provides us with a deep understanding of how institutional contexts shape relations inside firms, between firms and between firms and the local context (Hall and Soskice, 2001; Morgan *et al.*, 2005; Streeck and Thelen, 2005; Whitley, 1999, 2007). To a considerable degree this concerns the sorts of relationships which have been developed with others in the locality. Three obvious linkages are relevant. The first relates to the flexibility of local training institutions to respond to skill upgrading processes initiated by individuals, firms or trade unions. The second concerns relations between firms and in the locality. Are they engaged in processes of joint and cooperative development that link them together in supply chains or innovation chains? Finally, there is the role of linkages to local technological and scientific institutions. Where these have been developed into ongoing relationships that feed in to product development, local embeddedness is strong.

This literature, however, also suggests that the strength of local institutions will vary. For example, Germany and other Northern European societies have strong regulatory and institutional frameworks which firms must follow, whereas more liberal market economies tend to have looser institutional constraints. As a result the diversity in the types of firms which can evolve in liberal market economies is generally much larger than in the more coordinated economies. In this sense, there is an asymmetrical effect. MNC subsidiaries in the coordinated economies are invariably embedded in an existing strong network of social embeddedness whereas subsidiaries in more liberal market contexts are weakly embedded.

How do multinational subsidiaries relate to this social embeddedness? It seems clear that the subsidiaries of MNCs are embedded to varying degrees in local contexts (Morgan *et al.*, 2001). For example, it depends on whether the subsidiary has been set up from scratch by the MNC with foreign direct investment (a 'greenfield' investment) or whether it has been purchased by the MNC as a 'brownfield' investment. Where greenfield sites are established, MNC managers have the opportunity to seek to establish their own practices and may be much less bound to local institutional conditions. This is much more difficult in brownfield sites where local embeddedness may be strong, e.g. in cases where the site was originally an independent operator that was later bought by an MNC (see for example the discussion of Japanese subsidiaries in the UK which compare these forms of investment e.g. Sharpe (2001); Elger and Smith (2005)).

Further insights into these dynamics arise from recent analysis of the relationship between local linkages and global interdependencies within the MNC. Boehe, for example, looked at the degree to which subsidiaries in his survey were integrated into a global workflow and also into how far they were integrated into local outsourcing and local cooperative arrangements. He identified four main patterns:

- Dependent units which are weakly linked to the locality and to the global processes of the MNC, described as 'the most fragile regarding their scope of activities, global workflow interdependence, local linkages' (Boehe, 2007: 503).
- Isolated units which 'show a very low degree of global workflow interdependence with other MNC units' but have some in-house product development capacity and local outsourcing links.

- Dominant units with a moderate degree of global workflow interdependence with other MNC units but a high degree of counterdependence, meaning that other MNC subsidiaries were more dependent on the output of the dominant unit than the dominant unit was on them. These units were not strongly integrated with the locality.
- Integrated units where global workflow interdependencies were high as were local outsourcing links though local cooperative relations were low.

Social embeddedness is therefore a variable quality shaped by the nature of the investment and the role that the subsidiary is given (or more actively develops) within the MNC. Subsidiaries can play an active role in reshaping their mandate and developing it further; their social embeddedness becomes a resource in this process, not just a constraint (see e.g. Kristensen and Zeitlin 2005). What is the relationship between forms of social embeddedness and the taxation system previously described?

The Conflict Problem

We identify this as the conflict problem in MNCs. As the court society imposed its standards and its taxes on localities, conflict grew depending on the nature of the social embeddedness and the social actors in particular localities. What evidence do we have of analogous forms of conflict inside MNCs?

A simple starting point is Kostova's argument that the multinational subsidiary is in a situation of 'institutional duality' (Kostova, 1999; Kostova and Zaheer, 1999; Kostova and Roth, 2002). On the one hand, it is pressurized by the headquarters to adopt a particular set of practices derived from the home base of the firm; on the other hand, the subsidiary is pressurized by its host context to follow local practices. The subsidiary faces the question of which set of institutions are more important to it – those that make it legitimate within the multinational or those which legitimate it in its local context? The greater the 'institutional distance' between the home and host countries, the greater the difficulty for the HQ of successfully transferring practices from one to the other (Kostova and Roth, 2002; Xu and Shenkar, 2002) and the more likely host influences will prevail. Kostova and Roth's findings are that 'both dimensions of practice adoption, implementation and organization, vary across foreign subsidiaries as a result of two factors – the institutional environment in the host country and the relational context within the MNC' (Kostova and Roth, 2002: 227). By relational context is meant the degree of dependence, trust and identity between the subsidiary and the head office. In combination, institutional duality and the relational context produce four types of subsidiary response to head office initiatives – which they label as 'active', 'minimal', 'assent' and 'ceremonial' (at p. 229).

Kostova's interest in issues of transfer of practices reflects a broader stream of research which has looked at these processes. In a series of papers and books, Ferner et al. have shown how local contexts affect the degree to which HR practices are transferred within the MNC (see e.g. Almond and Ferner, 2006). Their interest in employment relations leads them to emphasize how patterns of workplace representation, the regulatory environment of work and linkages into broader social relations such as political parties and trade unions affect the transfer process. Edwards, Colling and Ferner state that:

'central to our model ... is the observation that ... attempts to shape local environments do not go uncontested and that the political power of actors is itself shaped by prevailing markets and institutions. Our data revealed some instances in which action taken by employees and their representatives, altered, to some extent, decision-making by management ... A practice that is the subject of transfer may be implemented in full in some countries, partially in others and not at all in others. Thus apparently homogenising policies can have the opposite impact, something that is especially likely when applied in a way that is not sensitive to local contexts.' (Edwards et al., 2007: 213–15)

Kristensen and Zeitlin in their study reveal the conflicts which occur between subsidiaries competing over mandates as well as the conflict with head office over processes of investment and change (Kristensen and Zeitlin, 2005). Edwards and Bélanger in their chapter in this book demonstrate how multinationals can be considered in terms of a series of contested terrains where actors compete and enter into conflict over a range of processes (see also Bélanger et al. (1999) on ABB as well as the studies by Geppert et al. (2003); Geppert and Mattern (2006); Geppert and Williams (2006); Dorrenbacher and Geppert (2005)).

In summary, our argument is that as multinationals develop into 'court societies', the tensions and conflicts become more acute. Tightening up on what we have described as the taxation extracted from the subsidiaries requires increased levels of monitoring, control and supervision. However, subsidiaries are socially embedded, to varying extents, in localities with distinctive sets of social relationships and expectations. Efforts to increase taxation lead to increasing conflicts. This creates a limit on the productive power of MNCs. The more actors engage in conflict, whether this is major or minor, overt or covert, the less able they are to combine effectively. How might these processes be 'civilized' using our court society analogy?

MNCs, the Shadow of the Future and the Obstacles to Constitution Building

We could sum up the implications of this by saying that the MNC has become a context for gaming between the various actors and the headquarters as groups find ways of using the rules in order to further their own opportunistic interests. A vast amount of unproductive activity takes place inside the MNC as actors play these games. Because the actors have no belief that there are credible commitments tying them to certain institutions and ways of acting for the foreseeable future, they act as though they are living in a context of high uncertainty which requires that they store up assets that can maintain their security and independence in the event that they are threatened with closure, down-sizing or divestment.

Given these adverse effects, why does this continue, or why has no multinational engaged in creating a new constitutional order? Clearly there are all sorts of reasons why groups continue to pursue their self-interest and resist cooperation and change but as we have already discussed even in the most extreme situations, societies have overcome this and created for themselves institutions and constitutions that were at least good enough to create relative certainty and credible commitments and thus set the seal on a framework of infrastructural power. In this section, we argue that there is one aspect of the context of MNCs which we have not yet discussed which adds a further strong constraining force on any process of civilizing. In order to balance our pessimism, however, we then describe some positive forces which do push towards 'civilizing'.

What makes this particularly problematic in relation to multinationals is the operation of financial markets. The headquarters of MNCs do not control their own destiny and cannot make credible commitments for one important reason. Many of them are located in a financial market situation where a range of actors are exercising their own powers over the MNC. Although the power and significance of these financial actors varies across different settings, they are nevertheless highly influential over the head office of multinationals. Thus credible commitments to internal actors within the MNC cannot be guaranteed because of the significance of these financial actors.

One of the issues here is the complexity and diversity of this group of actors. The rights and claims which they hold over the MNC vary widely; also the power of these actors varies across social contexts as discussed in the varieties of capitalism literature, e.g. Japanese MNCs are much less influenced by shareholder demands than publicly quoted UK MNCs. It is beyond the range of this chapter to specify all these different processes, contexts and actors. We concentrate on those areas where the basic dynamic is the pressure on managers to deliver shareholder value (see e.g. Erturk et al. (2008); Froud et al. (2000, 2006); Williams (2000)). As ownership of firms has moved into the hands of large institutional investors on the one hand and more activist investors such as hedge funds on the other hand, the direct pressure on managers to deliver shareholder value has increased. Failure to do so in the broad terms constructed by the financial markets has the consequence that share prices fall as some of the large investors divest themselves of stock. A falling share price makes it more difficult to sustain borrowing at the current interest rate, thus making it more difficult for the firm to grow itself out of its problems. Managers have to provide their shareholders with 'profit warnings' when expectations about performance are going to be seriously breached. Profit warnings lead to further share price falls. As well as potentially leading to senior managers being replaced, the larger consequence of these processes is that firms become vulnerable to corporate restructuring in general via merger and takeover. Managers seeking to resist this have few options other than to deliver more value from the existing business. This occurs predominantly through the derivation of larger cash funds from subsidiaries, sell-offs, restructuring and down-sizing, all of which is designed to increase the surplus available for distribution to shareholders (Lazonick, 2005; Lazonick and O'Sullivan, 2000). The speed with which such crises hit firms is a significant reason why credible commitments cannot be sustained. The deal between head office and subsidiaries can always be overridden by the perceived requirements of investors. In other words, subsidiaries are treated as if they were living under Louis XIV, where they had to continuously adapt their lives to the idiosyncratic whims of the ruler, being taxed accordingly.

If these pressures only occurred occasionally, it might be possible to argue that this need not necessarily influence the firm all the time. However, this is not the case; the pressures that come from the markets are continuous. As senior managers of MNCs prioritize being able to respond flexibly to these demands, they are in no position to make credible commitments with subsidiaries, who increasingly see a sovereign that ignores and misrepresents their interests, while increasing taxes to finance highly salaried managers and costly court-like arrangements towards financial institutions and shareholders.

From this perspective and in the light of the 2007 credit crunch and its continuing aftermath, it is of interest to note calls for new and more adequate forms of regulation of the financial markets. This might be rephrased as a call for the civilizing of financial markets. In this respect beyond the court society of the MNC there is the broader court society of the financial markets where those who direct capital (institutional investors and their agents, dealers, brokers, hedge funds, private equity etc.) engage with each other and with the senior management of MNCs.

This court society is under pressure to regulate itself. The forms of 'irrational exuberance' that developed in the late 1990s were followed by a brief crash and some new forms of regulation over corporations and financial markets, such as the Sarbanes-Oxley Act in the US and new forms of international accounting standards. However, by 2003, the financial markets were booming again with new instruments (credit derivative swaps, collateralized debt obligations amongst others) and new actors (particularly the rapid expansion of hedge funds and the growth of private equity). Since this phase came to a juddering halt in August 2007 and particularly since late 2008 when governments have been forced to rescue banks and prop up financial markets on the point of collapse, regulators, politicians and senior figures in the financial industry have begun to explore how to build a more civilized system, e.g. one where companies and individuals were not encouraged to take on such high risks.

Beyond this, some analysts (Aglietta and Reberiroux, 2005; Blackburn, 2006) have suggested that there is an inherent contradiction emerging between the savers of funds and the investors of those funds. Savers save because they have jobs and because they want security for the future. The collective institutional investors currently throw those concerns out of the window. They see themselves as having no concern for security of employment, only security of returns in the future so that they can pay pensions, a security which is supposedly achieved by allowing intermediaries to reap high returns on the basis of high risks - a strategy which has led the same institutional investors to huge losses in equity and bond markets in late 2008. It may be seen as illogical that the institutions holding the funds which represent one of society's most obvious investments in the civilizing process, i.e. the right to a dignified old age, should feel no responsibility to creating organizations that act in a civilized way towards the same people when they are at work. This suggests that gradually pension trustees will, under pressure from their members, shift from being strong advocates of shareholder returns to taking a more balanced view so that the employment conditions of their members during their working lives are considered alongside their requirements for an adequately funded old age.

Depending on how this evolves, the 'internal' context for civilizing the MNC may change. However there are three other areas where 'civilizing' pressures may emerge: trade union and worker organization, social movements and collective political action.

Trade unions: The dynamics of MNCs are based on the difficulty for local sub-sidiaries in communicating and cooperating with other parts of the subsidiary in a similar situation. Instead the logic is to create the sort of destructive internal com-petition which was described earlier. It follows from this that the development of mechanisms for bringing together representatives from different subsidiaries has the possibility of new forms of cooperation horizontally across the MNC. The develop-ment within the European Union of European Works Council is relevant here. Whilst the impact of these EWCs still appears relatively limited and minor, nevertheless they have begun to act as a means whereby different subsidiaries can discuss the way in which the MNC is working (Marginson *et al.*, 2004; Marginson and Sisson, 2004; Whittall *et al.*, 2007). Such international collective bodies are notoriously difficult to manage because their interests are so diverse in comparison to the interests of senior managers. Nevertheless they have some potential for shaping a collective response from subsidiaries to head office demands. Internationally trade unions have also become involved in activity to monitor the employment and conditions of work-places in developing countries. This clearly involves a delicate balancing act. Trade unions can justify forms of protectionism by claiming that products and services in developing markets are 'artificially' cheap and competitive because employees lack basic rights of collective bargaining, workplace representation etc. The result of protectionism *tout court* might be the retention of jobs but at the cost of higher prices and slower economic growth in developing economies. The 'civilizing' role, therefore, involves delicate negotiations amongst competing actors.

Social movements: If it is hard to assess the impact of phenomena such as EWCs it is equally difficult to know how significant social movements might be in terms of civilizing MNCs. There is evidence that MNCs with strong consumer brands have been forced to ensure that their actions in developing societies in their subsidiaries or their contractors meet with the standards expected in the developed world. Often these standards are the outcome of social movements that have revealed the range of practices that have gone on. Similarly there are social movements that publicize their monitoring activities on the web and criticize those firms who fail to provide them with appropriate information. Alongside ethical consumer bodies which pressurize MNCs to change, there are ethical investment funds that declare their unwillingness to invest in funds which do not meet their standards. There is a civilizing element to this which is mainly around the involvement of civil society movements in discussions about the actions of multinationals. Mostly, however, this is couched in rather limited terms concerned with transparency, accountability and standards in developing societies rather than with the impact of MNC policy on subsidiaries in the developed world. Here civil society involvement tends to be piecemeal, protesting at the closure of subsidiaries, the despoliation of the environment, the impact on social relations but not on confronting the forces beyond this other than in very general terms.

Governments, electoral politics and regulation: The third force for potentially civilizing the MNC is, of course, government and politics. Governments in the West since 1945 have taken on the role of civilizing the more extreme outcomes of market forces. Although the renaissance of neo-liberalism has challenged this role and public choice theories have attacked this sort of justification of governmental action, states remain to varying degrees centrally concerned with the welfare of citizens through mitigating the harshest consequences of the market in terms of income inequality and recognizing the right to a certain standard of living, health, employment and education. The obvious problem for national governments is the international nature of MNCs. Attempts to 'civilize' by one government run the risk that the MNC will relocate to other less fussy climes. In this sense, international collective action to 'civilize' seems most likely. Examples of this come from surprising sources. Firms are frequently involved in private collective international action in order to 'civilize' themselves. Firms actually need to place themselves under the shadow of the future – to recognize that there are limits to their own opportunism and pursuit of self-interests in certain contexts if the consequence might be a wider collapse of confidence in the system. Thus banks have been willing to agree to standards on capital adequacy and risk ratios that have been agreed in Basle because that places them all under the same constraint and gives nobody an extra advantage even if recent events in the financial markets have revealed firstly that some key institutions such as investment banks and hedge funds avoided this regulation and secondly its value in practice could be undermined by the speed with which assets could lose value, leaving banks little time to replenish their capital from private sources and pushing them into the arms of the state. Whether it is sufficient to protect against global financial collapse in which others outside the ruling councils and discussions of the Basle community have an essential interest is a question that has been raised. The UN Global Compact and the growing tendency for MNCs to adhere to this through Corporate Social Responsibility and Sustainability reporting is also significant. There is thus a wide amount of evidence of a shift towards some self-civilizing amongst MNCs even though there are powerful countervailing forces as we have described earlier.

Conclusion

From the perspective of somebody living in early seventeenth century Europe, there would have seemed little likelihood of the end of wars of religion, the decline of absolute monarchies, the rise of equality before the law and the establishment of liberal political systems which guaranteed the rights of property for individuals against the claims of their monarchs. Indeed this was a long time coming; the resistance was strong and the claims established often weakly accepted at first. Over time, however, these institutions were established in significant parts of Europe and North America primarily because the various groups came to the conclusion that they could not continue to engage in conflict if they wished to garner the rewards which appeared possible in a society based on these emerging new principles.

If we look at MNCs now, we see similar conflicts and similar uncertainties. International financial markets are a powerful force pushing MNCs further down the path of conflict and uncertainty but even here there seem to be reasons to think that a civilizing process may emerge from structural and regulatory changes currently occurring even though the autonomous dynamics of the financial markets may appear overwhelmingly powerful most of the time. On top of this, other actors are pushing towards a new constitution for the MNC, a new civilized model of international economic coordination. The rewards of achieving this would be large but the route and timing is uncertain. When the Chinese Communist leader Zhou Enlie was asked his view of the impact of the French Revolution, he stated that 'it is too soon to tell'. We could well remember the importance of the long-term view if we want to consider how MNCs might become civilized and reach the productive potential which has been frequently identified but less frequently achieved.

CASE STUDY: CADBURY-SCHWEPPES

In 2007, Cadbury-Schweppes, the large food and drink multinational, announced that they were going to close their plant in Keynsham near Bristol in the UK and move production to Poland. The company explained that they had to cut costs in order to meet shareholder demands and by moving to Poland they could take advantage of cheaper labour and more modern production facilities. For some months, workers in the plant fought a campaign against this move enlisting the local community in support and arguing for a local boycott of Cadbury goods. Cadbury management were unwilling to change their decision and a ballot of members of the workforce in January 2008 voted to accept the closure and to end the protests.

These activities took place in the context of a wider debate in the financial markets about the performance of Cadbury-Schweppes. This debate has been led by Nelson Peltz, the main owner of the hedge fund, Trian Investment Funds and the Qatari Investment Fund, both of which own around 3-4 % of the shares in Cadbury-Scheweppes. These investors have argued that the company is under-performing in the markets. They have called for more aggressive management and in particular for the separation of the two elements of the business – the chocolate/confectionary business (the original Cadbury part) and the drinks business (Schweppes). In March, 2008, it was announced that the two businesses would be demerged. It was anticipated that this would generate higher returns for shareholders at least in the short to medium terms as the value of the two separated units would be higher than the single integrated company.

These changes reflected the distance which Cadbury had travelled since it had been founded as a company by a Quaker family in the UK Midlands in the nineteenth century. Cadbury had gained a reputation as a paternalistic employer, building a model village for its employees (known after one if its products as Bournville). This model village provided employees with good housing, educational and religious institutions. Temperance was encouraged and pubs not allowed. Employees were given good working conditions and long-term employment prospects at a time when these were not generally available. In return they showed loyalty and commitment to the firm which was maintained in family control through to its recent history. Even in the 1990s, after ownership of the firm had become more dispersed, members of the Cadbury family played a role in the management of the company.

Questions

1. The workforce in Cadbury is not consulted about the demerger strategy and its concern about switching production is ignored. Should this be a matter of concern? What impacts might it have?
2. If you were seeking to provide a more consultative constitutional process for decision-making inside an MNC such as Cadbury, what sort of mechanisms and which social actors would you expect to be helpful in this respect and which ones would be a hindrance?
3. Are MNCs becoming more 'civilized'? If so, how and why?

Further Reading

Our ideas on societies are drawn partly form the writing of the German sociologist Norbert Elias whose books *The Civilizing Process* (1983) and *The Court Society* (2000) provide a much more detailed background. In terms of MNCs, the sorts of mechanisms in which we are interested appear most clearly in qualitative studies of MNCs such as that in Almond and Ferner (2006), Belanger *et al.* (1999) and Kristensen and Zeitlin (2005).

References

Aglietta, M. and Reberioux, A. (2005) *Corporate Governance Adrift: A Critique of Shareholder Value.* Cheltenham: Edward Elgar Publishing.

Almond, P. and Ferner, A. (eds) (2006) *American Multinationals in Europe.* Oxford: Oxford University Press.

Anderson, S. and Cavanagh, J. (2005) *Field Guide to the Global Economy.* New York: The New Press.

Bartlett, C. and Ghoshal, S. (1991) *Managing Across Borders: The Transnational Solution.* London: Century Business.

Bélanger, J., Berggren, C., Björkman, T. and Köhler, C. (eds) (1999) *Being Local Worldwide: ABB and the Challenge of Global Management*. Ithaca, NY and London: Cornell University Press.

Birkinshaw, J. (1997) 'Entrepreneurship in Multinational Corporations: The Characteristics of Subsidiary Initiatives', *Strategic Management Journal*, 18: 207–29.

Birkinshaw, J. (2000) *Entrepreneurship in the Global Firm*. London: Sage.

Birkinshaw , J. and Hood, N. (eds) (1998) *Multinational Corporate Evolution and Subsidiary Development*. London: Macmillan.

Birkinshaw, J. and Lingblad, M. (2005) 'Intrafirm Competition and Charter Evolution in the Multibusiness Firm', *Organization Science*, 16(6): 674–86.

Blackburn, R. (2006) *Age Shock: How Finance is Failing Us*. London: Verso.

Boehe, D. M. (2007) 'Product development in MNC subsidiaries: Local linkages and global interdependencies', *Journal of International Management*, 13: 488–512.

Bouquet, C. and Birkinshaw, J. (2008) 'Weight versus Voice: How Foreign Subsidiaries Gain Attention from Corporate Headquarters', *Academy of Management Journal* 51(3).

Burchell, G. (1991) *The Foucault Effect: Studies in Governmentality*. Chicago: University of Chicago Press.

Burrell, G. and Morgan, G. (1978) *Sociological Paradigms and Organizational Analysis*. London: Heinemann.

Dorrenbacher, C. and Geppert, M. (2005) 'Micro-political aspects of Mandate Development and Learning in Local Subsidiaries of Multinational Corporations', WZB Discussion Paper SP III 2005-202.

Edwards, T., Colling, T. and Ferner, A. (2007) 'Conceptual approaches to the transfer of employment practices in multinational companies: an integrated approach', *Human Resource Management Journal*, 17(3): 201–17.

Elias, N. (1983) *The Court Society*. Oxford: Blackwell.

Elias, N. (2000) *The Civilizing Process*. 2nd edn, London: Wiley Blackwell.

Elger, T. and Smith, C. (2005) *Assembling Work: Remaking Factory Regimes in Japanese Multinationals in Britain*. Oxford: Oxford University Press.

Erturk, I., Froud, J., Johal, S., Leaver, A. and Williams, K. (eds) (2008) *Financialization at Work: Key Texts and Commentary*. London: Routledge.

Foucault, M. (1979) *Discipline and Punish*. Harmondsworth: Penguin Books.

Froud, J., Haslem, C., Johal, S. and Williams, K. (2000) 'Restructuring for Shareholder Value and Its Implications for Labour', *Cambridge Journal of Economics*, 24: 771–97.

Froud, J., Johal, S., Leaver, A. and Williams, K. (2006) *Financialization and Strategy: Narrative and numbers*. London: Routledge.

Geppert, M., Williams, K. and Matten, D. (2003) 'The social construction of contextual rationalities in MNCs: An Anglo-German comparison of subsidiary choice', *Journal of Management Studies*, 40/3: 617–41.

Geppert, M. and Matten, D. (2006) 'Institutional influences on manufacturing organization in multinational corporations: the "Cherrypicking" approach', *Organization Studies*, 27/4: 491–516.

Geppert, M. and Williams, K. (2006) 'Global, national and local practices in multinational corporations', *International Journal of Human Resource Management*, 17/1: 49–69.

Hall, J. A. (1986) 'Capstones and Organisms: Political Forms and the Triumph of Capitalism', *Sociology*, Vol. 19, No. 2, 173–92.

Hall, P. A. and Soskice, D. (eds) (2001) *Varieties of Capitalism. The Institutional Foundations of Comparative Advantages*. Oxford: Oxford University Press.

Hedlund, G. (1986) 'The Hypermodern MNC – A Heterarchy?', *Human Resource Management*, 25: 9–35.

Hedlund, G. (1999) 'The Intensity and Extensity of Knowledge and the Multinational Corporation as a Nearly Recomposable System (NRS)', *Management International Review*, 1, special issue: 5–44.

Hirschmann, A. O. (1997) *The Passions and the Interests: Political Arguments for Capitalism before Its Triumph*. New edition, Princeton, NJ: Princeton University Press.

Kostova, T. (1999) 'Transnational Transfer of Strategic Organizational Practices: A Contextual Perspective', *Academy of Management Review*, 24, 308–24.

Kostova, T. and Roth, K. (2002) 'Adoption of Organizational Practice by Subsidiaries of Multinational Corporations: Institutional and Relational Effects', *Academy of Management Journal*, 45, 215–33.

Kostova, T. and Zaheer, S. (1999) 'Organizational Legitimacy under conditions of complexity: the case of the multinational enterprise', *Academy of Management Review*, 24, 64–81.

Kristensen, P. H. and Zeitlin, J. (2005) *Local Players in Global Games. The Strategic Constitution of a Multinational Corporation*. Oxford: Oxford University Press.

Lazonick, W. (2005) 'Corporate Restructuring'. In S. Ackroyd, R. Batt, P. Tolbert and P. Thompson. (eds) *The Oxford Handbook of Work and Organizations*. Oxford: Oxford University Press, 577–601.

Lazonick, W. and O'Sullivan, M. (2000) 'Maximizing Shareholder Value: a new ideology for corporate governance', *Economy and Society*, 29(1): 13–35.

Ling, Y., Floyd, S. W. and Baldridge, D. C. (2005) 'Toward a model of issue-selling by subsidiary managers in multinational organizations', *Journal of International Business Studies*, 36: 637–54.

Mann, M. (1986) *The Sources of Social Power*. Cambridge: Cambridge University Press.

Marginson, P. and Sisson, K. (2004) *European Integration and Industrial Relations: Multi-level Governance in the Making*. London: Palgrave Macmillan.

Marginson, P., Hall, M., Hoffmann, A., Müller, T. (2004) 'The Impact of European Works Councils on Management Decision-Making in UK and US-based Multinationals: A Case Study Comparison', *British Journal of Industrial Relations*, 42(2), 209–33.

Morgan, G., Kristensen, P. H. and Whitely, R. (eds) (2001) *The Multinational Firm: Organizing across Institutional and National Divides*. Oxford: Oxford University Press.

Morgan, G., Whitley, R. and Moen, E. (eds) (2005) *Changing Capitalisms? Internationalization, Institutional Change, and Systems of Economic Organization*. Oxford: Oxford University Press.

North, D. C. and Weingast, B. R. (1989) 'Constitutions and Commitment: The Evolution of Institutional Governing Public Choice in Seventeenth-Century England', *The Journal of Economic History*, 49, 4, 803–32.

Parsons, T. (1964) *The Social System*. New York: Macmillan, USA.

Poster, M.. (ed.) (2001) *Jean Baudrillard: Selected Writings*. 2nd edn, Cambridge: Polity Press.

Sharpe, D. R. (2001) 'Globalization and Change: Organizational Continuity and Change within a Japanese Multinational in the UK'. In Morgan *et al*. (eds) *The Multinational Firm: Organizing across Institutional and National Divides*. Oxford: Oxford University Press, 196–221.

Streeck, W. and Thelen, K. (eds) (2005) *Beyond Continuity: Institutional Change in Advanced Political Economies*. Oxford: Oxford University Press.

Te Brake, W. (1998) *Shaping History: Ordinary People in European Politics, 1500–1700.* Berkeley: University of California Press.

Thrift, N. (2006) *Knowing Capitalism.* London: Sage.

Weber, M. (1992) *Economy and Society.* Berkeley: University of California Press.

Westney, E. and Zaheer, S. (2001) 'The Multinational Enterprise as an Organization'. In A. Rugman and T. Brewer *The Oxford Handbook of International Business.* Oxford: Oxford University Press, 349–79.

Whitley, R. (1999) *Divergent Capitalisms. The Social Structuring and Change of Business Systems.* Oxford: Oxford University Press.

Whitley, R. (2007) *Business Systems and Organizational Capabilities.* Oxford: Oxford University Press.

Whittall, M., Knudsen, H. and Huijgen, F. (eds) (2007) *Towards a European Labour Identity: The Case of the European Work Council.* London: Routledge.

Williams, K. (2000) 'From shareholder value to present-day capitalism', *Economy and Society,* 29, 1: 1–12.

Xu, D. and Shenkar, O. (2002) 'Institutional Distance and the Multinational Enterprise', *Academy of Management Review,* 27, 608–18.

Chapter 9   The Multinational Firm as a Contested Terrain

Paul Edwards and Jacques Bélanger

This chapter studies relations between MNCs and their workers, a domain of politics we will conceptualize as a 'contested terrain'. As shown by several contributions in this book, MNCs comprise groups with differing interests, and these groups use their resources to pursue their own ends (see also Morgan and Kristensen, 2006). Yet such points take on additional salience in relation to lower-level employees (a term defined shortly) for three sets of reasons.

First, these workers commonly mobilize their own interests through trade unions or other representative institutions. This fact used to be a fundamental building block of both the practice and the theory of industrial relations. With the decline of unions in many countries, there has been a tendency, particularly in the US and the UK, to treat opposing interests and their representation through unions as of only historical importance. Yet unions retain substantial membership in many countries; and even where membership is low, notably France, they remain recognized as 'social partners' with influence greater than numbers might suggest. Representative structures independent of unions are also important in many countries, particularly the works councils of Germany; and this model of representation is now, through the Information and Consultation Directive, the standard across the EU states.

Second, whether or not workers are unionized, they have distinct sets of interests which relate to the interests of management in complex and contradictory ways. This theme is fundamental to the idea of a 'contested terrain' (R. Edwards, 1979) and is developed below.

Third, relations with workers as collectivities generally embrace interests from outside the MNC itself. This is true even of Japan, whose famous enterprise unions are organized on a firm-by-firm basis but which are also connected with other unions and which function as a group, notably in annual pay bargaining. As seen in many instances in the US and in Europe, unions also work with other bodies to campaign against MNCs, notably in relation to the threat of job losses arising from corporate re-structuring.[1]

As to who comprises lower-level employees, detailed definitional discussion is not necessary. We are dealing with employees below the level of first-line supervisor. It is true that in some organizations the relevant job titles may be absent, but such cases are less common than is often imagined and in any event there is generally a distinction between those who control an operation and those who do not. Studies of managers have thus found that the traditional managerial functions of control and coordination remain largely unchanged (Hales, 2005).

Analysis in terms of the contested terrain is well-established in, and is a central component of most approaches to, the field of employment relations. It is less established in business studies more generally, and we therefore begin with its core features. We then show how managing the employment relationship in an MNC has features that are different from those pertaining to large single-country firms. These themes are then illustrated in relation to some key aspects of relations with workers.

The fundamental message for managers is two-fold. First, though large firms commonly claim that 'people are our most important asset', they often fail to grasp the nature of the asset. In particular, employees have their own expectations and socially generated frames of reference, and imposing policies without taking these into account is likely to produce difficulties. It is a commonplace that new payment systems or forms of work organization fail to achieve their goals. This is for two classes of reason. In some cases, they are driven by specific sectional goals such as the pursuit of short-term profit or an effort by managers to show that they are 'in command'; managers who think that everything that they do is in the common interest are seriously deluding themselves. But more fundamentally many such changes are introduced with no appreciation of the context of a particular contested terrain or the social expectations of workers. Second, these issues take on increased salience in an MNC, where differences of national and local context heighten the differences of meaning and understanding between managers and workers.

The Contested Terrain

Academic perspectives are commonly defined in terms of what they are not. There is one such contrast that we need to make here. A contested terrain is sometimes taken to mean that there is a complete opposition between worker and manager around such things as the distribution of the 'pie' between wages and profits. Yet MNCs typically pay higher wages than local firms, and workers are often enthusiastic to work for them. What relevance can an approach in terms of conflict have?

The contested terrain perspective has never taken such a stark view. Leading studies argue that the management–labour relation has an inherent duality: workers are creative individuals, and managers aim to deploy this creativity, but at the same time it is used under the authority of other people and it is subject to control and organization in ways that workers may resent (Cressey and MacInnes, 1980). This approach often traces its roots to the work of Karl Marx, who, contrary to some misconceptions, did not see capitalism as wholly bad; on the contrary he underlined its progressive character, while also stressing that progress has losers as well as winners and that both the choice of goals and the means to pursue them are political issues and not matters of an objectively best solution (Desai, 2002). Workers and managers have shared and conflicting interests. Workers have interests in wages and working conditions, and also in a sense of dignity and pride in work (Hodson, 2001). These interests have short-term and long-term elements. In the short term, workers prefer higher wages over lower ones, but they have to balance this interest against the ability of their firm to survive. In the long term, they are interested in the development of the enterprise, and are thus concerned to see innovation in the operation of the firm.

These interests may clash with those of management in several respects. First, the managerial concern is profit, whereas workers have wider interests in the quality of jobs and also the provision of employment for future generations (Streeck, 1997). This is a conflict of *goals*. Second, there is an array of *means* to pursue an objective. Managements often devise programmes such as Total Quality Management and impose them; yet workers may have different and equally valid views as to how to secure the objective. Third, there are conflicts of *process*. Workers expect to be informed and consulted, and research evidence shows that such involvement improves performance.

Several implications arise from this perspective. First, workers have expectations that have developed as collective, shared, norms. This does not mean that these norms are unchanging. They are resources and ways of thinking that workers will use to make sense of managerial initiatives. These initiatives will be interpreted through expectations developed from past experience and available knowledge. Thus an objectively 'good' payment scheme may be viewed with scepticism if there is a history of failed experiments. Second, it is not the case that worker expectations are 'worse' than those of managers. Indeed, a long line of research shows that workers often rescue managers from their own failings by devising informal ways to make formal rules work in practice (Roy, 1954; P. Edwards, 1988). Accounts of worker expectations sometimes suggest that these are essentially narrow and ill-informed expectations and that the issue is one of finding ways round them. In fact, workers often know work systems better than do managers, and, crucially, they have a greater commitment to the work site than do managers, for their skills are more specific and for family and other reasons they are less geographically mobile. Third, managements need to be aware of their own political assumptions. Consider Ahlstrand's (1990) fascinating study of the US MNC Esso in the UK. It showed that changes in the regime for dealing with workers were introduced over many years even though their directly productive value was unclear. One key explanation of the paradox was managers' desire to show to superiors in the US that they were 'in charge'. Managements often have their own political projects serving specific ends. Finally, 'worker' interests may overlap with those of local managers: the managers of a particular site have interests in its continuing survival, whereas higher levels of management are interested only in the company as a whole and also their own careers (Jenkins, 2005). In short, productively oriented employees, whether 'managers' or 'workers', have interests in the efficiency of production units; these interests may cut across the financially driven goals of higher levels of management (Thompson, 2003).

Recent theory has formalized these arguments to show that workers and managements relate to each other around two sets of 'concerns': control of the immediate work process and the longer term development of the productive process (P. Edwards et al., 2006; Bélanger and Edwards, 2007). Within both these concerns, there are objectives that are consistent with those of the other party and others which potentially conflict. Thus, in spite of the structural division between management and labour, both sides, according to their distinct rationales, usually find benefits in cooperating to achieve efficient production and the reproduction of the employment relationship. Different patterns of contested terrain then arise according to the structural positions in which agents find themselves and their own strategies.

MNCs and Labour Practices

Until the 1980s, the dominant approach to MNCs in the employment relations field was one of neglect. There were useful studies of employment policy (Gennard and Steuer, 1971), but MNCs did not loom large: they were few in number; several appeared to adopt the practices of host countries, albeit with some variations; and national regimes were driven mainly by domestic structures of collective bargaining. These conditions all changed from the 1980s. On the part of MNCs, the arrival of Japanese transplants, in particular in the UK and the US, led to a focus on the new employment practices that they brought with them. An industrial relations scholar coined the term 'Japanization' (see Oliver and Wilkinson, 1992) and many others sought out what, if anything, was distinctive about Japanese firms (see Elger and Smith, 2005). At the same time, the erosion of collective bargaining institutions in these two countries increased the space available to these new actors and also allowed established firms to copy their behaviour. With the growth of global competition, there was also a sense of pressure to improve performance. There have always been rather few Japanese direct investors, and their impact has been limited to certain sectors such as car manufacture and electronics, but their indirect impact through the effects of imitation and a growing search for best practice was substantial. Consider for example Ford in the UK. The company had been established since 1925 and, though it attempted to compare its UK plants with (more efficient) German ones, the power of direct coercive comparisons was limited (Beynon, 1973). But as competitive pressures intensified, as constraints on management action weakened and as models from Japan became available, these comparisons began to bite (Mueller and Purcell, 1992).

In what respects do MNCs affect labour practices? Several domains can be distinguished.

- In relation to a firm's own employees, we identified above issues of goals, means and process. MNCs may have distinct approaches to some or all of these. In relation to goals, there are effects in terms of wages and conditions compared to those that workers could gain in domestic firms. Means of organizing work embrace systems of work organization such as teamwork: do MNCs deploy distinct systems? Process includes arrangements for communication with employees, of which whether or not trade unions are recognized has been a key distinction; but MNCs may also have distinct arrangements for direct communication, such as suggestion schemes.

- MNCs also affect other firms. This embraces supply chain relationships, wherein suppliers are put under pressure by customers to behave in certain ways. There are also the effects of copying. Supplier relations and copying involve deliberate action. But there are also indirect effects, notably the impact in a local labour market of the arrival of an MNC.
- MNCs can affect the wider climate of employment relations, for example through their attitude to employer associations and through their dealings with governments. Action in both arenas can undermine established assumptions, particularly where a country has a tradition of strong and inclusive corporatism. For example, by being apparently undecided on location decisions they can influence the behaviour of governments and unions (T. Edwards *et al.*, 1999: 300).

In addition to these separate domains, MNCs are far from homogeneous. A long line of research has pursued contrasts between those from various countries of origin. Rather less explicit attention has been paid to sectoral variation, but studies have identified clear effects. For example, early research on Japanese MNCs in the US suggested that they imported distinct employment practices such as teamwork. But study of electronics firms demonstrated that this image turned on a few large firms, mainly those in the car industry; in the electronics sector, firms generally behaved much as did their US counterparts (Milkman, 1991).

The result of these considerations is two-fold. First, the question of the effect of the MNC on labour needs to be reformulated to take account of distinct domains and distinct types of MNC. Moreover, even the idea of 'effects' is too simple. As the idea of the contested terrain emphasizes, projects are ambiguous because they have mixed objectives and operate in a context of contradictory dynamics. The early debate on Japanization, for example, sought out distinct 'Japanese' practices and asked how far they were generalized in a host country. Yet as research developed several points emerged.

Some practices were not 'Japanese' but were a response by firms to what they saw as issues in the host country. Thus Japanese MNCs in the US often located in small towns in an attempt to avoid union traditions in large cities and also possibly to secure a largely white work force (Kenney and Florida, 1993). (The latter point is itself contested, with some seeing this locational decision as driven by conscious motivation, while others saw it as the by-product of other preferences.) Other practices had to be adapted to the local environment. A good example is a preference in the UK to hire young women; they were expected to be tractable but were found to be 'hard to manage' and also not in ready supply, so that the local practice of hiring older women was adopted (Elger and Smith, 2005).

There is more conscious experimentation with other practices such as teamwork. MNCs have been found to use host country operations as sites in which to learn from practices that may not be established in the home country. German MNCs for example have used the UK to learn about merit-based payment systems (Ferner and Varul, 2000).

The results of unconscious adaptation, deliberate experimentation and the emergence of new practices over time led to the development of the image of the 'hybrid' rather than the transfer of practices. The development of employment practice is thus variable and uncertain, as a contested terrain view would expect.

Second, however, all is not mere complexity. Research in the contested terrain tradition has identified a framework though which the relevant processes can be grasped. It has certainly yet to generate decisive answers. This is partly because the necessary empirical research agenda is very demanding. An ideal research design would address all relevant domains (including non-MNC comparisons) across sectors and home and host countries. This agenda is itself shifting. In the past, it was primarily about either core countries' MNCs in other core countries (e.g. US firms in Germany) or the impact in less developed countries. But as new countries, notably China and those of eastern Europe, enter the global economy the issues become more complex. Research in both these regions shows that practices are not simply exported and that there is a complex process of adaptation, summarized in the neat question of 'who is hybridizing what?' (Meardi and Tóth, 2006). New questions continue to emerge, but there is a developing framework that can help us address them. The remainder of this chapter illustrates how this can be done and then identifies key areas for further analysis.

Political Resources within MNCs

We first identify types of resources, and then consider variations in the availability of these types according to the character of the MNC. Finally, we discuss the ways in which resources are negotiated politically.

Bargaining resources may be positive for a particular agent. The obvious example is the ability of the MNC to shift production from one country to another. But there are also negative attributes, such as a lack of knowledge of local institutions and customs. Resources are also of different kinds. For example, it has long been known that coordination and control systems include subtle and informal methods as well as such formal devices as performance targets (Martinez and Jarillo, 1989). These formal systems, moreover, 'depend on informal systems and the power relations these embody' (Ferner, 2000: 521). We follow the distinction between formal and informal arrangements. In broad terms, formal arrangements are relatively objective rules and procedures (most obviously, labour laws) and also structural resources such as the ability of an MNC to switch production between its sites. Informal arrangements

Table 9.1 Resources and constraints of MNCS and key interlocutors

	MNC	Workers	Other agents
Resources			
Formal	• production switching • coercive comparisons • country-of-origin and dominance effects	• national representation rights • international TU cooperation	• labour laws
Informal	• norms and meaning systems	• needs for compliance	• corporate campaigns
Constraints			
Formal	• compliance with laws • transaction costs	• national basis of representative structures • transaction costs	• national boundaries • competition to attract MNCs
Informal	• ignorance of local norms • managerial politics	• ignorance of corporate language & meaning systems	• ignorance of corporate language & meaning systems

embrace the social and political norms and expectations of MNCs and other actors, together with cultural issues such as language and meaning systems. MNCs have been shown to deploy ideological and symbolic resources to shape the agenda on global climate change (Levy and Egan, 2003), and similar processes are at work in labour relations, for example in relation to the claimed inevitability of global competition and the need for changed work practices as a result.

Table 9.1 gives illustrations of formal and informal resources, and also of positive resources and constraints. It identifies MNCs, workers and other key agents that may affect the MNC's relations with its workers.

MNC Resources

To begin with the MNC, the obvious formal resources stem from the fact of operating across borders: the ability to make 'coercive comparisons' (Mueller and Purcell, 1992) between sites and to switch production. Any large firm can of course do this within national boundaries, but MNCs have more resources, both quantitatively (more places to go to) and qualitatively (the difficulty of chasing footloose capital to regimes with very different economic and political traditions from the site losing the operation). Research evidence supports this economic interpretation. Cooke (2001) for example proposes that MNCs evaluate the relative labour costs of different industrial relations systems and also the flexibility (for example over the hiring and firing of labour) that the systems provide. He shows that foreign direct investment in one country rather than another is indeed shaped by compensation costs and the extent of restraints (both legal and arising from the collective bargaining system) on MNCs' freedom of action. Note, however, that this is not a simple 'race to the bottom' argument. Cooke also shows that education levels in a country promote FDI, as does the ratio of compensation to education, which he takes as a measure of unobserved skills. Countries high on labour costs are also likely to be high on education and skills, and MNCs need to balance the respective benefits and constraints.

There is also a further argument here, which Cooke recognizes in noting that countries need to provide returns to workers as well as to capital. Even if we look at the issue through the eyes of a purely self-interested MNC, there are arguments for acceptable labour standards. A country finding an 'optimum' trade-off between education and compensation might immediately attract FDI. But as Frenkel and Kuruvilla (2002) show, nation states also have to respect the 'logics' of industrial peace and employment and income security as well as that of competitiveness. A state ignoring these logics may well generate discontented workers. A self-interested MNC going to such a country might find itself facing such workers and possibly also political turmoil. Moreover, other interlocutors may become engaged; for example, MNCs are under increasing pressure from human rights organizations if they operate in authoritarian countries.

Even if an MNC were a purely economically rational body, it would face a difficult utilitarian calculation of costs and benefits. But it is also composed of people who consider what they see as right as well as what maximizes net benefits (Legge, 2006). And what is 'right' alters over time, as the growing acceptance of ideas of corporate social responsibility illustrates. Terrains of contest are multiple and shifting.

Further useful economics-based reasoning is provided by Schmitt and Sadowski (2003). They rightly note that lists of pressures or bargaining influences do not explain how firms behave, and argue for a cost-minimization approach. They therefore address the costs of centralization and decentralization, and use these to predict patterns of the transfer of labour practices by MNCs. Centralization has benefits in terms of economies of scale, but also costs. The costs notably include 'legitimacy', that is the need to maintain the consent of workers in host countries.

We need to note at this point the resources labelled 'country of origin and dominance effects'. These are discussed in more detail below. In essence the country-of-origin effect comes from an MNC's location in a distinct national system; this system promotes certain ways of dealing with workers; and basis in the system is a resource for an MNC in other countries. For example, opposition to unions is a feature of the US system, and firms imbued with its characteristics can carry their anti-union policies to other countries. Dominance effects mean that certain countries play a lead role in the capitalist system and that firms from them have resources which they can deploy in other countries (Smith and Meiksins, 1995).

Returning to Schmitt and Sadowski, the prediction is that there are country-of-origin effects, reflecting the fact that decentralization is costly and hence that MNCs will retain home country practices in their other operations. But host country effects will also be important because of the costs of centralization. The data (on US and

UK firms in Germany) confirm these expectations. The authors conclude, however, that a rational choice model provides only part of the story: 'much of the variation in personnel practices cannot be grasped by cost considerations but is subject to managerial attitudes and micropolitical processes ... [and] personnel policy is ... an idiosyncratic phenomenon to a large degree' (2003: 426).

Turning then to political issues, economic resources and motivations may be supported by the political rhetorics of the need to compete internationally and to meet international standards. The examples here are numerous, for example BMW's use of global standards to win concessions from workers in its German factories. A key point here is that the global standard need not in fact be 'real': its invocation may be enough, even though there may in fact be little evidence that producing elsewhere is cheaper.

Formal constraints on MNCs include the need to comply with labour laws. These constraints are far from unimportant, notably the European Union's promotion of requirements for European Works Councils and directives on working time and other issues. Despite arguments that regulation interferes with market efficiency, there is no systematic evidence that regulated economies perform worse than others. A common argument, for example, is that firms operating in Germany are required to engage in vocational training and so forth, and that this in turn generates efficiency: what Streeck calls beneficial constraints. Any one firm may prefer to escape such constraints, but it may nonetheless find collective benefits.

Other constraints under the head of 'transactions costs' include the difficulty and expense of monitoring subsidiaries and then using the information in some purposive manner. Informal constraints are strongly illustrated in Kristensen and Zeitlin's (2005) study of a British-based MNC. The head office lacked knowledge of its subsidiaries and their national contexts, and was thus open to countervailing power by these subsidiaries, which in some cases formed alliances with local trade unions to pursue their own agendas. This last practice has also been noted in other cases, and is thus not purely idiosyncratic (Martinez Lucio *et al.*, 2001: 60).

Workers and Other Agents

Workers' formal resources include (mainly national) rights to organize and to be represented through trades unions and works councils. Internationally, they can draw on trade union organization, in some cases with a degree of success, for example campaigns of seafarers and dock workers over international labour standards. Martinez Lucio *et al.* (2001) develop the concept of 'regulation space' to analyse unions' resources in the aviation industries of Britain and Spain: the fact of regulation at national and international levels allowed the unions to engage in bargaining with companies.

The label 'needs for compliance' under the informal head refers to the fact that firms need a minimal degree of compliance to operate effectively. A well-known example is that of Japanese firms in Telford, England: despite their non-union status, they were not able to establish their regimes at will, for they faced problems of quit rates and a lack of enthusiasm which called for a degree of attention to workers' expectations (Elger and Smith, 2005). Evident constraints include the national, and indeed often local, basis of trade union organization – Beynon's (1973) famous 'factory consciousness', which limited the ability of workers at a Ford UK factory to bargain with the firm at national, let alone global, level. It may also be very hard to respond to the meaning systems of firms which can argue strongly about globalization and 'inevitable' forces of competition.

In relation to other agents, we need to comment on only two issues. First, we have included corporate campaigns, such as the celebrated actions against Nike, Nestlé, Shell and other firms, as informal resources. This is because, in contrast to established legal rights, these campaigns are voluntary actions that may take off for idiosyncratic reasons (e.g. the action against Shell's planned disposal of its Brent Spar oil platform, an action that turned out to be based on inaccurate information and that may have led to a solution that was more environmentally damaging than that originally proposed). Second, a key constraint is competition among nation states to attract foreign capital; many countries, for example Ireland, have explicitly developed regimes of low corporate taxation and other benefits to attract MNCs, and competition may lead to a driving down of standards. This is the essence of the 'race to the bottom' argument.

Sources of Variation in MNC Power

A problem with much of the debate on MNCs and labour is that it is expressed in essentialist terms: a given resource or constraint is identified and assumed to be dominant. Thus the 'race to the bottom' view assumes that nation states can do little except compete for the favour of footloose capital. Empirical research has demonstrated that MNCs in fact negotiate around a large set of contingencies. They may, for example, be constrained to be in a given country for reasons of access to its market and also for more informal symbolic reasons. This thus reduces their resources in relation to switching production. Similarly, the more that a firm produces standardized goods the more it is able to use coercive comparisons between sites.

Bair and Ramsay (2003) take the two contingencies of the nature of the market and the degree of integration of production to produce a matrix of possibilities. For example, integrated production and remote supply is likely in petrochemicals and aluminium, whereas such production and the need to be close to the market is exemplified by hotels and fast food chains. These contingencies do not in themselves define the outcome of MNC relations with labour. This is most evident in relation to fast food chains, for the need to be close to the market might be expected to limit their bargaining resources. Yet research has consistently shown that the leading chains are able to impose their own preferred models, even in countries such as Germany (Royle, 2000). Reasons for this include: a clear centralized management strategy; the low skills and fragmentation of the work force, which makes collective worker organization difficult; and divisions between directly owned and franchised operations. In relation to the integrated production and remote supply cases, we have shown elsewhere in the case of aluminium that remote supply does not equal footloose: aluminium producers typically locate near supplies of cheap energy, and in several cases they are also tied in to local political settlements (Bélanger, Edwards, Wright, 1999). For example, the subject of our case study at the end of this chapter, Alcan in Canada, had a key role in Quebec which would make it hard in terms of national politics as well as political relations with labour to shift production to another country. In short, there are many contingencies that cannot be reduced to a few simple dimensions.

This point has been developed in relation to US MNCs, though much of the analysis can be applied to MNCs generally (T. Edwards and Ferner, 2002). Four influences on approaches to labour management are identified. One is the integration and standardization of production, as discussed above, with greater integration tending to lead to the use of centrally determined labour policies. The second is the country-of-origin effect. The well-known anti-unionism of American firms in their own country tends to be extended outside its borders. Note that this feature should not be read as some kind of cultural characteristic. It can itself be explained by the institutional context of the US, crucially the weakness of state agencies in regulating labour and the weight placed on direct relations on the shop floor (P. Edwards, 1981). The third contingency is the host country environment: labour laws and other aspects of the institutional context will constrain the export of any standard model.

The fourth influence is more complex. It is that of dominance effects, a thesis developed by Smith and Meiksins (1995). The core idea is that certain nation states play a leading role in the development of the capitalist system, and hence MNCs from those states will have their powers enhanced (Almond and Ferner, 2006). The US had a dominant position for much of the twentieth century, with the export of Fordism being the sharpest illustration. On some accounts, Japan has taken over this position, but this view focuses on only one aspect of global hegemony, the system of production. It is true that Japanese lean production had a major influence, but this was not connected with control of the global financial or political system. US MNCs thus retain some dominance influence as a result of their location in a powerful global economy. This can be seen in, for example, their influence in debates on intellectual property rights (P. Edwards and Wajcman, 2005: 242–4).

Edwards and Ferner go on to elaborate their account. First, the four influences are not fixed. The national identity of MNCs from a given country evolves over time. Second, the 'specific impact of each element . . . is dependent on how it interacts with the others' (2002: 100). For example, dominance and country-of-origin effects will reinforce each other where an MNC comes from a dominant country. Or they may clash, notably in the case of German MNCs which, it has been found, often strive to qualify their German characteristics by adopting 'dominant' Anglo-Saxon practices is such fields as pay and performance management. This is a key point. It is not just that the four influences interact in the sense of having greater effects than they would do singly. In addition, the nature of the effect of one influence depends on the context of the others. Americanness plus dominance effects could have powerfully reinforcing effects.

Choice, Path Dependency and Indeterminacy

The above discussion focuses on structural factors. But the interpretation of influences and political choices is important. Consider American MNCs in Germany. Country-of-origin, dominance and host country effects will be the same. If we consider large and integrated firms, then the nature of the production system will also be similar. Yet it is well-known that US auto firms acted in ways consistent with the German model, with Ford for example playing a lead role in the metal industry employers' association, while McDonald's went out of its way to escape German requirements for works councils. The different *motives* here probably reflect the extent of a firm's pursuit of 'American' values, with McDonald's being the more committed to non-union policies. The *abilities* to operate in this way reflect variation within the German (host) system. Trade unions in the auto sector were able to counteract any American anti-unionism, whereas such countervailing power was much more limited in fast food.

The terrain on which contest takes place is thus shaped by continuing patterns of social relations. As these patterns evolve, the nature of constraints shifts. MNCs in countries like Germany have found it growing easier to import hitherto foreign practices such as merit-based pay systems. Yet new constraints emerge, for example in relation to information and consultation as a result of the European Works Council Directive and through less formal means such as pressures around human rights.

Similar issues of politics and choice affect the take-up of practices. In other words, host country actors make choices on the basis of their resources and their preferences. There is thus evidence in the UK that the adoption of Japanese practices was encouraged by the fact that these were seen as leading edge methods. Some of the adoption of the practices may have reflected coercive factors, notably the need to be able to compete. But there were also elements of fashion and copying (Oliver and Wilkinson, 1992).

Work Organization and the Diffusion of Innovation within MNCs

The organization of work is one of the most fundamental ways in which any firm can relate to its employees: what kinds of jobs are provided and what discretion do they offer? In respect of MNCs, a key issue is how far models of work organization are transferred, both within an MNC and in terms of diffusion to other companies.

A good place to start is the development of Fordism in Europe after 1945, for this was a particularly substantial case of the adoption of a production system which also illustrates the themes of how practices are transferred (discussed above). A study of the adoption of Fordism in Europe found that the process reflected the construction of a successful model (an example of dominance effects) but also the role of modernizing elites in the recipient countries that consciously adopted American practices (Djelic, 1998). It occurred rapidly in France, for example, where the M-form corporation was largely unknown in 1950 but very common by 1970. There was, however, resistance to the US model, notably from Communist trade unions in France and Italy. It appears, though Djelic does not discuss the point, that Fordism at the point of production was inserted into a wider regime that retained national characteristics. Studies of French workplace relations certainly find Fordist features, with little worker autonomy or participation in decisions at the point of production (Linhart, 1978). At the same time, however, French unions retained their capacity for mass mobilization. Fordism as a production system did not imply a Fordist structure of workplace governance based on a management–labour accord.

Contrasts between France and Germany, on the one hand, and the UK on the other are also instructive. One might expect relatively ready transfer of Fordism to the UK, given the similarities with the US in terms of overall business organization (what would later be termed the liberal market economy model, as opposed to the coordinated model of much of Europe: Hall and Soskice (2001)). Yet the evidence suggests relatively slow transfer, in terms of corporate organization (e.g. use of the M-form) and shop floor practice. There were several reasons. First, the British tradition of 'unscientific management' continued to operate, and was to some extent reinforced by the country's wartime experience: the post-war push was towards 'business as usual' rather than radical modernization (Hyman, 2003). Second, the British political elite made little effort to impose a modernization strategy on companies (Hall, 1986); US Marshall Plan funds were used for debt repayment rather than industrial reconstruction (Djelic, 1998: 194). Third, given this context, British unions at shop floor level continued to bargain on an informal basis, and the shop steward was as familiar a figure in US-owned firms as in domestic industry. One of the later and most famous, and also largely unsuccessful, efforts to 'reform' workplace relations took place at the Fawley oil refinery, owned by the US MNC Esso (Ahlstrand, 1990).

The technology of Fordism was indeed fairly standard: car factories in different countries looked much the same in terms of assembly lines and so on. Yet the social relations of production differed substantially, and the type of labour relations associated with Fordism in the US (plant-based trade unions, elaborate grievance systems and a strongly articulated right to manage) remained largely limited to that country.

Turning to more recent evidence, perhaps the strongest argument for dominance effects has been made in relation to Japanese lean production methods, which, ever since the publication of *The Machine that Changed the World* (Womack *et al.*, 1990), have been seen as a global best practice. Yet the translation of lean production had the same complexities as those affecting Fordism. Even in the car industry, specific contingencies operated at national, company and local level to amend the lean production model (Kochan *et al.*, 1997). Rinehart *et al.* (1997) found substantial worker and trade union resistance to lean production in the Canadian subsidiary of a Japanese firm. This is probably an extreme case, for many Japanese transplants avoid unions and thus restrict overt opposition, but it illustrates the general point that local contexts shape the transfer of practices.

Barriers to any simple transfer of practices are evident. Closely allied to lean production is the principle of quality management. One might expect this to be widely diffused, given that the broad idea of quality is uncontroversial and that principles to improve quality may be relatively unthreatening to workers. But consider a study of a case where transfer is particularly likely: a strongly centralized US MNC (Kostova and Roth, 2002). Even here, the degree of implementation of quality practices in non-US subsidiaries was very limited, with the character of the adoption being described as 'ceremonial' in the largest number of cases. The study also found that, contrary to expectations, subsidiaries that were the most dependent on the head office were the least, and not the most, likely to implement quality management. It was felt that this reflected power symmetries between the subsidiaries and the head office, so that there were two-way dependency relations rather than one-way imposition.

Further location in the quality management literature explains this result. Quality practices have been found to be very nationally specific: they are seen as foreign in some business systems; and they require changes in work organization if they are to be effective (Psychogios, 2004). In particular, quality management, like lean production and teamwork, can be contested by workers.

Ortiz (1998) compared the reception of teamwork in General Motors plants in Spain and the UK. One might expect difficulties in Spain, given that the company was relatively new in the country and that teamwork might be viewed as a foreign Anglo-Saxon practice. In fact, the trade unions accepted teamwork because it was not seen as a challenge to their own ability to organize and represent workers. Armed with this knowledge, the manager in the UK might expect an even easier ride: GM was long established in the country, and in general the business system is similar to the American one. Yet teams were not welcomed. There were two sorts of reason.

First, in relatively formal and institutional terms, teamwork threatened to undermine trade union organization. This was in turn due to the unions' weak structural position. In contrast to Spain, they enjoyed no legal guarantees. In countries like Spain, the idea of social partnership is legally underpinned but is also an established norm, so that unions can have confidence in their right to exist and to be recognized as legitimate bodies. In the UK, this is not the case. Here, their strength rested on their ability to organize workers on the shop floor, and their fear was that teamwork would reduce traditional loyalties and promote direct relations between managers and workers. The result could be that the relevance of unions to workers' day-to-day lives was eroded.

Second, and a factor more implicit in Ortiz's account, is workers' own expectations. GM's UK plants had, like many other workplaces, gone through a series of reorganizations that promoted distrust in management. In many UK workplaces, initiatives such as teamwork are treated with suspicion because of a lack of trust in managerial motives and in some cases because workers question the technical competence of managers. This distrust is hard to manage because it is tacit and informal. It may also emerge unexpectedly if it is triggered by managerial action. A celebrated example is the US-owned company Gate Gourmet, which supplied on-board catering to airlines including British Airways. Workers were low-paid, and many were women of Asian origin. In 2003 the company dismissed some workers after what it saw as illegal unofficial action over new work practices, though the workers argued that the company had failed to communicate properly and had acted without warning. The upshot was a strike which was supported by BA workers and which led to several days of severe disruption to BA flights. The intensity of the strike was increased by the symbol of a large and uncaring US firm being opposed by low-paid women who would not normally be seen as militant.

This is a very unusual event, for reasons considered below. But it is not simply unique. It is an extreme illustration of a general phenomenon, namely, the fact that workers have their own expectations which can lie dormant and unrecognized until activated by some managerial action. These expectations, moreover, are collective, and they can be supported by the deployment of symbolic and other resources. A different example illustrating the same principle comes from workers in Japanese transplant factories, again in the UK (Elger and Smith, 2005). Here, there was no direct opposition to management, but there was a deep scepticism about the model of work practice, which manifested itself in high rates of quitting. The firms had to modify their practices as a result. For example, they had recruited young women in the belief that such workers would be tractable, but they found them hard to motivate and control, with the result that older workers were recruited. Further insight comes from an observational study in a different UK town (Webb and Palmer, 1998). This underlined very deep worker scepticism about Japanese work practices; workers bent quality standards when they had the chance, saw managers as distant and merely complied with standards of work effort.

Managers may not be exposed to such specific problems. But there is always the possibility that unexpected challenges will arise. Some reflect national expectations. For example, a study of working hours found that workers in different parts of an MNC had distinct views about how long they should be at work, and when (Warton and Blair-Loy, 2002). Others are more embedded in particular workplaces. Training in 'cultural awareness' and diversity may help to sensitize managers to them. But the issues are not simply ones of national culture. Workers in any country are likely to differ widely, and much of their response to MNCs will reflect the distinct experiences and traditions of individual workplaces.

The purpose of stressing these points is to underline the nature of the politics of production. MNC managers face inherent tensions. A company best practice, such as teamwork, may offer workers in another country benefits in terms of more job autonomy. But a series of other questions arises: what are the costs, such as work intensification; do workers in fact believe that the benefits are real; has previous experience led to scepticism about new initiatives; are there appropriate mechanisms in place to involve workers in teamwork, or is this a top-down initiative that is simply imposed; are local managers willing to embrace a system that may threaten their interests; is there commitment in the company as a whole, or is it likely that teamwork becomes a dead letter; and are conditions in place that allow time and resources to be devoted to workplace change, or will good intensions be undermined by short-term pressures to produce results? These political and economic questions will shape how teamwork is understood within the politics of production. We now turn to the question of the influences that may lead to particular outcomes.

In some cases teamwork is a corporate 'best practice' which is largely imposed on national subsidiaries. Coller and Marginson (1998) found this to be the case in a UK-based MNC making standardized food products; common methods could be identified and transferred readily. In other cases, this is more difficult. We give in our case study the detailed example of the Canadian MNC, Alcan. At first sight, it should be a case of the ready transfer of models of work organization since its product, aluminium, is in many ways even more standardized than are food products, for national tastes are unimportant and the product is traded globally. Alcan is also a long-established and highly internationalized firm, so that it has had time to develop mechanisms of transfer, and it should fit the model of the globally integrated MNC (Bartlett and Ghoshal, 1998). Third, the firm developed centrally a preferred approach to work organization, turning on employee involvement and participation. Yet multiple contingencies mediated the extent and nature of transfer.

This conclusion is reinforced by studies of American MNCs (T. Edwards et al., 2005; Almond and Ferner, 2006). It might be expected that the transfer of practices would be particularly easy here, given the lack of state regulation of employment and the frequency of organizational change. Yet several factors limited the diffusion of practices from other parts of the MNC. Edwards et al. (2005: 1277) discuss three, of which one is central to the present argument. The weakness of trade unions in the US might be a major opportunity for diffusion. But, the authors show, US MNCs managed their domestic operations through pre-existing employment policies that were shaped by a desire to avoid unionization. Adopting apparently attractive arrangements from other parts of the MNC could disrupt this delicate balance. This argument neatly illustrates the theme of the contested terrain: managers negotiate a fragile workplace order, and even where overt opposition through trade unions is weak they have to be sensitive to the need to generate consent and retain legitimacy.

Conclusions

Viewing the MNC as a contested terrain in relation to labour takes analysis further than other perspectives. It is true that many scholars have spoken in broad terms about the importance of a political view. And writers such as Bartlett and Ghoshal (1998: 39) recognize that MNCs may be 'captives of their past', thus acknowledging that political forces may constrain a pursuit of 'best practice'. But such analysis remains at the obvious level of organizational interaction. It does not locate such interaction in the inherent tensions facing MNCs. In particular, it does not treat the negotiation of consent as a central issue, and it thus offers a bland view of the difficulties of managing MNCs. We have laid out an alternative view, which has three main features. First, the contradictory nature of the labour relation is made central. Second, the distinct ways in which this contradiction is played out in MNCs have been explained. Third, we have indicated some of the contingencies which lead to specific outcomes.

Developing the view of an MNC as a contested terrain now needs to proceed in three main ways, in relation to theory, method and empirical focus. In terms of theory, there has been a tendency in many empirical accounts to stress the complexity and uncertainties of workplace relationships. Causal explanations have been rare, or have focused on explaining a particular case and not its wider significance. We have endeavoured to set cases alongside each other, to point to potential causal influences. These embrace the market context of the firm, its national origin and the nature of its technology. Future analysis needs a more systematic treatment of such influences.

Theoretical issues are linked to those of method. Much research has been of a detailed case study kind, which explores processes in great detail but finds it hard to develop causal accounts. Some recent research, such as that discussed at the end of the last section, uses multiple case studies and can thus offer comparative analysis. Moreover, as cases become more common it is possible to extract causal accounts from them, as we have done above. But more systematic attention could be given to such methods and also to survey-based studies. The authors are currently engaged in a systematic cross-national survey of MNCs, the design of which was shaped by insights from qualitative study. There are major opportunities for more engagement of this kind between research methods.

Empirically, the obvious fact is the emergence of new economies such as China and India, which embraces not just MNC operations in those countries but also the practices of national firms in them as they become multinationals. There are enormous challenges of developing research here. These embrace funding, research access and the application of the contested terrain perspective. A great deal of research on MNCs operates at a relatively superficial level, relying for example on self-completion questionnaires often with low response rates. It has the benefit of being cheap and not raising large demands for access. A contested terrain view needs much fuller access, which implies more extensive funding. Given that the key questions are comparative in nature, it is generally likely to call for research in several firms in at least two countries, which is costly and demanding. A contested terrain view is also foreign to the research traditions of many countries. To deploy it in new terrain requires researchers who know the country and speak the language, literally and metaphorically. They then need to be absorbed into a critical perspective.

All that said, the contested terrain view has developed a new a distinctive image of the MNC. It is well placed to progress further.

CASE STUDY: TEAMWORK IN ALCAN SMELTERS: IMPLEMENTING INNOVATION ON A CONTESTED TERRAIN

Because of the nature of the management–labour relation (discussed in the opening section) and of the specificities of each production unit, the diffusion of innovations in work organization within a given multinational corporation is not an easy process. While one can certainly observe the influence of corporate policies on this matter, the implementation of 'best practices' tends to be demanding in matters of work organization, as both technical and social forces generate idiosyncrasies. New work rules have to be adapted to the ongoing compromise between management and labour. We will illustrate this social process by looking at the development of teamwork in three Alcan aluminium smelters where we have conducted direct observation, interviews and questionnaires over the years.[2]

Teamwork is perhaps the most common contemporary experiment in work reorganization, and an extensive research literature places much emphasis on the gap between its promises and its more modest achievements. In the best scenarios, employees can have significant autonomy in the organization of their daily routine and the application of their know-how, with the group also taking charge of many aspects of coordination and monitoring, sometimes without any direct supervision. But such instances are only observed under the best conditions.

At first sight, Alcan aluminium smelters represent a favourable ground for a model of work organization based on teamwork.

- First, although this is a highly competitive product market, aluminium ingots are a standard commodity, traded globally, and these highly capital-intensive workplaces tend to be relatively insulated from the winds of competition. Such conditions, where the stability of production over a long period of time is the key for the corporation, allow management to offer a relatively high degree of employment security.
- Second, continuous process technology, where workers apply their tacit skills to the monitoring of a flow of production, demands little direct supervision and creates a favourable terrain for teamworking.
- Third, and relatedly, teams are in continuity with the culture of these workers, who value their expertise and autonomy and had prior experience of various forms of informal crew systems or group work.
- Fourth, Alcan corporate management had adopted the general principle of teamwork as far back as 1986; but this with a conscious choice not to launch a central programme. Each plant had to experiment and develop its own model. The corporation favoured direct participation but also knew, and accepted quite well, that some plants were much more advanced than others in this direction. Teams were preferred, but not required, and the outcome of adopting a team model was not predetermined: it was one factor taken into account in essentially qualitative judgements as to a plant's viability.

What are the factors accounting for such limited isomorphism between the smelters, and for the acceptance of this situation by the corporation?

Besides the specificity of every workplace—its history and embeddedness in local institutions and communities, and the pattern of relations between management and labour—at least two structural factors may also account for this lack of a single corporate model. First, investments in aluminium smelters are very costly; these are dedicated assets which cannot be transferred elsewhere. Switching technology between sites being impossible, this weakens the value and impact of coercive comparisons. Second, though the product is largely standard, ways of manufacturing it are not. Different generations of smelters have different technological characteristics. These differences are heightened by local and highly specific adaptations to the core production methods. Direct comparisons of performance are only optimal within a given generation of technologies, hence limiting the possibility of a single best practice model. Indeed, the three smelters where we conducted fieldwork during the 1990s represent different generations of technology, and teamwork was observed at three stages of development. In the Alcan case, it is not so much that various plants resist in a strategic way engagement in mutual learning, a pattern well documented elsewhere by Kristensen and Zeitlin (2005), but that there are objective limitations to the transfer of 'best practices', at least in the sphere of work organization.

The smelter at Lynemouth in the UK, for example, was set up in 1970 with shop floor arrangements that were quite advanced for the time. But it was not until the early 1990s that teamwork was implemented. Direct supervision in production areas was abolished, the position of team leaders created, and job rotation implemented. Teams were given some responsibilities for monitoring output, quality, aspects of safety and, in certain areas, budgeting. Teamwork initially led to some resistance, mainly from local managers rather than unions. Overall, the progress of teamwork was significant and workers had a positive response to it. While they felt their workload may have increased, they appreciated that their knowledge of the production system was better used (Wright and Edwards, 1998). At the Isle-Maligne smelter, in the province of Quebec, production was launched in 1943. When we conducted fieldwork in the early 1990s, a limited form of teamwork was implemented. Direct supervision was reduced significantly, as well as the number of job classifications, some degree of job rotation was observed and some of the teams took charge of coordination tasks, although the picture varied very much between teams. Closer study showed that, in spite of the acceptance of the principle of teamwork by most participants, the evolution towards more flexible work arrangements was limited because such arrangements conflicted, in practice, with the system of work rules enshrined in the collective agreement (Bélanger and Dumas, 1998). Most of these tensions between teamwork and the traditional system of work rules were resolved in the Laterrière smelter where we conducted fieldwork in 1997. Located in the same region, this modern smelter began operation in 1989. From the start, it was agreed that this greenfield site would be unionized and would operate on the basis of an advanced form of teamwork, with absolutely no direct supervision for most of the working time, a very limited number of job classifications, and systematic job rotation (Bélanger, Edwards and Wright, 2003). All of the 450 hourly workers worked according to such principles, organized in 52 teams all across the plant, with no team leader. The system allowed for a high degree of efficiency while also preserving equity among employees and their collective identity and logic of action.

There was no single model of teamwork in Alcan smelters. Although, in the long run, in a rather polycentric fashion, a learning process certainly was at play within the corporation, it remains the case that patterns of work organization have to be part of a social compromise between management and labour, in a specific context. In short, in spite of corporate intent, the diffusion of workplace innovation can never be taken for granted; it is part of social regulation between management and labour. In these three smelters, hourly workers were unionized. In each case, the workplace union was open to the principle of teamwork, although its support was sometimes equivocal, usually reflecting workers' reluctance to accept some of its facets and implications. In other words, gaining formal union approval is a critical condition for management to initiate change in work organization with significant chances of success, but this condition does not ensure that work rules will be transformed easily. It is through the resolution of the issues arising in day-to-day production, in connection with long-standing work rules and routines, that a workplace compromise evolves, with the active or passive support (or opposition) of union delegates. This sphere of micro-politics, which is shaped by the labour relations institutions of a given country or region, is also part of the contested terrain of the workplace.

Questions

1. If teamwork has clear advantages in a firm like Alcan, why do MNCs take so long to implement it? What are the constraints on 'organizational learning'?
2. Why might local managers of an MNC resist a teamwork model?
3. From the point of view of (a) workers and (b) trade unions, what factors need to be taken into account in responding to managerial proposals for advanced forms of teamwork, such as that practised at Laterrière?
4. Teamwork and related efforts at work redesign often fail. What can MNC managers do to reduce the risk of failure in implementing workplace innovation?
5. Teamwork is presented above as a contested and political issue, rather than 'best practice'. What does this mean, and what are the advantages and limitations of such a perspective?

Further Reading

Bélanger, J., Berggren, C., Björkman, T. and Köhler, C. (eds) (1999) *Being Local Worldwide: ABB and the Challenge of Global Management*. Ithaca, NY: Cornell University Press.

An international study of ABB, a cosmopolitan corporation long heralded as a trendsetter in global management policies. Field research was conducted in power transformer plants in six countries. Despite the rhetoric, 'global management' was hard to achieve and more of a project than an end point. Most plants had some success in preserving their relative autonomy from corporate policies, and they also had to adjust to their institutional environment and to make arrangements with employees and local unions. By mediating between global markets and production constraints, the MNC is portrayed as a rich field of internal politics. Nevertheless, international management was making progress in introducing various benchmarking programmes on key measures of productivity, throughput times, quality control, etc., seeking to foster emulation and learning between organizations. Although local managers initially found 'excuses' for below standard performance, corporate management also had resources (such as investment decisions, allocation of mandates for export markets, and career management) to induce subsidiaries to consider corporate policies seriously.

Kristensen, P. H., and Zeitlin, J. (2005) *Local Players in Global Games: The Strategic Constitution of a Multinational Corporation*. Oxford: Oxford University Press.

A very rich empirical study within a British-owned MNC specializing in food- and drink-making equipment, which looks closely at three subsidiaries (in Denmark, the US and England) and the London headquarters. It consists of a sociological analysis of the ways in which the MNC was socially constructed, through the long evolution of small and medium-sized firms in many different institutional environments, which later became part of the company. The authors show the varied degrees of success these subsidiaries later had in playing 'global games', and explore the ways local actors (such as the union leader on the Danish site) successfully made use of national and local institutional arrangements as levers to improve their strategic position in their local community and within the multinational. The power resources and strategies of local actors, at the point of production, were such that the head office appeared to lack any clear strategic view. The book helps understand how the relationships between HQs and subsidiaries are complex because none of the constituents had a monopoly of strategic resources, of expertise in the understanding of market opportunities or of a 'global vision'.

References

Ahlstrand, B. (1990) *The Quest for Productivity*. Cambridge: Cambridge University Press.

Almond, P. and Ferner, A. (eds) (2006) *American Multinationals in Europe: Managing Employment Relations Across National Borders*. Oxford: Oxford University Press.

Bair, J. and Ramsay, H. (2003) 'MNCs and Global Commodity Chains'. In W. N. Cooke. (ed.) *Multinational Companies and Global Human Resource Strategies*. Westport, Conn.: Quorum.

Bartlett, C. and Ghoshal, S. (1998) *Managing across Borders: the Transnational Solution*. 2nd ed. London; Random House.

Bélanger, J., Berggren, C., Björkman, T. and Köhler, C. (eds) (1999) *Being Local Worldwide: ABB and the Challenge of Global Management*. Ithaca, NY: Cornell University Press.

Bélanger, J. and Dumas, M. (1998) 'Teamwork and Internal Labour Markets: A Study of a Canadian Aluminium Smelter', *Economic and Industrial Democracy*, 19(3): 417–42.

Bélanger, J. and Edwards, P. (2007) 'The Conditions Promoting Compromise in the Workplace', *British Journal of Industrial Relations*, 45(4): 713–34.

Bélanger, J., Edwards, P. and Wright, M. (1999) 'Best HR Practice and the Multinational Company', *Human Resource Management Journal*, 9(3): 53–70.

Bélanger, J., Edwards, P. and Wright, M. (2003) 'Commitment at Work and Independence from Management: A Study of Advanced Teamwork', *Work and Occupations*, 30(2): 234–52.

Beynon, H. (1973) *Working for Ford*. Harmondsworth: Penguin.

Coller, X. and Marginson, P. (1998) 'Transnational Management Influence on Changing Employment Practice', *Industrial Relations Journal*, 29: 4–17.

Cooke, W. N. (2001) 'The Effects of Labour Costs and Workplace Constraints on Foreign Direct Investment among Highly Industrialized Countries', *International Journal of Human Resource Management*, 12: 697–716.

Cressey, P. and MacInnes, J. (1980) 'Voting for Ford', *Capital and Class*, 11: 5–33.

Desai, M. (2002) *Marx's Revenge*. London: Verso.

Djelic, M.-L. (1998) *Exporting the American Model*. Oxford: Oxford University Press.

Elger, T. and Smith, C. (2005) *Assembling Work*. Oxford: Oxford University Press.

Edwards, P. (1981) *Strikes in the United States, 1881–1974*. Oxford: Blackwell.

Edwards, P. (1988) 'Patterns of Conflict and Accommodation'. In D. Gallie. (ed.) *Employment in Britain*. Oxford: Blackwell.

Edwards, P., Bélanger, J. and Wright, M. (2006) 'The Bases of Compromise in the Workplace', *British Journal of Industrial Relations*, 44(1): 125–46.

Edwards, P. and Wajcman, J. 2005. *The Politics of Working Life*. Oxford: Oxford University Press.

Edwards, R. (1979) *Contested Terrain*. London: Heinemann.

Edwards, T. and Ferner, A. 'The Renewed "American Challenge": A Review of Employment Practice in US Multinationals', *Industrial Relations Journal*, 33: 94–111.

Edwards, T., Rees, C. and Coller, X. (1999) 'Structure, Politics and the Diffusion of Employment Practices in Multinationals', *European Journal of Industrial Relations*, 5: 286–306.

Edwards, T., Almond, P., Clark, I., Colling, T. and Ferner, A. (2005) 'Reverse Diffusion in US Multinationals', *Journal of Management Studies*, 42: 1261–86.

EIRO (European Industrial Relations Observatory) (2002) 'Industrial Relations Aspects of Mergers and Takeovers', www.eurofound.europa.eu/eiro/2001/02/study/ tn0102401s.htm.

Ferner, A. (2000) 'The Underpinnings of "Bureaucratic" Control Systems', *Journal of Management Studies*, 37: 521–39.

Ferner, A. and Varul, M. (2000) '"Vanguard" Subsidiaries and the Diffusion of New Practices', *British Journal of Industrial Relations*, 38: 115–40.

Frenkel, S. and Kuruvilla, S. (2002) 'Logics of Action, Globalization and Changing Employment Relations in China, India, Malaysia and the Philippines', *Industrial and Labor Relations Review*, 55: 387–412.

Gennard, J. and Steuer, M. (1971) 'The Industrial Relations of Foreign-owned Subsidiaries in the United Kingdom', *British Journal of Industrial Relations*, 9: 143–59.

Hales, C. (2005) 'Rooted in Supervision, Branching into Management: Continuity and Change in the Role of the first-line Manager', *Journal of Management Studies*, 42: 471–506.

Hall, P. (1986) 'The State and Economic Decline'. In B. Elbaum and W. Lazonick., (eds) *The Decline of the British Economy*. Oxford: Clarendon.

Hall, P. and Soskice, D. (2001) *Varieties of Capitalism*. Oxford: Oxford University Press.

Hodson, R. (2001) *Dignity at Work*. Cambridge: Cambridge University Press.

Hyman, R. (2003) 'The Historical Evolution of British Industrial Relations'. In P. Edwards. (ed.) *Industrial Relations*. 2nd edn, Oxford: Blackwell.

Jenkins, J. (2005) 'From Collective Bargaining to "Procedural Individualisation"'. PhD thesis, University of Keele.

Kenney, M. and Florida, R. (1993) *Beyond Mass Production*. Oxford: Oxford University Press.

Kochan, T., Lansbury, R. and MacDuffie, J. P. (eds) (1997) *After Lean Production*. Ithaca: ILR Press.

Kostova, T. and Roth, K. (2002) 'Adoption of an Organizational Practice by Subsidiaries of Multinational Corporations', *Academy of Management Journal*, 45: 215–33.

Kristensen, P.H. and Zeitlin, J. (2005) *Local Players in Global Games: The Strategic Constitution of a Multinational Corporation*. Oxford: Oxford University Press.

Legge, K. (2006) 'Ethics and Work'. In M. Korczynski *et al.* (eds) *Social Theory at Work*. Oxford: Oxford University Press.

Levy, D. L. and Egan, D. (2003) 'A Neo-Gramscian Approach to Corporate Political Strategy', *Journal of Management Studies*, 40: 4, 803–29.

Linhart, R. (1978) *L'établi*. Paris: Les éditions de minuit. (English edition, *The Assembly Line*, 1981.)

Martinez, J. I. and Jarillo, J. C. (1989) 'The Evolution of Research on Coordination Mechanisms in Multinational Corporations', *Journal of International Business Studies*, 20: 489–514.

Martinez Lucio, M., Turnbull, P., Blyton, P. and McGurk, J. (2001) 'Using Regionalization', *European Journal of Industrial Relations*, 7: 49–70.

Meardi, G. and Tóth, A. 2006. 'Who Is Hybridizing What?' In Ferner *et al. Multinationals, Institutions and the Construction of Transnational Practices*. Basingstoke: Palgrave Macmillan.

Milkman, R. (1991) *Japan's California Factories*. Los Angeles: Institute of Industrial Relations, University of California.

Morgan, G. and Kristensen, P. H. (2006) 'The Contested Space of Multinationals: Varieties of Institutionalism, Varieties of Capitalism', *Human Relations*, 59(11), 1467–90.

Mueller, F. and Purcell, J. (1992) 'The Europeanization of Manufacturing and the Decentralization of Collective Bargaining', *International Journal of Human Resource Management*, 3: 15–34.

Oliver, N. and Wilkinson, B. (1992) *The Japanization of British Industry*. Oxford: Blackwell.

Ortiz, L. (1998) 'Union Response to Teamwork', *Industrial Relations Journal*, 29: 42–57.

Psychogios, A. (2004) 'Towards the Adoption of New Management Methods in a Modernising Business System?' PhD thesis, University of Warwick.

Rinehart, J., Huxley, C. and Robertson, D. (1997) *Just Another Car Factory?* Ithaca: ILR Press.

Roy, D. F. (1954) 'Efficiency and "the Fix"', *American Journal of Sociology*, 60: 255–66.

Royle, T. (2000) *Working for McDonald's in Europe: the Unequal Struggle*. London: Routledge.

Schmitt, M. and Sadowski, D. (2003) 'A Cost-minimization Approach to the International Transfer of HRM/IR Practices', *International Journal of Human Resource Management*, 14: 409–30.

Smith, C. and Meiksins, P. (1995) 'System, Society and Dominance Effects in Cross-national Organisational Analysis', *Work, Employment and Society*, 9: 241–68.

Streeck, W. (1997) 'Beneficial Constraints'. In J. R. Hollingsworth and R. Boyer. (eds) *Contemporary Capitalism*. Cambridge: Cambridge University Press.

Thompson, P. (2003) 'Disconnected Capitalism', *Work, Employment and Society*, 17: 359–78.

Warton, A. S. and Blair-Loy, M. (2002) 'The "overtime culture" in a global corporation', *Work and Occupations*, 29: 32–63.

Webb, J. and Palmer, G. (1998) 'Evading Surveillance and Making Time', *British Journal of Industrial Relations*, 36: 611–27.

Womack, J. D., Jones, P. and Roos, D. (1990) *The Machine that Changed the World*. New York: Rawson.

Wright, M. and Edwards, P. (1998) 'Does Teamworking Work, and if so, Why? A Case Study in the Aluminium Industry', *Economic and Industrial Democracy*, 19(1): 59–90.

NOTES

1. See EIRO (2002), and the European Industrial Relations Observatory website for more recent examples (www.eiro.eurofound.eu.int).
2. More recently, in October 2007, Alcan was acquired by Rio Tinto. The aluminium business was consolidated within Rio Tinto Alcan, one of the five product groups now operated by Rio Tinto.

Chapter 10 The Multinational Firm as a Locus of Learning along Networks

Ray Loveridge

Introduction

This chapter begins by acknowledging the focus of much of the currently prescriptive literature upon technological innovation as a strategic driver in the attainment of global competitive advantage for the multinational corporation (MNC). It interrogates this view through the lens of the MNC as the locus of multi-layered networks of relationships that may give rise to widely differentiated shared identities and aspirations. In this respect it seems important to distinguish the kinds of 'conflicting isomorphic pressures' (Westney, 1993; Kostova, 1999) that shape the action repertoires of both expatriate and indigenous managers in more particular terms than those provided by more holistically functionalist and, usually, after the fact, prescriptive analysis often found in the field of international business strategy.

This is not to deny the importance of intentionality to be discerned in the practice of strategic decision-making in the MNC, both informal and formal. Nor, by implication, do I wish to deny the sometimes heuristic utility of an assumed actor 'rationality' embodied in transaction cost and resource dependency approaches to business management. It is to say that these rationales or logics of action are shaped by negotiated meanings and ideational frames arising within the shifting social contexts of both strategists and implementers of organized projects (Karpik, 1972). Therefore the assumed universality of value transitivity present within rational choice approaches to the analysis of business decisions can often be dangerously misleading. There may, indeed, be greater historical evidence for the periodicity of mimetic 'fashions' in the ideational framing of perceived problems in business and in the wider political economy among cross-national elites (Clark, 2004).

However the language of neo-institutionalist analysis often fails to encompass the problematic and temporarily constrained nature of the processes by which

Images of the Multinational Firm   Edited by Simon Collinson and Glenn Morgan
© 2009 John Wiley & Sons, Ltd

individual and collective interests and identities are aligned within complex organizations. Likewise, much of the more functionally oriented analysis of 'knowledge management' assumes away the possibility that the so-called social capital present within networked relations gains its potential value through its generation of differential returns, both financial and symbolic, for community members (Bourdieu, 1980). Intra-organizational learning, whether collective or personal, can possess a value for the learner quite other than that possessed in its instrumental use by a corporate elite. Appropriative closure rather than collaboration with 'the other', be that a distant home country executive or an even more distant and temporary presence of a private equity owner, can sometimes seem a feasible, if equally transient, strategy for a knowledgeable group of employees. Ideal types of the 'knowledge-based firm' (see for example Kogut and Zander, 1993) seem often to ignore the effects that a dynamically contested context can have on the commitments of internal knowledge-communities. Many business analysts appear to assume that member 'trust' in organizational procedures can be generated and judiciously applied by strategic management as an all-purpose and least-cost relational lubricant (Weick, 2008). Those firms fortunate enough to be based in national systems whose institutions promote a more diffused trust in corporate authority are, thus, often construed as sharing a national competitive advantage (Dore, 1973; Lane, 1996).

The defining characteristic of the MNC is, in fact, that of the dispersed nature of business decision-making across geographical, institutional and cultural space. Much of the earlier literature has focused on the manner in which formal structure has followed attempts by the parent firm's executive management to control and to orchestrate entry into overseas locations and to monitor and sustain local operations thereafter. This process has been well summarized by Bartlett and Ghoshal (1989). More recently MNC structures have been seen to reflect an increased willingness on the part of corporate elites to mandate operational authority to overseas affiliates (see Cantwell and Zhang in this volume). This may reflect a growing importance placed on embedding affiliates within the institutional networks provided by host settings (Andersson and Forsgren, 1996). In some part it can also denote a more significant trend towards the outsourcing and offshoring of many formerly internally provided services (Sako, 2003). Taken together with a now familiar pattern of cross-border alliances between suppliers, customers and competitors, this is seen by some observers as denoting an epochal change in the nature of the firm towards Network or Alliance Capitalism (Castells, 2001; Dunning, 2003).

While not discounting the significance of such inter-organizational linkages, or 'extended bureaucracies' in the production of technological change and innovation (Child and Loveridge, 1990), I would like to suggest in this chapter that the success of such contractual arrangements is intimately and ultimately dependent upon the reflexive management of both the substantive meaning of information exchanges and the processes of translation along inter-personal networks (Czarniaska and Joerges, 1996). This is not solely a matter of the ability to codify transmissible information (Kogut and Zander, 1992). Nor indeed are inter-personal networks shaped solely by formal organizational goals, though formal organizational structures represent dominant shaping influences by virtue of their significance in wider society. In this chapter I will build on the conceptual schema suggested by Naphapiet and Ghoshal (1998) to focus on the signification of organizational hierarchy/career expectations, of formal education and tacit knowledge and of national and ethnic identity in the shaping of networks and knowledge translation. In all cases, language, both 'natural' and vocational, provides asymmetries in access to resources along extended layered relationships that constitute the MNC (Vaara *et al.*, 2005).

Shifting Terrains: The Contextual Dynamics of Change

An important ideational strand of the current globalization paradigm is one that sees 'appropriative learning' by MNCs and by nation states as the basis for competitive (or monopolistic) advantage in a Schumpeterian contest between firms and between nation states for technological advantage (Schumpeter, 1912; Teece, 1986; Ostry and Nelson, 1995). It has long been asserted that the MNC can serve as a conduit in the transportation of 'external' or market knowledge and information across national boundaries and different jurisdictional regimes (see Vernon (1966), Buckley and Casson (1976)). Within this efficiency perspective, the organizational capability of the MNC in the coordination, recombination and relocation of spatially separated and socially distant sources of local knowledge is seen to provide it with a competitive advantage over dispersed and isolated local competitors (Dunning, 1993; Kogut and Zander, 1993).

However, the surge in foreign direct investment (FDI) recorded since the mid-1980s can be attributed to a confluence in a number of perceived contextual factors that has served to make the multinational mode of production and distribution increasingly more attractive and more technically possible for strategic elites. Among these factors the emergence of Pacific Asian nations as effective contestants and investors in overseas markets might be seen as stimulating an emulative response within both 'mature' Western systems and in other 'late developing' or 'transitional' capitalist business systems, such as those of mainland China and India. Over the same period, Schumpeterian analytical perspectives have gained fresh appositeness from continuing waves of commercially successful technological innovation that has accompanied the spread of cross-national firms (Freeman and Louca, 2001). These seem often to have had the effect of eroding institutionalized sectoral boundaries and/or re-aligning inter-organizational relationships within them, sometimes producing new fields based on a fusion of existing technologies (Kodoma, 1992; Kaonides, 1999). These latter, in turn, can often be seen to be accompanied by convergences upon new specializations within underlying scientific and professional disciplines (Murmann, 2007). A widely experienced phenomenon across all sectors has been the transformative usages of communications and information technology (CIT). These can be seen as of particular consequence in their effects on the ease of transacting over distance and across national boundaries and in greatly adding to the overall velocity of innovative change (Perez, 1985).

Within this context the development of the N-form or alliance structure of formal organization has become increasingly evident. The main focus of much of the analysis of intra-organizational relations within the MNC has, as in the past, been on centre–periphery relations and on attempts by head office (HO) to orchestrate activities in overseas subsidiaries (Birkinshaw and Hood, 1998). These overseas ventures have often been part-owned by indigenous agents as a host government condition for gaining entry to their sovereign territory and so have, more aptly, been entitled as 'affiliates'. But, as Cantwell observes elsewhere in this volume, over the past quarter century it has become increasingly common for MNCs to enter into overseas alliances with other MNCs (Kang and Sakai, 2000). Such alliances have been justified in terms of a number of strategic objectives, increasingly often in terms of providing complementary technological capabilities or the opportunity for mutual technological learning (Chesborough, 2006). In many rapidly changing sectors or fields, alliances with both competitors and suppliers or customers (horizontal or vertical) have been seen as providing means of sharing the costs and risks of both long-term R&D and/or shorter term design and development (D&D). Both arrangements can offer flexibility through loose-linked and project-focused relations with collaborators but, sometimes, can develop into longer and more broadly based collaborations (Fine, 1998; Vanhaverbeke et al., 2002).

The Sectoral Context

Cross-border changes in inter-firm relationships have moulded the technical forces affecting emergent sector boundaries (Loveridge and Mueller, 1999; Powell et al., 2005). In some new fields such as biotechnology this has been portrayed as a few large pharmaceuticals sponsoring multiple external R&D projects over a long gestation period. In others, such as software development, time horizons in product development may be shorter, but the customized provision of a turn-key system and integration of specialized after-sales services in maintaining the system are more important in determining the significance of orchestrator and conductor. In many cases the role of the 'flagship firm' located at the node of a complex system of networks can be seen to possess a potential capability to shape the structure of emergent fields through the development of protocols for collaboration and for the cooption of new entrants (Powell, 1998; Powell et al., 2005).

In these circumstances the emergence of nascent fields can appear to follow two parallel paths. One is marked by a growing concentration in the ownership of such strategically positioned 'flagships' through a process of regionally focused M&A (Rugman and D'Cruz, 2000). The other is that of the emergence of clusters of relatively small artisanal producer-designers, often located in close proximity after the manner of Silicon Valley (Morgan, 1997). Here, collaborative relations between competitors can be shaped by a shared vocational enthusiasm for exploring the new field. Similarly, successful relations between technological 'artisans' and scientists and technologists in nearby universities and research institutes tend to be based on a mutual recognition of the other's contribution to new knowledge and of the importance of its commercialization (Powell and Owen Smith, 1998). The interface between the more bureaucratically structured frame of the D&D technologist in the flagship firm and that of the university scientist is often seen to be mediated by the artisanal *bricoleur* within the context of the small venture company. The opportunity for 'spill-overs' of useful information along densely clustered local networks and through very active labour mobility is also seen by many economists to be a major attraction for MNCs. For those artisanal technologists unsuccessful in creating a 'boundary-less career' this externalization of risk by the MNC can prove to be something of a two-edged sword (Audretsch and Feldman, 1996; Arthur and Rousseau, 1998).

The National Context

At this point we should note the part played by US government agencies in the establishment of these new sectors. The US National Institutes of Health (NIH) has held a nodal position in the inter-organizational networks in the emergent field of biotechnology from the 1980s to 2000 (Powell *et al.*, 2005). Its financial contribution in the early years far outstripped that of commercial investment and, even by the year 2000, amounted to over $17 billion compared with the aggregated internal R&D expenditure of all major world pharmaceutical and biotechnology firms of just over $26 billion. Venture capital contributions are described as 'episodic' and only topped $1 billion from 1997 onwards. A similar story can be constructed around the role of the US Defence Department's investment in Silicon Valley since WWII (Nelson and Rosenberg, 1993).

At the national level the promotion and protection of technological innovation has long been associated with the development of the industrialized nation state (Landes, 1969; Freeman, 1987; Whitley, 2007). Ostry and Nelson (1995) extend this description to one in which the present contest for national advantage in technology could be described as a historically grounded form of 'techno-nationalism'. Earlier, Chalmers Johnson (1982) made the distinction between the interventionary role played by government in the 'developmental state' and the more arm's length position taken in the 'regulatory state'. It is a distinction that has been repeatedly challenged, only to be reproduced in a number of similar analytical taxonomies. Recent comparative institutional analyses of national business systems tend to position national contexts between polar structures of more or less socially integrated institutionalized contexts. Hall and Soskice (2001) present these as the 'Liberal Market Systems' (LMS) at one end of a relational spectrum and the 'Coordinated Market Systems' (CMS) at the other. These are exemplified in the US and German systems respectively. It is a spectrum more minutely extended by other analysts (e.g. Whitley (1999), Amable (2003)). Hall and Soskice advance two important conjectures. The first is that LMS will adapt more readily to exogenous shocks such as radical technological change more readily than CMS. A number of comparative studies of the development emergent sectors such as ICT and biotechnology seem to confirm this (Casper and Whitley, 2004). A second hypothesis stresses the need for complementarity in form between key institutionalized activities functional to capitalist systems, mainly those concerned with the provision of capital or credit and those of labour socialization and transformation (Hall and Soskice, 2001). Again, some historical evidence can be provided to support this conjecture (Gospel and Pempleton, 2005).

In spite of the limited role as a regulatory state attributed to the US government in these typologies, since WWII at least it seems to have supported state funded agencies in the field of technology to an extent probably unmatched in aggregative financial terms and 'scientific' resources by any other country. Most national governments are, in fact, currently engaged in what has been described as 'locational tournaments' for FDI (Dicken, 2007: 238). More particularly, the regional cluster or technopole, modelled on that of Silicon Valley, is seen as a means of attracting overseas investment in 'a centre of excellence' (Holm and Pederson, 2000). This is the label often claimed for a facility that provides global or regional R&D/D&D services for a guest MNC, though in my own research I have found it to be often applied to local servicing laboratories for reasons of public and political relations (see Loveridge, 2007). Robert Reich (1991), a former member of the US administration, has gone so far as to suggest that the 'work of nations' is to graduate sufficient 'symbolic analysts' to make that country the preferred locale for strategic and technological 'problem solving' on behalf of the 'country-less' global MNC. Other, largely American, historians and political scientists have written in a similar vein.

For the most part international policy agencies have, hitherto, measured the absorptive or technical learning capacity of a nation much more mechanistically in terms of 'human capital' (Schultz, 1961; Becker, 1964). Their indices include data such as the proportion of the relevant cohorts to have passed through higher education and the number of product patents filed in the USA (United Nations Trade and Development (UNCTAD), 2005). (The relationship between the two indices is represented in a simple economic growth equation.) More recent recognition of the part played by the wider context of national institutions is to be found in UNCTAD reports. For a short period of years from 2000 the World Bank actually created a research unit devoted to finding measures of 'social capital' and its contribution to the economic performance of national economies (World Bank, 2001).

The MNC as a Confederation of Internally Networked Communities

Within this context the importance of the knowledge basis of the firm's activities has gained in operational and analytical significance (Grant, 2003). The complementary metaphors of 'dynamic capabilities' (Teece and Pisano, 1994) and 'absorptive capacities' (Cohen and Levinthal, 1989) reflect a perceived need for continuous learning, adaptation and recombination of member skills in order to maintain the capacity for innovation required for corporate survival. The exploration of new ideas and their exploitation in novel products and processes has become elevated to that of a strategic precept. The notion of absorptive capacity lays emphasis on a capacity to import knowledge and to recombine it with an existing stock of capabilities that enables the organization, firm or nation to produce a unique and inimitable product. Attempts to operationalize these, perhaps rather evident, concepts in a universally prescriptive way have sometimes seemed to bring greater variety in situational explanation than universal elucidation (Eisenstadt and Martin, 2000). Instead, there has been an enormous emphasis in scholarly analysis on the notion of tacitness and of its persistent recursiveness in the development of task knowledge within 'communities of practice' that exist within all large organizations (Polanyi, 1966; Wenger, 1998; Brown and Duguid, 1991). Successful knowledge management is often seen to involve the appropriation of experiential learning and its recombination in more formal design systems, a goal not too far distant from that of the commodification of knowledge associated with traditional scientific management. The weight attached to the subjective involvement assumed to be necessary in reflexive learning within and between internal communities can be significant in distinguishing between the kind of prescriptions offered by academics and consultants.

Again, the Japanese exemplar can be seen to have been significant in moving Western practice towards an emphasis on the harvesting of practical experience through devices such as continuous improvement, autonomous team working and inter-disciplinary project management. A central capability to archive such tacit knowledge has been seen to lie in social mechanisms for its articulation and codification, the most cited of these being taken from the Japanese practice of 'Ba' (Nonaka and Takeuchi, 1995). The advocacy of such participatory organizational devices has become part of a burgeoning knowledge management literature that has gained considerable credibility across apparently incommensurable academic approaches such as those of transaction cost economics and critical cultural theory (Schuller, Baron and Field, 2000). As suggested above, this literature puts emphasis on the notion that tacit or enacted knowledge is generated through collaborative relationships along networks based on trust between members. The existence of this trust can be seen to constitute a 'social capital' from which members can draw a stream of shared rewards which may be economic, symbolic or simply affectively sentient (Adler and Kwon, 2002). Possibly the most comprehensive application of this approach to innovation within the MNC is that of Naphapiet and Ghoshal (1997). Their analysis distinguishes between the structural shaping of ties within intra-organizational networks, the depth of identity and normative obligation attached to these relationships by members, the cognitive meaning of information and knowledge generated in this way and, finally, to its appropriability through representation in shared codes and narratives.

The analysis of these authors is unusual both in its attempted exploration of the dimensionality of networked relationships and of their significance in giving variety of meaning and identity to actant behaviour in ways that may or may not complement those of 'the organization'. There is little in the more exhortative literature of knowledge management that acknowledges the exclusiveness of networks and their appropriative, not to say *expropriative*, nature. Yet this is, indeed, the role attributed to *habitus* in the accumulation of social and symbolic capital by Bourdieu (1977,

1991) whose work is used extensively by institutional theorists. Indeed, in much of the international business literature of all persuasions it is assumed that inter-personal networks complement a holistic logic on each side of inter-organizational alliances. Resistance is seen as 'frictional' to the eventual attainment of the over-riding functionality of purpose attributed to organizational processes. As Whetten and Godfrey (1998) concede, identity with 'the organization' may be difficult to achieve without a predisposition towards such a normative commitment in the employee. This is evidently more possible within particular circumstances, such as small artisanal enterprises, or when bureaucratic authority chimes with a normative commitment to a wider communal frame as, for example, is seen to occur in the 'manorial' Japanese firm (Dore, 1973).

However, the inherent contradictions between the institutional context within which such social technologies were first developed, that of Japan, and those to which they have been subsequently translated in the Western world have become increasingly evident (Swan and Scarbrough, 2005). Within the latter context the relational basis of 'Ba' has given place to a more market-based notion of services encapsulated in regulatory systems such as lean production, Six Sigma (statistical process control) and, more widely, in the so-called 'flexible firm'. The latter is usually characterized by an increasing dependency on a 'contingent' labour force and upon outsourced services – including the fractionation and dispersal of professional design and development activities (Shutt and Whittington, 1987; Powell, 2001). Within the more formally specialized division of labour that exists across much of mainland Europe this 'flexibility' in task and career has been widely resisted. Across a wide variety of MNCs Casson et al. (1998) discovered that a significant proportion of managerial employees felt threatened by the introduction of 'flexible' working and employment conditions and had experienced a widespread breakdown of corporate trust. Paradoxically perhaps, in many developing economies such as mainland China, there sometimes appears a lack of underlying bureaucratic socialization required for the effective operation of autonomous group or project-based systems (Hitt et al., 2002; Child and Heavens, 2003; Warner and Witzel, 2004).

Thus the role of the MNC in the creation of internal structures that act as conduits for conveying such design archetypes across national boundaries becomes problematic (Greenwood and Hinings, 1993). HQ executives will attempt to incorporate the prevailing fashion in organization modelling within the codes and standards of affiliated hosts, while attempting the assimilation of appropriate attitudes and styles by distant colleagues and stakeholders. Within the N-form organization these negotiated frames of meaning/action have to be severally agreed and implemented within the differently structured arenas of partner organizations, some more immediately exposed to market competition than others. Along the journey, models, both abstract and concrete, become translated in terms that provide legitimation for the actant's view of his or her situated authority in each of many bureaucratic arenas encountered in transit. Equally, they are retranslated in the subsequent day-to-day interchanges with local agencies. Thus, the idea becomes re-embedded and re-enacted over time in the remote context of localized social relations and beliefs. As a bridging text or 'boundary object' the original mission statement may become the basis upon which communications are legitimated, performance measures are constructed and computer systems are programmed (Star and Greisemer, 1989). Yet, even where, as in many American parented MNCs, great efforts are made to ensure complete standardization of local operations across national borders, it is likely that the meanings attributed to procedural norms will vary greatly (Czarniawska and Sevon (eds), 1996). Such differences can sometimes come to light when the computerized system 'fails' or, equally commonly, when customers fail to communicate their perceived needs to operators in remote call centres.

In the following sections I attempt a brief exploration of three sources of social closure in the creation of factional identities within interdependent transnational communities. For the purposes of this chapter I confine my analysis to the significance for actants of i) organizational hierarchy, ii) formal occupational knowledge/education and iii) their membership of national and ethnic communities. All of these have been demonstrated to provide socio-political boundaries, and possible obstacles, to the recombination of ideas in the creation of technological innovation. Of the many other likely collective identifiers, gender is only lightly touched upon in this chapter, but can be seen as especially important in the context of developing countries (Jack and Lorbiecki, 2007).

The Signification of Hierarchy

Few, if any, organizations can be described as constitutional democracies. Even fewer public corporations offer more than limited procedural 'voice' to external stakeholders. Often the intentions of boards of directors seem more influenced by their perceived reputation among peers and, more especially, along those networks that conjoin the firm with financial and regulatory intermediaries in the performance of what has become known as corporate governance (Gourevitch and Shinn, 2005; Coffee, 2006). These are described by Gupta and Govindarajan (1991) as the 'capital networks' of the MNC, ones that are often most closely monitored. It is likely that symbolic and social capital will play an important bonding and bridging role in establishing their members' reputation for creditworthiness, but equally they can provide limits for the enactment of risky investment decisions.

This is well illustrated by Kristensen and Zeitlin's (2005) study of a British engineering firm that attempted to expand overseas through a process of acquisition over a decade and a half from the early 1980s to the late 1990s. Of the 200 or so subsidiaries that thus constituted the loosely linked MNC, the authors focus on the tactics adopted by local management and trade union representatives in three acquired businesses, one British, one American and one Danish, to illustrate the influence that each developed in the negotiated process of strategy formulation within the group. The ascendancy of the Danish management within this struggle is seen largely to derive from the knowledge capabilities of the workforce and from the institutional setting within which these were shaped. A second theme in their narrative is that of the influence of the financial networks of the City in which the group's executives were seen to be firmly embedded. The need to maintain their financial reputation is seen to have precipitated both the board's initial move to internation-alize the firm's activities and, later, to have led to its eventual demise through a series of mergers with rivals in which its local subsidiary plants were closed or found other corporate identities. In much of the authors' concluding commentary one can discern echoes of a long-standing criticism of the financial 'short-termism' of City of London bankers. Kristensen and Zeitlin interpret the rationale for the group's eventual demise as deriving from a financial evaluation of shareholder returns from a 'restructuring of assets', seen to outweigh any technical assessment of their op-erational efficacy. This is a world made more significantly complex by the several waves of M&A activity over the last 25 years and by the contributory roles played by financial deal-makers and the enormous growth in entrepreneurial opportunities created by de-regulation in the fields of global venture capital and private equity (Guler and Guillen, 2005, Coffee, 2006).

The growing complexity of control and coordination within and across boundaries might well be seen to combine with contextual turbulence in bringing about a large measure of mandated responsibility for operational management (Pugh *et al.*, 1969). Students of international business have generally put greater explanatory emphasis on a strategic need for the MNC to respond to local markets and/or to exploit local resources, particularly when seeking an active embeddedness in regional R&D clusters (Dunning, 1993; Cantwell and Zhang in ch. 3). On the other hand, some executives, such as the CEO of IBM, see the attainment of a globally sourced value chain as leading to increased surveillance and a more minutely modelled continuous delivery of 'systems servicing' worldwide (Palmisano, 2006). Devolution of authority in this view has more to do with the modularization of geographically dispersed HQ functions whilst leaving more ultimate power at the MNC's centre (Sako, 2003).

There is, then, scope for wide differences in strategic responses to perceived con-tingencies across changing and emergent contextual fields. But, as suggested above (Casson *et al.*, 1998) much of the strategic uncertainty is seen ultimately to have been absorbed by operative staff and middle management. Yet it remains the case that within case studies these conduits seem crucial both to the orchestration of innovation within the MNC and, increasingly, across its layered interfaces with alliance partners. As Wenger (1998) suggests: 'The job of brokering is complex. It in-volves processes of translation, co-ordination and alignment between perspectives. It requires enough legitimacy to influence the development of practice, mobilise attention and address conflicting interests.' (p. 109) A second level in micro-politics of frame alignment is to be seen in the day-to-day creation and maintenance of local management authority both in the eyes of HQ and those of their workforce (Bacharach, Bamberger and Sonnenestuhl, 1996). Success in the first is likely to en-hance authority within the local plant and in the networks in which it is embedded. In fact the boundaries often encountered by local managers can be doubly drawn. First, can come the difficulties of translating local operating conditions into the criteria used to create standardized procedures for reporting to the centre. Second, can come their own perception of their marginal social identity within parent-based networks. Both can help to obscure HQ recognition of their technical accomplishments. These tensions attached to boundary-spanning positions are also likely to occur in the management of joint ventures as encountered in the study by De Rond (2003). Evidently the corporate elite in the well integrated MNC can attempt to alleviate these tensions through the use of reflexive mentoring and frequent face-to-face meetings between management at every level. At the same time the origins of conflicts in the enactment of their roles and, indeed, of the multiple networks they conjoin, derive from the nature of the contestual environment in which they operate.

As a result of recent trends towards extensive 'de-layering' and outsourcing to 'global business service firms', the close-knit stability of networks within many MNCs can be seen to have become much more fragmented or extended over modularized networks of suppliers. Westley (1990) talks of the 'micro-politics of inclusion' among operational managers and this is perhaps most evident in contests that occur between both patriate and expatriate managers of acquired plants in overseas locations. This can be particularly the case after a cross-border merger or acquisition when local managers are attempting to establish the significance of the potential contribution of their plant for their new masters (Dorrenbacher and Geppert, 2006). Expatriate operational managers of overseas affiliates can also be seen to feel the vulnerability of their career position and to seek to 'repair the effect that distance has on their know-ability' through the continuous servicing of their HQ networks and the establishment of parent country patrons (Goodall and Roberts, 2003). Nohria and Ghoshal (1990) find homophily, or common socialization, across HQ and subsidiary managers to be a significant predictor of intensity of communication between the two. In my own research (see case study at the end of this chapter) I seek to show the effect that membership of one or other network had on the manner in which innovations were valued and translated within HQ, the overseas affiliate and within the socio-political context of the host country. The nature of the embeddedness of the role played by the incumbent, in each of these contexts, was critical to the manner in which new technologies were interpreted and enacted. Andersson and Forsgren (1996) demonstrate that the possibilities of imposing central standards may be highly circumscribed by the extent of the existing embeddedness of an acquired subsidiary or partner in their local networks. Yet, other researchers (Westney and Sakakibara, 1985; Lam, 2003) stress the importance of feedback from local networks to successful product development and to R&D.

Historically relations between R&D networks and those of both strategic and operational managers have been reported in many studies as being poor and, even, conflictful (Conway, 1995). My own study of 20 European MNCs in South East Asia (Loveridge, 2007) revealed the fragility, not to say, hostility, often expressed in relationships between disparate R&D groups and between them and operational management. The role played by overseas R&D was often discounted in rivalries with the parent R&D laboratory. The responsiveness of the latter to the client needs of overseas affiliates was often reported as being ignored in the central R&D's pursuit of 'cutting-edge technology'. In other studies of mergers and international joint ventures similar rivalries can lead to the ultimate failure of the project. Powell (1998) describes a variety of misunderstandings that took place between large bureaucratically organized pharmaceutical firms and their more artisanally organized partners in biotechnology. Yet he suggests: 'I have rarely seen presentations where such difficulties are openly discussed' (p. 271). In De Rond's (2003) rich account of three alliances between British biotechnology firms and their US sponsors in pharmaceuticals rivalries and breakdowns in trust between the corporate partners emerged at different levels in each organization and at different interfaces. That is to say, rivalries emerged across the respective groups of scientists, of operational managers and of senior executives. Disputes over strategies on intellectual property also arose between scientists and their corporate executives. The mode of 'up-scaling' of discoveries to be adopted led to differences between scientists and operational management. Strategic interventions by corporate boards provided additional departures from the original purposes of the R&D project. In other words, there seemed often to be a perennial tension between institutionalized expectations held along different, hierarchically shaped internal networks and the need for coordination in the purposive exploration and exploitation of new knowledge (Teece and Pisano, 1994).

Educational and Occupational Signification

As suggested earlier, for some time the emphasis in the analysis and teaching of knowledge management techniques has been on the importance of encouraging the verbalization, harvesting and archiving of the tacit or experiential task knowledge of operatives at all levels of the organization. In its emphasis on listening and categorizing information according to its situational significance for organizational objectives it can be seen as contrasting with the top-down imposition of standards according to some universal models of efficiency and optimization used in traditional scientific management. It is, of course, equally instrumental as the latter in its attempt to gain a monopolistic advantage for the firm over external rivals in the field through the appropriation of idiosyncratic knowledge. The nature of the contest is such that possession of such uniqueness in the construction of new meaning systems may provide the basis for positional leverage in a new knowledge field and product market.

Yet the model of the translation process presented by Nonaka and Takeuchi (1995), and other similar analyses, is curiously devoid of reference to any possible existing mode of categorization within which tacit knowledge might become articulated. Indeed, across this whole school of management analysis there is a discounting of formal structures of knowledge as being dysfunctional to the exploration of new understandings of task and task environments. By way of contrast we may refer back to the manner in which there has been an ever-increasing social demand for educational qualification in established disciplines (Dore, 1976; Schofer and Meyer, 2005), allied with the overwhelming importance attached to the notion of 'human capital' by competing national governments (UNCTAD, 2005). A considerable literature in the USA, for example, has been devoted to anxious comparisons between the present and future production of scientists and engineers in that country and those of the more rapidly growing economies of China, India and Russia (Reich, 1998; Yang and Jiang, 2007).

Much of the burgeoning global demand for vocational qualification might be seen to derive from a societal demand for credentialism that is not directly – in Japan often not at all – related to the eventual task skills or required career knowledge of employees (Dore, 1976).Yet the attainment of the symbolic and social capital provided by a formal education – more especially by a short stay at a university and, increasingly, an even shorter stay in a business school – is evidently seen as an asset by would-be students (Bourdieu and Passeron, 1977; Whitley, Thomas and Marceau, 1981). The probability of entrance to formal education is, of course, still significantly affected by the socio-economic position of the applicant's family in wider society; this is especially so in the 'less developed' countries. But, it may be unwise to consider the symbolic and social investment in formal education as its primary source of ongoing value – especially for employers. The substantive content of academic disciplines taught throughout the formal education system provides the basis for a set of underlying ontological and epistemological assumptions that have co-evolved with a steepening trajectory in technological design across Western economies over the last three centuries (Murmann, 2003). In this sense, both the economist's and employer's view of formal education as 'human capital', or the basis for developmental capability, can seem historically justifiable.

This is not to say that the intellectual assumptions of formal disciplines have been 'true' in the sense that no other explanation for a 'problem' existed or that they themselves were not disputable or subject to fashion (Kuhn, 1970). Neither is it to say that workable theoretical solutions have not, even today, derived from 'trial and error' experience, especially in pursuit of practical need or commercial opportunity. But, as Nonaka and Takeuchi correctly observe, the design capability of the firm will critically derive from an ability to model experience in an abstract way and to translate 'practice' into law-like solutions that can be codified and archived. (In this regard this process reproduces historical movements in the creation of formal academic disciplines (Whitley, 1984: 2000).) But, by the same token the day-to-day operational recipes of employees are assumed to be shaped by differential frames of meaning through their respective experiences of formal education. However, within the context of current technological innovation the tasks they are given can often bridge established knowledge fields. This can demand a re-combination of widely separated disciplines in the provision of a solution. The very depth of abstract meaning attributed to the problem in terms used by competing disciplines can lead to disputes that originate outside of respective workplace roles and instantiated powers. Project based multi-disciplinary design teams are not new (see Whitley (2007)). But, as the above case studies illustrate their management across design disciplines remains problematical.

Yet some observers see the erosion of expert power as increasingly imminent (Reed, 1996). To a large extent this view is predicated on the belief that large-scale bureaucracies have, through their colonization of new knowledge creation, assumed the role previously played by 'free professions' and autonomous universities in determining the nature and content of expertise. Yet the widespread spinning-off or outsourcing of expert labour might be seen as an admission that hierarchical modes of control over design activities have not only failed, but have actually constrained the strategic elite's ability to explore new avenues of technological opportunity. This strategy may have contributed to a marked diminution in attempts to create self-regulating occupational associations of the traditional kind in emergent sectors. But it seems premature to dismiss the 'invisible colleges' or occupational networks seen by Powell and Grodal (2000) to exist in Silicon Valley as a passing phenomenon or one that will not take up a more associational form. Equally it is difficult to believe that exchange relations between local university departments and MNCs are entirely assymetrical in form (Guston, 2000; Owen Smith, 2003). At both the collective and at the micro level occupational claims to expertise remain potent sources of closure. This has, traditionally, been expressed through the creation of specialized languages combined with claims to their situational interpretation (Jamous and Pelloille, 1970). Yet, the tension between intellectual exploration and commercial application may have a deeper meaning for both the identity of protagonists and its meaning for civil society than can be analysed as a local struggle for workplace control.

This is especially true when transacting across geographical as well as social space where often hierarchical authority can complement claims to scientific authenticity in communicating between parent R&D facilities and those of overseas affiliates. Resistance to the adoption of new technology can be reinforced by the mobilization of ethnic or national identities in response to the unconscious or perceived use of such discourse and symbols by the head office (Loveridge, 2007). Hakanson (2007) sees the development of cross-national epistemic communities as requiring a like response from employers in their recognition of the importance of textually bonded groups. This may be especially so in their choice of text-based boundary objects (Star and Griesemer, 1989) that attempt to draw together disparate knowledge-based, global communities.

The Signification of Nationality and Ethnicity

In the cases of the joint ventures described earlier (De Rond, 2003) differences in orientation between US managers and British scientists display both hierarchically and occupationally shaped responses to the treatment of the recombinant 'discoveries' made by the latter. These differing perspectives on the proprietorship and treatment of the outcomes from their collaboration was given a third interpretative dimension in the differing *national* frames provided by each of the would-be collaborators. Interfaces between partners in cross-national alliances seem frequently to display such national differences in partner orientation that contribute to their wide-spread failure (Doz and Hamel, 1998; Faulkner and De Rond, 2000). It is also noteworthy that the micro-politics described by Kristensen and Zeitlin (2005), as well as by Dorrenbacher and Geppert (2006) can be seen as arising out of contests for recognition between recently acquired MNC subsidiaries in *different* countries.

The sources of these conflicts might well be ascribed to what cultural psychologists describe as 'cultural distance' between territorially dispersed in-groups (Shenkar, 2001). Comparative studies of formal management structures, styles and values carried out over the last half century offer evidence of the persistence of these differences (Child and Kieser, 1979). Other analysts place more emphasis on the effects of wider societal institutions in configurative systems that span generations and 'lock-in' widely shared orientations and ways of conducting business. Evidently the ideal types of Liberal and Coordinated Market Capitalisms (Hall and Soskice, 2000) are widely used examples of this genre. With varying degrees of explicitness much comparative analysis in management is in fact undertaken with a view to adjudging the competitive effectiveness of national or regional structures and processes. Its focus over the last half century can be seen to have shifted from the USA, to Federal Germany, and on to Japan, thence to South Korea before, most recently, encompassing India and China. For some social analysts like Ostry and Nelson (1995) this is evidence of a nationalistically driven contest between states, a notion extended most explicitly by Greenfeld (2001). In practice, expressions of nationalistic resistance to local changes may be more symptomatic of the indigenous workforce's experience of a series of foreign owners over as many years; an experience which can lead them to value the protection of a national or ethnic identity more highly than their latest corporate identity.

Familiarity with host institutions, including language, may, nevertheless, be one important factor in shaping FDI decisions on accessibility to particular overseas locations taken by corporate elites (Birkinshaw and Hood, 1998). But, in a much less conscious way, so also might the cultures and national institutional context that has shaped the organizational archetype underlying the parent, i.e. founding, MNC. Whitley (2007) has perhaps been most particular in seeing a nationally contingent reflection of its externally institutionalized environment in the configuration of relationships existing within any parent MNC. One of more important predictions of the Hall and Soskice (2001) loose–tight dichotomy of national systems was that the loosely knit LMC would adapt to exogenous technological change more quickly than that of the more tightly integrated CMC. This observation might be seen as based on the relatively short-term experiences of the German and Japanese economies over the decade of the 1990s when compared with that of the turnaround in the USA. But these observations have also led to a reconsideration of the value of the social capital produced in bonding relationships along networks in a way that inhibits the creation of new relationships provided by bridging roles across differentiated networks (Adler and Kwon, 2002). In a recent study of two Japanese MNCs by Collinson and Wilson (2006) the authors suggest that great importance was placed upon the acquisition of general managerial skills within the context of intimate collaborative relationships with colleagues in partner organizations. The multi-layering of interdependencies resulted in an embedded inertia that precluded the exploration of overlapping new fields. A strong routinization of cross-functional learning and associated control routines also confined innovation to path-dependent improvements. This precluded the development of specialized expertise in new areas – often through the de-selection of specialists in the R&D function. The experiences of the Japanese MNCs in their study are contrasted with those of a British competitor which is seen to have created multiple interfaces with specialized research groups in universities and institutes. Social capital generated in one field by the Japanese companies is seen to have circumscribed their movement into others (Adler and Kwon, 2002). A similar observation has been made of the weakness of strong regional ties in Germany (Grabher, 1993). By way of contrast, Whitley (2007) raises the paradox that MNCs parented in the more 'arm's-length' environments of the LMC may produce more meritocratically based career structures for local overseas personnel and so, he implies, invoke a greater sense of internal justice and social integration. This is seen to be less possible within MNCs whose parent HQ is embedded in the more tightly woven networks present within more 'collaborative' institutional settings.

Competitive Disadvantages?

Crouch (2005) recently estimated that no more than 25 nations were regularly incorporated in academic comparisons of business systems, out of a population of 294 national state members of the UNO. These are, evidently, the more successful economies and, as suggested above, their numbers within academic business studies have recently expanded to take in 'emergent economies'. The existence of stable institutions that coincide with a Western archetype of the organized means of reproducing capital and labour might be one important consideration for the analyst. Most often it is the existence of a viable means of creating and enforcing property and contractual rights that is seen as defining a stable national system in comparative business studies (Whitley, 2007). This generally implies a capability in state agencies to enforce these rights. A lack of access to such means to enforce rights in an impartial way can be described as an 'institutional void' to be filled by relations between the extended family, tribe or ethnically based organization (Khanna and Palepu, 1997, 2002). The universal mediation of particularistic relations can inhibit the authority and capabilities of more formal rules-based agencies of the state (Li et al., 2004). The exchange of gifts or fees for service are seen to play a predominant role in the enactment of rules in a way often described as 'corrupt' by international agencies (Kauffman, 2005). Perhaps equally as important for the technologically innovative newcomer can be a lack of effective legal protection for intellectual property such as patents, copyrights and trademarks. Evidence of widespread unauthorized copying of product design by small local manufacturers can be found in most Asian street markets. When major indigenous firms enter new sectors by copying the product designs of guest MNCs outside of licensed agreements the matter often provokes inter-governmental exchanges that can lead to bilateral agreements at international level. Indeed, historically, a mark of the technological development of a host country can be the adoption of a more aggressive pursuit of patents or copyright for their own innovations by local firms (Pitkethly, 2001).

However, the problem of negotiating coalitions between ethnic interests in national government can be seen as a major distraction and a widespread constraint on technological development in post-colonial countries even where, as in South East Asia, rapid economic growth has been experienced over the last 20 years (Doner, Ritchie and Slater, 2005). In choosing a local partner the foreign MNC is likely to find an apparent fluidity and complexity of interfaces that reflects that of personal strategies deployed by local partners along highly affective networks. Khanna and Palepu (1997, 2002) suggest that partner operational units are likely to be part of a broadly diversified and family-owned business group in which decisions made in relation to investment in the technological innovation will be adjudged against a wide portfolio of varied opportunities. Direct access to government in more focused national or turn-key projects can, of course, bring a more intensive effort to the transfer of knowledge in systems design and maintenance. Generally, however, the foreign MNC may find itself operating a dual system of formal and informal rules in which knowledgeable 'go-betweens' play an important bridging role in interpreting the likely effects of the use of one set of rules on the enactment of the other when both are applied at critical junctures in their relationship (see attached case and Loveridge (2007)).

At other times the MNC management will make exceptions to 'usual practice'. For example Jack and Lorbiecki (2007) describe how management interviewees within BAE Systems explain the unsuitability of women technologists for employment on their extensive military projects in Saudi Arabia. Such, often trivial, adjustments in the interpretation of the 'arm's-length' relations seen as typical of liberal civil societies might well be seen as pragmatic adjustment to the institutionalized customs and beliefs of the host society. Equally and more worryingly, they can be seen as undermining the beliefs underpinning the archetypes of corporate governance presented to burgeoning numbers of students from 'developing' countries in Western business schools. Either way the MNC will often be leaving an imprint on societal practices that goes far beyond the transfer of workplace technology (Bies *et al.*, 2007).

Discussion–Innovation as the Micro-mobilization of Networks

The movement towards alliance capitalism contains within it many such contradictory tendencies and accompanying managerial rhetorics that are often partial and largely inconsistent. In spite of the weight of exhortative literature on the importance of trust in the building of social capital between corporate partners along intra- and inter-organizational networks, insufficient attention has been paid to the complexity of this process across multiple communities of practice that have to be engaged in bringing about cross-national transfers of technology. This requires the recognition of the variety of potentially conflicting identities, interests and languages of interest by which technology is constructed, translated and transported along different networks and across the different internal and external communities that sustain them. In much of the strategic and organizational literature conflict is treated as frictional. In this regard there is ultimately little to choose between the latter's underlying assumptions concerning the ultimate attainment of organizational purpose and those of the economic modellers they so often critique. In this chapter I have suggested ways in which aspects of the formal division of labour within the MNC provide continuing significance to its members in the creation of socially closed networks. Differences in institutionalized structures such as the hierarchies of formal authority, of education (or formal knowledge), and of nationally specific identities and modes of transacting tend to produce their own forms of collective closure and resultant social capitals.

Some scholars believe that successful organizational innovation in the dispersed context of the N-form MNC can resemble a strategic attempt to create a global social movement (Hargrave and Van de Ven, 2006). This process is designed to align competing frames with the aid of coopted key agencies that span intra-organizational networks. Through these locally assimilated agencies movements can be mobilized towards the attainment of corporate goals (Bacharach et al., 1996). Kaplan et al. (2003) see operational management as key to this alignment, thus focusing on the management of overseas affiliates as translators of innovation along several networks. The personal tensions accompanying their so-called 'dual alliances' in relation to their internal and external roles have been explored in the HRM literature over a long period (Black and Gregerson, 1992). The implications of these conflicts for the translation of technology transfer from other parts of the MNC or from their local context – and its implications in terms of political and commercial risk – is not so well documented. This may be seen as critical for the MNC's success in many circumstances. Where the parent is expanding through overseas acquisition, the local significance of central recognition can take the form of overt 'global gaming' between affiliates in an attempt to realign the corporate strategy towards the survival and development of local capacities. Quite clearly in the case described by Kristensen and Zeitlin interpersonal networks were drawn upon by actants to shape the perceptions of powerful allies and to create a narrative favourable to the proposed changes.

It seems possible that the top-down strategic use of intermediary agencies can be more successful in socially and technically well integrated organizations whose overseas affiliates are the result of 'organic' growth rather than of a merger with or acquisition of existing overseas enterprises (Loveridge, 2000). In the bipolar categorization of national systems discussed above, these MNCs are, of course, likely to be found in CMCs such as Germany and Japan. In such circumstances the foundational experiences of the local affiliate and its subsequent development have been moulded by its foreign parent's cultural norms. The resultant local reactions to strategic shifts are likely to better understood by the parent. Feelings of alienation from the centre, and from peer plants in other countries, are, by the same token, more likely to occur among employees in acquired plants where conflicts surrounding the recognition of hierarchy, vocational accreditation and even of pride in national or ethnic identity can be complementary and reinforcing in effect. Much the same phenomenon can sometimes be encountered in the case of cross-border alliances between MNCs. In practice other factors can mediate the significance, and therefore influence, given to these structures in framing their workplace situation by local actants. It is, for example, evident that both Japanese and German MNCs have been highly successful in overseas production in many assembly sectors such as automobile manufacture and much less so in others such as professional services. It seems feasible then, that the manner in which national institutions have shaped the division of occupational or task knowledge within particular sectors may differ across parent MNCs and may well affect their successful embeddedness within the host systems in which they seek to operate (Whitley, 2007).

Conclusion

Innovation management can thus be characterized as a continuous political process in which ideological rhetoric and discourse intermediate in the interpretation and adjustment of broad strategic goals along multiple networks. It also involves the stimulation and mobilization of commitment to orderly change within widely various operational contexts while responding creatively to 'external' stimuli (Kaplan, 2008). For senior executives these are likely to be felt most insistently along networks of corporate governance – most particularly from changes in their financial reputation or creditability or from the politically generated changes in the regulatory context. But, their success in creating the absorptive capacity of their enterprise is likely to depend on the maintenance of both working and latent coalitions across the multiple layered inter-personal networks that make up the *confederal MNC* – an entity that usually extends beyond the boundaries of its hierarchical jurisdiction. The co-optation of key intermediaries that span internal networks and can construct performance metrics and incentive structures in terms meaningful for the accumulation of symbolic and social capital along local networks has been seen to be a characteristic of some such successful confederations (Hargrave and Van de Ven, 2006). In this sense the knowledge capabilities of the MNC can be usefully seen as relationally shaped, more fluid than concrete, and more kinetically potential than simply limitational. But, limitational it clearly is. A walk down any business school corridor reveals the extent to which the accumulation of intellectual capital takes place within socio-political boundaries. The reflexive business student can, perhaps, provide an archetype for both the creative consumer and reflexive strategizer in providing synthesis in the application of contradictory frames of supplier expertise.

At the macro level, movement towards the dispersed or market-linked forms of the N-form corporation can be seen as attempts by corporate elites to externalize risks presented by internal boundaries created by communities of practice. Concurrently they might be seen to maximize their chances of innovative options through the maintenance of a wide range of loose-linked relationships with artisanal providers in geographically and socially dispersed knowledge hubs (Shutt and Whittington, 1987). This, at least, is the justification provided within the currently dominant neo-liberal market model. As such this movement can be seen to have led to an attempted radical restructuring of internal relations within many MNCs. In turn, this has been reflected in changes in wider occupational markets, not least in the migration of skilled jobs to overseas locations. On the other hand, as Hakanson and other observers suggest the recent growth in communication between cross-national 'invisible colleges' has been phenomenal, thanks largely to the *textual* revolution contained in CIT. Other influential epistemic communities find their roots in already existing regulatory professions in fields such as law and accountancy (Morgan, 2001). These continue to set directional limits to the global contest in technological innovation and to the ideas by which it is legitimated.

It seems likely therefore that the construction of boundaries delineating fields of new knowledge production will not be entirely in the hands of corporate customers, leaving fragmented suppliers of expertise with little countervailing strength to resist a consequent standardization of form and substance. Indeed, as Powell has observed, the discovered value of contemporary hi-tech artisanal modes may lie precisely in the scope for exploration that rests with the supplier. The corporate customer for new knowledge might appear to have every incentive for retaining this source of flexible capacity in the supply of services. At the same time it can evidently provide a potential threat for their sponsor. The rate of growth in some start-ups in new fields can be exceptional. Diversification up the value chain still remains an attractive option for these newcomers in the extended use of their 'core capabilities', e.g. Microsoft. Increasingly such competition is coming from within newly developing countries, most recently from the so-called BRIC countries. But, beyond the immediate sources of contestual pressures, the physical effects of climate change, as well as the spreading fear of 'irrationally' motivated violence, seem to have brought more collectively felt issues up the agenda of both political and corporate elites. So far this is, perhaps, most evident in somewhat hesitant attempts by national governments to meet their obligations under the Kyoto Protocol on the release of carbon emissions and in the more localized effects of the branding of 'socially responsible' products for niche markets. However, as Schumpeter (1912, 1934 (trans.)) recognized, in the history of technological development it would not be unknown for ideas of collective self-interest to be brought to bear on the shaping of future trajectories in ways that restrain the extent of allowable 'creative destruction'. The future shaping of global technological contests may rest as much on such politically determined changes in the rules of the game as on the players' tactical interpretations.

CASE STUDY: SOUTH EAST ASIA SUBSIDIARY MANDATES IN EUROPEAN MULTINATIONAL CORPORATIONS

Over the period 1997 to 1999 I conducted an interview and observational study of 20 European-based multinational corporations with affiliates in South East Asia (Loveridge, 2007 (below)). Interviews were conducted with divisional executives and R&D heads in the parent central offices and with affiliate senior executives and local R&D heads in ASEAN locations. I also interviewed officials from local development agencies and local university academic staff. The sample contained a wide range of sectors and most of the MNCs were large (20–50 thousand employees) and over 80 years old. Of the 78 management interviews, all but eight were with Europeans, that is to say that expatriates predominated. The focus of the study was on variations in the local mandate in matters of product and process development allowed across the different nationalities present within the sample (UK, France, Germany, Netherlands, Sweden).

In practice the degree and the focus of the mandate afforded each plant seemed more related to the *sector* in which the MNC operated. However, the effects could be best seen in terms of the manner in which significant negotiations were acted out at different levels of the MNC and its host institutions, bringing into play different types of formal and informal networks. These could be seen to be grouped around strategic, operational and R&D activities. All of the firms contained such clusters of activity-based inter-personal networks, but there was a marked difference in the way they operated and the style and backgrounds of the actants. Along strategic networks a role that I labelled 'Diplomat' was often critical. Actants in this role were generally rewarded in the highest salary banding and had appropriate lifestyles. Their home contacts were at board or divisional level but they played an itinerant role which included top-level trouble-shooting and directing early access into new markets. Their local contacts were likely to be at government, ministerial or princely level.

Senior managers of local affiliates tended to be either fast-trackers or locals. The former were on three to five-year assignments and, like the expatriates surveyed in most HRM studies, regarded their present posting as a rung in their corporate career that would end in promotion. They therefore saw their local achievements in these terms. By contrast the local saw his or her career in terms of a permanent place in the local community into which they would, eventually, retire. As in the Black and Gregerson (1992) study they were often referred to in HQ interview as having 'gone native'. A sub-group, also in the latter study, were expatriate locals who had been recruited from other MNCs in the region. All of the affiliate laboratory heads interviewed in my sample, together with their university or research contacts were local citizens.

The activities of 'diplomats' seemed most significant in banking (capital financing), petrochemicals and in turn-key infrastructural or defence projects. Technology transfer in these sectors often involved the MNC in a long-term association with a client government in an industrialization project. It could also involve the commitment of financial subsidies or other support from the national government of the parent MNC. For example the delivery of aircraft and ships, and the accompanying new airfield and harbour, by the British defence supplier in my sample committed the Royal Air Force and Royal Navy to an ongoing, and already strong, training relationship with the local, Brunei, military. (My interviews with the British management were conducted in the Defence Procurement Agency of the British government.) Similarly the Swedish telecommunications firm in the sample was committed to the creation of a Multimedia Corridor outside Kuala Lumpur to the extent of providing a large academy and other training in the management and maintenance of this billion dollar project. Throughout the region the activities of the two large oil companies in my sample made them important allies for their national host governments in a range of activities including patriotic campaigns to increase the productivity of citizens in every area of their lives. In all of these cases local adaptations of centrally designed technology had often to be reported to a government committee and, where considered significant, agreed between the parties at a diplomatic level.

The activities of fast-trackers among affiliate plant managers in the sample seemed most significant in the more footloose subsidiaries of auto-components and micro-electronic assembly firms. Their approach to their fellow indigenous directors was, as to the workforce, courteous but calculative. While encouraging local adaptations in product and process to the marketplace they were also acutely aware of the need to meet centrally required global standards and the transient needs of HQ fashions in strategic management. (This could lead to long working hours and to consequential family tensions.) Their local contacts were with district rather than national agencies. They reported their relationships with such district agencies in terms of bargaining in a professional but confrontational manner. While anxious to recruit appropriately educated labour, particularly in D&D, they often showed little interest in, or knowledge of, the provision of local education beyond their own need to provide remedial in-house training for local employees. Indeed, much of their local knowledge seemed often to be acquired from conversations with other expatriates after local meetings of the European or American Chamber of Commerce. By contrast locals seemed to spend more time in activities along inter-family or co-religionist local networks in which they sometimes held considerable status. They were much more aware of the need to translate ideas emanating from HQ in a way that might embed them within local practice. In doing so, there might be occasions when their transactions might be seen to have offended good 'professional' standards.

Sometimes the innovative achievements of locals could be discounted, or even disrupted, by HQ initiatives. In a Dutch/Swedish chemical group a local subsidiary manager had achieved considerable success in collaborating with a Singaporese entrepreneur in the use of the firm's adhesive product in the production of chip-board from old palm tree waste from Malaysian plantations. Members of his local D&D laboratory were justifiably proud of their part in this project. Shortly afterwards they received a visit from a young and enthusiastic Operations Management expert from the Swedish HQ who spent six months installing a statistical process model of quality management in the laboratory. At the time of my interviews most of the, also young and ambitious, local scientists were planning to move to other MNCs based in Singapore. The local manager was contemplating an early retirement. The juxta-positioning of the HQ initiative in re-organization with an apparent lack of sufficient acknowledgement of the creativity of the local team was seen to characterize a discounting of their efforts – a view that all too often in my interviews was equated with ethnocentricity or even racism.

Questions

1. How far does the path by which new technological models or archetypes travel, arrive and, eventually, get implemented in new cultural locations affect their translation into local practice?

2. How far does the type of MNC network that transports ideas across time and space affect their acceptance and continued translation within the context of host networks? (e.g. hierarchical basis, educational basis, national or ethnic basis).
3. How far can a strategic realization of the presence of layered intra- and extra-organizational networks inform the way in which innovative movements for socio-technical change are organized and mobilized across spatially and culturally dispersed communities of practice?

Further Reading

For a comprehensive analysis of how bridging and/or bonding relationships between social networks can facilitate or inhibit learning behaviour within organizations and communities see: Adler, P. S. and Kwon, S. (2002) 'Social Capital: prospects for a new concept', *Academy of Management Review*, 27, 17–40.

For an analytic frame that attempts a distinction between the value of formulated knowledge within 'epistemic communities' and that of the tacit knowledge possessed by 'communities of practice' see: Hakanson, L. (2007) 'Creating Knowledge: the power and logic of articulation', *Industrial and Corporate Change*, 10, 1093–175.

For empirical studies of the effect on learning of the relational embeddedness of MNC managers in local networks of overseas subsidiaries see: Andersson, U., Forsgren, M. and Holm, U. (2002), (2007) 'The Strategic Impact of External Networks on Subsidiary Performance and Competence Development in the Multinational Corporation', *Strategic Management Journal*, 23, 11, 979–96.

Loveridge, R. (2007) 'Embedding the Multinational: bridging internal and external networks in transitional institutional contexts', in J. H. Dunning and T.-M. Lin (eds), *Multinational Enterprises and Emerging Challenges of the 21ˢᵗ Century*. Cheltenham UK: Edward Elgar, ch. 10, 324–60.

For approaches to the micro-politics of technology transfer within the MNC and across inter-alliances see: De Rond, M. (2003) *Strategic Alliances as Social Facts: Business, Biotechnology and Intellectual History*. Cambridge, UK: Cambridge University Press.

Dorrenbacher, M. and Geppert, M. (2006) 'Micropolitics and conflicts in multinational corporations: current debates, re-framing, and the contributions of this special issue', *Journal of International Management*, 12, 251–65.

References

Adler, P.S. and Kwon, S. (2002) 'Social Capital: prospects for a new concept', *Academy of Management Review*, 27, 17–40.

Amable, B. (2003) *The Diversity of Modern Capitalism*. Oxford: Oxford University Press.

Andersson, U. and Forsgren, M. (1996) 'Subsidiary Embeddedness and Control in the Multinational Corporation', *International Business Review*, 5, 5, 425–46.

Arthur, M. B. and Rousseau, D. M. (eds) (1998) *The Boundaryless Career*. Oxford: Oxford University Press.

Audretsch, D. B. and Feldman, M. P. (1996) 'R&D spillovers and the geography of innovation and production', *American Economic Review*, 86, 630–40.

Bacharach, S. B., Bamberger, P., Sonnenestuhl, W. J. (1996), 'The Organizational Transformation Process: the Micropolitics of Dissonance Reduction and the Alignment of Logics of Action', *Administrative Science Quarterly*, 41, 3, September, 477–506.

Bartlett, C. and Ghoshal, S. (1989) *Managing Across Borders*. Boston, MA: Harvard Business School Press.

Becker, G. (1964) *Human Capital: a theoretical and comparative analysis with special reference to Education*. Princeton NJ: Princeton University Press.

Bies, R. J., Bartunek, J. M., Fort, T. L. and Zald, M. N. (2007) 'Corporations as Social Change Agents: Individual, Interpersonal, Institutional, and Environmental Dynamics', *Academy of Management Review*, 32, 3, 788–93.

Birkinshaw, J. and Hood, N. (eds) (1998) *Multinational Corporation Evolution and Subsidiary Development*. London: Macmillan.

Black, J. S. and Gregerson, H. B. (1992) 'Serving Two Masters: managing the dual allegiance of Expatriate Employees', *Sloan Management Review*, 33, 4, 61–71.

Bourdieu, P. (1980) 'Le capital social', *Actes de la Recherche en Sciences Sociales*, 31, 2–30.

Bourdieu, P. (1991, 1995 edn) trans. G. Raymond and M. Adamson *Language and Symbolic Power*. Cambridge: Polity Press.

Bourdieu, P. and Passeron, J.-C. (1977) trans. R. Nice *Reproduction in Education, Society and Culture*. London: Sage.

Brown J. S. and Duguid P. (1991) 'Organizational learning communities of practice: toward a unified view of working, learning and innovation', *Organization Science*, 2/1: 40–57.

Buckley, P. and Casson, M. (1976) *The Future of the Multinational Enterprise*. London: Macmillan.

Casper, S. and Whitley, R. (2004) 'Managing Competences in Entrepreneurial Technology Firms: a comparative institutional analysis of Germany, Sweden and the UK', *Research Policy*, 33, 89–106.

Casson, M., Loveridge, R. and Singh, S. (1998) 'Human Resource Management in Multinational Enterprises: Styles, Modes, Institutions and Ideologies'. In G. Hooley, R. Loveridge and D. Wilson (eds) *Internationalization: Process, Context and Markets*. Basingstoke: Macmillan.

Castells, M. (2001) *The Information Age, Volume 1: The Rise of the Network Society*. Oxford: Oxford University Press.

Chesborough, H. (2003) *Open Innovation: the new imperative for creating and profiting from innovation*. Boston, MA: Harvard University Press.

Child, J. and Heavens, S. J. (2003) 'The Social Constitution of Organizations and the Implications for Organizational Learning'. In M. Dierkes, A. Berthoinantal, J. Child and I. Nonaka *Handbook of Organizational Learning & Knowledge*. Oxford: Oxford University Press, 308–26.

Child, J. and Kieser, A. (1979) 'Organization and managerial roles in British and West German companies: an examination of the culture free thesis'. In C. J. Lammers and D. J. Hickson (eds) *Organizations Alike and Unlike*. London: Routledge and Kegan Paul.

Child, J. and Loveridge, R. (1990) *Information Technology in Europe: toward a Microelectronic Future*. Oxford: Blackwell.

Clark, T. (2004) 'Strategy viewed from a management fashion perspective', *European Management Review*, 1, 105–11.

Coffee, J. C. (2006) *Gatekeepers: the professions and corporate governance*. Oxford: Oxford University Press.

Cohen, W. M. and Levinthal, D. A. (1990) 'Absorptive Capacity: a new perspective on learning and innovation', *Administrative Science Quarterly*, 35, 128–52.

Collison, S. and Wilson, D. (2006) 'Inertia in Japanese Organizations: Knowledge Management Routines and Failure to Innovate', *Organization Studies*, 27(9) 1359–87.

Conway, S. (1995) 'Informal Boundary-spanning Links in Successful Technological Innovation', *Technology Analysis and Strategic Management*, 7(3), 327–42.

Crouch, C. (2005) *Capitalist Diversity and Change*. Oxford: Oxford University Press.

Czarniawska, B. and Joerges, B. (1996) 'The Travel of Ideas'. In B. Czarniaska and G. Sevon (eds) *Translating Organisational Change*. Berlin: de Gruyter, 13–48.

De Rond, M. (2003) *Strategic Alliances as Social Facts: Business, Biotechnology and Intellectual History*. Cambridge: Cambridge University Press.

Dicken, P. (2007) *Global Shift*. London: Sage.

Doner, R. F., Ritchie, B. K. and Slater, D. (2005) 'Systemic Vulnerability and the Origins of Developmental States: Northeast and Southeast Asia in Comparative Perspective', *International Organization*, 59, Spring, 327–61.

Dore, R. (1973) *British Factory-Japanese Factory: the Origins of National Diversity in Industrial Relations*. Berkeley, CA: University of California Press.

Dore, R. (1976) *The Diploma Disease: Education, Qualification and Development*. London: George Allen and Unwin.

Dorrenbacher, C. and Geppert, M. (2006) 'Micro-politics and conflicts in multinational corporations: current debates, re-framing, and contributions of this special issue', *Journal of International Management*, 12, 251–65.

Doz, Y. and Hamel, G. (1998) *Alliance Advantage*. Boston, MA: Harvard Business School Press.

Dunning, J. (1993) *Multinational Enterprises in the Global Economy*. Wokingham, UK: Addison-Wesley.

Dunning J. H. and Boyd, G. (eds) (2003) *Alliance Capitalism and Corporate Management; Entrepreneurial Cooperation in Knowledge Based Economies*. Cheltenham, UK: Edward Elgar.

Eisenstadt, K. and Martin, J. (2000) 'Dynamic Capabilities: what are they?', *Strategic Management Journal*, 21, 1105–21.

Faulkner, D. and De Rond, M. (eds) (2000) *Cooperative Strategy: Economic, Business and Organizational Issues*. Oxford: Oxford University Press.

Fine, C. H. (1998) *Clockspeed: winning industrial control in the age of temporary advantage*. New York: Addison Wesley, Longman.

Freeman, C. (1987) *Technology Policy and Economic Performance*. London: Pinter Publishers.

Freeman, C. and Louca, F. (2001) *As Time Goes By*. Oxford: Oxford University Press.

Goodall, K. and Roberts, J. (2003) 'Repairing managerial knowledge-ability over distance', *Organizational Studies*, 24(7): 1153–75.

Gospel, H. and Pendleton, A. (eds) (2005) *Corporate Governance and Labour Management: an International Comparison*. Oxford: Oxford University Press.

Gourevitch, P. A. and Shinn, J. (2005) *Political Power and Corporate Control: the New Global Politics of Corporate Governance*. Princeton, NJ: Princeton University Press.

Grabher, G. (1993) 'The weakness of strong ties: the lock-in of regional developments in the Ruhr area'. In G. Grabher (ed.) *The Embedded Firm. On the Socio-Economics of Industrial Networks*. London: Routledge.

Grant, R. M. (2003) 'The Knowledge Based View of the Firm'. In D. O. Faulkner and A. Campbell (eds) *The Oxford Handbook of Strategy*. Oxford: Oxford University Press, 203–30.

Greenfeld, L. (2001) *The Spirit of Capitalism: Nationalism and Economic Growth.* Cambridge, MA: Harvard University Press.

Greenwood, R. and Hinings, C. R. (1993) 'Understanding Strategic Change: the contribution of archetypes', *Academy of Management Journal*, 36, 1052–81.

Guler, I. and Guillen, M. F. (2005) *Knowledge, Institutions and Foreign Entry: the Internationalisation of the US Venture Capital Firms*, Wharton School Working Paper, University of Pennsylvania (http://www-management.wharton.upenn.edu> downloaded September 2007).

Gupta, A. K. and Govindarajan, V. (1991) 'Knowledge Flows and the Structure of Control within Multinational Corporations', *Academy of Management Review*, 16/4, 75–84.

Guston, D. H. (2000) *Politics and Science: assuring quality.* Cambridge: Cambridge University Press.

Hakanson, L. (2007) 'Creating knowledge: the power and logic of articulation', *Industrial and Corporate Change*, 10, 1093–175.

Hall, P. and Soskice, D. (eds) (2001) *Varieties of Capitalism: the Institutional Foundations of Comparative Advantage.* Oxford: Oxford University Press.

Hargrave, T. J. and Van de Ven, A. (2006) 'A Collective Action Model of Institutional Innovation', *Academy of Management Review*, 31, 4, 864–88.

Hitt, M. A., Lee, H. U. and Yucel, E. (2002) 'The importance of social capital to the management of multinational enterprises; relational networks among Asian and Western firms', *Asia Pacific Journal of Management*, 19, 353–68.

Holm, U. and Pederson, T. (2000) *The Emergence and Impact of the Multinational Corporation Centres of Excellence.* London: Macmillan.

Jack, G. and Lorbiecki, A. (2007) 'National Identity, Globalization and the Discursive Construction of Organizational Identity', *British Journal of Management*, 18, 79–94.

Jamous, H. and Pelloille, B. (1970), 'Changes in the French University Hospital System'. In J. A. Jackson. (ed.) *Professions and Professionalisation.* Cambridge: Cambridge University Press.

Johnson, C. (1982) *MITI and the Japanese Miracle.* Stanford, CA: Stanford University Press.

Kang, N.-H. and Sakai, K. (2000) *International Strategic Alliances: their role in Industrial Globalisation.* Paris, France: OECD.

Kaonides, L. C. (1999) 'Science, Technology, and Global Competitive Advantage', *International Studies of Management and Organization*, Spring, 29, 1, 53–80.

Kaplan, S. (2008) 'Framing contests: Strategy Making under Uncertainty', *Organization Science* 19, 5, 729–752.

Karpik, L. (1972) 'Les politiques et les logiques d'action de la grande enterprise industrielle', *Sociologie du Travail*, 1, 82–105.

Kauffman, D. (2005) *Corruption in Developing Countries.* Washington DC: World Bank Institute.

Khanna, T. and Palepu, K. (1997) 'Why Focussed Strategies may be wrong for Emerging Markets', *Harvard Business Review*, July–August, 41–51.

Khanna, T. and Palepu, K. (2002) 'The Future of Business Groups in Emerging Markets: Long Run evidence from Chile', *Academy of Management Journal*, 41 (3): 260–85.

Kodoma, F. (1992) 'Technology fusion and the new R&D', *Harvard Business Review*, 70–178.

Kogut, B. and Zander, U. (1993) 'Knowledge of the Firm, Combinative Capabilities and the Evolutionary Theory of the Multinational Corporation', *Journal of International Business Studies*, 4: 625–45.

Kostova, T. (1999) 'Transnational transfer of strategic organizational practice: a contextual perspective', *Academy of Management Review*, 24, 308–24.

Kristensen, P. H. and Zeitlin, J. (2005) *Local Players in Global Games: the Strategic Constitution of a Multinational Corporation*. Oxford: Oxford University Press.

Kuhn, T. S. (1970) *The Structure of Scientific Revolutions*. Chicago Ill: University of Chicago.

Lam A. (2003) 'Organizational Learning in Multinationals: R&D networks of Japanese and US Multinational Enterprises in the UK', *Journal of Management Studies*, May, 40, 3, 673–703.

Landes, D. (1969) *The Unbound Prometheus: Technological Change and Industrial Development in Western Europe from 1750 to the present*. Cambridge: Cambridge University Press.

Lane, C. (1996) 'The Social Constitution of Trust', *Organization Studies*, 17/3: 365–95.

Li, S., Park, S. H. and Li, S. (2004) 'The Great Leap Forward: the transition from relation-based governance to rule-based governance', *Organizational Dynamics*, 33, 1, February, 63–78.

Loveridge, R. (1983) 'Sources of diversity in internal labour markets', *Sociology*, 17, 44–62.

Loveridge, R. (2000) 'The Firm as Differentiator and Integrator of Networks: Layered Communities of Practice and Discourse'. In D. O. Faulkner and M. De Rond (eds) *Cooperative Strategy: Economic, Business and Organizational Issues*. Oxford: Oxford University Press, 135–72.

Loveridge, R. (2007) 'Embedding the Multinational :bridging internal and external networks in transitional institutional contexts'. In J. H. Dunning and T.-M. Lin (eds) *Multinational Enterprises and Emerging Challenges of the 21st Century*. Cheltenham, UK: Edward Elgar, ch. 10, 324–60.

Loveridge, R. and Mueller, F. (1999) 'Globalisation in Telecommunications: the dynamics of Firms, Governments, and Technologies', *Competition and Change*, 4, 61–91.

Morgan, G. (2001) 'The Multinational Firm: organizing across institutional and national divides'. In G. Morgan, P.-H. Kristensen, R. Whitley (eds) *The Multinational Firm: Organizing Across Institutional and National Divides*. Oxford: Oxford University Press.

Morgan, G. (2001) 'Transnational communities an business systems', *Global Networks*, 1, 2, April, 113–30.

Morgan, K. (1997) 'The learning region: institutions, innovation and regional renewal', *Regional Studies*, 31, 491–503.

Murmann, J. P. (2003) *Knowledge and Comparative Advantage: the co-evolution of firms, technologies and national institutions*. New York: Cambridge University Press.

Naphapiet, J. and Ghoshal, S. (1998) 'Social Capital, Intellectual Capital and Organizational Advantage', *Academy of Management Review*, 23, 242–66.

Nelson, R. R. and Rosenberg, N. (2000) 'Technical Innovation and National Systems'. In R. R. Nelson (ed.) *National Innovation Systems*. Oxford: Oxford University Press.

Nohria, N. and Ghoshal, S. (1990) *The Differentiated Network: Organizing Multinational Corporations for Value Creation*. San Francisco, CA: Jossey Bass.

Nonaka, I. and Takeuchi, H. (1995) *The Knowledge Creating Company*. Oxford: Oxford University Press.

Ostry, S. and Nelson, R. (1995) *Techno-nationalism and Techno-globalism: Conflict and Co-operation*. Washington DC: Brookings Institute.

Owen Smith, D. (2003) 'From Separate Systems to Hybrid Order: accumulative advantage across public and private science', *Research Policy*, 32, 6, 1081–104.

Palmisano, S. (2006) 'The Globally integrated Enterprise', *Foreign Affairs*, 85, 3, May/June, 127–35.

Perez, C. (1985) 'Microelectronics, long waves and world structural change', *World Development*, 13, 441–63.

Pitkethly, R. (2001) 'Intellectual Property Strategy in Japanese and UK Companies: Patent Licensing Decisions and Learning Opportunities', *Research Policy* 30, 3, 425–442.

Polanyi, M. (1966) *The Tacit Dimension*. London: Routledge & Kegan Paul.

Powell, W. W. (1998) 'Learning from Collaboration: Knowledge and Networks in the Biotechnology and Pharmaceutical Industries', *California Management Review*, 40, 3.

Powell, W. W. (2001) The Capitalist Firm in the Twenty First Century: Emerging Patterns. In DiMaggio, P. (ed) *The Twenty First Century Firm*. Princeton NJ; Princeton University Press, 33–68.

Powell, W. W. and Grodal, S. (2000) 'Networks of Innovators'. In Fagerberg, J., Mowery, D. C. and Nelson, R. R. (eds) *The Oxford Handbook of Innovation*. New York: Oxford University Press, 56–85.

Powell, W. W. and Owen Smith, J. (1998) 'Commercialism in Universities: Life Sciences Research and its linkage with Industry', *Journal of Policy Analysis and Management*, 17, 2, 253–77.

Powell W. W., White, D. R, Koput, K. W. and Owen-Smith, J. (2005) 'Network Dynamics and Field Evolution: the growth of inter-organizational collaboration in the Life Sciences', *American Journal of Sociology*, January, 110, 4, 1132–205.

Pugh, D. S., Hinings, C. R. and Turner, C. (1969) 'The context of organization; structures of work organization', *Administrative Science Quarterly*, 14, 115–26.

Reed, M. I. (1996) 'Expert power and control in late modernity: an empirical review and theoretical synthesis', *Organizational Studies*, 17, 573–97.

Reich, R. B. (1991) *The Work of Nations: preparing ourselves for 21st Century Capitalism*, New York: Alfred A. Knopf.

Rugman, A. M. and D'Cruz, J. R. (2000) 'The Theory of the Flagship Firm'. In D. Faulkner and M. De Rond (eds) *Co-operative Strategy: Economic, Business and Organizational Issues*. Oxford: Oxford University Press.

Sako, M. (2003) *Modularity and Outsourcing: the nature of coevolution of product architecture and organizational architecture in the global automobile industry*. Oxford: Oxford University Press.

Schofer, E. and Meyer, J. W. (2005) 'The Worldwide Expansion of Higher Education in the Twentieth Century, *American Sociological Review*, 70, December, 898–920.

Schuller, T., Baron, S. and Field, J. (2000) 'Social Capital: a review and critique'. In S. Baron, J. Field and T. Schuller (eds), *Social Capital; critical perspectives*. New York: Oxford University Press.

Schultz, T. W. (1961) 'Investment in Human Capital', *American Economic Review*, 1, 2, 1–17.

Schumpeter, J. A. (1912, 1934) trans. *The Theory of Economic Development*. Cambridge, MA: Harvard University Press.

Shenkar, O. (2001) 'Cultural Differences Revisited: Towards a More rigorous Conceptualization and Measurement of Cultural Differences' *Journal of International Business* 32, 3, 519–535.

Shutt, J. and Whittington, R. (1987) 'Fragmentation Strategies and the Rise of Small Units', *Regional Studies*, 21, 13–23.

Star, S. L. and Griesemer, J. R. (1989) 'Institutional ecology, "translations" and boundary objectives: amateurs and professionals in Berkeley's Museum of Vertebrate Zoology 1907–39', *Social Studies of Science*, 19: 387–420.

Swan, J. and Scarbrough, H. (2005) 'The politics of networked innovation', *Human Relations,* 58, 7, 913–43.

Teece, D. J. (1986) 'Profiting from technological innovation; implications for integration, collaboration, licensing and public policy', *Research Policy,* 15, 285–305.

Teece, D. J. and Pisano G. (1994) 'The Dynamic Capabilities of Firms: an Introduction', *Industrial and Corporate Change,* 3, 537–56.

United Nations Conference on Trade and Development (2005), *World Investment Report: Transnational Corporations and the Internationalization of R&D.* UNCTAD, New York/Geneva: United Nations.

Vaara, E., Tienan, R., Piekkan, R. and Saentti, R. (2005) 'Language and the Circuits of Power in a Merging Multinational Corporation', *Journal of Management Studies,* 42, May, 3, 595–618.

Vanhaverbeke, W. P. M. (2001) 'Realizing regional core competences', *Entrepreneurship and Regional Development,* 13-2, 97–116.

Vernon, R. (1966) 'International Investment and International Trade in the Product Cycle', *Quarterly Journal of Economics,* May: 190–207.

Warner, M. and Witzel, M. (2004) *Managing in Virtual Organization.* London: International Thomson Business Press.

Weick, K. E. (2008) 'Trust: a bigger picture' Book Review Symposium: Handbook of Trust Research, (eds) R. Bachmann and A. Zaheer, *Academy of Management Review,* 33, 1, 271–74.

Wenger, E. (1998) *Communities of Practice: Learning, Meaning and Identity.* Cambridge: Cambridge University Press.

Westley, F. R. (1990) 'Middle management and strategy: the microdynamics of inclusion', *Strategic Management Journal,* 11, 337–51.

Westney, D. E. (1993) 'Institutionalization Theory and the Multinational Corporation', in S. Ghoshal and D. E. Westney (eds) *Organization Theory and the Multinational Corporation.* New York: St Martins Press, 53–76.

Westney, D. E. and Sakakibara, D. (1985) 'Comparative study of the training, careers, and organization of engineers in the computer industry in Japan and the United States' Mimeograph, MIT-Japan Science and Technology Program.

Whetten, D. A. and Godfrey, P. C. (eds) (1998) *Identity in Organizations: Building Theory through Conversations.* Thousand Oaks, CA: Sage.

Whitley, R. (1984, 2000 edn) *The Intellectual and Social Organization of Science.* Oxford: Oxford University Press.

Whitley, R., Thomas, A. and Marceau, J. (1981) *Masters of Business? Business science and business graduates in Britain and France.* London: Tavistock Publications.

Whitley, R. (1999) *Divergent Capitalisms.* Oxford: Oxford University Press.

Whitley, R. (2007) *Business Systems and Organizational Capabilities: the Institutional Structuring of Competitive Competences.* Oxford: Oxford University Press.

World Bank (2001) *World Bank Development Report: Attacking Poverty.* New York: Oxford University Press.

Yang, Q. and Jiang, C. X. (2007) 'Locational advantages and subsidiaries: R&D activities in emerging economies', *Asia Pacific Journal of Management,* 24, 3, September, 341–58.

Chapter 11 The Multinational Firm as an Instrument of Exploitation and Domination

Raza Mir and Diana Rosemary Sharpe

In this chapter, we critically reflect on the multinational corporation (MNC), drawing on the image of the MNC as an instrument of exploitation and domination. As discussed in other chapters, a lens may be seen as a specific way of focusing in which we are sensitized to specific kinds of questions and issues that become the focus of analysis. In this chapter we will reflect on what a critical lens, based on the analysis of the MNC as exploitative and dominating, can contribute to our understanding of the MNC and its internal and external behaviour.

Morgan has noted how 'being skilled in the art of reading a situation' is important for people working in organizations, and that skilled leaders are aware that new insights can emerge as one looks at a situation from different angles. In this chapter we introduce the image of the organization as an instrument of domination and sensitize the reader to the 'readings' or understandings of the MNC that are placed in focus by this image. As noted by Morgan (1997: 4), a metaphor uses evocative images and can create powerful insights whilst being inherently paradoxical in that by elevating some ways of seeing it will also create ways of not seeing – by highlighting some ways of seeing, others are ignored. Morgan also notes that 'we have to accept that any theory or perspective that we bring to the study of organization and management, while capable of creating valuable insights, is also incomplete, biased and potentially misleading' (1997: 5).

This chapter argues that the image of the MNC as an instrument of domination can indeed provide a counter image of the multinational to that which predominantly underlies mainstream accounts. Introducing a critical perspective on the MNC enables us to reflect on the ethical issues surrounding the behaviour of MNCs and sensitizes us to the need and the potential for changes in the way in which their

---

Images of the Multinational Firm Edited by Simon Collinson and Glenn Morgan
© 2009 John Wiley & Sons, Ltd

activities can be regulated. On an individual level, it can sensitize us to how our own actions as managers and members of MNCs impact on different stakeholders and particularly in terms of the abuse of power and exploitation of vulnerable groups. In terms of policy and action, it can also sensitize us to areas where policy and regulation of MNCs are needed, for example concerning the exploitation of local communities and in labour-management relations.

In summary, the metaphor of the MNC as a system of exploitation highlights the awareness of these corporations as independent, powerful stakeholders. Privately held MNCs represent many of the largest global economic entities, larger than many countries, amounting to 13 of the 50 largest economic entities (Palmer, 2001). This image of the MNC brings into focus the ways in which these firms can misuse their power. Critics claim that many MNCs are not fulfilling their part of the implicit social contract. Whilst these practices may be within the legal frameworks of the countries in which they operate, there are several ethical issues that need to be highlighted. For example, MNCs may protect their core technology and research and development in a way that keeps host countries as consumers not partners or producers. They may create a brain drain attracting expertise out of the host country. They may disturb local government planning and business practices by controlling how infrastructure is developed and deployed. Finally, they may significantly displace customs, values and traditions of the local culture. Whilst these criticisms do not apply to all MNCs, they represent the concerns of host country and developing country governments that have suffered from the abuses of MNCs over the years (Weiss, 2003). MNC practices have also included exerting undue political influence and control and damaging the physical environment and human health. Weiss argues based on empirical analysis that a significant percentage of MNCs (11 % of 1043 MNCs studied) were involved in one or more major white collar crimes or frauds over a 10-year period. The crimes included foreign bribery, kickbacks and improper payments (Weiss, 2003: 285).

Theoretical Underpinnings

Existing as they do in multiple national environments characterized by divergent levels of development, MNCs are uniquely positioned to extract arbitrage advantages from two simultaneous phenomena: the relative infancy and feebleness of institutions of global governance, and the inability of individual nation states to police an entity whose reach extends beyond national boundaries. The image of the MNC here is of an entity that takes advantage of several factors to exploit the global poor, such as corrupt local governments, an increasing global turn toward neoliberal governance mechanisms (making MNC-based investments lucrative and necessary for poor nations), support from international regimes like the IMF, World Bank and WTO, technological innovations that render labour extraction possible without recourse to large-scale migrations, and the inability of the global poor to organize better across national boundaries. *Exploitation* or the appropriation of surplus value by capitalists has been a feature of industrial society. Our image of the MNC is one where this feature continues to be refined in the age of globalization.

Exploitation, as used in the Marxian sense (Bottomore, 1983: 157–8), is defined as the ability of a capitalist institution or apparatus to appropriate the surplus value generated by labour. The power of the capitalist to exploit labour is predicated upon three conditions. First, the ownership of productive assets has to be rendered limited; ownership rights are vested in a propertied class and the bulk of the population is excluded from such ownership. Second, workers have nothing to sell but their labour power; their only possible means of livelihood is to enter the labour force as wage employees. In the Marxist argument, the cost of labour is lower than its productive potential and the difference makes up the surplus value which is expropriated from the employee. Finally, this system is sustained by a variety of institutions, the most important of which is the state.

While these three conditions are general conditions of the capitalist system, they are especially visible in the conduct and the governance of MNCs. First, MNCs are controlled by relatively small numbers of individuals whose accountability rests mainly with actions in the capital markets. The vast sums of capital controlled by MNCs may derive from the savings of individuals but these individuals have little impact on MNC policies. Once these savings are aggregated into large investment pools by fund managers in international banks control is again vested in the hands of a relatively small number of institutional investors whose actions in the capital markets influence the strategies of MNCs. In effect, whether these savings come from Kansas or Shanghai, they flow into London and New York where their manipulation generates huge fortunes for insiders within the financial system and exacerbates global (and national, regional and urban) inequalities.

Second, MNCs are increasingly associated with actions that Marx termed 'primitive accumulation', the act of dispossessing peasants across the world of their lands, thereby moving them from precapitalist modes of accumulation into a situation where they have little to trade except their labour. In the words of Harvey (2005: 159), 'the main substantive achievement of neoliberalization has been ... the commodification and privatisation of land and the forceful expulsion of peasant populations (and) the conversion of various forms of property rights (common, collective, state, etc) into exclusive private property rights'. While the term 'primitive' suggests a temporal antecedent to the practice of capitalist accumulation, the process remains continuous even in present times. As Hardt and Negri argue in their book *Empire*, 'Primitive accumulation is not a process that happens once and then is done with; rather, capitalist relations of production and social classes have to be reproduced continually. What has changed is the model or mode of primitive accumulation' (Hardt and Negri, 2000: 259). For instance, in an exquisite irony, primitive accumulation is often carried out on behalf of the MNC by the state itself. The Chinese government regularly dispossesses peasants of their multi-cropped lands to enable the setting up of 'Special Economic Zones' for MNCs (Holmstrom and Smith, 2000). Likewise, land has been forcibly acquired from farmers by the state in Liberia (Ibrahim, 2004) and Russia (McCauley, 2001). The government of India's controversial 2006 acquisition of multi-cropped fields for the South Korean MNC POSCO provides a recent example of this phenomenon. Reports quoted Jeong Tae Hyun, the CEO of the giant steel corporation as saying that 'we came to India for the iron ore and will go forward with the plan only if we are given a captive mine'.

Of course, the concept of exploitation has undergone a transformation in the past several decades. Within democratic systems, the state plays a role in mitigating the more egregious effects of exploitation by capital (Chatterjee, 2007). Likewise, the rapid erosion of regimes of feudalism, the spread of education and political consciousness among the dispossessed, and the patterns of urban migration seen in countries like India and China mean that exploitation becomes a much more nuanced phenomenon than earlier conceptualizations would have described it (Sanyal, 2007). However, we argue that at the heart of this complicated enterprise, the fundamental nature of exploitation remains the same, especially for the poor in the Third World.

In what sense is the MNC a more sophisticated agent of exploitation than any other capitalist organization? In this section, we contend that the exploitative behaviour of MNCs per se can be grouped in three areas. First, in their efforts to break down the barriers to global capital, MNCs often reduce the protective barriers which in the past have shielded infant economies from the predatory attacks of speculators and global carpetbaggers. This is not so much a withering away of the nation state, as part of a broader effort of MNCs to reshape states to their own benefit by reducing their welfare role while strengthening their ability to control their populations in the interests of creating a workforce available for use in MNCs (Pooler, 1991). Second, MNCs aim to privatize public goods through mechanisms such as global intellectual property regimes. To that end, they can be accused of 'confiscating public creativity' (Perelman, 2002). Third, MNCs perpetuate a culture of inappropriate consumption that is ecologically irresponsible and socially infeasible. This again is a process-related effect of MNC presence; by exacerbating the inequalities in an already unequal society, MNCs end up laying the groundwork of a situation where consumption patterns are skewed in the direction of the rich, and upset the balance of production, consumption and rejuvenation that characterize more slowly developing economies (Kahn and Landler, 2007).

The Nation State Lives

Some theorists of the MNC have often been quick to predict the demise of the nation state as a consequence of the emergence of a unitary global economy (Ohmae, 1995). The reality of course is that the more globalized the world becomes, the more dependent transnational institutions (including corporations and international regimes like the WTO) become on the nation state, to secure intellectual and other property rights, to maintain law and order and to provide facilities conducive to business (Dicken, 2003: 122–63). At the same time, international regimes are deployed to twist the arm of the nation state into self-weakening moves such as the reduction of corporate taxes, lifting tariffs that might have provided protection to local infant industries[1] and reduced government involvement in industry.

Ultimately, these twin pressures push the nation state simultaneously into a position of prominence as well as a position of diminished strength in its ability to wield its sovereign authority against MNCs (Pitelis, 1991).

Intellectual Property Rights and Inequality

Stiglitz (2002) notes that we have a system that might be called global governance without global government, in which a few institutions, the World Bank, the IMF (International Monetary Fund), the WTO (World Trade Organization) – and a few players – the finance, commerce and trade ministers, closely linked to certain financial and commercial interests – dominate the scene, and many people affected by their decisions are left almost voiceless. The 'failures' of globalization to work for many of the world's poor and for the environment are traced to the prevalence of commercial and financial interests and mind-sets within international economic institutions.

The worldwide protests over globalization which began to hit headlines occurred during the WTO meetings in Seattle in 1999. The WTO was perceived as the most obvious symbol of the global inequities and the hypocrisy of the advanced industrial countries. A particular area of concern raised in the Doha development round of trade negotiations (November 2001) was that of intellectual property rights. Whilst these are important if innovators are to have incentives to innovate, the rights and interests of potential users also need to be considered – not only users in developing countries but researchers also. In the Uruguay negotiations it was thought that the agreement had put producers' interests over users with the consequence that life-saving medicine might be denied to the poor. This issue later received considerable attention within the context of the provision of HIV-AIDS medicine in South Africa. Stiglitz notes (2002: 245) how it was the growth of international outrage that forced the drugs companies to back down despite initially being supported by the US government. A further development has been where international companies have patented for example local traditional medicines or foods, what is now known as bio-piracy.

In the 1999 protests, activists in Seattle argued that a few bureaucrats allied with global corporations had begun to set the agenda for world trade, without any regard to democratic process or national sovereignty (Cockburn and St Clair, 2001). The Multilateral Agreement on Investments, a proposal that eventually failed because of immense protests, actually sought to codify such immunity into international law, proposing that all MNCs be exempted from local statutes against various violations including pollution, minimum wage and labour laws (Waters, 2001). The regime of intellectual property rights has functioned to deprive farmers of their rights over their seeds, as exemplified by the efforts of Monsanto Corporation to patent seeds (Pringle, 2005). MNCs are the primary beneficiaries of these property rights, and often have attempted to dispossess citizens of the poor nations of the world of the most indigenous of products, as exemplified by the application by WR Grace and Company to patent neem[2] or the attempts by RiceTec to patent basmati.[3] MNCs are constantly attempting to deploy intellectual property rights as a means of earning monopoly rents from public goods.

The Culture of Consumption

MNCs shape consumption processes as part of their efforts to create markets and this process can have perverse results, e.g. Nestlé implicitly encourages mothers to undernurse their children;[4] Unilever uses sophisticated marketing techniques to sell skin whitening creams to dark-complexioned Asians and Arabs.[5] These are classic examples of MNCs producing a culture of consumption that not only strains the social fabric, but diverts valuable social and economic resources toward a Veblenesque fetishism of consumption.

   The ability of MNCs to create global brands and logos is central here. As Klein notes: 'The astronomical growth in the wealth and cultural influence of multinational corporations over the last fifteen years can arguably be traced back to a single, seemingly innocuous idea developed by management theorists in the mid-1980s: that successful corporations must primarily produce brands, as opposed to products' (Klein, 2001: 3). Klein (2000) describes the impact of MNC advertising as well as supply-chain dynamics on poorer nations and poor people in the West. By the fetishistic production of demand for consumer goods, MNCs have a substantial impact on the impoverishment of the middle class, and the heightening of exploitative tendencies, as the haves in society perceive themselves as deprived of the ability to consume even more goods, and heighten their exploitation of the have-nots to achieve the capability of being able to engage in 'consumer society'. Klein notes how companies no longer just brand their own products but also brand the outside culture as well by sponsoring cultural events and using imagery to equate products with positive cultural or social experiences. In this way Klein notes how the effect is to nudge the host culture into the background and make the brand the star – i.e. to be the culture.

   In the agricultural sector, pressures placed by MNCs on local farmers (through market control as well as changing the contours of the credit system) have drastically altered the crop-growing patterns in various regions, shifting the focus to commercial crops over food grains (Pearson, 2006), altering financial arrangements leading to farmer impoverishment (Vakulabharanam, 2004) and accelerating the process of environmental degradation (Jacques, 2006). Overall, MNCs have been accused of systematically shifting consumption patterns across the world toward the zone of unsustainability, and by implication, increasing the exploitative tendencies in the regions of their operation.

   In the next section, we focus on the effect of the MNC at various analytical levels, both within the firm and across the environment.

MNC Impact

To place the exploitative tendencies of MNCs into analytically discrete categories is an exercise in futility. These corporations act in a variety of inter-related ways, in the economic as well as the cultural domain, in the national as well as the transnational space, involving global as well as local subjects. However, at the risk of being reductive, we have chosen to analyse MNC impact at three levels. *Intra-firm level* relationships constitute the manner in which the headquarters and subsidiaries of MNCs are implicated in a power relationship, which may show exploitative tendencies of its own. *Firm level* analytics refer to the manner in which the corporation presents itself as a whole, either to states or to interest groups (Geppert, 2005). Finally, *macro level* interventions by groups of MNCs are often carried out through strong states where MNCs are typically headquartered, through international institutions like the WTO or IMF, or through inter-firm coalitions (Barnet and Cavanaugh, 1995).

In examining the interaction of three different levels with three different terrains, we are dealing with nine sets of relationships, which are represented in Table 11.1. As the table shows, many of these relationships exhibit potentially exploitative tendencies. In other words, MNCs deploy a variety of levels to a variety of contexts, and many of those linkages heighten regimes of exploitation. We will briefly describe all nine relationships, but hasten to add that our descriptions are meant to be illustrative rather than exhaustive.

Interactions with the Nation State

At the macro level, MNCs act in concert with nation states to reduce the bargaining power of the workforce. The issue of Foreign Direct Investment (FDI) becomes especially relevant here. The 1990s in particular constituted a decade of neoliberalization all over the world. The World Development Report of 2000 estimated that in the 1990s, over 100 nations enacted reforms making life easier for MNCs, reducing their tax burdens and making exit easier. Following a neoliberal economic logic, nation states enacted the twin strategies of stabilization (through curbing the rate of inflation) and structural adjustment. Policy changes included redefining the role of the state (to a less active player in the day-to-day running of organizations), reducing the regulation and licensing process affecting MNCs and FDI, making foreign investment more attractive through tariff reduction, and financial liberalization. The effect of these actions has been quite disastrous for the poor of the world in many ways (Chandrasekhar and Ghosh, 2002). Poverty levels have risen dramatically, infant industries the world over have suffered, and environmental legislation is a casualty, all pointing toward increasing exploitative pressures.

Escobar (1995: 165) notes how the World Bank continues to be the official policy guide in developing countries, itself collaborating on mutual assistance agreements with UN agencies. Most of the loans of the World Bank are disbursed based on

Table 11.1 MNC impact at different levels across different terrains

	Macro Level	Firm Level	Intra-Firm Level
Nation State	• Changed local laws on capital investment • Removal of entry/exit barriers • State used as punitive device on behalf of MNC	• Immunity from local laws • Reduced tax payments • Transfer pricing • State procures land/resources for MNC	• Tighter control over subsidiary • Less recourse to legal system by subsidiary • Linkages between MNC labour and local labour discouraged
Local Knowledge	• New IPR regime • Inappropriate consumption • Nexus between MNC products and (atavistic) local pre-modern practices.	• Appropriation of local knowledge • Patenting indigenous knowledge • Destruction of local practices	• Subsidiary-level knowledge destroyed in the name of 'standardization' • Local practices devalued within the MNC
Extant Inequalities	• Exacerbated divide between rich and poor nations • Widening of within-nation inequalities • State loses welfare role	• Infant industries rendered more vulnerable • Mistreatment of contractors and suppliers	• Undercutting the ability of unions to protect local workers • Rewarded compliance with HQ strategy • Severe punishment for dissent against HQ

international bidding and most often go to multinational corporations and experts from the developed countries (a total of $80 billion at the end of 1980). In this way, the World Bank maintains intellectual and financial hegemony in development and provides the conditions and institutional systems and practices that enable multi-nationals from developed countries to engage in exploitative practices. For example the World Bank opens up new regions to investment through transportation, elec-trification and telecommunications projects; it contributes to the spread of MNCs through contracts; it deepens dependence on international markets by insisting on production for exports, it opposes protectionist measures of local industries and fosters the loss of control of resources by local people by insisting on large projects that benefit national elites and MNCs.

At the firm level, organizational theorists working on the issue of MNCs and global corporate responsibility (Wokutch, 2001) have noted that the pressures that can be exerted by sovereign nations on firms is small and hence MNCs tend to wring major concessions out of even quite powerful governments. In 1995, for example, DuPont signed an agreement with the Indian government where they insisted on and received an 'exemption' releasing the corporation from any liability for claims of environmental degradation or a large-scale industrial accident (Cohen and Sarangi, 1995).

At the intra-firm level, the issue of MNC governance is usually framed within the discussion of 'knowledge transfer'. Knowledge is usually embodied in organizational routines (Nelson and Winter, 1982). In order to transfer it across national boundaries, MNCs need to codify knowledge. However, the challenge here is that the more codifiable the knowledge, the easier it is to imitate (Zander and Kogut, 1995). The absorptive capacity of the recipient unit in organizations is believed to be a key contingency variable in knowledge transfer (Cohen, 1998). Motivational and dispositional issues at the level of the source unit can affect knowledge transfer (Szulanski, 1995).

One major critique of MNCs and their attitude to knowledge relates to their po-tentially ideological approach. Interest groups at MNC headquarters tend to valorize their interests as the interests of the corporation as a whole, without examining the role played by subsidiaries, or their needs and dispositions. Moreover, they conceive of organizational processes as moving toward a singular goal, thereby treating all conflict as pathological, and rewarding compliant behaviour (Mir and Mir, 2007). To that end, MNCs 'universalize sectional interests', or position the interests of certain organizational sub-groups (usually shareholders) as the interests of the firm itself (Alvesson and Willmott, 1995; Shrivastava, 1985).

Interactions with Local Knowledges

At the macro level, MNCs are at the forefront of the push for intellectual property rights, the privatization of public goods, and the extension of monopoly rights to corporate patents across the world (Perelman, 2002). In an earlier section, we have discussed some of the controversies that surround the WTO, and allegations that it functions on behalf of MNCs. To add to that discussion, we have the unfortunate prospect of living organisms and genes being patented in the United States, a consequence, according to Crichton (2007) of 'a mistake by an underfinanced and understaffed government agency. The United States Patent Office misinterpreted previous Supreme Court rulings and some years ago began – to the surprise of everyone, including scientists decoding the genome – to issue patents on genes.' MNCs were quick to jump on the bandwagon. Gene patents now make it exorbitantly expensive for individuals and universities to do research on diseases like Hepatitis C or breast cancer; their only recourse is to pay upwards of a million dollars to patent-holding MNCs. Needless to say, research is suffering, just as agricultural innovations by local farmers are suffering because of the IPR barriers erected by MNCs.

At the firm level, MNCs take advantage of the misery of suffering populations, such as the case of AIDS in Africa (Bond, 1999), where corporations charged exorbitant rates to suffering people, who had neither any hope of paying the prices demanded for therapy, nor were in any danger of diluting world demand for those drugs. Monsanto's 'terminator seeds' are a singular case in point; the MNC spent millions of R&D dollars to produce a seed that would 'terminate' after one crop, thereby preventing farmers from practicing the millennia-old practice of replanting part of their crop as seed (Graham, 2001). The impact of MNCs on local knowledge at the firm level has most certainly been exploitative.

At the intra-firm level, local knowledge at the subsidiary level is often delegitimized and derided by headquarters of MNCs. Empirical research on MNC knowledge transfer has tended to follow one of two assumptions. Either knowledge is perceived as flowing into a vacuum (Wheelwright and Clark, 1995), or that knowledge flows play the role of agents of creative destruction, destroying old knowledge and replacing it with new (Dewar and Dutton, 1986). In order to prevent such an understanding from degenerating into an exploitative pattern, we need to take a more complex and contextualized view of knowledge, and move beyond these two perspectives. Also, as philosophers like Bakhtin (1981) as well as organizational theorists like Nonaka (1994) have stressed, knowledge that resides in individuals or isolated bodies can only be integrated into a larger framework through a spirit of social sharing, conversation and dialogue, which is often absent in the exploitative relationship between MNC headquarters and their subsidiaries.

Effect on Extant Inequalities

At the macro level, MNCs exacerbate the inequalities between rich and poor nations, and increase the class divides within societies. In a damning analysis, Banerjee and Linstead (2001: 684) define globalization as a rhetoric that is tailored to respond to 'public criticisms on the dismantling of social institutions, redundancies or plant closing'. To them, the talk of an emerging globalization thus becomes the ideological arm of privatization, wealth concentration, neoliberal ingress of MNCs into third world nations, and of global capitalism in general. After all, it is not as if the growth and spread of international corporate activity has contributed in any measure to world employment. In fact, through the combined use of technology and the threat of flight, corporations have also been able to control the labour force far more efficiently than in the past. Between 1980 and 1995, the asset base of MNCs increased seven-fold to $4 trillion, while their labour pool shrank by 7 % (Klein, 2000).

At the firm level, excesses by MNCs against sovereign nations (BP in Iran, ITT in Chile, Shell in Nigeria) have prompted critiques by theorists like Ahmad (2000) who find the globalization espoused by these corporations to be little more than a euphemism for the conquest of the poor nations of the world by the West in general and the US in particular, a form of imperialistic recolonization. As an empirical hook into the topic, let us consider the July 2004 issue of *Fortune* magazine, which reported its annual list of 500 corporations, noting that most of its members derived over 50 % of their revenues from foreign operations (Fortune, 2004). Topping the list was Walmart with annual sales in excess of $260bn. Interestingly, Walmart did not even have a single store outside the US till 1990. In a highly appreciative case study, Hill (2003: 3–4) notes that by cleverly leveraging the global economy, including supply chain management, Walmart reached a position whereby it had over 1300 stores and 305 000 'associates' (its euphemism for employees) outside of the US in 2002, generating revenues in excess of $35bn. The case is meant of course to extol the ability of Walmart, explicitly to succeed in a competitive environment, and implicitly, to tap into a win–win situation in the global marketplace.

In a counter-ideological and counter-discursive framing of this situation, we must first acknowledge and if necessary, highlight alternative elements of Walmart's 'international' presence. For example, Walmart has been accused of taking advantage of the precarious situation of illegal immigrants in the US to reduce its labour cost, employing them at sub-minimum-wage levels with no benefits.[6] Lesser known is its reputation for eventually bankrupting its international suppliers (Fishman, 2003). Walmart's presence in local communities as well as international markets is viewed with alarm not only by competitors, but also by the workforce in the region who fear the eventual erosion of their hard-fought gains on the pay and benefits front.

Finally, at the intra-firm level, the ability of the subsidiary workers to organize is often undercut by the headquarters with an implicit threat by the MNC that they will exit and close down the subsidiary unless their demands are met. Walmart has been known to close operations and leave in countries where the workforce has sighted success in its attempt to form a union.[7] Overall, the increase in FDI by MNCs in a nation has often been correlated with the decline of labour power in that nation (Chandrasekhar and Ghosh, 2002). The level of MNC coverage of any national space or economy is also directly proportional to the increase in power distance between the headquarters and the subsidiary, which can be interpreted as a special case of exploitation.

The closing case, with the example of the maquila workers, provides insights into the exploitative nature of MNC activity in export processing zones.

Resisting MNCs

In the course of this chapter, we have tried to highlight the role of MNCs as agents of exploitation and domination. We suggest that the exploitative tendencies of MNCs work through their manipulation of nation states and the regime of intellectual property rights, their role in the exacerbation of inequalities between and within nations, their appropriation of local knowledges and by increasing the power distances between headquarters and subsidiaries. The control of MNCs is currently beyond the coercive power of any national institution, since MNCs are often more powerful than the nation states in which they operate. Likewise, international regimes like the IMF, the WTO and the World Bank are currently co-opted by MNCs to a point where the task of controlling them cannot be entrusted to these beholden institutions.

Whilst this chapter focuses directly on MNC exploitation at the macro level, the firm level and the intra-firm level, a further step in the analysis can bring the micro level into focus. Such an approach could link individuals' experiences of work and social relations within the context of the MNC to macro-level issues such as the global division of labour (Sharpe, 2006).

Two legitimate theoretical issues arise upon reading our analysis of the negative effects of MNCs: why do these corporations participate in such a patterned behaviour that produces negative consequences for a large section of the world population, and is our analysis not dismissive of the positive impact of MNCs in different parts of the world?

In brief response to the first issue, this analysis is not merely of the effects of one corporation or of behaviour over a short time-span, but the impact over a long time of many corporations, not necessarily acting in coordination. Nevertheless, the negative effects of MNCs can be collectively attributed to the growing power disparity between global capital and local control mechanisms. Nation states or communities are increasingly powerless to place checks and balances on MNCs. To use the language of game theory, exploitative behaviours by MNC, despite their negative long-term impacts on MNC reputations, constitute equilibrium in terms of behaviour. In the absence of effective governance, such exploitative behaviour becomes a short-term norm in the economic logic of the MNC.

Our decision not to spend much time highlighting some of the positive contributions of global capital in different parts of the world is also deliberate. There exist substantial analyses by organizational theorists that are celebratory of global capital or attempt to take a 'neutral' stance. This however, is not our project. To that extent, the theoretical approach we have chosen to foreground represents an 'entry point' into the discourse of the MNC, as one way to enter its overdetermined theoretical terrain. As the historian Sudipta Kaviraj (1992: 38) remarks with respect to subaltern historiography, 'the interstices of every narrative are filled with semblances rather than truth. Thus, the telling of true stories in history would not rule out the telling of other stories different from the first, which are also true.'

If our story of MNC exploitation indeed rings true, where should one look to for ways in which MNCs can be corralled? It appears that the only space for intervention against the MNCs' push toward domination and hegemony comes from organized acts of resistance by citizen groups and social movements. These resistance forms occupy the space of 'political society' (Chatterjee, 2004). Political society as used here is distinct from civil society, which often degenerates (as a result of the active collusion between MNCs and local governments) into being nothing more than 'the closed association of modern elite groups, sequestered from the wider popular life of the communities, walled up within enclaves of civic freedom and rational law' (Chatterjee, 2004: 4). On the other hand, political society includes large sections of those who do not relate to the laws of the state in the same way that the middle classes do. They lack the citizenship rights that are the hallmark of civil society, but do make their claims on states through unstable arrangements arrived at through direct political negotiations. Political society is the realm of populations, of instrumental alliances between marginalized groups, and an attempt to wrest some concessions from a society where the status of its constituents is beyond the pale of legality (Mir, Marens and Mir, 2008).

In examining the power of social movements recent examples illustrate the ways in which they are seeking and gaining influence. In April 2000, AIDS activists, unions and religious groups were ready to begin a lawsuit and picketing campaign denouncing the Pfizer corporation as an AIDS profiteer for the high prices it was charging for AIDS drugs. Pfizer suddenly announced that it would supply the drug fluconazole, used to control AIDS side effects, for free to any South African with AIDS who could not afford it. A few weeks later, US, British, Swiss and German drug companies announced that they would cut prices on the principal aids drugs, anti-retrovirals, by 85 to 90 % (Brecher et al., 2002: 28). When the Japanese-owned Bridgestone/Firestone (B/F) demanded 12-hour shifts and a 30 % wage cut for new workers in its American factories, workers struck. B/F fired them all and replaced them with 2300 strikebreakers. American workers appealed to B/F workers around the world for help. Unions around the world organized 'Days of Outrage' protests against B/F. In Argentina a two-hour 'general assembly' of all workers at the gates of the B/F plant halted production, while 2000 workers heard American B/F workers describe the company's conduct. In Brazil Bridgestone workers staged one-hour work stoppages, then 'worked like turtles', the Brazilian phrase for a slow down. Unions in Belgium, France, Italy and Spain met with local Bridgestone management to demand a settlement. US B/F workers went to Japan and met with Japanese unions, many of whom called for the immediate re-instatement of US workers. Five hundred Japanese unionists marched through the streets of Tokyo, supporting B/F workers from the US. In the wake of the worldwide campaign, Bridgestone/Firestone unexpectedly agreed to re-hire its locked out American workers (Brecher et al., 2002: 28).

Signs of the engagement between political society and MNCs emerged when labour and trade activists spectacularly disrupted the WTO's third meeting of ministers in Seattle in 1999 (Thomas, 2000). The WTO was cast into the public spotlight by the Seattle riots, a consequence it had avoided in the nearly five prior years of its existence since its inception in January 1995. Since then, people have been taking it on everywhere. Likewise, public action against Nike for supporting sweatshops,

Exxon for its environmental irresponsibility, Halliburton for its questionable role in Iraq, Nestlé for its role in African public health, Walmart for its treatment of workers, Coca Cola for its privatization of water resources and a variety of global and local initiatives provide reasons for hope. The everyday interactions between world citizens and MNCs are the sites of resistance to class exploitation, institutionalized racism, alienation, the re-constitution of worker subjectivity, the gendering of labour, the diminished power of intra-organizational bargaining, and sometimes, of relations of imperialism and cultural dislocation. Similarly, these acts of resistance all over the world form the true 'weapons of the weak' (Scott, 1985), and stand between the MNC and the triumph of its exploitative agenda.

CASE STUDY: EXPLOITATION OF WORKERS IN EXPORT PROCESSING ZONES – THE CASE OF THE MAQUILA WORKERS

The image of the multinational as an instrument of exploitation is maybe nowhere quite as starkly presented as in the Export Processing Zones or free trade zones of countries including Indonesia, Mexico, Vietnam and the Philippines for example.

A rare inside glimpse into working conditions within the free trade zone of El Salvador led to the publication by the US National Labour Committee of a report in 2001. Eighty-five thousand maquila workers, mainly young women sewing garments for companies including Nike, Jordan, Adidas, Gap, Kohl's and Walmart were systematically being denied their rights and paid wages of abject poverty. A suppressed Salvadoran government investigation of working conditions in the free trade zones, funded by the US Agency for International Development, documented below subsistence wages, forced overtime, abusive working conditions, unsafe working conditions, limited access to health care (in the majority of cases, the workers had to give up their regular medical care because of the bosses' and supervisors' refusal to allow them to attend their appointments, arguing that their presence is needed to cover production goals), complete denial of freedom of association and government complicity and corruption.

The report documented how the Salvadorian government has provided the maquila factories and free trade zones with complete impunity to violate the most fundamental, internationally recognized worker rights. The study revealed how workers at Nike were paid 29 cents for each 140 dollar Nike shirt they were sewing, 20 cents for each $14.99 child's dress they were sewing for Kohl's, 11.5 cents for each $12.99 Gap T-shirt and 74 cents for each $198 Liz Clairborne jacket (US National Labour Committee Report May 2001). At the time of the study Nike insisted that the 60 cents an hour base wage in El Salvador which amounts to $4.80 a day was both fair and adequate. The researchers took the example of a single mother working at the Hermosa factory sewing Nike Garments. Their response gives a different insight. She had three children, and her daily expenses were outlined:

Round trip bus fare (to get to and from work) $1.14
Small breakfast (coffee, plantain, beans, 2 rolls, sour cream) $0.91

Lunch (stuffed peppers, rice, tortillas and lemonade – the main meal of the day) $1.37

At the end of the day she is left with $1.38.

Rent for the crowded two rooms that she and her children share with three other adult relatives costs $1.68 a day, which is more than she has left. This is excluding gas and electricity, supper for her family and powdered milk for her children. There is no money for medicine or shoes for her children so that they can go to school. 'We asked this woman – who gets up at 4.30am, every morning and frequently returns home at 8.15pm after working a 12 hour shift sewing $140 dollar Nike shirts if she had any savings. 'No', she replied, 'but we do have debts. Sometimes we cannot pay the rent' (US National Labour Committee Report, May 2001, p. 81).

The report raises the question ... In today's global economy, just what leverage do poor developing countries have over giant multinationals roaming the world in search of low wages, no taxes, no unions, no environmental or health and safety constraints, no red tape?

El Salvador in 2000 had a gross domestic product (from all goods and services produced) of $13.2bn. Walmart, for example, had annual sales of $193.3bn in 2000, 14.5 times larger than the entire country of El Salvador. The Salvadorian government's entire general budget for 2000 was $2.08bn.

Gap's sales in the 12-month period to 31 January 2001 totalled $13.7bn, 6.5 times larger than the government's budget. It would also take all 85 000 workers in El Salvador 84 years (if they did not spend any of their wages) – to earn what Nike's Phil Knight was worth – 12.3bn dollars (US National Labour Committee Report, May 2001, p. 82).

Question

1. There are now a large number of websites monitoring the actions of MNCs in developing countries, export processing zones and maquiladora plants. MNCs themselves use their websites to defend themselves against accusations of exploitation. Use the internet to research how one particular company is affected by this. Obvious companies to research are Nike, Walmart, Gap, Monsanto, one of the oil companies (such as Shell). Is exploitation endemic? Are MNCs self-regulating to reduce exploitation? Are there effective forms of regulation emerging at the international level, e.g. the UN Global Compact? Are national governments losing the power to regulate MNCs?

Further Reading

Naomi Klein's *No Logo* is a good source of materials on how large corporations and their abilities to create brands, influence governments and shape international agreements and institutions contribute to the formation of a global society riven with inequalities and what Marx termed 'commodity fetishism'. Hardt and Negri's monumental work *Empire* and its follow-up *Multitude* range across many of these issues in a more provocatively political style though their language is dense and often unclear and their musings idiosyncratic and tangential. Both Klein and Hardt and Negri have, however, been influential in developing an intellectual basis for resistance to globalization and the activities of MNCs.

References

Ahmad, A. (2000) 'Globalisation: A society of aliens?' *Frontline*, 17(20): 31–3.

Alvesson, M. and Willmott, H. (1995) 'Strategic Management as Domination and Emancipation: From Planning and Process to Communication and Praxis'. In P. Shrivastava and C. Stubbart *Advances in Strategic Management: Challenges from Outside the Mainstream*. Greenwich, Conn.: JAI Press.

Bakhtin, M. (1981) *The dialogic imagination: Four essays by M. M. Bakhtin*. M. E. Holquist (ed.), C. Emerson and M. Holquist (trans.). Austin: University of Texas Press.

Banerjee, S. B. and Linstead, S. (2001) 'Globalization, multiculturalism and other fictions: Colonialism for the new millennium?' *Organization*, 8 (4): 711–50.

Barnet, R. and Cavanaugh, P. (1995) *Global Dreams: Imperial Corporations and The New World Order*. New York: Simon & Schuster.

Bond, P. (1999) 'Globalization, Pharmaceutical Pricing, and South African Health Policy: Managing Confrontation with U.S. Firms and Politicians', *International Journal of Health Services*, 29(4): 765–92.

Bottomore, T. (1983) *A Dictionary of Marxist Thought*. Cambridge, MA: Harvard University Press.

Brecher J. (2002) *Globalization From Below*. Cambridge, MA: South End Press.

Chandrasekhar, C. P. and Ghosh, J. (2002) *The Market That Failed: A Decade of Neoliberal Economic Reforms in India*. New Delhi: Leftword Books.

Chang, H.-J. (2003) *Globalisation, Economic Development and the Role of the State*. New York: Zed Books.

Chatterjee, P. (2004) *The Politics of the Governed: Reflections on Popular Politics in Most of the World*. New York: Columbia University Press.

Chatterjee, P. (2007) 'Democracy and Economic Transformation in India', unpublished manuscript, Center for the Advanced Study of India http://casi.ssc.upenn.edu/events/khemka_series.htm (accessed 30 January 2008).

Cockburn, A. and St Clair, J. (2001) *Five Days That Shook the World: The Battle for Seattle and Beyond*. New York: Verso.

Cohen, D. (1998) 'Toward a knowledge context: Report on the first annual U.C. Berkeley forum on knowledge and the firm', *California Management Review*, 40(3): 22–39.

Cohen, G. and Sarangi, S. (2002) 'DuPont: Spinning its Wheels in India', *Multinational Monitor*, 16(3): 8–14.

Crichton, M. (2007) 'Patenting Life', *New York Times*, 13 February 2007, p. 23.

Dewar, R. D. and Dutton, J. E. (1986) 'The adoption of radical and incremental innovations: An empirical analysis', *Management Science*, 32 (11): 1422–33.

Dicken, P. (2003) *Global Shift: Reshaping the Global Economic Map in the 21st Century*. London: Guilford Publications, Inc.

Escobar, A. (1995) *Encountering Development: The Making and Unmaking of the Third World.* New Jersey: Princeton University Press.

Fishman, C. (2003) 'The Wal-Mart you don't know', *Fast Company*, 77: 68–72.

Fortune (2004) 'Who's on top? The 2004 global 500', *Fortune* (19 July 2004).

Geppert, M. (2005) 'Multinational Companies are not "Stateless" Enterprises', *Organization*, 12(2): 302–4.

Graham, G. (2001) 'Learning from the Terminator debacle', *International Journal of Biotechnology*, 3(3–4): 260–6.

Hardt, A. and Negri, A. (2000) *Empire*. Cambridge, MA: Harvard University Press.

Harvey, D. (2005) *A Brief History of Neoliberalism*. Oxford: Oxford University Press.

Hill, C. (2003) *International Business: Competing in the Global Marketplace*. New York: McGraw-Hill Irwin.

Holmstrom, N. and Smith, R. (2000) 'The Necessity of Gangster Capitalism: Primitive Accumulation in Russia and China', *Monthly Review*, 51 (2): 1–21.

Ibrahim, J. (2004) *Democratic Transition in Anglophone West Africa*. East Lansing, MI: Michigan University Press.

Jacques, P. (2006) 'The Rearguard of Modernity: Environmental Skepticism as a Struggle of Citizenship', *Global Environmental Politics*, 6(1): 76–101.

Kahn, J. and Landler, M. (2007) 'China Grabs West's Smoke-Spewing Factories', *New York Times*, 21 December 2007, A1.

Kaviraj, S. (1992) 'The imaginary institution that was India'. In R. Guha (ed.) *Subaltern Studies: VII*. New Delhi: Oxford University Press, 1–27.

Klein, N. (2000) *No Logo: Taking Aim at the Brand Bullies*. New York: Picador.

Klein, N. (2002) *Fences and Windows: Dispatches from the front lines of the Globalization*. New York: Picador.

Marx, K. (1939, 1973). *Grundrisse: Foundations of the Critique of Political Economy*. London: Penguin Classics.

Marx, K. (1977) *Capital (Vol. 1)*. New York: Vintage. (Original: 1868.)

McCauley, M. (2001) *Bandits, Gangsters and the Mafia: Russia, the Baltic States and the CIS Since 1991*. New York: Pearson Education.

Mir, R. and Mir, A. (2008) 'From the Corporation to the Colony: Studying Knowledge Transfer Across International Boundaries', *Group and Organization Management* (forthcoming June 2008).

Mir, R., Marens, R. and Mir, A. (2008) 'The Corporation and Its Fragments: Corporate Citizenship and the Legacies of Imperialism'. In A. Scherer and G. Palazzo (eds) *The Handbook of Corporate Citizenship*. London: Edward Elgar Press, 819–52.

Morgan, G. (1997) *Images of Organization* 2nd ed. London: Sage.

Nelson, R. R. and Winter, S. (1982) *An evolutionary theory of economic change*. Cambridge, MA: Harvard University Press, New Jersey: Princeton University Press.

Nonaka, I. (1994) 'A dynamic theory of organizational knowledge creation', *Organization Science*, 5(1): 14–37.

Ohmae, K. (1995) *The End of the Nation-State: The Rise of Regional Economies*. New York: The Free Press.

Palmer, E. (2001) 'Multinational Corporations and the Social Contract', *Journal of Business*, 31(3): 245–58.

Pearson, T. (2006) ' "Science", representation and resistance: the Bt cotton debate in Andhra Pradesh, India', *The Geographical Journal*, 172(4): 306–21.

Perelman, M. (2002) *Steal This Idea: Intellectual Property Rights and the Corporate Confiscation of Creativity*. New York: Palgrave Publications.

Pitelis, C. (1991) 'Beyond the Nation-State? The transnational firm and the Nation-State', *Capital and Class*, 43: 131–52.

Pooler, S. (1991) 'The State Rules, OK? The Continuing Political Economy of Nation-States', *Capital and Class*, 43: 65–82.

Pringle, P. (2005) *Food, Inc.: Mendel to Monsanto–the Promises and Perils of the Biotech Harvest*. New York: Simon & Schuster.

Sanyal, K. (2007) *Rethinking Capitalist Development: Primitive Accumulation, Governmentality and Post-Colonial Capitalism*. New Delhi: Routledge.

Sharpe, D. R. (2006) 'Shop Floor Practices Under Changing Forms of Managerial Control: A comparative ethnographic study within a Japanese multinational', *Journal of International Management*, 12(3): 318–39.

Shrivastava, P. (1985) 'Is strategic management ideological?' *Journal of Management*, 12: 363–77.

Stiglitz, J. E. (2002) *Globalization and its Discontents*. New York: W.W. Norton.

Szulanski, G. (1995) 'Unpacking stickiness: An empirical investigation of the barriers to transfer best practices inside the firm', *INSEAD Working Paper*, November 1995.

Thomas, J. (2000) *Battle in Seattle: The Story Behind and Beyond the WTO Demonstrations*. New York: Fulcrum Books.

U.S. National Labour Committee. (2001) May. 'Worker Rights in the Americas? A Rare Inside Glimpse' available from http://www.cleanclothes.org/ftp/NLCelsalv.pdf.

Vakulabharanam, V. (2004) 'Agricultural growth and irrigation in Telangana: A review of the evidence', *Economic and Political Weekly*, 39(24): 1421–6.

Waters, A. (2001) 'NGOs, Business, and International Investment: The Multilateral Agreement on Investment, Seattle, and Beyond', *Global Governance*, 7(1): 51–73.

Weiss, J. (2003) *Business Ethics: A Stakeholder and Issues Management Approach*. 3rd edn, South-Western, Div of Thomson Learning.

Wheelwright, S. C. and Clark, K. B. (1995). *Leading product development: The senior manager's guide to creating and shaping the enterprise*. New York: Free Press.

Wokutch, R. (2001) 'Nike and its critics: Beginning a dialogue', *Organization & Environment*, 14(2): 207–38.

Zander, U. and Kogut, B. (1995) 'Knowledge and the speed of the transfer and imitation of organizational capabilities', *Organization Science*, 6(1): 76–92.

NOTES

1. As an example of the ideological nature of pro-MNC research, the infant industry argument continues to be 'discredited' by the mainstream literature in organizational studies and economics, despite historical evidence showing that most industrialized nations prospered in the initial stages of their development through the active use of tariffs, subsidies and protectionist policies (Chang, 2003).

2. http://www.domainb.com/economy/general/2005/20050402_patent.html.

3. http://www.american.edu/projects/mandala/TED/basmati.htm.
4. http://www.ibfan.org/english/pdfs/btr04.pdf.
5. http://www.africanbynature.com/eyes/openeyes_whiteningthearab.html.
6. http://www.brennancenter.org/content/resource/wal_mart_makes_workers_pay/.
7. http://www.commondreams.org/headlines05/0210-13.htm.

Index

ABACUS 136–7
ABB 16, 60–1, 129–38, 158, 182
Abbey National 27, 28
'absorptive capacity' 222–3
Acer 80, 101–2
acquisitions *see* mergers . . .
Adidas 260
'administrative heritage' 11
affiliates 4, 81–2, 103–4, 234
   see also networks
Africa 71, 74–5, 105, 167, 251, 259, 260
agricultural sector, exploitation issues 252, 256
Ahmad, A. 257
Alcan 203, 208
Aldrich, Howard 118, 121, 123–4, 135–6
Alliance Unichem 27, 28
alliances 54–60, 82, 85–6, 177, 218–20, 226–38
aluminium producers 203
'ambidextrous organizations' 121
Americas 9–10, 23–44, 105, 146
   see also individual countries; US
ancillary organization MNE linkages 82–3, 220–1,
   232
Anglo-Saxon common law model 33
anti-dumping laws, barriers to entry 42
anti-trust laws 41–2
   see also competition policies
APV 126, 130–3
arbitrage advantages 34–5, 248–9
arm's length institutional regimes 148–62, 221–2,
   232–3
ASEA 60–1, 136–8
Asia 9–14, 23–44, 55, 71, 80–1, 101–8, 227–8, 236–8
   see also individual countries
aspirations, locus of learning along networks 17,
   217–38
asset-seeking FDI motives 8–9, 34–5, 54–60, 107–8

assets 8–10, 23–44, 54–60, 71–6, 78, 81–6, 93–115,
   249–61
   see also intangible . . .
AstraZeneca 25–6
Australia 25, 107
authority-sharing benefits, concepts 146–62, 218
auto firms 29, 30, 32, 70, 85–6, 103–4, 146, 154–5,
   167, 196–7, 201, 202, 204–5, 206, 234–5
autonomous variation processes, concepts 121–6,
   131–6
aviation industries 201–2

Ba, Japan 223–4
BAE Systems 233
Bakhtin, M. 256
banking services, regional nature of MNE activities
   29, 32
banks 4–5, 29, 32, 148–62, 186, 225–6
   see also institution . . .
bargaining power 75, 198–204
Barnard, Chester 134–5
Barnevik, Percy 136–8
barriers to entry 10, 15, 24, 41–2, 53–5, 250, 253–5
Bartlett, C.A. 10–12, 16, 17, 125–38, 145, 174–5, 208,
   218–19
Basle community 186
basmati rice 252
Baum, Joel 119–20
Bélanger, Jacques 16, 182, 193–216
Belgium 38, 259
beliefs 168–9
benchmarking 158, 175–7
Berlin Wall 15
biotechnology 18, 221–2, 227–8, 230–1, 256–61
biregional firms 24–30
Birkinshaw, Julian 11–12, 16, 128–9, 145, 175–9
BMW 30, 201

Images of the Multinational Firm   Edited by Simon Collinson and Glenn Morgan
© 2009 John Wiley & Sons, Ltd

Botswana 105
bottom-up evolution of MNEs 53–5
'bottom-up' theory, institutional change 96–7
'boundary objects' 224–5
bounded evolutionary systems, concepts 117–38, 224–5, 236
Bourneville model village 187–8
BP 25–6, 160, 257
brain drain problems 248
'branch plant economies' 12
brands 75, 252, 261–2
Brazil 127, 236
breast cancer 256
Brent Spar oil platform 202
BRIC countries 236
    see also Brazil; China; India; Russia
'bridge-building enterprise' 13
Bridgestone/Firestone (B/F) 259
Britain see UK
British Airways 207
British Empire 4–5
Brown Boveri (BBC) 60–1, 136–8
Burgelman, Robert 121–2, 131
Burrell, G. 2–4
business models 41–2, 128–36, 138

Cadbury-Schweppes 187–8
call centers 52, 225
Cambodia 105
Canada 25, 38, 203, 205–6, 208
Cantwell, John 9, 45–67, 82–3, 158, 220
capabilities 16–18, 54–5, 81–4, 94–109, 145–62, 167–88, 217–38
capital flows 70, 73–80, 148–62, 183–8, 249–50
capitalisms 10, 15, 18–19, 23, 32–44, 54–60, 75, 82, 85–6, 97, 172–3, 177, 179–81, 183–5, 194–5, 218–20, 221–2, 226–38, 247–61
    see also exploitation issues
career expectations 17–18, 146–62, 167–88, 219–38
Caribbean 5
Casson, Mark 97
'catching up' models 58, 80, 84–6, 209
    see also 'leapfrogging effects'
categories of MNEs 10–12, 57–8
centers of excellence 52–60
Central and Eastern Europe 106–8, 198
central-for-local innovation processes 131–6
centralized processes 10–11, 45–67, 200–1
Centrica 27, 28
Chandler-Redlich corporate hierarchical structure 50–1, 59
change 8–10, 12, 13–14, 16–19, 23–44, 45–67, 70–92, 93–115, 135, 138, 146–62, 171–88, 217–38, 248–61
    see also institutional change
charters, subsidiaries 175–7
chemicals/pharmaceuticals industry, regional nature of MNE activities 29, 32
Chery 86

Chile 105, 257
China 5, 15, 52, 58, 70, 75, 80–1, 85–6, 101–3, 187, 198, 209, 219–20, 224, 231, 236, 249–50
choice of entry modes, institutional distance 107–8, 181–2
Christianity 5
CIT see communications and information technology
Citigroup 31
'civilization' 5, 170–3, 182–8
'civilizing process', societies 170–1, 173, 182–8
co-evolution concepts 49, 55–60, 119–22, 125–6, 133–6
Coca Cola 28, 30, 260
codes of conduct 96–7, 148–62
    see also institution . . .
codified knowledge, dangers 255
collaborative institutional regimes 148–62
Collinson, Simon 1–22, 69–92
collusion 53–5
Colombia 105
colonial MNEs, authority-sharing/careers/ capabilities characteristics 153–4, 161–2
commercial risk 234
commitment levels, labour 224, 235
commodification processes, exploitation issues 18, 249–61
communications and information technology (CIT) 219–20, 236, 255
communism 205
Compaq 101
comparative advantages 32–44, 48–67, 221–2
competence-creating activities, innovative MNEs 9, 45–67, 93–115, 121–2
competing theories, economic development 70, 71–2
competition policies
    see also anti-trust laws
    barriers to entry 41–2
competition process, subsidiaries 175–82
competitive advantages 8–10, 17, 32–3, 37–40, 73–6, 79–82, 84, 94–109, 136–8, 217–38
competitive disadvantages 232–3
competitive markets, Imperialism 5
compliance needs, labour resources 201–2
'conduct of conduct' 173
confederal MNCs 235–6
conflict problems 18–19, 181–2, 186–7, 247–61
constitutions 172–88
'consumer society' 252
consumption cultures, exploitation issues 250, 252–3
'contested terrains' 16, 182, 193–212
contextual dynamics of change 219–28
contingencies 202–4
continuous improvements 223–5
Cooke, W.N. 199–200
coordinated market economies, varieties-of-capitalism approach 35–7, 180–1, 183–5, 221–2, 231–2

copying practices 31, 55, 78, 86, 203, 232–3
corporate governance 33–4, 37–8, 95, 99–100,
    105–6, 225–8, 233, 248–50
corporate social responsibilities (CSRs) 18, 98–100,
    185–6, 236, 247–61
corrupt governments 248–50
costs
    economies of scale 10–11, 24, 59, 137, 200–1
    FDI decisions 34–5, 199–200
    labour 15–16, 73–6, 82–3, 85–6, 100, 136–8,
        187–8, 199–200, 257, 260–1
    MNE market power 48–9
countervailing duty laws, barriers to entry 42
country risk analysis 74–5, 105–6
country-of-origin effects 203–4
country-specific advantages (CSAs) 32–3, 73–6, 100,
    203–4
    see also varieties-of-capitalism
'court-society' 170–1, 173–87
'creative destruction' 236, 256
creativity, dispersion of creativity 9, 45–67,
    204–12
creators of institutional change 9, 93–115
'credible commitments' 18, 172–88
credit crunch 184
criminal activities, MNEs 248
Croatia 107
cross-border knowledge exchange systems 17, 54–5,
    146–62, 174–5, 217–38, 255–61
Crouch, C. 232
CSAs see country-specific advantages
CSRs see corporate social responsibilities
cultural issues 10, 11, 14, 23–44, 54–5, 59–60,
    97–109, 146–62, 176–7, 219, 225, 230–8,
    247–61

D&D see design and development
Darwin, Charles 119–21
databases 9–10, 23–44
De Rond, M. 227–8, 230–1
decentralized processes 9, 10–11, 45–67, 200–1
decision-making
    FDI decisions 34–5, 199–200
    locus of learning along networks 17, 218–38
    make-or-buy decisions 106–7
delegated managerial MNEs, authority-sharing/
    careers/capabilities characteristics 157–8,
    162
delegated professional MNEs, authority-sharing/
    careers/capabilities characteristics 157,
    162
delegation see authority-sharing…
Dell 101
demergers 187–8
democracy effects, exploitation issues 250
Denmark 149, 167, 225–6
Depression of the 1930s 4
deregulation 34–5, 256–7
design and development (D&D) 220–1, 238

developing countries 5–6, 9, 18, 71, 82–3, 93–4,
    117–18, 247–61
Diageo 25–6
'diamond of national competitive advantage' 37–9
differentiation 24, 46–7, 145
diffusion of innovation 9, 45–67, 204–12
discipline, societies 172–3
dispersion of creativity 9, 45–67, 205–12
distinctive capabilities 16–17, 81–4, 94–109, 145–62,
    236
    see also capabilities
distortions, metaphors 3, 136, 247–8
diversification up the value chain 236
division of labour, specialization 5, 148–62, 233–4,
    258–9
domestically dominated MNEs, authority-sharing/
    careers/capabilities characteristics 154–5,
    161–2
domination critique 18–19, 48–9, 203–4, 247–61
    see also exploitation issues
dormant expectations, labour 207
'double diamond' mindset, strategy perspectives
    38–9
Dunning, John H. 8–9, 12, 69, 74–5, 81–2, 84,
    93–115
DuPont 255
dysfunctions of 'court-society' 178–82

East India Company 4
ECLA see European Commission for Latin America
'eclectic paradigm' 8, 14–15, 94, 97–109
    see also OLI paradigm
economic perspectives 1–2, 4, 6–10, 19–20, 23–44,
    54–60, 69–92, 93–115, 123–4, 135, 138, 167–88,
    248, 257, 261
economies of scale 10–11, 24, 59, 137, 200–1
education systems 17, 71–2, 75–82, 96–7, 223–5,
    228–38, 250
Edwards, Paul 16, 182, 193–216
effective leadership 41
efficiency issues 3, 6, 7–8, 13, 14–15, 73–6, 84,
    95–109, 118–19, 123–4, 128–38, 199, 201,
    205–6, 217–18, 224
El Salvador 260–1
Electrolux 130
elementally chlorine free (ECP) pulping 104
Elias, Norbert 188
EMAS 104
embedded resources, subsidiaries 56–8, 179–82
employees see labour
employment FDI drivers 73–7, 199–200
endogenous growth theory, evolutionary theory 72
energy industry, regional nature of MNE activities
    29, 32
engines, variation, selection, and retention processes
    14, 118–38
Enlie, Zhou 187
enterprise unions, Japan 193
entrepreneurs 12, 97

environmental co-evolution, innovative MNEs 49, 55–60, 119–22, 125–6, 133–6
environmental impacts 1–2, 9, 69–92, 119–22, 125–6, 196–7, 236, 255
epistemology 3–4
Esso 195, 205
ethics 9, 93–115, 168–9, 247–61
ethnic identities, social closure sources 219, 225, 230–8
euphemisms, globalization critique 257
European Commission
    for Latin America (ECLA) 71
    Microsoft dispute 41–2
European Union (EU) 9–10, 15, 23–44, 103, 107–8, 149–50, 168–73, 180–1, 185–7, 201, 236–8
    see also individual countries
    South East Asia subsidiary mandates 236–8
    trade wars 24, 41–2
'evolution of evolution' 122
evolutionary models 12–15, 49, 51–60, 72, 117–44, 145, 174–88, 218–19, 220–1, 225–6, 230–6
expatriate employees, Japan 154–5
experimental movements, innovative MNEs 49, 53–60
experts 147–50, 230
exploitation issues 5–6, 18, 71, 82–3, 93–4, 117–18, 247–61
    commodification processes 18, 249–61
    concepts 18, 247–61
    consumption cultures 250, 252–3
    definition 249
    maquila workers 257, 260–1
    'political society' resistance 25–60
    population expulsions 249–50, 253–5
    'primitive accumulation' 249–50, 253–5
    privatization issues 249–50, 255–7, 260
    protective barriers of infant economies 250–1, 253–5
    protests 251–2, 259–60
    resistance methods 258–9
    US 256–7, 259–61
    Veblenesque fetishism of consumption 252
export promotion 74–80, 85–6, 137–8, 255, 257, 260–1
extant inequalities, exploitation issues 254, 256–7
'extended bureaucracies' 218–19
externality ('free rider') FDI effects 78
Exxon 260

face-to-face social relationships 169–73, 179–81, 227–38
'factory consciousness' 202
fashioners of institutional change 9, 93–115
Fawley oil refinery 205
FDI see foreign direct investment
federations of national firms 17, 145–62, 235–6
Ferner, A. 16–17, 182, 188, 203–4
feudal lords 170–1, 173, 177
finance and accounting studies 5–6

financial markets 17–18, 183–8, 225–8
financial power FSAs 75
Finland 149
firm-specific advantages (FSAs) 33–4, 75, 98–109, 145–62
First World War 4, 5
'flexible firms' 224
Ford 30, 146, 167, 196–7, 202, 204–5
foreign direct investment (FDI)
    see also multinational enterprises
    concepts 4–5, 9, 24, 34–5, 39–40, 52–60, 69–92, 93–115, 178–9, 199–204, 219–20, 222, 249–61
    exploitation issues 249–61
    unintended consequences 77–9, 84, 86
Foucault, M. 172–3
fragmentation of production 9, 46–67
France 5, 25–8, 38, 172, 187, 205, 237, 259
Friedman, Tom 5
front-back organizational structures 138
FSAs see firm-specific advantages
Fujitsu-Siemens 101
function evolutionary subsystem 128–36, 138

game theory 41, 182–3, 234, 258–9
Gap 260–1
Gate Gourmet 207
GDP statistics 4, 71, 75, 122, 167–8, 248, 257, 261
Geely 86
General Electric (GE) 41, 102, 127, 130
General Motors (GM) 167, 206
genetic modifications 18, 251–2, 256–61
genome patents, exploitation issues 256
geographic evolutionary subsystem 128–36, 138, 230
'geographic fiefdoms' 129
geographical hierarchies of activity, innovative MNEs 49, 51–60, 128–36, 230
Germany 5, 15, 25–8, 33–4, 38, 61, 107, 146, 149, 152, 180, 188, 193, 198, 201, 202–3, 204–5, 221–2, 231–2, 234–5, 237, 259
Gerstner, Lew 129
Ghana 105
Ghoshal, S. 10–12, 14–15, 17, 125–38, 145, 174–5, 208, 218–19
Gladstone, William Ewart 5
GlaxoSmithKline 25–6
'global firms' 11
global strategies 23–8
globalization 1, 5–6, 10–11, 18–19, 23–44, 50–1, 71, 81, 82–3, 93–4, 95–109, 117–18, 221–2, 247–61
    definition 256–7
    exploitation issues 5–6, 18, 71, 82–3, 93–4, 117–18, 247–61
globally-linked innovation processes 131–6
GM 30, 85–6
goal conflicts, 'contested terrains' 195–6
governments see nation states
Greece 167
Greve, Henrich 124

Hall, John 169
Hall, P. 221–2
Halliburton 260
headquarters (HQs) 11–14, 16, 45–67, 80–1, 117–18, 121–38, 146–62, 174–88, 193–212, 220–38, 253–61
hedge funds 183–4, 187
Hennart, J.-F 7–8, 13, 123
Hepatitis C 256
Hewlett-Packard 101
'high modernism' 2–3
highly integrated MNEs, authority-sharing/careers/capabilities characteristics 158–62
Hirschman, Albert 132
HIV/AIDS 251, 256, 259
Hobson, J.A. 5
Hofstede's cultural model 14, 176–7
Honda 86
Hong Kong 71, 80, 101–2
host countries see nation states
HQs see headquarters
Hudson Bay Trading Company 4
human capital 71–2, 135, 219–38
human nature 96
human resource management 5–6, 33–4, 135, 234, 237
    see also labour
Hymer, S. 9, 47–60
'hyper-reality' 2–3
Hyun, Jeong Tae 250
Hyundai 80

IB see international business studies
IBM 28, 101–2, 109, 129, 226
Identities 17, 217–38
ILO 16
images of multinationals 1–22, 46–7, 69–70, 71, 82–3, 84, 93–4, 117–18, 167–73, 174–88, 209, 247–61
    see also multinational enterprises
    concepts 1–22, 46–7, 69–70, 117–18, 167–73, 247–61
    definition 2
IMF see International Monetary Fund
Imperialism 5, 257
import substitution 74–80
indeterminacy concerns, evolutionary models 135–6
India 5, 52, 58, 85, 209, 219–20, 231, 236, 249–50
indigenous developments, nation states 77–84, 117–18, 217–38
indigenous/expatriate management conflicts 217–38
Indonesia 167, 260–1
induced variation processes, concepts 121–2, 131–6
industrial relations 5, 15–17, 33–4, 148–62, 185–8, 193–212, 259–60
    see also trade unions
initiatives, subsidiaries 176–7
innovation management 217–38
    see also locus of learning along networks

innovations, definitions 46–7, 131
innovative MNEs 1–2, 9, 17, 19, 45–67, 69–92, 117–18, 125–36, 146–62, 174–7, 181–2, 196–212, 217–38
INSEAD 12–13
inside-out views of MNEs 83–4
insights, images of multinationals 3–4, 247–8
institutional arbitrage 34–5, 248–9
institutional change 8–10, 12, 13–14, 16–19, 23–44, 93–115, 146–62, 171–88, 231–2
institutional distance, choice of entry modes 107–8, 181–2
'institutional duality' 13–14, 181–2, 234–5
institutional investors 184–5, 249–50
institutions 8–10, 12, 13–14, 16–19, 23–44, 75, 93–115, 146–62, 171–88, 198–202, 221–5, 231–2, 236
    concepts 32–44, 75, 93–115, 146–62, 171–88, 198–202, 221–5
    definition 96–7
    exploitation issues 249–61
    roles 94–7, 107–8, 148–62, 221–2
    types 40, 96–7, 148–62, 199, 221–2, 232
insurance companies, regional nature of MNE activities 31
intangible assets 54–8, 71–2, 78, 81–6, 219–38
    see also knowledge; technological developments
intellectual property 31, 55, 78, 86, 203, 219–38, 250, 251–2, 253–6, 258–61
    see also knowledge; patents
internal dynamics of MNEs 18–19
internalization theory, concepts 7–10, 81–2, 84, 94–109
international business studies 14–18, 69–92, 94–109, 123–6
International Monetary Fund (IMF) 248, 251, 253, 258–9
international political economy (IPE) 10, 23–44
internationalization, concepts 4–5, 72–3, 122–3
Internet uses, exploitation issues 261
intra-organizational level 17, 84, 85–6, 119–38, 217–38, 253–8
'invisible hand of the market' 5, 78–9
IPE see international political economy
IPR see intellectual property
Iran 105, 107, 257
Iraq 260
ISO 9000 104
ISO 14000 104
isomorphism 13–14, 34–5, 181–2, 217–38
Israel 167
Italy 5, 25, 205, 259
ITT 127, 257

Japan 13–14, 24–8, 32, 47, 59–61, 104, 107–8, 149–53, 154–5, 158, 183, 193, 196–8, 201–2, 203–6, 223–5, 231–2, 234–5, 259
Johnson, Chalmers 221–2
joint ventures 58–60, 78, 82, 85–6, 123
Jordan 260

Kaviraj, Sudipta 258
keiretsu system, Japan 59–60
Kingfisher 27, 28
Klein, N. 252, 261–2
Knight, Phil 261
know-how 7–8, 98, 155
knowledge 7–8, 17, 45–67, 71–2, 74–5, 80–6, 94–109,
    128–36, 145–62, 174–5, 217–38, 253–61
    see also intellectual property; tacit knowledge
    importance 54–7, 71–2, 74–5, 80–4, 94–109,
        146–62, 256
    political power 56–7, 174–5
Kogut, Bruce 14, 69, 123–4
Kohl 260
Kostova, T. 13–14, 181–2
Kristensen, Peer Hull 17–18, 125–36, 167–91, 201,
    225–6, 230–1, 234–5
Kyoto Protocol 236

labour 5–6, 15–18, 33, 71, 73–6, 82–3, 85–6, 117–18,
    136–8, 146–62, 179–82, 187–8, 193–212,
    217–38, 247–61
    see also management issues
    authority-sharing benefits 146–62
    division of labour 5, 148–62, 233–4, 258–9
    exploitation of the workforce 5–6, 18, 71, 82–3,
        117–18, 247–61
    lower-level employees 193–4
    maquila workers 257, 260–1
    motivations 194–6, 207–8
    problem-solving employees 146–62, 167–88
    productivity issues 3, 71–2, 75–7, 195–6
    skills 146–62, 167–88
    teamwork mistrust 206–8, 210–12
    trade unions 5, 15–16, 148–62, 185–6, 193–212,
        225–6, 259–60
    vocational training 33–4, 71–7, 82, 85–6, 201, 225,
        228–38
    women 197–8, 207, 233, 260–1
    works councils 15, 185, 193–212
languages 161–2, 231–2
'latecomer firms' 80
'law of uneven development' 9, 47–60
LDCs see less-developed countries
leadership
    see also management . . .
    effective leadership 41
lean production methods 205–6, 224
'leapfrogging effects' 80, 84, 86, 209
    see also 'catching up' models
learning 17, 54–5, 59–60, 80, 82, 84, 85–6, 145,
    146–62, 217–38
legal regimes 33–4, 148–62, 171–3, 199–201, 253–61
    see also institution . . . ; regulations
Legend 101–2
legitimacy concerns, evolutionary models 134–5,
    200–1
Lenin 5
Lenovo 101–2, 109

less-developed countries (LDCs) 71–5
Lg Semicon 80
liberal economies 35–7, 107–8, 180–1, 183–5, 186,
    221–2, 231–2, 249–50, 253–61
Liberal Imperialism 5, 257
Liberia 249–50
licensing activities 58
local knowledge, exploitation issues 253–6, 258–61
local-for-local innovation processes 131–6
locally leveraged innovation processes 131–6
locational factors, concepts 8, 9, 45–67, 73–6, 81–4,
    94–109, 125–36, 174–7, 181–2, 200–1, 220
locus of learning along networks 17, 84, 85–6,
    217–38
Loveridge, Ray 17, 217–46
lower-level employees 193–4
Lundan, Sarianna M. 8–9, 69, 84, 93–115
LVMH 28, 30–1

McDonalds 5, 30, 204
macro organizational level 119–38, 253–6, 258
make-or-buy decisions 106–7
Malaysia 102, 105, 238
management issues 16, 17, 35–7, 75, 95–109, 125–6,
    129–38, 146–62, 182, 193–212, 221–5, 217–38
    see also labour
managerially coordinated MNEs, authority-sharing/
    careers/capabilities characteristics 155–7,
    161–2
manufacturing MNEs 4–5, 28–32, 79–80, 82–3,
    154–5
maquila workers, exploitation issues 257, 260–1
market economies, varieties-of-capitalism approach
    35–7, 180–1, 183–5, 221–2, 231–2
market power of MNEs 18–19, 48–9, 53–5, 59, 129,
    202–4, 247–61
market shares 34–5, 73–9
market-based systems 35–7
market-seeking MNE motivations 34–5, 73–80,
    85–6, 100, 104–6, 252–3
marketing studies 5–6
Marx, Karl 6, 71, 72, 194–5, 249, 262
mass production methods 103–4
matrix case 16, 193–212
Matsushita 127
mature stage of MNE development 54–5
Mazda 86
means conflicts, 'contested terrains' 195–6
media 4, 5–6, 19–20
medicines 251, 256, 259
merchants, historical background 4–5
mergers and acquisitions 101–3, 126–7, 129–30,
    136–8, 183–4, 187–8, 220–1, 225–6, 234–5
metaphors, distortions 3, 136, 247–8
'methodological weaknesses' 11
Mexico 260–1
Meyer, Marshall 119
MG Rover 86
micro-mobilization of networks, innovation 233–6

Microsoft 39, 41–2, 236
minority investors, legal regimes 33
Mir, Raza 18–19, 247–65
mission statements 224–5
Mitsubishi 167
MNEs *see* multinational enterprises
modularization of technologies 9, 46–67
monopolistic advantages 53–5, 59
Monsanto Corporation 251–2, 256, 261
moral hazard 106–7
morals 9, 93–115, 168–9, 247–61
Morgan, Gareth 2–3
Morgan, Glenn 1–22, 167–91
motor vehicle industry *see* auto firms
multidivisional organizations 103–4
multinational enterprises (MNEs)
  beneficial impacts 69–92, 108–9, 117–18, 167–9,
    258–9
  'court-society' analogy 174–87
  critique 5–6, 18–19, 48–9, 69–92, 108–9, 117–18,
    145–62, 167–9, 247–61
  CSR 18, 98–100, 185–6, 236, 247–61
  definitions 23–4, 37, 48–9, 94–5, 218
  economic perspectives 1–2, 4, 6–10, 19–20, 54–60,
    69–92, 93–115, 123–4, 167–88
  environmental impacts on host countries 1–2, 9,
    69–92, 196–7, 236, 255
  exploitation issues 5–6, 18, 71, 82–3, 93–4,
    117–18, 247–61
  financial markets 17–18, 183–8, 225–8
  historical background 4–5, 6–19, 47–51, 58–9,
    71–2, 103–4, 125–6, 129–30, 133–4, 174–7
  largest 500 firms by country 24–30, 41, 122, 257
  market power 18–19, 48–9, 53–5, 59, 129, 202–4,
    247–61
  motivations 4–5, 7–14, 34–5, 54–5, 72–80, 85–6,
    93–115, 122–4, 145–7, 178–9, 199–204, 217–38,
    249–61
  non-economic objectives 108–9
  OLI paradigm 8, 81–2, 84, 94–109
  organizational structure perspectives 7, 8–9,
    10–19, 47–9, 50–1, 93–115, 128–38, 145–62,
    167–88, 204–9, 218–38
  political perspectives 1–2, 4, 8–10, 14, 17, 19–20,
    48–9, 56–8, 71–2, 93–115, 168–88, 194,
    198–212, 225–38, 247–61
  purely global MNEs 24–30, 41
  social perspectives 1–2, 4, 6–7, 8, 9, 14, 17, 19–20,
    69–92, 93–115, 117–38, 148–62, 168–88,
    219–38, 247–61
  as societies 17–18, 167–8, 174–88
  statistics 4, 24–30, 41, 77, 81, 167–8, 248, 257, 261
  strategy perspectives 5–7, 10–14, 23–4, 31–2,
    35–40, 56–8, 78–9, 82–3, 121–2, 132–6, 167–88,
    225–38
  theories 6–14
  types 10–12, 57–8, 153–62
'multinational' firms 10–11, 57–8
multiplier effects, economic perspectives 73–7

N-form corporations, concepts 47, 205, 220, 224–5,
  234–6
NAFTA 10, 15–16, 24, 31, 35–6, 39
Nanjing Motors 86
nation states 5–7, 8–9, 10, 11, 12, 14, 23–44, 49,
  54–5, 59–60, 69–92, 93–115, 146–62, 176–7,
  186–7, 219, 225, 230–8, 247–61
  attractiveness factors 72–80, 85–6, 105–8, 202,
    222, 248–61
  cultural issues 10, 11, 14, 23–44, 54–5, 59–60,
    97–109, 146–62, 176–7, 219, 225, 230–8,
    247–61
  economic impacts 9, 69–92, 196–7
  environmental impacts 1–2, 9, 69–92, 196–7, 236,
    255
  ethnic identities 219, 225, 230–8
  exploitation issues 5–6, 18, 71, 82–3, 93–4,
    117–18, 247–61
  government assistance 8–9, 12, 32–3, 49, 73–80,
    85–6, 93–115, 202, 222, 248–61
  indigenous developments 77–84, 117–18, 217–38
  protective barriers of infant economies 250–1
  regulations 32–3, 35, 41–2, 73–6, 86, 96–109,
    148–62, 179–81, 184–7, 198–201, 221–5, 236,
    248–61
  roles 12, 32–3, 49, 73–80, 85–6, 93–115, 250–1
  social development 9, 69–92
  tax revenues 73–7, 171, 178–9, 182, 202, 250–1,
    253–5
  unintended consequences of FDI 77–9, 84, 86
national context, locus of learning along networks
  221–5
national institutions 8–9, 35–7, 75, 93–115, 125–6,
  221–2
  see also institutions
'national subsidiaries' 127–36
  see also subsidiaries
nationalistic resistance, social closure sources 230–8
NEC 127
neoinstitutionalism 13
Nestlé 202, 252, 260
Netherlands 25–8, 38, 237–8
networks 9, 11, 17, 19, 45–67, 83–4, 100–4, 131–6,
  145, 217–38
  see also affiliates
'new realities of globalization' 69–70, 81–92
newly-industrial countries (NICs) 71, 73–6, 80
NICs *see* newly-industrial countries
Nigeria 257
Nike 30, 31, 202, 259–61
non-core activities 30–1, 51, 52, 82, 129–30, 180–1
non-economic objectives 108–9
Nonaka, I. 223–30, 256
norms of behaviour 96–109, 148–62
  see also institution . . .
North America 9–10, 23–44
  see also Canada; US
North, Douglass 96–7
North Korea 105

Norway 167
Novell 42

occupational knowledge, social closure sources
    223–5, 228–30, 235–6
OECD 37, 70, 81
oil companies 25–6, 160, 195, 205
OLI paradigm 8, 81–2, 84, 94–109
ontology 3–4
operational management, R&D conflicts 227–8,
    230–1
opportunism 106–7, 146–62, 183–8, 226
organization theory scholars 12–15, 117–38
organizational hierarchies, social closure sources
    225–8
organizational structure perspectives, concepts 7,
    8–9, 10–19, 47–9, 50–60, 93–115, 128–38,
    145–62, 167–88, 204–9, 218–38
organizations 2–6, 7, 8–9, 10–19, 47–9, 50–60,
    93–115, 118–22, 128–38, 145–62, 167–88,
    204–9, 218–38
    see also multinational . . .
Ottoman Empire 5
outsourcing 30–1, 51, 52, 82, 129–30, 180–1,
    218–19, 224, 230
overview 1–22
ownership competitive advantages, OLI paradigm 8,
    81–2, 84, 94–109

P and O 42
Pakistan 105
parallel evolutionary models 135–6
parliamentary developments, societies 171–2
particularistic institutional regimes 148–62
PATAC 86
patents 31, 55, 75, 222–3, 232–3, 251–2, 253–6
    see also intellectual property
pension funds 184–5
perfect competition 99
Pfizer 259
pharmaceutical firms 228, 251, 256, 259
Philippines 260–1
Philips 127
Poland 167, 187–8
political perspectives 1–2, 4, 8–10, 14, 17, 19–20,
    23–44, 48–9, 56–8, 71–2, 93–115, 168–88, 194,
    198–212, 225–38, 247–61
political risk 234
'political society' resistance, exploitation issues
    25–60
population ecology 121–2
population expulsions, exploitation issues 249–50,
    253–5
Porter, M.E. 37–8
portfolios
    institutional portfolios 100
    knowledge 82–3
POSCO 250
'postmodernism' 2–3

poststructuralist philosophy 3
pound sterling, historical background 4–5
power 18–19, 48–9, 53–5, 59, 75, 129, 169–88,
    198–204, 247–61
    see also exploitation . . .
prices 48–9, 104, 106–7, 137–8, 253–5
'primitive accumulation', exploitation issues 249–50,
    253–5
prisons 172–3
privatization issues 137–8, 249–50, 255–7, 260
problem-solving employees, concepts 146–62,
    167–88
process conflicts, 'contested terrains' 195–6
process-oriented view, economic growth 75–7
product life cycle theory 6, 82
productivity issues 3, 71–2, 75–7, 195–6
protective barriers of infant economies, exploitation
    issues 250–1, 253–5
Protestant work ethic, capitalism 97
protests over globalization 251–2, 259–60
purely global MNEs 24–30, 41

QQ 86
'quality of life' concerns 104–5
quality management processes 104, 195, 206

R&D 9, 13, 31, 51, 61, 70, 80–2, 86, 123, 135, 158,
    220–8, 232, 236–8, 248, 256
'race to the bottom' arguments 202, 222
rational agents 6, 108
raw materials 4–5, 72–6, 85–6, 203, 249–61
realities, images of multinationals 2–4, 19–20,
    69–70, 81–92, 247–8, 258–9
RealNetworks 42
recommended reading list 19, 43, 61–2, 87, 109–10,
    139–40, 163, 188, 212–13, 239, 261–2
reflexive mentoring 227–38
regicides 171–3
regional nature of MNE activities 9–10, 23–44,
    46–67, 75, 79–80, 84, 85–6, 94–109, 125–38,
    146–62, 221–5, 226–7, 236, 247–61
    concepts 9–10, 23–44, 125–36
    critique 40–2, 247–61
    statistics 24–30, 41, 77, 81
    trends 31–2, 81
regulations 32–3, 34–5, 41–2, 73–6, 96–109,
    148–62, 179–81, 184–7, 198–201, 221–5, 236,
    248–61
    see also institution . . .
relational contexts
    locus of learning along networks 217–38
    subsidiaries 13–14, 16, 181–2, 193–212, 253–61
relationship-based systems 35–40
relativism, transcendental truth 2–4
religions 169–71, 186–8
reputations 7–8, 151–2, 176–7, 225
resource-based view of the firm 33–5, 53–60,
    94–109, 193–212, 217–18
respondents to institutional change 9, 93–115

retention aspects
  definition 123–4
  variation, selection, and retention processes 14,
    118–38
'retention' environments 84
returns to workers 200–1
Ricardo, David 72
RiceTec 252
rights 171–3, 179–81, 186–7
Rostow's linear growth stages 71
Roth, K. 13–14, 181–2
routines 14, 118–38
Rugman, Alan 9–10, 18–19, 23–44, 73
Russia 5, 236

SAIC 85–6
Samsung 80
Sarbanes–Oxley Act 184
Saudi Arabia 233
savers 184–5
Schumpeterian evolutionary approach 72, 219–20,
    236
'scramble for Africa' 5
sectoral context, locus of learning along networks
    220–1
segmented collaborative institutional regimes
    148–62
selection aspects, variation, selection, and retention
    processes 14, 118–38
'selection' environments 84
semiconductors 80
service MNEs 28–32, 79–80, 82–3
shareholder capitalism 99–100, 108–9, 183–5,
    249–50, 255–61
Sharpe, Diana Rosemary 18–19, 247–65
Shell 160, 202, 257, 261
Singapore 71, 80, 102, 105, 238
Singh, Jitendra 119–20
Six Sigma 224
skills 17–18, 145–62, 167–88, 219–38
Slovenia 107
Smith, Adam 5, 72, 78–9, 96
SMT 80
social capital 8, 219–38
social closure sources 225–36
social embeddedness problems, dysfunctions of
    'court-society' 179–82
social movements 185–6
  see also corporate social responsibilities
social order 168–88
social perspectives 1–2, 4, 6–7, 8, 9, 14, 17, 19–20,
    69–92, 93–115, 117–38, 148–62, 168–88,
    219–38, 247–61
social responsibilities see corporate social
    responsibilities
social sciences, images 2–3
societies
  capitalism history 172–3
  'civilizing process' 170–1, 173, 182–8

'court-society' 170–1, 173–87
  definition 168–9
  historical background 168–73, 186–7
  laws 171–3, 186–7
  MNEs as societies 17–18, 167–8, 174–88
  parliamentary developments 171–2
  power sources 169–88
  religions 169–71, 186
  rights 171–3, 179–81, 186–7
  tax revenues 73–7, 171, 178–9, 182, 202, 250–1,
    253–5
  wars 169–71, 173, 221–2
'sociological paradigms' 2–3
solidaristic collaborative institutional regimes
    148–62
Sölvell, O. 145–6
Soskice, D. 221–2
South Africa 74, 167, 251, 259
South East Asia subsidiary mandates case studies
    236–8
  see also Asia
South Korea 71, 80, 105, 231, 250
Spain 201, 206, 259
specialization, division of labour 5, 148–62, 233–4,
    258–9
Sri Lanka 107
stakeholders 8–9, 18, 33, 70–92, 93–115, 167–88,
    193–212
standardization 23–4, 30–1, 103–4, 201, 224–8, 236,
    253–5
Stiglitz, J.E. 251–2
strategic assets 8–9, 34–5, 54–5, 72–6, 81–6, 95–115,
    249–61
strategic thinking, needs 78–9
strategy perspectives 5–7, 10–14, 23–4, 31–2, 35–40,
    56–8, 78–9, 82–3, 121–2, 132–6, 167–88, 221–2,
    225–38
subsidiaries 11–14, 16, 45–67, 80–1, 117–18, 121–38,
    146–62, 174–88, 193–212, 220–38, 253–61
  'civilizing process' 173, 182–8
  'court-society' analogy 174–87
  definition 128–9
  exploitation issues 253–61
  innovative MNEs 9, 45–67, 80, 146–62
  MNEs as societies 174–88
subsystems, evolutionary models 128–36
Sudan 71, 74–5
Sun Microsystems 41–2
supply chains 197, 247–61
Sweden 60–1, 136–8, 237–8
Switzerland 25, 60–1, 136–8, 259
synergies 137–8

tacit knowledge 7–8, 17, 80–2, 223–38, 255
  see also knowledge
Taiwan 71, 80, 105
takeovers see mergers . . .
Takeuchi, H. 223–30
tariffs 251

tax revenues 73–7, 171, 178–9, 182, 202, 250–1, 253–5
teamwork mistrust problems 206–8, 210–12
Tech Semiconductor 80
'techno-nationalism' 221–2
technological developments 9, 45–67, 70–92, 93–115, 135, 138, 146–62, 217–38, 248–61
'terminator seeds' 256
Tesco 25–6
theories of multinationals 6–14
TI-Acer 80, 101
Total Quality Management 195
Toyota 86, 167
trade unions 5, 15–16, 148–62, 185–6, 193–212, 225–6, 259–60
  see also labour
trade wars 24, 41–2
  see also barriers to entry
trademarks 232–3
trading companies, historical background 4–5
transaction cost economics 7–8, 13, 84, 95–109, 118–19, 123, 199, 201, 217–18
transcendental truth, relativism 2–4
transfer pricing 104, 137–8, 253–5
'transnational firms' 11–13, 17, 57, 105–6, 125–36, 145–62, 174–5
transnational skills 17, 145–62
triad-based capitalism 18–19, 23–44
TRIPS 55
trust 8, 148–62, 223–4
truth, images 2–4, 19–20, 247–8, 258–9
TSMC 80
two-way exchange, economic perspectives 75–7, 83–4

UK 4–5, 25–9, 33–4, 38, 104, 146, 151–2, 158, 171–2, 183, 187–8, 193, 196–8, 201–2, 205–8, 211, 225–6, 230–2, 237, 259
UN Global Compact 261
UNCTAD's World Investment Report 4, 9, 77, 81, 168, 222, 228
uneven development, 'law of uneven development' 9, 47–60
Unilever 252
unintended consequences of FDI 77–9, 84, 86
US 15–16, 23–44, 59–60, 61, 101–4, 146, 151–3, 172, 193, 195, 196–7, 200–1, 203, 204–7, 221–2, 225–9, 230–1, 256, 259–61

value chains 30–4, 80, 84, 85–6, 94–109, 128–36, 226–7, 236
values 168–9
variation, selection, and retention processes 14, 118–38
  see also evolutionary models
varieties-of-capitalism approach 10, 15, 18–19, 23, 32–44, 75, 179–81, 183–5, 221–2
  concepts 32–44, 75, 179–81, 183–5, 221–2
  definition 32–3
Veblenesque fetishism of consumption 252
venture capital 32–3, 221
Verbeke, Alain 9–10, 23–44
Vernon, R. 6–7, 55
Vietnam 105, 107, 260–1
virtuous circles 18, 77–9, 167–88
vocational training 33–4, 71–7, 82, 85–6, 201, 225, 228–38
Vodafone 26, 28
VW 30, 85–6

Walmart 31, 41, 167, 257, 260–1
Ward, Steve 101
wars 4–5, 169–71, 173, 221–2
Welch, Jack 102
Wenger, E. 226–7
Westney, D.Eleanor 12–15, 84, 117–44, 227
'white man's burden' 4–5
Whitley, R. 16–17, 75, 145–66, 231
Wolseley 25–6
women workers 197–8, 207, 233, 260–1
works councils 15, 185, 193–212
World Bank 222, 248–9, 251, 253–5, 258–9
World Trade Organization (WTO) 49, 248, 250–1, 253, 256, 258–60
WR Grace and Company 252

Yuanquing, Yang 101

Zander, I. 145–6
Zander, Ugo 123
Zeitlin, Jonathan 125–36, 201, 225–6, 230–1, 234–5
Zhang, Yanli 9, 45–67
Zimbabwe 105